Livin' Just to Find Emotion

Livin' Just to Find Emotion

JOURNEY

AND THE STORY OF AMERICAN ROCK

DAVID HAMILTON GOLLAND

ROWMAN & LITTLEFIELD
Lanham • Boulder • New York • London

Published by Rowman & Littlefield
An imprint of The Rowman & Littlefield Publishing Group, Inc.
4501 Forbes Boulevard, Suite 200, Lanham, Maryland 20706
www.rowman.com

86-90 Paul Street, London EC2A 4NE

British Library Cataloguing in Publication Information Available

Library of Congress Cataloging-in-Publication Data

Names: Golland, David Hamilton, author.
Title: Livin' just to find emotion : Journey and the story of American rock / David Hamilton Golland.
Description: Lanham : Rowman & Littlefield, 2024. | Includes index. |
Summary: "Journey boasts an undeniable position at the top of rock 'n' roll superstardom. This is the story of their remarkable career—from formation in San Francisco and meteoric rise to disintegration and astonishing return. Incorporating exclusive interviews with members of the band, this biography provides a definitive and thrilling ride" —Provided by publisher.
Identifiers: LCCN 2023034358 (print) | LCCN 2023034359 (ebook) | ISBN 9781538187012 (cloth) | ISBN 9781538187029 (epub)
Subjects: LCSH: Journey (Musical group) | Rock musicians—United States—Biography.
Classification: LCC ML421.J68 G65 2024 (print) | LCC ML421.J68 (ebook) | DDC 782.42166092/2 [B]—dc23/eng/20230817
LC record available at https://lccn.loc.gov/2023034358
LC ebook record available at https://lccn.loc.gov/2023034359

For Zelda and Jerry
and
In memory of George Tickner and Hillel Swiller

Contents

Foreword

How did Journey turn out to be a timeless band? So many of their contemporaries from the FM rock dial of the late '70s—Foreigner, Styx, REO Speedwagon—disappeared without a trace as soon as the hits stopped, in an instant, like a light switch had been turned out. Who knew that "Don't Stop Believin'" would become an enduring classic and "Feels Like the First Time" would vanish in the ether like it never existed?

By all rights, the Journey story should have ended with the controversial *Raised on Radio* album and tour, after vocalist Steve Perry completed his leveraged takeover of the band and drove it into the horizon. But the rock gods had other plans and Journey stumbled, tumbled, and fell into a miraculous second life as their trademark song echoed in sports stadiums and the final episode of *The Sopranos*.

Journey emerged in the post-hippie San Francisco scene, after Bill Graham closed the Fillmore West and the original bands—save for the good old Grateful Dead—had fractured, splintered, and devolved into barely recognizable versions of the groups that made the Summer of Love famous. There was a new ethos guiding the musicians—music was no longer a calling; it was now a business.

Journey rose out of the ashes of the original Santana band, which had crashed and burned after three enormously successful albums, establishing a worldwide following after a breakout performance at the Woodstock festival, and setting new standards in drug abuse. Santana equipment manager Walter "Herbie" Herbert pulled together organist and vocalist Gregg Rolie and teenage guitar phenom Neal Schon from Santana with bassist Ross Valory and guitarist George Tickner from the East Bay band Frumious Bandersnatch, where Herbert worked before Santana.

Herbert took responsibility for the strategy and direction of the band. The initial plan was to create a kind of flexible rhythm section—along the lines of Memphis's Booker T. and the MGs—that could back other musicians in recording studios, but with the immense virtuosity they assembled, the musical direction quickly shifted into a dense instrumental sound along the lines of the Mahavishnu Orchestra.

The San Francisco music scene was no longer a cultural phenomenon. After the hippie ballrooms produced a string of landmark rock groups—from Jefferson Airplane to Creedence Clearwater Revival—music business professionals took note. Columbia Records bought a San Francisco recording studio and opened a branch office, bringing from New York the label's top producer, Roy Halee, the man behind the company's best-sellers, Simon & Garfunkel. He started by supervising the first solo albums by both Simon & Garfunkel at the San Francisco studio.

San Francisco ballroom impresario Graham had expanded his empire from running dance halls in San Francisco and New York, after closing both the Fillmore West and Fillmore East in 1971, into managing acts like Santana, booking bands like the Grateful Dead, and running two record labels with former Columbia Records staff producer David Rubinson, where they recorded bands such as Tower of Power and Cold Blood while still presenting concerts every week at San Francisco's Winterland and other halls around Northern California.

There was real money involved, and the young musicians found they could support lavish and unconventional lifestyles. Guitarist Carlos Santana, who grew up stuffed into a two-room apartment with a family of eight, lived in a faux medieval castle in the hills of Mill Valley. Vocalist Grace Slick of the Airplane drove around in an Aston Martin she purchased for cash, after the salesman scoffed at her ability to afford such a car.

So the musicians forming Journey had been around, knew the score, and came together on purely professional terms, which was something of a new attitude for the customarily more casual San Francisco bands. "We're a San

Francisco band," Huey Lewis once said. "We found the five nearest musicians and started playing."

This underlying commitment to commercial success guided Journey's path through its serpentine march to the top of the pops. This was not like one of the early British rock groups smitten with the sound of American rhythm & blues or the first wave of psychedelic bands intent on expanding the boundaries and vocabulary of the music. From day one, Journey was an industrial enterprise, and the marketplace would determine its design. In 1973, that was a novel, almost revolutionary, concept in the rock world.

The first album was a temperamental mismatch between the band and producer Roy Halee, a fussy, exacting engineer who once held up a Journey session for several hours waiting for a specific microphone to be delivered while the musicians cooled their heels playing pinball, drinking coffee, and growing angry. Still, "Of a Lifetime" is a stark representation of the powerful instrumental sound the band could muster.

By the second album, Journey had slimmed down to a four-piece with the departure of Tickner, but by the third album, there was a sense of desperation creeping into the program as keyboardist Rolie added his "Black Magic Woman" vocal sound to a Beatles cover. The band's favorite track was left off the album because the label wanted something more commercial than the hard-bopping instrumental "Cookie Duster."

Herbert had the band touring endlessly. The more bodies he could put Journey in front of, the better. After a long series of dates with hard-rock band Kansas, the other band went home and retooled a riff from a Journey song they heard the band play every night into "Carry On Wayward Son." The band spent years going from the road to the studio and back out on the road. They took vocal lessons. Herbert stressed that every concert had to be an Academy Award–winning performance and they must train like Olympic athletes.

They realized the band needed a vocalist to sing songs that could get on the radio. Herbert found Robert Fleischman, a pint-size Robert Plant out of Denver who was drafted to join the band in time for a summer tour. Although he instantly developed personality problems with the other band members, Fleischman and Schon sketched out the song "Wheel in the Sky," which would ultimately become a radio breakthrough for the band. Just not with Fleischman.

Herbert had the Alien Project tape for quite a while, and he had been fascinated with the sound of the vocalist. By the time he reached out, the band had dissolved and the vocalist, Steve Perry, was shoveling turkey shit on his family farm in Visalia. With Herbert employing a modest bit of subterfuge to get Fleischman out of the way, Perry tried out with the band during a sound check in Long Beach, and that was all they needed to hear.

Perry brought the voice the band needed. He worked his way into the band, sharing vocal responsibilities with Rolie and writing with Schon. He brought a song he had begun, called "Lights." With Queen producer Roy Thomas Baker behind the console, Perry was fully onboard with the next album, *Infinity*. With "Wheel in the Sky" on the FM radio, Journey set out on the band's first headline tour that would last more than a year and play 172 cities in the United States, Canada, and Europe. The album would be Journey's first million seller, and the tour established the band as a major concert attraction. By the time they toured behind the next album, *Evolution*, with the Top 20 hit "Lovin', Touchin', Squeezin'," the band was filling baseball stadiums.

The departure of Gregg Rolie, the band's sole remaining connection to the Fillmore era, paved the way for Jonathan Cain to leave the Babys and join Journey in time to write and record the band's ultimate masterpiece, the *Escape* album. From the platform the band had created with three consecutive platinum albums, *Escape* exploded Journey into the leading rock band of 1981. They had juggled personnel, behind-the-scenes teams, repertoire, styles, and sounds until they found the stroke.

Of course, in classic *Behind the Music* style, such success was hard to duplicate, and the resulting frustrations led to dissension within the band, political infighting, and Perry practically holding hostage an entire album project while he dithered with the recording endlessly, having taken tyrannical charge of the band's music. That ultimately spelled the end of Journey.

As Perry disappeared into a reclusive lifestyle, the remaining survivors grouped and regrouped and tried out various side projects without any great success (Bad English, the Storm, etc.). Journey loomed over anything they did. Their road back was as fraught and complicated as the first time—who could imagine Schon finding a Perry replacement on YouTube?—but Journey climbed out of the oblivion to which they had been consigned, back into a glory that many of the band's original peers could only envy.

How did this happen to Journey? This turgid tale of art and commerce, aspirations and inspirations, calculations and coincidences couldn't have been planned, but the principals who steered the band kept Journey between the gutters and off the sidewalks. The music had been designed for commercial acceptance and drawn from the experiences of musicians coming up in the Fillmore era. Schon was less influenced by Muddy Waters and Howlin' Wolf than by '60s British guitar heroes such as Jeff Beck, Peter Green of Fleetwood Mac, Alvin Lee of Ten Years After, or Eric Clapton. It was music that had its roots in the Woodstock generation and had smoothed out the rough edges of any more unruly elements.

Of course, Journey was trying to make music for their time, not the ages. Somehow, in their ceaseless efforts to crash the best-selling charts, they crystalized some essence of contemporary rock before the incursion of new wave and punk, in the final days of classic rock. Along with Huey Lewis and the News and Pablo Cruise, Journey represented the post-countercultural San Francisco music scene, an often confusing mélange of styles and influences without a single overarching direction other than commercial success. When one of my reviews referred to the Journey juggernaut as "the military-industrial complex of rock," Herbert took it as a compliment.

Journey has long deserved a richly detailed account of the band's meandering, complicated history. Their tremendous belief in what drove their rise to the top—that is, their own destiny—dashed by the vagaries of success and subsequent personality issues, also served to restore the band in an unexpected second coming. Nobody who was around the grubby, hustling early days of Journey could have imagined the band posing for photos fifty years later in the Oval Office with a disgraced and disgraceful president, but no telling what happens when you don't stop believing.

Joel Selvin

Box Office
The Portuguese Cousin

A nervous Steve Perry waited backstage at Long Beach Arena. After a decade of failure, could this be his big break?

The band was tremendously talented. He had first met Neal Schon back in '71, when the sixteen-year-old guitar prodigy was playing with Santana. Gregg Rolie, on keyboards, had also been with Santana back then; he sang their biggest hit, "Black Magic Woman." The drummer, Aynsley Dunbar, had played with David Bowie and Jeff Beck and Frank Zappa—and Perry had listened to every one of those albums. Even the bass player, Ross Valory, was a superstar: he cut his teeth with the legendary Steve Miller Band. But . . . Steve Perry? Journey certainly didn't need him.

They also didn't want him. Perry was a crooning tenor with a singing style straight out of Motown. His favorite artists were African American. Journey was progressive rock—muscular, chest thumping, head banging—and very, very white. Schon and Rolie had long ago left behind the Afro-Latin rhythms of Santana, and Dunbar and Valory had forsaken the blues for a style of music that some critics called "heavy space."

But the record label wanted better sales, so their manager, "Herbie" Herbert, forced Journey to take on a lead singer. First they tried a screamer named Robert Fleischman. Then Herbie got a tape of a singer from a band called Alien Project that had broken up after their bass player died in a freak car crash on the Fourth of July. Perry was the voice on that tape.

1

But the singer had given up on his dreams and was back on his stepfather's ranch fixing turkey coops. Herbie convinced him to come down to Long Beach to sing with the band. To keep anyone—especially Fleischman—from suspecting his plan, he told the crew that Perry was a roadie's Portuguese cousin.

Now Perry waited for that moment when he could take the stage. Was he setting himself up for just another disappointment? Or was this the start of something new?

The band paused. He walked onstage. The crowd waited in anticipation. What was next? Who was this?

Steve Perry closed his eyes and opened his mouth. And everything changed.

That seemed like so long ago now, as he sat in his well-appointed, if understated, home. He looked around at all the things that money could buy and thought about his mother, and how there was nothing his fame and fortune could do to bring her back, to bring back all the years they had lost while he had been out pursuing his dreams.

This was why he knew that, despite the band's successful reunion and its Grammy nomination, he would not go out on the road for another extended tour.

He looked at his hip. It hurt, off and on, but especially when he exercised, and sometimes just standing up. He knew he needed the surgery, but he was scared. Even with the best medical attention in the world, he had been in enough hospitals to know that anything might happen on that operating table.

The phone rang. He knew who it was. He was dreading this call.

It was Jonathan Cain, Journey's longtime pianist and songwriter. "We're not going to go behind your back," he said. "So if you hear we're auditioning for new singers, it's true."

"Don't break the stone," Perry pleaded. "I don't know if we can come back if you do." But his entreaties fell on deaf ears. Cain and their old friend Neal Schon, who was listening in on another line, were resolved to keep the band going—with or without him.

Finally, in exasperation, he ended the conversation, his hip throbbing. "Just lose my phone number," he said.

The idol of millions had somehow lost control of the band he had taken to superstardom. How had it come to this?

*   *   *

"Just a small-town girl, living in a lonely world." Few lyrics have so closely captured the identity of a listener and the zeitgeist of an era. "Don't Stop Believin'" was released in October 1981 to rapidly ascend the *Billboard* Hot 100. In its fifty-year history, Journey has sold more than ninety million albums, including forty million of their number-one 1981 LP *Escape*, which contains "Don't Stop Believin'" and four other hits. As of the week of July 8, 2023, *Journey's Greatest Hits* has been on the *Billboard* album chart for an astonishing seven hundred weeks; only Bob Marley's *Legend* and Pink Floyd's *Dark Side of the Moon* have enjoyed longer runs. Journey sold just over one million tickets on their last full tour, at an average ticket price just under $100. Today Journey is one of the most popular touring bands on a billion-dollar heritage circuit, and that song has continued to influence popular culture, from the 2003 film *Monster* to the final scene of *The Sopranos*, from the TV show *Glee* to its adoption as an underdog anthem by several professional baseball teams. But why?

Like so much of what has moved American history, Journey's popularity has to do with *race*. It was made possible by a unique combination of Black-oriented Motown and white-oriented progressive rock, a cultural appropriation made palatable to the white teenage audience of the post–civil rights era. Journey's popularity was made possible because it was white. In a modern form of minstrelsy, these white musicians safely provided "Black" music to white audiences.

Prior to the advent of rock and roll, popular music was segregated: the blues, gospel, jazz, and ragtime had been considered "race music" because of their origins in the African American community and appeal to Black listeners. People of color were considered "racial," while white people were considered "normal"—and therefore "without" race. White audiences enjoyed country, music hall, operetta; their exposure to race music was through "acceptable" white interlocutors like the jazz impresario Paul Whiteman, "white gospel," and, of course, minstrelsy—the original cultural appropriation.

For a brief moment in the mid-1900s, rock and roll integrated popular music. The genre took seed in a time of national optimism following victory in World War II, much as jazz had grown in popularity after World War I. It flowered during the social revolution of the 1960s, much as jazz had during the Roaring Twenties. The baby boom generation was reordering society—or at least they were trying. This revolution integrated popular music at the same time that it integrated buses, public schools, lunch counters, and *Star Trek*. "Rock and roll did more for integration than the church," said civil rights leader Andrew Young, who succeeded Martin Luther King Jr. as head of the Southern Christian Leadership Conference, "and if I was going to choose who I was going to let into the Kingdom . . . I might have to choose Elvis."

While it lasted it was glorious. Elvis Presley, Little Richard, and other pioneers combined Delta blues, country, gospel, and rockabilly; the Young Rascals demanded that their opening acts include musicians of color; British bluesmen like John Mayall, Peter Green, and Eric Clapton explicitly duplicated the Black Delta sensibility; Aretha Franklin borrowed from Mick Jagger and Mick from Aretha; the Santana Blues Band combined mariachi heritage with Afro-Cuban rhythms and psychedelic surf, joining Jimi Hendrix and Sly and the Family Stone for a triumphant performance before an interracial audience at Woodstock. Often in spite of their parents, the baby boom teenagers ate it all up. Rock and roll seemed to be leading the way to an interracial future—and having a lot of fun doing so.

But it ended with disillusionment, thanks to the war in Vietnam, the urban crisis, and stagflation, much as the promise of the Roaring Twenties ended with the Great Depression. As society sought familiarity in old patterns, popular music resegregated too. By the 1970s, with the South under orders to integrate, more of the battle for civil rights moved to the North, where it stalled over busing, affirmative action, and police brutality. Oil shocks, deindustrialization, and recession replaced the optimism of the 1950s with an overwhelming anxiety, a sense of malaise. The nation saw a backlash against the achievements of the civil rights era and against those who opposed the war in Vietnam. As the hippies, peace signs, and patchouli receded, Hendrix was replaced by Lynyrd Skynyrd; Led Zeppelin eclipsed the British blues; and Santana disintegrated. Cutting-edge Black artists abandoned the inoffensive rhythms of Motown as their brethren in the civil rights movement turned to more militant forms of protest, spurning Chuck Berry and Ray Charles for Sam and Dave and James Brown. Rock and roll resegregated, dividing into *rock*, primarily performed by and marketed to a white audience, and *soul*, which was by and for Black people. By 1973, one could no longer hear Marvin

Gaye on the same station as the Allman Brothers, despite their similar musical structure and roots.

Journey was founded later that same year by manager Herbie Herbert,
guitar prodigy Neal Schon, and singer-organist Gregg Rolie, all formerly of
Santana, with Ross Valory, Steve Miller's former bass player, and a second
guitarist, George Tickner who had worked with the Grateful Dead's Jerry
Garcia. They were soon joined by Aynsley Dunbar, the noted British blues
drummer. These were young, energetic musicians at the cutting edge of musicality and closely tuned to the latest currents in popular music. They were a
supergroup, and they promptly failed to meet expectations.

Fifty years later, Journey is one of the most popular touring bands on a
multimillion-dollar nostalgia circuit. Neal Schon remains in the band, with
longtime pianist-songwriter Jonathan Cain.

Neither the 1973 Journey nor the 2023 version, however, fully represents
the band's history, as neither includes the individual most closely associated
with its sound. That is singer Steve Perry, who led Journey to superstardom
and whose controversial departure still represents its most devastating loss.
The technically proficient and immensely talented musicians Perry joined in
1977 were under threat of losing their contract with Columbia Records. No
album since he left the band has received either lasting airplay or comparable
sales; indeed, in keeping with that 1977 threat, Columbia dropped the band
after their first album without Perry's emblematic voice. But during his years
at center stage, the band experienced an unrivaled heyday at the heart of
popular culture.

Rock and roll had always been a business, but with the rise of Bob Dylan
and the Beatles and the founding of periodicals like *Rolling Stone* and *Creem*,
some began to see it as an art form untethered to capitalist realities. This was
true of the early years of Journey, which produced experimental, progressive
jazz-fusion rock. Admiring critics called their style "heavy space," yet few
rock fans bought their albums.

But the music business remained a business, and successful musicians
learned to adapt. In 1981, with a marketing and merchandise operation
netting tens of millions of dollars a year (at one point earning $7 million
in T-shirts alone), Journey epitomized a trend toward "corporate rock,"
and Herbie, a former hippie, epitomized corporate management. He pioneered point-of-sale advertising, pushing retailers to play Journey music in

showrooms. He made all band decisions, from venue choice to contracting minutiae to personnel changes (including hiring and firing band members). He established wholly owned subsidiaries to handle trucking, lighting, and sound for the band's tours, so they could profit from—rather than pay for— these services. He sold corporate sponsorships to the likes of Budweiser beer. He even licensed a Journey video game, with a home version as well as a coin-operated one for arcades.

This is not to say that Journey was not musically innovative. In fact, like Paul Whiteman and Al Jolson, Journey's musical innovation was in cultural appropriation. It combined the best of rock, Motown, and the blues into a form pleasant to the ears of millions of mostly white teenagers. When Perry crooned, he combined his father's big band sound and Portuguese *fado* ancestry with the Motown of his adolescence: a white Sam Cooke aspiring to be a white James Brown. Schon poured Eric Clapton and Jimi Hendrix into his guitar solos, with an occasional nod to Carlos Santana. Cain combined the country music of his Arkansas heritage with the polka of his Chicago youth into a songwriting talent to rival Bruce Springsteen.

Their most enduring hit, "Don't Stop Believin'," combines all of these multiracial, trans-American elements with a simple, familiar chord progression used by both the Beatles and the Rolling Stones. The lyrics speak to the angst of the era: yearning, wistfulness, transition. And by inverting the sensibility of Jim Weatherly's "Midnight Train to Georgia," which spoke of defeat (specifically the failure of most southern Blacks to achieve success in the de facto segregated North), they added a hint of promise, a road out of the darkness into which the country had seemingly fallen: "the midnight train going anywhere" accompanied by an accelerating guitar transit. It was the perfect complement to Ronald Reagan's "Morning in America," and it appealed to the same electorate.

Music and dance allow people to be more in touch with their emotions, especially repressed sexuality. Polite Western European culture considers emotion and sexuality to be carnal, animalistic, and uncivilized, revealing instincts better left repressed. Much of the history of racism is based on the idea, generated by white people (slavers, imperialists, and even common folk seeking advantage) that Black people are sexually primitive, childlike, and uncivilized. This has no basis in fact; African Americans and whites engage equally in "acceptable" and "unacceptable" sexual behaviors, for example.

And there is no racial disparity in innate artistic talent; race is socially constructed and not biologically determined, and natural melanin production is genetically unrelated to natural talents like musical pitch and rhythm. But just as Black people's perceived sexual freedom has titillated repressed whites, Black people's music, dance, and other artistic contributions have been simultaneously marginalized and covertly admired by white people restrained by society's rhythm-denying straitjacket.

Actually becoming Black, however, is a bridge too far for most white people. The long history of racial rape, murder, and pillage is well understood even if publicly denied. White people, then, have historically sought only a temporary flirtation with dangerous Blackness. That's where minstrelsy came in. Minstrelsy allowed white people to temporarily revel in the rhythms that connected them to their innate, barbaric emotions and sexual desires, "to escape periodically into an exotic world of pleasure, sensuality, and emotional freedom traditionally denied or suppressed within Western European culture," as historian Michael Bertrand puts it.

Journey's continued popularity in recent decades, both in MP3 downloads and on the largely white "heritage" tour circuit, has been no less instructive in how Black musical styles continue to influence white musical tastes. The use of "Don't Stop Believin'" on *The Sopranos* is but one example. Albeit fictional, Tony Soprano represents the white suburban teenager of the 1970s, all grown up and no less anxious; the violent plotline stands in for the continuing fears of a generation that moved from Reagan's "Morning in America" to Donald Trump's "Make America Great Again." As music historian Dewar MacLeod has written, "Music shapes our identity, music makes us feel human, music brings us together. But music can also alienate and divide us." By 2016, Journey was no less caught up in the nation's tribal divisions than were its political parties.

But the song's meaning and interracial origins allow it to be fluid and dynamic. The band hired a new lead singer, a Filipino named Arnel Pineda, expanding the group's cultural reach to the immigrant community; for him, and for so many other fans of color, "Don't Stop Believin'" is about Dr. Martin Luther King Jr.'s dream. In 2020, given the opportunity to replace two members, the band chose two Black mainstays of the San Francisco music scene, including bassist/A&R* executive Randy Jackson, a longtime judge on

---

* Artists & Repertoire—the record company professionals who recruit and directly work with talent and music.

American Idol. In the era of Black Lives Matter, the band once known for rocking the "red states" became majority-minority and reminded the world of the roots—and continuing impact—of African American music on rock.

Meanwhile, Journey remains corporate, a brand as much as a band. Its parent company, Nightmare Productions, Inc., rakes in more than $30 million per year from the band's tours (barring pandemics); it is owned by the five musicians who were in the band in 1981 (only two of whom remain in the group), as well as the estate of former manager Herbie Herbert. Not much has changed since 1981—except that none of this is innovative anymore.

Livin' Just to Find Emotion does not just tell the story of how changes in race relations since the civil rights era have affected popular music. It is also a reappraisal of the role of race in rock. Carefully following the development of Journey from a failing progressive rock group to Motown-influenced superstardom, *Livin' Just to Find Emotion* demonstrates the continuing impact of resegregation and cultural appropriation in the genre.

The story also involves three of the most important and colorful men in 1980s rock. One, of course, was Steve Perry, whose path from starving artist to bandleader was strewn with the bodies of as many friends and enemies than the plot of Macbeth. There is also Neal Schon, the teenage wunderkind who helped found the band and struggled to take on the mantle of leadership after Perry left. Finally, there is Walter "Herbie" Herbert, the larger-than-life manager who went from Santana guitar tech to respected industry mogul. Herbie made the fateful decision to hire Perry as Journey's lead singer against the wishes of the band members and his own better instincts, and their eventual showdown destroyed them both.

Taking its title from a poignant lyric in Journey's emblematic "Don't Stop Believin'," *Livin' Just to Find Emotion* speaks to the yearning of the white American teenager for something more "real" than the false optimism of disco or heavy metal's oppressive Klaxon. Just like their grandparents when it came to jazz, the emotion white rock fans were "livin' just to find" could only come from soul music. But white racial identity prevented them from following that genre instead of Journey's brand of rock.

This book explores how the story of Journey—its music, its players. and its business—illuminates the story of racial resegregation in American popular music.

*   *   *

This book is the product of historical scholarship. I am a professionally trained and tenured historian, and I applied the methodology of that training to this work. In order to appeal to a mass audience, however, readers will not find any citations here. Instead, you are urged to visit www.journeyhistory book.com, where you will find fully-referenced endnotes, a bibliography, music playlists, and other interactive material.

But I was a Journey fan long before I became a scholar. In the summer of 1982, at a decrepit old resort in the borscht belt of *Dirty Dancing* fame, I was shooting pool when someone put a quarter in the jukebox. I was no stranger to music, of course; my mother, who had been a folk singer, favored the "easy listening" of New York's WPAT, so I was well versed in the Carpenters and ABBA. Dad, on the other hand, was tone-deaf but status-conscious: when he was in the driver's seat—and he usually was—we listened to WQXR, the city's classical station. But this was different. For the next four minutes I just stood there, entranced by Journey's "Don't Stop Believin'." Unlike Dad's classical or Mom's easy listening, this music spoke directly to *me*. As "a city boy . . . livin' just to find emotion," I yearned to meet that "small-town girl" on "the midnight train going anywhere." When I bought my first car, like so many other Journey fans, I ordered a vanity license plate: in my case, JRNYDV, for "Journey Dave."

Soon after the dawn of the World Wide Web, my personal Journey led me to create the website that ultimately became the Journey Zone (http://www.journey-zone.com/), a journalistic tribute site dedicated to the music of Journey, the solo acts of the current and former members of the band, and connected acts like Santana and Bad English. At its heyday, the Journey Zone boasted more than twenty editors and reviewers, all volunteers, all Journey fans like me. It was thanks to that site that I scored some of my first interviews, including my exclusive with former Journey lead singer Robert Fleischman, as well as with original Journey/Santana lead vocalist and keyboardist Gregg Rolie, longtime Journey drummer Steve Smith, original Santana *conguero* Mike Carabello, and Kevin Chalfant, lead singer of the Storm. The site also got me backstage a few times, where I found myself cheek by jowl with guitarist Neal Schon, pianist and primary songwriter Jonathan Cain, bassist Ross Valory, and Steve Augeri, the first replacement of longtime vocalist

Steve Perry. Eventually I got a real coup: an interview with George Tickner, one of Journey's founding guitarists and the composer of much of the band's early progressive material; sadly, Tickner died as this book went to press.

Meanwhile, I went to grad school, earning a master's from the University of Virginia and a PhD from the City University of New York. I became a scholar of race in American history. My first book, *Constructing Affirmative Action: The Struggle for Equal Employment Opportunity* (University Press of Kentucky, 2011), explored race and labor; my second, *A Terrible Thing to Waste: Arthur Fletcher and the Conundrum of the Black Republican* (University Press of Kansas, 2019), looked at race and politics.

It was in December 2020, during the pandemic winter, that it first occurred to me that I might combine what had previously been two distinct interests—that I could write a history of Journey. Someone gave me a copy of Neil Daniels's book *Don't Stop Believin'* (Omnibus, 2011), and while it was enjoyable, it was a missed opportunity. There was so much more Daniels could have said if he had approached the work as a historian.

Undertaking such a project was no easy decision. I was certainly familiar with the band's story, as were so many other fellow fans—one need only read Joel Selvin's liner notes to Journey's 1992 box set to get the basics. But to apply the historian's craft to a topic is to dedicate months and years to the research. And historians work on spec: a book contract is rarely a guarantee. Ultimately, I decided that the story needed to be told, that it needed to be told well, that it needed to be told thoroughly, and that it needed to be told by me.

The sources I consulted are divided into what we call "primary" and "secondary." Put simply, primary sources are written at or near the time period being discussed or are recollections by people who lived through the events. Secondary sources are after-the-fact commentary and analysis—like books by historians. I consulted more than 2,300 primary sources for this book, mainly newspaper and magazine articles from the likes of the *San Francisco Chronicle*, *Rolling Stone*, *People*, and the *New York Times*; interviews with current and former members of the band and associated acts; Jonathan Cain's memoir (*Don't Stop Believin': The Man, the Band, and the Song That Inspired Generations* [Zondervan, 2018]); documents housed at the Rock and Roll Hall of Fame Archives in Cleveland; legal and corporate documents filed with such offices as the California Secretary of State and the US Patent and Trademark Office; and, of course, the music itself—I listened carefully to every single

Journey song ever released (and quite a few never publicly released) as well as the first four Santana albums, Frumious Bandersnatch, and William Penn and His Pals; the Aynsley Dunbar Retaliation and Dunbar's albums with Bowie, Zappa, and Flo & Eddie; the Jonathan Cain Band and the Gregg Rolie Band; Vital Information, Schon & Hammer, and HSAS; all the Perry and Schon solo material; Bad English, Hardline, the Storm, Abraxas Pool, and Soul SirkUS; and pretty much everything else I could find. Secondary sources, meanwhile, included about forty books on just about every aspect of the history of popular music.

What historians do is read, analyze, and interrogate sources, put them in context, draw evidence-based conclusions about the past, and write those conclusions into a narrative. And when I say interrogate, I mean just that: it's as if the source is a witness in a trial and the historian is the opposing counsel. We think about motivation and faulty memory and try to poke holes in what we're reading or being told, all to better glean some kernel of truth.

All histories tell stories, but the best of them find ways to change how we think. I started the work thinking I was simply writing the history of a rock band, divorced from my previous scholarship. As I engaged with the sources, however, I discovered a scholarly thesis that surprised me. Now I conceive of this book as the third part of a trilogy on race. Whereas my first book looked at race and labor, and my second race and politics, this book considers the role of race in popular culture. I hope it changes the way you think about rock music.

As with any scholarly work, however, I'm certain I made mistakes, both of fact and of interpretation. Knowing my fellow fans, I'm sure my errors will be pointed out in short order. That's fine. Let's make this book the start of the conversation, rather than its definitive end.

Opening Acts

There were cars abandoned, parked on highways, it was wild. I would've probably gotten stage fright if I'd known it was gonna be this big.

—*Gregg Rolie*

California's Central Valley is famous for its agriculture. The swath of land from Bakersfield to Redding is known for raising everything from asparagus to zucchini—and especially almonds: most of the world's almond supply, in fact, comes from here. One can raise almost anything in the three fertile watersheds that constitute the Central Valley. Almost anything, it turns out, including rock singers.

Stephen Ray Perry was born in 1949 in Hanford, in the heart of the Central Valley's San Joaquin County, to Portuguese immigrants Ray Perry (né Pereira) and Mary Quaresma. An only child, he quickly displayed an aptitude for singing. "I was 3 years old when I started singing around the house. Mom couldn't believe it. She told me I'd hit these high screaming notes that would go right through her head. Poor thing, I must have driven her crazy." At age seven, after his parents' divorce, he and his mother moved to nearby Lemoore to join his maternal grandfather, Manuel. Despite Manuel Quaresma's influence on Steve's personality, and Mary's subsequent remarriage to local turkey farmer Marv Rottman, however, his father made a lasting mark. Ray Perry was a singer and big-band leader who performed songs by Count Basie and Duke Ellington. They did not have many years together, but before the divorce, "my Dad always sang to me, especially at bedtime." It was not long before Steve was singing in a barbershop quartet: "[W]e would perform for the Chamber of Commerce and other city functions."

Lemoore was an unlikely town to host an aspiring rock star. Although several commentators, including Perry himself, have likened it to the town in the film *American Graffiti*, George Lucas's paean to postwar teenage life, with cars, hamburgers, angst, and rock and roll, the real-life basis for the film, Modesto, had little in common with Lemoore besides a quaint, western-style main drag (Ninth Street in Modesto, D Street in Lemoore). According to the 1960 census (when Perry turned eleven, and two years before the setting of *American Graffiti*), Modesto boasted a population of 36,585, while Lemoore counted only 2,561 souls. Even combined with Hanford—a virtual metropolis by comparison—the area had a population of only 12,694. In fact, life in Lemoore must have been downright lonely for the aspiring drummer-singer.

But a small-town boy in the early 1960s was never truly lonely. Indeed, to borrow a phrase, Steve Perry was quite literally raised on radio. Lemoore was roughly equidistant from Los Angeles and San Francisco, and AM signals from both cities easily bounced off the ozone to the boy's set. And it was on the radio, riding in his mother's Thunderbird, that he first heard Sam Cooke. "I heard 'Cupid,'" Perry recalled, "and I about died." The irrigation canals of the valley came with many a "make-out point," where Perry and his dates would listen to the music, perhaps hoping that Cooke's voice would make Cupid draw back his bow and let that arrow flow straight to their lover's heart.

Lemoore High School, fortunately, was integrated: Tommie Smith, who went on to raise a Black-power fist at the 1968 Olympics in Mexico City, attended the school five years ahead of Perry, and the youngster had at least some Black acquaintances with whom he could discuss the latest hits. "Through some of my friends of color, I discovered R&B music ... and I wanted to know why it felt the way it did, why it made me feel the way it did. And I wanted to know why Sam Cooke killed me the way he did. And why Jackie Wilson was slaying it like he did."

Notwithstanding his father's connections to the industry, it was on the radio that Perry also heard the great crooners of the era. They sang with a sophisticated, earnest style that mixed urbane jazz—the boring type that tended to do well with upper-class white audiences—with light opera, carefully enunciating the lyrics yet offering a smooth, emphatic delivery. There was Bing Crosby, whose 1942 hit "White Christmas," by Irving Berlin, captured the spirit of soldiers hoping for a quick return home and a nation looking for a quick end to the war. He learned about the power of race and culture in music when he heard Perry Como's 1949, number-one hit from Rodgers & Hammerstein's "Some Enchanted Evening," the theme from the Broadway musical *South Pacific*, about a forbidden love affair between a white American sailor and a girl from the islands. In 1958, Bobby Darin transformed the theme from the Weimar German *Threepenny Opera* by Kurt Weill and Bertolt Brecht into the hugely popular "Mack the Knife." And of course there was Frank Sinatra, who covered all of those songs and so many more in his six-decade career as a musical heartthrob. Most importantly, the crooners told *stories* with their songs. Stories of heartbreak, of unrequited love, of adventure. Stories that made the listener think as much as sing along. Stories to capture the imagination of a lonely boy in Lemoore.

Rock and roll music, also growing in popularity during Steve Perry's childhood, was less for making listeners think than for making them *move*. Born of a combination of folk, country, and most importantly rhythm and blues—which at the time was called secular "Negro" music or, often, "race" music—rock and roll's early years were likewise tied to the inclusion of vocals. Indeed, some rock and roll singers needed no backup instruments at all. Doo-wop acts consisted of harmonized singers, well dressed in matching outfits, with minimal accompaniment. Usually at least one member would have a bass voice so deep as to effectively serve as a vocal rhythm section. Unlike the great crooners, who shed their immigrant origins and strove for urbane respectability, the doo-wop acts embraced their roots. The Platters—named for the shellac or vinyl records played in jukeboxes at 78 or 45 revolutions per minute—proudly combined the blues with Black church music, while Dion and the Belmonts overtly appealed to the Italian immigrant sensibility of New York City and environs that Sinatra seemed to have forsaken. And not all acts were male: by the time Perry entered Lemoore High in 1963, three Black women in bejeweled evening gowns had taken over the radio. The Supremes, with their lead singer Diana Ross, helped put Berry Gordy's Detroit-based Motown Records on the map.

Elvis Presley, the "King of Rock and Roll" whose "greatest attribute may have been an ability to communicate and convey effectively the dreams and values of his audience," a trait Perry would one day emulate, grew up attending both the Black and white churches in his hometown of Tupelo, Mississippi. Presley combined all of these styles and had the mixed reputation of both offending middle-class white parents with his overtly sexual swinging hips and simultaneously making "race" music palatable to white audiences. Even more authentic was Steve Perry's idol, Sam Cooke, who started out recording church music before finding a secular crooning career more lucrative. Cooke's blockbuster recordings included hits like "Cupid," the repurposed African American folk tune "Frankie and Johnny," "Chain Gang," "Good Times" (which Perry would later record with Journey), and "You Send Me." His tragic 1964 murder by a Los Angeles motel owner coincided with the arrival of the Beatles in New York. Rock and roll had reached maturity; the British Invasion had begun; and Steve Perry put together his first band.

The Sullies looked, at first, like just about any other mid-'60s high school band. But like similar acts near the San Francisco Bay, they had big dreams. Once organized, this group consisted of Bill Bilhou on keyboards, David Geffken on bass, Rick Stephens on guitar, and Perry on drums—with all four members sharing vocal duties. They played regular club shows, driving up to Sacramento each week in their van. At one point they entered the Calaveras County Battle of the Bands and beat out dozens of other groups—which came with a chance to open at Bill Graham's Fillmore Auditorium in San Francisco. "[W]e dressed in our [Nehru] jackets and were ready," Perry remembered. "The crowd dug us.... Then Janis Joplin, with her explicit adoption of African-American performance styles, stepped on stage with [Big Brother and] the Holding Company and tore it up!! She was great! Then Steve Miller and Boz Scaggs (who was in the band at that time) came out and sang all my favorites off the first LP," *Children of the Future*. "I really wanted to get into the music Biz after that." The Sullies stayed together after graduation, continuing to play their weekly gigs even as Perry went off to College of the Sequoias, half an hour east of Lemoore in Visalia, where he took band, choir, and speech classes.

Perry had nothing but positive things to say about the Sullies. "They were one of the finest groups I've ever heard in my life with some of the finest musicians that ever played," he unabashedly told *Hanford Sentinel* reporter Ruth Gomes in 1978 (although he may have been trying to spare the feelings of readers of the hometown paper, some of whom surely knew his former bandmates—and members of his own family).

After college, Perry was determined to make it in the music industry. He moved to Los Angeles and took a job at Hollywood's Crystal Studios as a second engineer, hoping to learn another side of the business. And that he did, watching such acts as Barbra Streisand, Jimi Hendrix, the Jackson 5, the Doors, and the Byrds lay down tracks from behind the glass in Crystal's Vine Street headquarters. Once, after seeing an Azteca concert in 1972, he even got a ride home from Neal Schon; he came to admire the guitarist and later saw Journey every time they appeared at the Starwood Club.

But proximity to the stars did not lead to stardom. "Working at Crystal kept me alive for a while but [I] found out it was taking time away from what I was doing musically . . . so I got out."

The stars he met at Crystal were helpful in one regard: as he observed their behavior, he learned what *not* to do. "They were not career oriented," he told journalist Robyn Flans. "They were partying musicians and were not thinking any further than that. Every time I turned around, they would be late, not show up for rehearsals. That kind of thing." Perry's exacting standards helped him develop his own identity and behavior on the job, which eventually led him to the pinnacle of stardom, but his high expectations of those around him cost him more than a few relationships along the way.

When Perry said that his Crystal Studios job "kept me alive," he was speaking literally. Once he left Crystal and gave up that steady paycheck, he became so single-mindedly focused on his career as a singer that he nearly starved to death. His meager earnings from the few bands he played with—unknown names like Ice, the Privilege, the Nocturns, the Dollar Bills—did little more than cover the rent. But he was getting more experience, honing his craft as a front man, picking up a little piano and guitar, and further developing his voice. The Privilege, for instance, made him an international singer: "[W]e ended up in Quebec and Montreal . . . we stayed at the Chateau Frontenac and my big thrill [there] was having onion soup." And it wasn't as if he only sang with nobodies: in 1976 he linked up with former Vanilla Fudge bassist Tim Bogert in a short-lived group called Pieces; he also recorded songs with singer/songwriter Forrest McDonald. But success was not forthcoming, and malnutrition turned to gum disease. "I was eating a lot of pork and beans. [A] dentist said . . . I ought to have all my teeth out."

In early 1977, Perry finally joined a band that seemed to be going places. The Alien Project was "a pure rock and roll band . . . with a style that allowed me to stretch out as a singer." The band included bass player Richard Michaels Haddad, formerly of the Detroit rock act SRC; guitarist Steve DeLacy; and drummer Craig Krampf. "We were good together," Perry recalled. They recorded a demo titled "If You Need Me, Call Me," which was standard late-'70s hard rock inspired by the 1963 Wilson Pickett hit "If You Need Me," with lyrics that speak of being available to a former lover after a breakup. It showcases Perry's clean and clear vocal style, where he gets multiple notes out of each line's final syllable. A standard verse-chorus-verse-chorus-bridge-chorus format, the song has elements of the blues and strong harmonies.

Its radio potential was quickly recognized. Word on "the street" in Hollywood that the band members were up-and-comers became loud enough that they considered changing their name to "Street Talk" (which Perry would later repurpose for a solo album). And it wasn't just on the street. They lined up meetings in early July to discuss possible deals with Columbia Records as well as Chrysalis, the British label that included such acts as Nick Gilder, Billy Idol's band Generation X, the Babys, and Procol Harum. Everything finally seemed to be coming together.

Then tragedy struck. On July 4, 1977, while the nation celebrated its founding and three of the band members were celebrating their impending success, bass player Haddad died in a car crash. His devastated mates immediately suspended the band. A shaken and distraught Perry returned to his mother's home in Lemoore. He had failed as a musician, he thought, and resolved to spend the summer working on his stepfather's turkey farm while he considered his future.

That's when he got a phone call that would change his life.

*   *   *

It's a five-minute walk to the Capitol Records Building, up Vine Street from Sunset Boulevard. Five minutes or three years, depending on how you look at it. In June 1968, the tall record stack–shaped building where Nat King Cole, Frank Sinatra, and the Beach Boys had recorded albums seemed to stare down Vine Street, almost taunting the sweaty band of musicians who had come from San Francisco to open for the Byrds at the Kaleidoscope Club, a top Los Angeles rock venue. The gravity of the moment was not lost on this little-known band with a curious name—Frumious Bandersnatch.

The Byrds, with their number-one smash hit covers of Bob Dylan's "Mr. Tambourine Man" and Pete Seeger's "Turn! Turn! Turn!"—and their own original hits "Eight Miles High" and "Mr. Spaceman"—were a constant on the airwaves from coast to coast. Elvis Presley grouped them with the Beatles when asked about "new" music, famously mispronouncing their name as "the beards." The Byrds (actually pronounced "birds") had a dedicated fan base of hippies that the opening act hoped to attract. "Byrd freaks" "went anywhere the Byrds did" and "smelled of patchouli and hash and wore long flowing things," according to Derek Taylor, the press agent they shared with another California rock act, the Beach Boys. Their set naturally garnered the first paragraph of music columnist Michael Etchison's review of the show in the *Los Angeles Herald Examiner*.

But that was only a brief and cursory statement, overshadowed by the writer's impressions of opening act Frumious Bandersnatch. Etchison compared their psychedelic sound favorably with an act that had also, like the Byrds, achieved national success: Buffalo Springfield, the Los Angeles–based folk-rock group that included Stephen Stills and Neil Young. And while Frumious Bandersnatch could occasionally delve into folk rock, as with their "Love Is Blind" (which the reviewer found "especially impressive"), they wowed the crowd even more with "Woodrose Syrup," a ten-minute romp with multiple guitars and sudden, unexpected changes in tone and style, covering everything from funeral dirge to toe-tapping rhythm & blues to British Invasion–style rock. This versatility was not lost on Etchison, who called the band "strong both vocally and instrumentally," adding that they "should be brought back."

The Bay Area in 1967, home to Frumious Bandersnatch, was a cauldron of musical churn, with groups like Sly and the Family Stone, the Grateful Dead, and the Santana Blues Band forming and reforming as the baby boom generation came of age and experimented with sex, drugs, and rock and roll. The version of Frumious Bandersnatch that opened for the Byrds at the Kaleidoscope—the version that music critic Alec Palao later called "the great lost psychedelic band"—arose from the garage bands of Lafayette, across the San Francisco Bay and over the Berkeley Hills. In 1967, Seattle-born guitarist Jimmy Warner invited Ross Valory, who played bass clarinet in the Lafayette

High School band, to "rent a bass and an amp . . . we'll have some fun and make a little change."

He meant the kind of bass with strings, of course, and the kind of change that jangled in the pocket. Together they created Little Jimmy and the Good-Timers and quickly built a local reputation playing James Brown–style soul music in church halls. Valory had been raised in a musical household, "playing ukulele at the age of four" at the urging of his mother. He described their sound as going over the heads of the listeners, who danced "their stiff surf stuff." Like the white TV-studio audiences when Sam Cooke performed on the *Ed Sullivan Show*: minuscule knee bends and snapping fingers. Nothing like how the music was meant to be enjoyed: hot and sweaty and sexy, as at a Black juke joint.

One day "at the local Presbyterian church . . . [t]he back doors fly open and this huge guy in just a dirty T-shirt, jeans and tennis shoes comes in and does the skate all the way right up the middle aisle, gets in front of us and does all the real soul dances from the west side of the tracks in Berkeley." This was Walter "Herbie" Herbert, a local white kid who dug Black music and wanted nothing more than to "hang out and help." He fixed up his 1956 Chevrolet panel truck and became their roadie and manager, which gave the Good-Timers the opportunity to travel further afield.

The Good-Timers were not the only band to come out of Lafayette High School that year. Drummer Jack King and guitarist George Tickner had a psychedelic band called Shades Blue that ended up on a blacklist after a series of teenage pranks. "Usually it would involve a girl, or something would get stolen," King later said. "We were punks, we were reprobates . . . we went out on Los Lomas High football field and 'donutted' the whole field, just tore it up." Tickner, born in Syracuse, New York, and raised in Lafayette where he studied alto saxophone in elementary school, had "switched over to guitar when all the bands started happening . . . when I was a freshman in high school."

Refusing to quit, Shades Blue changed their name to Frumious Bandersnatch, a pun borrowed from the Lewis Carroll poem "The Jabberwocky." Inspired by the 1967 Jefferson Airplane song "White Rabbit," which explores the narcotic references of another Lewis Carroll work, *Alice in Wonderland*, they gathered local musicians into the group, including guitarists David Denny and Bret Wilmot, with Brian Hough on bass. Vocalist Kaja Doria provided a lyric tone similar to the Airplane's Grace Slick. This version of the Bandersnatch appeared at such Bay Area venues as the Ark, a scuttled wheel boat in Sausalito, and Bill Graham's Fillmore Auditorium. Also in San Francisco they played several "Dance Class" gigs in the city's nascent rock ballroom scene, including one at the O'Farrell Theater in San Francisco's Polk Gulch. But they were still often perceived as simply an "East Bay" band. *San Francisco Chronicle* music critic Herb Caen mentioned them in a humorous story of a trip to "dread O-k-l-nd," where "the owner of a nearby factory called The Squirkenworks . . . said that the rock'n'roll band playing at the end of the pier was called the Frumious Bandersnatch. No matter how many trips I make to the East, I will never get used to their language."

This version of the band came to an unfortunate end, however, after a burglary at the warehouse where they stored their equipment. Jack King blamed the crime on members of the local police department "because they'd always come down there and harass us." But in the end, "we were just 19-year-old hippies with no dough . . . breaking up not because we didn't want to continue but because we couldn't play." Tickner added that it "was the nature of the beast in those days. It took a while to get . . . new equipment."

It was at a Good-Timers gig in Reno that Herbie Herbert learned of the poor fortune that had befallen Frumious Bandersnatch. As much as he loved soul, his burgeoning business sense told him there was more of a future in psychedelia, at least for white musicians. That's when he had the sort of eureka moment that would later help him bring Journey to the pinnacle of success: use the best of the Good-Timers to reform Frumious Bandersnatch.

He paired Jack King and David Denny of Bandersnatch with Warner and Valory of the Good-Timers under the general management of the Bandersnatch's Jim Nixon. They recruited a soulful lead singer named Bobby Winkelman, from the Epics, a moderately successful band out of Concord that had recently recorded a punk rock hit "Humpty Dumpty," in what music critic Palao later called a "literal" kidnapping. Winkelman himself called it "a friendly abduction," noting that he "went smiling . . . because I wanted to do something different." Guitarist George Tickner, who harbored no ill will at being left out as he was starting school at California State University, continued to associate with the group, teaching them his songs.

Of critical importance to this "classic" lineup of the Bandersnatch was the Valory homestead. Whereas the original lineup had collapsed when their instruments were stolen, Ross Valory came from a family of some means.

His mother, Kaye, was a Republican fundraiser who had helped elect Ronald
Reagan to the statehouse; the family had a ranch in Lafayette where the band
ate, slept, and—most importantly—wrote and rehearsed. It was something of
a musical saturnalia, with various locals popping in from time to time, including Steve Miller.

After a gig with a new group called the "Santana Blues Band" at San Francisco's Balboa High School, in April 1968 Frumious Bandersnatch entered
Pacific High Recorders in Sausalito to lay down some tracks that would be
collected in compilation discs many years later. Their sound is representative
of late-'60s psychedelic rock, which the scholar Seth Bovey perhaps unfairly
defines as "ponderous songs filled with meaningless guitar solos." The drum
solos are actually longer, if less meaningless. Although lead vocalist Winkelman is no one to write home about, and the mixing and engineering are lacking, the guitars of Warner and Denny are fantastic, the Valory-King rhythm
section gets ample opportunity to showcase their developing talent, the songwriting is creative, and the music is delightfully unpredictable.

The songs themselves are an eclectic mix; this was a band that knew how
to rock. "Chain Reaction" is reminiscent of the Youngbloods' "Get Together."
"Rosemary's Baby" is a lyrical tribute to the 1968 Roman Polanski film of the
same name, with harmonies in the slow parts similar to the style of the Beatles. "What Is a Bandersnatch?" includes Lewis Carroll–inspired music, in this
case almost reminiscent of Gregorian chant over minimalist acoustic guitar.
"Now That You've Gone" is a lullaby that unfortunately makes Winkelman's
voice seem harsh, while "45 Cents" begins with a strange homophobic spoken
interaction, devolving into frenetic psychedelia, mostly instrumental, with
competing guitars, hand clapping, and a strong bass and beat. "Pulpit Huff,"
structured like a sermon or extended prayer (even concluding with a harmonized "amen"), includes a bass solo and simple harmonies with multiple
voices. "Paper," literally a celebration of paper of all kinds and uses, is probably, in the context of "Pulpit Huff," a tribute to the doobie-rolling variety.
The song includes a spoken-word portion that could double as a commercial
for the "Acme Paper Company." "Cheshire" begins with a two-minute instrumental and includes references to *Alice in Wonderland*, with clear similarities
to Jefferson Airplane's "White Rabbit" in the ten-minute track. "Black Box"
is a short, thoughtful ballad, while "Can-A-Bliss," an obvious play on words,
is a twelve-minute indulgence showcasing Denny's guitar. Like "Woodrose

Syrup," it goes through multiple style changes, and it features the best lead vocals and harmonies of the lot and an incredible five-minute drum solo by King that leads to a jazzy finale.

An outtake contains some beautiful vocal harmonies otherwise lacking in Bandersnatch. "Hearts to Cry," structured like an act of lovemaking, is at turns cacophony and funeral march, with a prominent bass line that climaxes in an extended vocal orgasm. Given the ever-present Lewis Carroll themes, the song title is likely an allegory to an imagined liaison with the Queen of Hearts, a character from *Alice in Wonderland*—possibly as a dominatrix. According to music critic Palao, the "repeated whiplash at the start of the central rave-up section [is] Valory hitting a volume pedal on his amp." Finally, "Misty Cloudy" is an up-tempo departure for the group, reminiscent of the sound of the TV rock group the Monkees.

They also recorded themselves opening for the Youngbloods at the Straight Theater, "an old movie house in the Haight that some hippies fixed up," resulting in a raucous, mostly instrumental live track, "Medley: You've Gotta Believe/Judgement Day," which includes a call-and-response (a musical form from the Negro spiritual tradition) where the backing vocals are sadly hard to hear. Then they joined Buddy Guy at a "dance-concert" at the Avalon Ballroom in Polk Gulch and opened for Santana twice more, on Muir Beach and at the Avalon. Following the June show with the Byrds in Hollywood, they played a free concert in Berkeley's Provo Park with Memphis bluesman Charley Musselwhite, returned to Muir Beach, and joined Santana and the Steve Miller Band for a benefit at Bill Graham's Fillmore West. With the release of a few tracks as an "extended play album" in August, they seemed on their way; by November they were back at Fillmore West opening for the British group the Moody Blues and for the Chicago Transit Authority (who later shortened their name to Chicago).

But their manager, Jim Nixon, was unreliable. According to Jack King, "[t]he more Jim Nixon got into drugs and alcohol . . . his arrogance just alienated everyone, including Bill Graham," lord of the San Francisco music scene. This may have contributed to Ross Valory's decision to leave the band at the end of the year. Valory later said he was following George Tickner, now in college, and indeed the two briefly joined keyboardist James Trumbo in a band called Faun, which recorded a single, eponymous album—an eclectic combination of ragtime, fifties-era Broadway, folk, jazz, psychedelia, proto-seventies rock, and English traditional, with a variety of instruments, including flute, sitar, harpsichord, and trumpet. The remaining members of Frumious Bandersnatch left the group one by one in 1969, only occasionally being replaced, and the gigs dwindled. Roadie Herbie Herbert stayed on until it was clear it was over, but eventually he too left—to work for Santana.

Frumious Bandersnatch had an interesting coda. An old friend from the Valory ranch days had hit it big and needed musicians. In January 1970, Jack King, Bobby Winkelman, and Ross Valory joined the Steve Miller Band. At that point it might even have been called "Frumious Bandersnatch featuring Steve Miller," with every member but the eponymous bandleader himself a Bandersnatch alum, except that the music—a psychedelic-informed blues-rock—was all Miller's. They toured nationally, often joined by another Bandersnatch alumnus, David Denny, on rhythm guitar.

Valory, Winkelman, King, and Denny provided a tight, controlled backup to Miller, a far cry from their Bandersnatch days. No longer playing free-form psychedelic rock, theirs was a maturing musicianship. They recorded some of their live performances, resulting in the three tracks on side 1 of the album *Rock Love*. And in the summer of 1971, they went into the studio to record the tracks for side 2—at none other than Capitol Records in Los Angeles. Three years after their appearance opening for the Byrds at the Kaleidoscope at Sunset and Vine, Frumious Bandersnatch—or at least four of its members—had made it up the street to the towering record stack.

*   *   *

Any list of important 1960s San Francisco rock acts would be incomplete without the Santana Blues Band, which featured a Palo Alto organist on lead vocals. Seattle-born Gregg Rolie, who bore a passing resemblance to Scottish singer-songwriter Donovan, "grew up listening to the Beatles, Rolling Stones, Chuck Berry, Bo Diddley, [and] Dave Brubeck," and reported falling in love with the jazzy sound of the Hammond B3 organ at age eleven when first hearing Jimmy Smith's "Walk on the Wild Side." This performer, who would achieve so much success as founding lead singer of Santana and Journey, got his start in a garage band called William Penn and His Pals, a typical white 1960s surf band. After the group's first drummer, Mickey Hart, left to join the Grateful Dead, the group consisted of Neil Holtmann on vocals, Mike Shapiro on lead guitar, Ron Cox on drums, Steve Leidenthal on bass, Jack Shelton on rhythm guitar, and Gregg Rolie on Vox organ. Once the rest of the band heard his smooth tenor, Rolie quickly took over lead vocal duties.

William Penn and His Pals recorded "Swami," which achieved some moderate local airplay, and recorded a one-minute musical commercial, with a voice-over by their manager Vernon Justus, for Pacific Southwest Airlines. They played a number of gigs around the Bay Area in 1966, appearing with Fred Cole's band, the Lords, at the under-twenty-one Wildcat A-Go-Go in Berkeley's Claremont Hotel, and they opened for Van Morrison at the Oakland Auditorium Arena, for the Dave Clark Five at the Circle Star Theater in San Carlos, and for the 13th Floor Elevators at the birthplace of San Francisco folk rock, Longshoreman's Hall. At one point they opened for Paul Revere and the Raiders, whose hit songs included "Kicks" and "Just Like Me." This pairing would have made for an entire evening of Revolutionary War costumes, if not for the performances of four other garage bands with equally fanciful names like Peter Wheat and the Breadmen, and a last-minute decision by William Penn to trade their breeches for motorcycle-gang black leather. The group even had a fan club based in San Lorenzo; a young woman named Lauretta Pica served as its president.

High school ended, the band ended, and singer-organist Rolie went off to college to study architecture. William Penn and His Pals might have faded into obscurity as just another short-lived garage band except for a random moment of serendipity that speaks to the ferment of musical talent developing in the Bay Area—"the epicenter of multidimensional consciousness," one musician called it—during those years.

A wonderful thing happened one evening at the Fillmore. Rolie's friend, Tom Fraser, went to see a group of some renown called the Butterfield Blues Band, but the bandleader, Paul Butterfield, showed up "stoned on acid" and unable to play, so the band just started jamming without him. Fraser knew the guitarist, Mike Bloomfield, and asked if another friend of his, a dishwasher at a nearby restaurant, could sit in. That dishwasher was Carlos Santana, and that night was his big break.

Mexican-born Carlos Santana attended Mission High School in San Francisco, where he gathered his friends regularly in one band after another. As soon as he could, he struck out on his own and disappeared into the hippie scene, losing contact with his family for several years. But he was building a

new family, and during this absence he returned to Tijuana to learn guitar
from several blues practitioners there. Back in San Francisco, he took odd
jobs and whatever gigs he could get around town.

Introduced by Tom Fraser, Rolie had an instant chemistry with Carlos.*
"We played in this house in Mountain View, which is where Shoreline
[Amphitheatre] is now, and it was like, you know, an old farmhouse or
something and we were out there playing in the middle of the farm fields,"
he recalled. "And of course there was grass [cannabis] around. So the cops
started [to] come. We heard the sirens, saw the cars. I turned around and
said, 'Look, Carlos, we better get out of here.' And he was already 50 yards
down the road. . . . And so we ended up hiding in a tomato patch . . . till the
cops left."

In late 1966, Carlos and Rolie formed a band with Tom Fraser on rhythm
guitar, high school chum Gus Rodriguez on bass, Rod Harper on drums, and
Michael Carabello on congas. But the group had no name and no clear direction. "We were playing songs like 'Mary Ann' by Ray Charles and 'Misty' and
'Taste of Honey,' only with Latin percussion," Carlos said later. "To me it still
wasn't music. It was just a process of learning, you know."

After a 1967 hospital stay for tuberculosis, Carlos got back together with
Rolie and Carabello to try something new. Joined by David Brown on bass,
Jose "Chepito" Areas on timbales and Michael Shrieve on drums, they called
themselves the Santana Blues Band. "It was Carabello who came up with
the idea," remembered Carlos, noting that their one constant musical style
was the blues; they were admirers of the Butterfield Blues Band; and none of
the names of the other members sounded right. "He thought my last name
had the most ring to it." To non-Latinos it sounded like the jolly man who
delivers presents on Christmas Eve, which gave the name a ring of kindness
and expectation; Latinos heard the contraction of Santa Anna, an important
nineteenth-century Mexican general and president, which added power and
strength.

They played whatever gigs they could get, slowly building a reputation
as an interracial blues-rock band, experimenting with a sound that would
come to define Afro-Cuban rock. In 1968 they appeared with Frumious
Bandersnatch at Balboa High School and at Dino and Carlo's Bar; opened for

---

* Throughout this section, I refer to Carlos Santana by his first name, to distinguish him from his
eponymous band.

Steppenwolf for three nights at the Avalon Ballroom; and, of course, played Bill Graham's Fillmore West. The group started attracting local press. Music columnist Ralph Gleason of the *San Francisco Chronicle* called them "one of the most impressive of the new young groups," while the *San Francisco Examiner*'s Philip Elwood called Carlos "sometimes exciting" and the band "a loud, racially mixed hard-rhythm group, and potentially a major force hereabouts."

Still, most observers in the Bay Area would have been surprised if told that Santana would be national rock stars by the following summer. The group was still building their reputation at venues like the Santa Clara and Merced County fairgrounds, the College of San Mateo, and the "Fun House" in South Lake Tahoe. But Bill Graham saw something in them. Agreeing to serve as their manager on a "handshake contract"—an informality he would later regret—he booked them to open for Crosby, Stills & Nash on a tour of the Midwest in the spring of 1969, brought them home in May to appear with blues legend Albert King at the Fillmore West, and secured a record contract with Columbia. They went into Pacific Recording in San Mateo in May to lay down tracks for an album, while Graham arranged an East Coast tour. He showcased them at the Atlantic City Pop Festival, where Carlos, from the stage, announced a name change: "It's just 'Santana.' After you hear us play a few numbers you'll see why" (they no longer emphasized the blues). Then it was up to Graham's New York outpost, the Fillmore East. Almost as an aside, Graham booked them to appear at something called the "Aquarian Celebration" that summer in upstate New York for the meager sum of $1,500.

The idea for Woodstock grew out of the success of the annual jazz and folk festivals at Newport, Rhode Island; Monterey, California; and Montreux, Switzerland, which started in the mid-1950s and had gained popularity during the 1960s. One of these saw a major moment in rock history: Bob Dylan appeared at the Newport Folk Festival in 1965 with an electric band for the first time. A popular folk music phenomenon ended that day, arguably the moment when rock and roll began to split between "white" rock and "Black" soul. In that sense, Woodstock and the subsequent success of Santana served as a last hurrah for interracial rock and roll (with headliner Jimi Hendrix, tragically, its sacrificial lamb). Henceforward, with some notable exceptions, white rock fans expected their music to be performed by white musicians, often with country roots, such as the Eagles, the Allman Brothers, or Lynyrd Skynyrd; or with a touch of English folk, such as Led Zeppelin, Jethro Tull, or the Who. "The little white girl in school loved to dance to Chuck Berry," music mogul Ahmet Ertegun observed, "but somehow John Lennon looked more like her dream." All grown up, with love beads around her neck and flowers in her hair, she might have swooned at the sound of Carlos Santana's guitar, but she ended up in Gregg Rolie's hotel room.

Over the decades, the music festival at Max Yasgur's dairy farm in Bethel, New York, has taken on something of a mythical aura. The three day "exposition" included concerts by such well-known acts as Joan Baez, Janis Joplin, Jimi Hendrix, Jefferson Airplane, and Joe Cocker, and it helped launch the careers of Richie Havens and Sha Na Na (the latter going on, most famously, to record six songs on the soundtrack to the 1978 major motion picture *Grease*). But what most of the actual attendees remember is the mud—acres and acres of mud—and the traffic—miles and miles of backed-up roads in all directions. The promoters did not expect the volume of attendees. Folks showed up for the show, with or without tickets. They camped in the nearby fields, with or without tents. The organizers failed to get the fence built on time, failed to provide sufficient food and water in the midsummer heat, failed to provide adequate medical care, failed to rent enough porta-potties. Ultimately, they succeeded only in getting most of the performers to the gig—by helicopter.

What made the festival a success was the attendees. In a public rebuke to authorities from the Nixon White House to the concert organizers themselves, the "hippies" of Woodstock organized themselves to share food and water and even assembled a health brigade comprised of medical students and nurses. The signature photo from Woodstock—taken during Santana's set on day 2, August 16, 1969—is not of the stage but the people. Thousands and thousands of them: men, women, and children of various races, colors, and styles of dress.

The movie *Woodstock*, several hours long, includes footage of Santana playing their original song "Soul Sacrifice." The outstanding stars are Carlos, of course, mostly toward the back of the stage, almost hiding from the crowd and letting his guitar say everything he needed to say; Mike Carabello, a flurry of motion on the congas; "Chepito" Areas, likewise akimbo at the timbales; and Gregg Rolie, who stands at the organ almost like a hippie King Kong, puffy hair cascading past his shoulders, long arms extending down to the keys. "I can remember watching his posture and how he'd get into it so

deeply, watching the veins appear in his throat, all that tension and convic-
tion," said Carlos, adding that "the whole arrangement was based on Gregg's
solo."

"We were flown in by helicopter, over all these people . . . and I don't think
we were really paying attention to the crowd at the time," said Rolie. "We had
a 35 minute set, and . . . it was a really great experience. That night, after our
set, we watched Sly & The Family Stone perform. . . . Now, instead of flying
us out like they had flown us in, they drove us out in a few cars. That's when
it really hit home. . . . There were cars abandoned, parked on highways, it
was wild. I would've probably gotten stage fright if I'd known it was gonna'
be this big."

The next month, Columbia Records released the band's eponymous first
album. *Santana* uses African rhythms, church organ, and even a touch of
psychedelia under the overall umbrella of "Latin" rock. Employing the writing skills of all six regular band members as well as conga player Marcus
Malone, the nine tracks include four instrumental numbers and two cover
songs that became hits for the band and eclipsed their original releases:
"Jingo," by Nigerian drummer Babatunde Olatunji, and Clarence Henry's
"Evil Ways," included at the insistence of Bill Graham. The front cover design
features the faces of the six musicians combined to form an image of a lion's
head. The album quickly climbed into the top 10, peaking at number four on
the *Billboard* 200 on November 14, 1969. By February 1970 it had garnered
more than $1 million in sales. Carlos, who used his first royalty check to buy
a house for his mother, wasn't living on dishwasher wages anymore.

With a triumphant return to the Fillmore West in September and gigs
through the end of the year at such venues as Philadelphia's Convention
Hall, where they headlined the Quaker City Rock Festival; Chicago's Kinetic
Playground, resulting in a gushing review; and Sacramento's Memorial Auditorium, where they opened for Sly and the Family Stone, Santana had taken
rock music in a new direction, achieving a truly remarkable feat by helping
the listening public find an appreciation for a style most hadn't expected they
would like: Afro-Cuban-Latin jazz-blues rock.

They found even more success in 1970. The band headlined Fresno's
Selland Arena, performed at Orlando Stadium, and joined Miles Davis at the
Tanglewood Music Festival in Massachusetts in front of 17,432 fans. They
appeared at San Bernardino's Swing Auditorium, with Bread as their opening

act, and returned to San Francisco at the end of the summer for four dates
headlining—yet again—the Fillmore West. Bill Graham attempted to take
Santana and Jefferson Airplane on a benefit tour of Vietnam to entertain the
troops, arguing that the soldiers were "a little weary of Bob Hope, Martha
Raye, and Miss Whatever 1970," but he met resistance from the Department
of Defense. There was only one way these young men could get to Vietnam,
and they all definitely wanted to avoid *that*.

They released a second album that year, *Abraxas*, considered by many critics the best of the Santana catalog. All band members save bass player David
Brown and drummer Michael Shrieve participated in the writing, but again,
the two hit singles were cover songs. "Black Magic Woman," an expansive,
experimental take on a song originally written by Peter Green of Fleetwood
Mac, showcases Rolie's smooth, insistent vocal and an extended guitar conclusion by Carlos that was emulated nearly a decade later by Joe Walsh of the
Eagles in "Hotel California." The song went to number four on the *Billboard*
weekly charts—and was only recorded because Rolie, who heard something
special in the Fleetwood Mac version, insisted on it. Tito Puente's "Oye Como
Va," roughly translated as "listen to my rhythm," made it to number 13. That
one Carlos insisted on over Rolie's objections: "[I]t turned out to be . . . one
of my favorite songs," the organist recalled. "But when I heard it initially, I
was just like, 'Wow, I don't know what to do with this.'" Two original songs
received moderate airplay but did not chart: "Hope You're Feeling Better,"
by Rolie, with a hard rock power fueled by Rolie and Shrieve ("I had finished
the lyrics right before we went on stage . . . I had them written out so I could
see them right in front of me"); and "Samba Pa Ti," by Carlos, translated
as "samba for you," a melancholy instrumental featuring a plaintive guitar.
The concluding track, "El Nicoya," by Areas, while not a hit, is nevertheless
notable for its brief lyric, translated as "it's itchy, let's go Chepito," as if the
band is saying to Areas, "[L]et's wrap this up"—with a nod to Chepito's serial
dalliances with groupies that may have led to the *timbalero*'s various brushes
with venereal disease. Featuring cover art by German artist Mati Klarwein,
Abraxas quickly topped their previous effort, going all the way to number one
on the *Billboard* 200.

Superstar rock groups face a unique sort of pressure: keep producing successful music, but do it differently than before. For Santana, that meant adding to the membership. Their 1971 album, simply called *Santana*, like their

first (but usually referred to as "Santana III"), included jazz percussionist Coke Escovedo as well as the Tower of Power horn section. There is an evolution evident. For one thing, the album includes more tracks written by Carabello, attempting to assert himself as an equal member to Carlos, despite the band's name. Although this one also included a cover song—Puente's "Para los Rumberos"—otherwise it was mostly a band-authored album, and the hits "Everybody's Everything" (by Carlos, Milton Brown, and Tyrone Moss) and "No One to Depend On" (by Carlos, Rolie, and Escovedo) helped drive it, like its predecessor *Abraxas*, to number one on the *Billboard* 200.

The album also included a second lead guitarist: teenage wunderkind Neal Schon. Gregg Rolie and Michael Shrieve had first met Schon at the Poppycock Club in Palo Alto one evening in 1970. Always interested in hearing great music, they were struck by this incredibly talented guitarist with a sound remarkably like British bluesman Eric Clapton, playing "a lot of Little Richard tunes and old, like, rock and roll" with a band called Old Davis. As friends of the bass player, Rolie and Shrieve were invited onstage. "We ended up jammin' the whole night and they closed down the club, kicked everybody out and we sat up and played 'til about six in the morning," Schon recalled. Before long, he was part of Santana.

Carlos claimed he did not regret the decision to add a second lead guitarist. "I wasn't threatened by the idea . . . we had some new tunes we were doing . . . that I wanted to play with two guitar players." It was hardly a pioneering move—the Yardbirds had included both Jeff Beck and Jimmy Page on lead guitar in 1966—but some critics saw the move as indicating a certain laziness on his part, as the bandleader would often "hide behind the congas" while Neal played brazenly up front. Indeed, for several 1971 shows, Schon played for both Santana and their opening act Booker T. and Priscilla—one of Bill Graham's pairings designed to head off the growing resegregation of rock and roll. However, according to critic John Sadler of the Vincennes, Indiana, *Sun-Commercial*, the high school dropout from San Mateo "seems to have revitalized the group."

Although the band gave the press the impression that their newfound success had not changed their personalities and all was well in Santana-land, with *Philadelphia Inquirer* music columnist Jack Lloyd going so far as to note in late 1969 that Carlos had a "[h]umility . . . rarely encountered in rock performers," several incidents shook the band's fragile cohesiveness.

First, they foolishly terminated their association with Bill Graham after the Tanglewood gig in 1970. Santana was generating lots of money and attracting less-than-honest people interested in taking it from them. Graham, who had been instrumental in the band's success by booking them with Crosby, Stills & Nash and at the East Coast venues in the summer of 1969, including Woodstock, later claimed to have made less than $20,000 from his association with the group. He correctly predicted that without his steady hand, the band would fall prey to the worst sort of vultures. Their official manager, Stan Marcum, had no experience managing a rock band; his prior professional experience was as a barber. Marcum started hiring disreputable folks, including an accountant who embezzled "in six figures," an attorney subsequently fired "for misrepresentation," and even an astrologer. Someone calling himself Ralph Salazar fraudulently booked the Hollywood Bowl for a Santana show and pocketed an advance; had Graham still been involved, he would have told venue officials that no person named Ralph Salazar worked for Santana, but at that point he had no idea who was on staff.

The band headed to Peru to perform at the University of Lima to benefit the victims of a recent earthquake there. After being welcomed by the mayor and performing three gigs, "nine musicians and four technicians . . . were held in jail for six hours before being put on a Braniff Airlines flight at midnight Thursday for Los Angeles." Apparently a right-wing student group had protested their presence from the start, and the government justified the expulsion—which resulted in the loss of more than $100,000 worth of equipment—because the group "offended the good customs of the people and violated the military regime's morality campaign." They stood accused of obscene "gestures and attitudes." Carlos, no stranger to narcotics himself, felt that Mike Carabello's increasing drug use was over the top and had contributed to the incident.

After a gig in Oklahoma City later that year, Herbie Herbert, the East Bay kid who had left the defunct Frumious Bandersnatch to work for Santana and apprentice with Bill Graham, was arrested with two other roadies on drug possession charges. At least one article referred to them as "members of the rock music group," failing to distinguish between musicians and employees; one bore the headline "Santanans," in a bit of ethnic prejudice that drew the eye to the page as surely would "Satanists." The three were given a two-year suspended sentence after agreeing "never to return to Oklahoma" on pain of "five years at hard labor." The feeling was surely mutual but, given their later travels, seems to have expired after the sentence concluded.

Even the racial and ethnic mixture that had helped form the group's unique sound led to difficulties within the band. The forces in popular music that were defining African American performers as "soul" rather than "rock" even before the death of Black rocker Jimi Hendrix (despite the continuing musical similarities of such artists as Aretha Franklin and the Rolling Stones) were felt in Santana, where two of the white musicians—Rolie and Schon— started balking at performing such numbers as "Oye Como Va" because "it didn't sound like Cream or Hendrix or The Doors." They preferred progressive rock songs like "Hope You're Feeling Better." Carlos and Carabello, for their part, "used to tease Gregg about the fact that he walked like John Wayne," recalled Carlos. "We'd imitate the way he talked, too."

The moment that led to the breakup of the "classic" Santana lineup revolved around band members' various responses to the temporary medical absence of timbalero Chepito Areas for a head injury, which coincided with David Brown's leaving the band for his own medical reasons. Carlos wanted to replace them and keep gigging, but Carabello wanted to wait, at least until Areas recovered. Carlos was moving in a new spiritual direction, both personally and musically, having become a follower of guru Sri Chinmoy, even taking a new given name, Devadip, from the swami. Drummer Mike Shrieve and percussionist Coke Escovedo pushed him toward more experimental music akin to what Miles Davis was then exploring, while Rolie, Schon, and Carabello wanted to keep performing and recording the commercially successful Afro-Latin rock that had brought the band so much success. Rolie was particularly dismayed by Carlos's devotion; his hit with William Penn and His Pals, "Swami," poked fun at exactly the same type of cynical Indian healers under whose spell the guitarist had fallen.

Ultimately Carlos's growing feud with Carabello led to a threat not to perform so long as the master *conguero* was still in the group. Carlos recalled that it was about Carabello's drug use: "I'm not going [on tour] unless we get rid of Stan Marcum and Carabello, because they're supplying the band with the heavy stuff and we sound like shit." When the others did, in fact, perform without him for two weeks, Carlos was dangerously close to losing the band that bore his name, but then Carabello, sensing increasing concern among his bandmates over Carlos's absence, left on his own. Coke Escovedo departed as well, realizing that he, too, was a source of tension, and noting in a subsequent interview with *Rolling Stone* that "[w]hen it got to the point that I was unhappy, I left."

The remaining players from the first two albums—Carlos, Rolie, Areas, and Shrieve—limped into the studio in 1972 with Neal Schon and a variety of other musicians chosen by Carlos to produce what "should have been an unmitigated disaster," according to music writer Hal Miller. Instead, they recorded an instrumental showcase for a growing, evolving band, now boasting fifteen members and a clear leader in its namesake. The tunes on *Caravanserai* are eclectic, including a space-age synthesizer effect presaging Steve Miller's 1976 smash hit "Fly Like an Eagle." It opens with the sound of crickets, and Hadley Caliman's solitary saxophone sounding almost like a shofar. "Stone Flower," with music by Brazilian composer Antonio Jobim and lyrics by Carlos and Shrieve, includes a rare lead vocal by Shrieve, with Carlos on backing vocals, and is an example of the growing spirituality in the music and the changes afoot, while "Song of the Wind," according to Schon, is "simply a couple chords that Carlos came up with, and we started jamming in his studio one day, and they rolled tape, and I ended up playing the first solo and he comes in in the middle, and then I played the last solo going out, and we're just improving." The album yielded no major hit songs but nevertheless soared to number six on the *Billboard* 200 album chart, largely thanks to name recognition. The final track, a nine-minute instrumental by Shrieve called "Every Step of the Way," seems like a farewell.

And indeed, a farewell it was. Rolie quit after the recording sessions to move to Seattle and use some of his earnings to open a restaurant with his father, and Schon quit to focus full-time on Coke Escovedo's new band, Azteca, with whom he had already cut one album and was poised to do another. Santana continued under Carlos's unchallenged leadership and that fall embarked on a "19-city, 27 show barnstorming tour of Europe," Carlos cultivating a sound that one reviewer dismissed as "impersonating McLaughlin impersonating Coltrane." Roadie Herbie Herbert, now the band's production manager, stayed with Carlos for a few months until it was clear that without Rolie—and without playing the hits on the road—Santana was no longer selling out arenas. He too jumped ship and became road manager for Steve Miller's European tour in early 1972.

*   *   *

So why did Santana "make it" while so many other groups, like Frumious Bandersnatch, William Penn and his Pals, and Steve Perry's myriad bands, did not? Some of it was luck, but much of it was cohesiveness, the centrality of one member (Carlos), and the mutual agreement to pursue a cutting-edge musical style at a moment when popular music was in flux, leaving behind blue-eyed surf music and experimental psychedelia. Getting a record deal and an East Coast tour made a huge difference—not to mention the unpredictable success of Woodstock.

Santana's success was rare in that the critics by and large celebrated their music despite the group's commercial popularity. That is not usually the case. The commercial success of musical acts of the era tended to occur when three factors were present: first, the act had absolute technical proficiency; second, it captured an existing cultural zeitgeist; and third, it pushed that zeitgeist in a new direction. The first is a prerequisite, while the second is difficult to attain, relying on a random match between the performer and the culture—in other words, *luck*. Nirvana could not have succeeded in 1980, the Beatles could not have succeeded in 1950, and Elvis could not have succeeded in 1940, no matter how technically proficient all were. But the third, pushing the zeitgeist, tends to offend critics, who are often either frustrated artists themselves or not musically creative—and so usually can only appreciate creativity that has already been accepted. Grunge rockers were dirty. The Beatles had silly haircuts. Elvis was overtly sexual.

Steve Perry, Frumious Bandersnatch, and William Penn and His Pals all had the requisite technical proficiency. The Bandersnatch succeeded, to the extent they did, by reflecting the cultural desire of the era for psychedelic rock, but their attempts to expand and move the culture fell flat; the musicians either left the business or took gigs with successful acts with different musical styles. Santana took a similar risk by combining their own musical interests to create something new—Afro-Cuban-Latin jazz rock. It might have also fallen flat, but they got lucky—they expanded their musical repertoire in tandem with changing cultural tastes. While the surf sounds foundered on the shoals, and psychedelia floated away in a puff of the magic dragon, Santana scored a hat trick—at least until they ran into human nature, the toughest of goaltenders.

Gregg Rolie, Herbie Herbert, and Neal Schon learned lessons from their years with Santana that they would employ successfully in their future careers. For Rolie, the lesson stemmed from his decision to leave. He learned not to hesitate to leave a successful band if it was moving in a musical direction he didn't like or included too many clashing personalities. For Herbie,* the lesson came from the band's treatment of Bill Graham. Herbie learned to put everything in writing and not be afraid to regularly remind musicians what he had done to build their success. But Schon took a very different lesson, gleaned from Carlos's split with Michael Carabello. For him, the lesson was that when the bandleader departs, you need to go on without him—or he might come back and kick *you* out.

---

* Throughout, I will usually refer to "Herbie" by his nickname, which is a version of his surname, Herbert.

First Set

"To Play Some Music," 1973-1976

We wanted to say, hey—there's something sophisticated that can go on with music. Music can really take you somewhere.

—*Herbie Herbert*

The months after the breakup of the classic-era Santana were a time of musical churn for its former members. Guitarist Neal Schon was particularly prolific. In late 1972 he recorded another album with Coke Escovedo's Azteca. Then he joined folk-rock guitarist Terry Dolan in the studio to record *Inlaws and Outlaws*, an album produced by Jefferson Starship keyboardist Pete Sears (and which sadly remained unreleased for decades). After that, he and Sears joined Azteca and Sly and the Family Stone alumni Larry Graham and Gregg Errico to form Graham Central Station. And when Errico produced the funk-rock debut album of Betty Davis, wife of legendary jazz trumpeter Miles—an album that included Merl Saunders, glam disco singer Sylvester, and the Pointer Sisters—naturally he brought in Graham, Sears, and Schon to help as well.

Another member of the band Dolan assembled for *Inlaws and Outlaws* was drummer Prairie Prince of the Tubes. Prince had garnered some small attention in San Francisco for painting a mural at Cliff House with another artist "by walkie-talkie," taking turns on the scaffolding and down below for perspective. Harvesting a penchant for unusual sightings, the "21-year-old art student and rock drummer" was found jumping high on his trampoline, viewed in flight by "passengers from the nearby Hyde Street Cable Car." Stranger still, as he started to gain national attention as a musician providing drums for Nicky Hopkins's album *The Tin Man Was a Dreamer*, columnists for at least two newspapers in the South thought he might actually be dapper Rolling Stones drummer Charlie Watts, working under a fake name to skirt the terms of his record contract. And he caught the attention of a number of San Francisco music professionals, including former Santana roadie Herbie Herbert.

Herbie spent much of 1972 in Europe, helping to manage the Steve Miller Band. Returning to the states to work Hawaii's Crater Festival for Santana and manage Schon, he was looking for something new. And San Francisco was still a crucible for rock music. He formed the suggestively named Spreadeagle Productions with Lou Bramy, a former promoter for Warner Brothers and Famous Music, and got to work.

One musician who soon came back into Herbie's orbit was George Tickner. Having graduated college, the original guitarist and songwriter for the defunct Frumious Bandersnatch still had the musical bug and was ready to play. Herbie introduced him to another friend of no small repute: Jerry Garcia. His band, the Grateful Dead, was in flux following the death of rhythm guitarist Ron "Pigpen" McKernan. Garcia was considering forming a new band altogether, and in 1975 he would birth the Jerry Garcia Band. But at this point, the spring of 1973, he was simply open to new ideas. He put together a group with Merl Saunders, John Kahn, and Bill Vitt that appeared throughout that spring at Keystone Berkeley and Homer's Warehouse in Palo Alto; Tickner played with that group about ten times and may even be an uncredited musician on the resulting album *Live at Keystone*. But he wasn't looking for a permanent gig, he told me; he was just "having fun for a while."

Herbie's primary goal was finding a way to work with Gregg Rolie again. The organist also still had the musical bug and wasn't fully committed to his Seattle sandwich shop, which was not going so well in any event. He later said that "jumping into the restaurant business from the music business is like going from the pan to the fryer. Forget it. It's horrible." The restaurant had a small stage, and when *Rolling Stone* reporter Ben Fong-Torres interviewed the remaining members of Santana, he first met them performing at Rolie's Seattle café. In early 1973, Rolie and Carlos appeared in Honolulu at the Red

Noodle nightclub in Waikiki, albeit separately billed. The big show in Hawaii, of course, was the Sunshine Festival, an annual January affair that Santana had played for several years—but not this year. The stars were a new group that one reporter erroneously called "Happy Birthday" when in fact they preferred to be known as "Schon, Errico, and Sears"—three parts of the original Graham Central Station—and none other than Gregg Rolie sat in with them on their last number. That June, with Santana continuing to find little success with their new musical direction, *Honolulu Advertiser* columnist Ken Rosene confirmed that "Gregg Rolie, ex-organ player for Santana, has been asked to rejoin the group on organ and much-needed vocals." But Herbie had other plans for him. And at this point, Herbie wanted nothing to do with Carlos.

Schon and Rolie worked well together, the guitar prodigy and the organist-vocalist providing a complementary vibe that resembled the relationship Gregg had once shared with Carlos. Rolie had seemed open to joining Schon, Errico, and Sears, but two of them were now in Graham Central Station. Schon seemed willing to strike out on his own from that group, so Herbie added to Schon and Rolie from his current stable, bringing them together with Tickner. Tubes drummer Prairie Prince, keen on recording an album with them at least as a side project, came on as well.

All that was left was bass, and for that the aspiring manager needed look no further than the Steve Miller Band. Miller's former bass player, Ross Valory, was out of work. Valory had met Rolie back when Frumious Bandersnatch shared a bill with the Santana Blues Band and had long been aware of Schon's talents, having been introduced by a gushing Herbie back when the manager was first pushing Carlos to take on the guitar prodigy. "At the time I met him I think was at Pacific Studios in San Mateo," Valory recalled. "He was in the front office and there was carpeting on the floor . . . and he had this little . . . amplifier face down in the carpet so the people in the other room were disturbed by it, 'cause he's sitting there playing all these solos and licks and he's got this thing faced into the carpet." Valory also knew George Tickner, who had written most of the original songs for Frumious Bandersnatch and with whom he had played in Faun. Given the opportunity to join a band with Schon and Rolie, Valory jumped at the chance.

At first, the idea was that this new group, which they called the Golden Gate Rhythm Section, would serve as a backup for local artists in need of a tight instrumentality, something of a San Francisco version of the Muscle

Shoals Rhythm Section, the house band at FAME Studios in Alabama that supported such stars as Aretha Franklin and Wilson Pickett. They were not the first to have this idea; a group of musicians in Georgia had been calling themselves the Atlanta Rhythm Section since 1970.

But these players were more than just a backup band, and they very quickly began collaborating on original material. Notwithstanding the fact that Santana had broken up over Carlos's new musical direction, his sound had nevertheless influenced Schon and Rolie. They were also "influenced by the raw energy of British bands like Led Zeppelin, Deep Purple and the Who." It would be wrong to argue that they "settled" on a particular style, however; the music they produced might be correctly characterized with the wordy description "avant-garde progressive jazz-rock fusion," but it had its own unique character. Guitarist "Tickner supplied many of the blueprints," argued one reporter. "Some of his compositions were little more than chord changes with whimsical names like 'Sketches of Pacheco,' but he laid out a unique floorplan for the band." According to Rolie, Tickner "had these massive hands and he would de-tune his strings and come up with these voicings that nobody else could." Schon concurred. "He had all these really great chording ideas that [I had] never seen before . . . with different tunings, and moving his thumb around. . . . I learned a hell of a lot from him." Indeed, while some music writers have subsequently referred to Tickner as Journey's original *rhythm* guitarist, his role was much closer to the one Schon had played in Santana—second *lead* guitarist.

Top-notch talent recruited, the band simply hoped that they could influence the cultural zeitgeist as Santana had, but first they would need to change their name. All agreed that "Golden Gate Rhythm Section" did not even begin to describe what they had set out to do, but none of the players or even their stalwart, rotund manager could think of a catchy alternative. They cut a few demo songs and the disc jockeys at KSAN-FM put them into rotation, asking for listeners to suggest names.

The results were not promising. They included "Rumpled Foreskin and the Mound-Pounders" and "Hippie-Potamus," seemingly as strange as "Frumious Bandersnatch" or "William Penn and His Pals," but without any of the literary or historical inspiration. Finally, roadie John Villanueva, in one of those cannabis-induced hazes that had gotten him arrested with Herbie in Oklahoma, suggested "Journey." It stuck, and they invented a fictitious fan who suggested it, one Toby Pratt—so that the radio station and the band alike could avoid the embarrassment of not having ultimately chosen a listener-suggested name. When an actual San Franciscan named Toby Pratt came forward to collect the prize—lifetime free admittance to Journey concerts—"the whole thing kind of backfired," said Rolie.

In the renamed band's first appearance, they opened for Santana at the Winterland Ballroom with Malo (a group formed around Jorge Santana, Carlos's younger brother) and Herbie Hancock. Both the *San Francisco Chronicle* and the *San Mateo Times* erroneously called the band "Journeys" and spelled Schon's given name "Neil," with the *Chronicle* also misspelling Gregg's first name ("Greg") and Neal's last ("Schoen"). But when they performed the following week at Sunshine '74 in Hawaii, following the annual tradition Schon and Rolie and Herbie had kept with Santana, the reporters got it right. In both cases, though, the group received "warm critical notices."

As tight as they were musically, their hastily recruited rhythm section was already coming apart. Prairie Prince had never actually left the Tubes. Unable to be in two places at once, the drummer chose the more-established group. The Tubes "were more artistic [and] I felt like it was more my band," he said. At the time, the choice made sense; a local newspaper listed the Tubes, like Santana, as among the best rock bands "presently living and working in the Bay Area"; Journey did not make that cut. Prince left after recording a demo with Journey they called "Charge of the Light Brigade" and playing only two public performances. The Tubes, of course, went on to chart several hits on the *Billboard* Hot 100, most notably "She's a Beauty" in 1983.

But this left Journey—which comanagers Herbie and Bramy incorporated as a "General Partnership" in the Office of the San Mateo County Clerk—with a full calendar and no one behind the drum set. They auditioned more than thirty before Herbie had another of his eureka moments. British drummer Aynsley Dunbar, an alumnus of Frank Zappa's Mothers of Invention who had recently recorded *Diamond Dogs* with David Bowie, was looking for a home for his eclectic musical interests. All agreed to offer him the spot. "After working with Bowie, I had these messages on my answering machine back in America," Dunbar recalled. "They asked me to get together with them, and I did all that, got the gig, and moved up to San Francisco." Although not technically the band's first drummer, Dunbar was offered full membership for the life of the band and an equal share in all profits, as a de facto original member.

Now complete, and stable, this original Journey gave its first performance at San Francisco's Great American Music Hall on February 1, 1974.

The result was a match made in musical heaven, according to at least one critic. *San Francisco Chronicle* columnist Joel Selvin, at the start of what would become a decades-long love affair with the band, wrote that since Carlos Santana "cut his hair and changed his name . . . altered his musical directions along with his consciousness . . . Journey has stepped forward to fill that space," further gushing that "[j]ust as certain as there is an audience ready and waiting, Journey will find its way there. No new band in San Francisco in the past twelve months (at least) has been such an obvious smash."

Merriam-Webster defines "supergroup" as "a rock group made up of prominent former members of other rock groups," and Wikipedia defines it similarly, as "a musical performing group whose members have successful solo careers, are members of other groups, or are well known in other musical professions." Oxford, unsurprisingly, is more selective, defining it as "a very successful and very famous band that plays rock music, especially one whose members have already become famous in other bands." Even as the phrase "very successful and very famous" is relative—one could argue that having a record contract and a national tour would qualify—the original Journey clearly fit the bill. All members except George Tickner had been part of successful rock acts, with Gregg Rolie and Neal Schon having played in Santana, Ross Valory in the Steve Miller Band, and Aynsley Dunbar with Bowie and Zappa. Even Tickner met the lowest of the standards, having been a "member of other groups," like Frumious Bandersnatch, and having performed with the "very successful and very famous" Jerry Garcia.

Valory considered the original Journey a supergroup, and at least two contemporary observers agreed. When *Rolling Stone*'s Fong-Torres, in his post-mortem on Santana, had relayed a rumor that Rolie and Schon were forming a band with a member of the Steve Miller Band, he reported that Santana bassist David Brown thought it would be "a superstar Cream group or something like that," referencing Eric Clapton's 1966–1968 band Cream—which rock historians consider the first supergroup. Connie Rumney of the British Columbia *Victorian* was more explicit, referring to the "new supergroup Journey" in her May 1974 review of the band's appearance as opening act for blues legend B. B. King.

Tickner, no stranger to rock stars, was nevertheless in awe of his new band-mates. Neal Schon "was magical . . . he was like a savant on the guitar." Gregg Rolie "was super talented . . . not only could he play the organ but the electric piano, and he obviously sang, and . . . he bought a place in Marin County and I moved in there with him." As for the drummer, Aynsley Dunbar "was fantastic . . . that was the stuff of dreams, really an excellent timekeeper and showman, and it was just part of the magic." Schon agreed, noting that while Rolie and Tickner spent much of their time writing, "we'd grab a song, figure out a good solo section, and then Aynsley and I would go to town on it."

Despite their supergroup status, Journey started out with a very distinct place in the artistic pecking order. They were headliners several times in 1974, including at Winterland Ballroom, the Great American Music Hall, and Chumash Auditorium at San Luis Obispo's Cal Poly, providing a draw for opening acts Redwing (which had themselves already released three albums), Niteshift, and Sapo (a band formed by former members of Jorge Santana's Malo). But nonetheless, they were more often among the opening acts for established bands like Santana, Steely Dan, Rare Earth, Hot Tuna, and even Graham Central Station, one of Schon's former bands.

Some of their pairings drew the ire of critics. Selvin at the *San Francisco Chronicle* was particularly incensed by the choice to have Journey open for Sam Cooke's former guitarist Bobby Womack at the Berkeley Theater in March 1974, calling their "especially loud, crunching rock music . . . totally lost on the predominately black audience," noting that "they will never make it as a soul act," a sarcasm clearly intended for the promoters and managers—but which played into the growing rift between the Black and white descendants of rock and roll, a rift that promoter Bill Graham was struggling to prevent with just such pairings. Later, when the band opened for Graham Central Station there in June, he called the choice "another mistake." Richard Cromelin of the *Los Angeles Times* was somewhat more forgiving in his review of their appearance with Hot Tuna at the Santa Monica Civic Auditorium. "Its strong set was almost enough to salvage the evening," he wrote of the performance with the Jefferson Airplane members' side project, "and no doubt would have done so had the billing been reversed."

Still, the reviews of the original Journey that first year were overwhelmingly positive. John Hurst of the *Sacramento Bee* called their show at Selland Arena in May "nicely done . . . with lots of rhythm and power and a knack for getting a crowd cooking." Dave Everard, reviewing their appearance with B.B. King at Vancouver Arena for *The Victorian*, especially liked their song "Kohoutek," a Schon-Rolie tune inspired by the appearance of a comet that was visible for much of 1973 and 1974, but added that they would need "a few years to get to know one another (musically) [to] become one of the best bands around." Connie Rumney added in a review on the same page that "Aynsley Dunbar on drums . . . provided the foundations of the band." Philip Elwood, reviewing their appearance opening for Santana at Winterland, worried that "the audio imbalance and microphonic overkill almost capsized Journey's powerful musical voyage," but "Rolie often sings beautifully and . . . Schon comes through as a remarkable imaginative guitarist." Joel Selvin likewise entered a glowing review of that show, and the *Santa Maria Times* called the band "little-known but tremendously talented."

Given the lengthy touring experience of the band members, there was little question they would garner positive reviews of their road show; they knew how to entertain a crowd. What remained was to get a record contract. The major impediment was Rolie's encumbrance with Columbia Records, which held the contract for Santana. Rather than attempt to get Rolie out of that or have him appear under a *nom de musique* like former Turtles Mark Volman and Howard Kaylan (a.k.a. Flo & Eddie)—Journey already had too much baggage finding a band name, let alone trying to rename its members—comanager Bramy brought the group into negotiations for a contract with Columbia. By the end of June, "after a long legal battle," the band signed with Columbia for a seven-figure deal. By August they were in Automatt Studios in San Francisco working on an album with producer Roy Halee.

*   *   *

Journey released their eponymous first album in the spring of 1975 to mostly rave reviews. After industry members got a preview "at CBS Studio A on Folsom street," Joel Selvin of the *San Francisco Chronicle* wrote that the album was "[p]ropelled substantially by superb work from drummer Aynsley Dunbar," highlighting how the band "moves through an array of time signatures, colors, modes, and densities. Rolie's full-throated keyboard work," he added, "brims behind every rhythm track and Schon's piercing guitar style is fully exposed for probably the first time on record." Jim Knippenberg of the

Cincinnati Enquirer agreed, calling the offering from the "star studded lineup ... star studded music ... extremely creative and inventive beyond what you normally hear from a new group ... not exactly inaccessible, but ... definitely complex ... [t]he instrumentals are the album's chief delight."

"Something good very well could be coming in the group called Journey," gushed Pete Bishop of the *Pittsburgh Press*. "Dunbar and Schon are the stickouts." The reviewer identified "[s]everal songs [with] above-average appeal: 'To Play Some Music' ... 'Kohoutek' and 'Topaz,' particularly the latter with its shimmering delicacy yielding to full fledged boogie," adding, however, that Rolie is "no great shakes as lead singer." Joseph Bensoua called Journey "the biggest surprise of the year" in his overwhelmingly positive review. He joined *Rolling Stone* in labeling "To Play Some Music" as "commercial," noting that the "musical patterns on the album are ever-changing with no over-dabbling in electronics." Rich McGrath's more sober account in *Richmond Review* called *Journey* "[n]ot bad, at first listen, with interesting musical arrangements and Rolie's usually unintelligible singing ... more reminiscent of the vibrant early days of Santana ... obviously English rock-influenced. ... Intelligent overall."

Other reviewers were less kind. Mike Diana of the *Newport News Daily Press* called *Journey* "a well-executed but below average musical morsel." Covering the album in depth, the reviewer pronounced "Of a Lifetime" "proficient, but devoid of life," adding that "Kohoutek" "sounds like a cross between cuts from two [of John McLaughlin's Mahavishnu Orchestra] albums ... similar in its seemingly never-ending length." "To Play Some Music" earned "the high marks ... for droning mediocrity and non-funky Top 40 cutie pie and down hominess," while "Topaz," "written by rhythm guitarist, George Tickner ... shows why he should always stay one" since the song contained "every hackneyed cliche used and reused in the last ten years of Rock 'N Roll." Finally, "In My Lonely Feeling," he noted, "is the only cut that shows even the slightest bit of sensitivity ... after Rolie closes his mouth." Gary Deane of the *Saskatchewan Leader-Post* found the work derivative and unoriginal. "'Of a Lifetime,'" he wrote, "might well have been taken from [Santana's] *Abraxas*," calling Schon's guitar work "fiery and molten, the rhythms thick and black ... [s]ix or seven years ago, we would have called this acid rock ... [n]ow it's righteously called jazz, and it's still boring." Ultimately, he found, "Journey proves no more viable than anything else that happened to the members of Santana since the demise of the original band."

These reviewers had a point. Although a competent producer, with credits that included folk duo Simon & Garfunkel and singer-songwriter Laura Nyro, Roy Halee is to blame for the album's lack of breakthrough success due to its subdued sound. The style of music called for explosive loudness, but on this first effort, the band was more often held back than allowed to soar. "He had never produced a rock band before," critic Joel Selvin said, "and recorded the scorching, shrieking music at low volume levels that left evident amounts of tape hiss on the finished master." The producer had been brought in by the president of Columbia Records, but his "desk littered with Grammy awards" did not help here. The record made it only as high as number 138 on the *Billboard* 200, doing moderately better in Japan. "At that time the band sold more tickets than we did records," Rolie recalled.

But *Rolling Stone*'s Cynthia Bowman disagreed. Calling the group "not merely a spinoff" of Santana, like Azteca and Malo, but one that offered "more energetic and less contemplative music than Carlos Santana has been making lately," she specifically credited producer "Roy Halee [who] has contributed to the group's original sound by placing Rolie's piano within the rhythm section and leaving Schon's guitar as lead instrument. His sensitive mix prevents the lackluster vocals from intruding on the band's instrumental strength. . . . A strong beginning."

A strong beginning indeed. "Of a Lifetime," by Rolie, Tickner, and Schon, begins with an organ- and bass-heavy full-minute instrumental. Rolie sings the first verse smoothly and calmly, building to a frenetic culmination. This pattern repeats and is followed by a Schon guitar solo. The rock is strong and heavy, emblematic of where the band is musically. The bass line is prominent, if not particularly complex. The theme is haunting. It is not short—nearly seven minutes long. It speeds up into a guitar solo at the end to showcase Schon's fast fretwork. "In the Morning Day," by Rolie and Valory, begins with piano, soon joined by organ and then vocals. With a more conventional length at about four and a half minutes, the song starts as a teasing romantic ballad, with two verses building up but then pulling back. About two minutes in, following Led Zeppelin's playbook, they add some space-age guitar pyrotechnics, sped by Dunbar's machine-gun drums and backed by church organ and vocal hoots. The final minute includes another fast-fingered guitar solo by Schon.

Side 1 of *Journey* concludes with "Kohoutek," a seven-minute instrumental by Schon and Rolie. It begins with piano accentuated by rhythm guitar, soon joined by drums and then spacey lead guitar pyrotechnics. This was the song that inspired the album cover (band members on a moonscape in low gravity) and was itself inspired by the thousand-year comet that passed near Earth in 1973 and 1974. Two minutes in, it's off to the races, with Dunbar's drums setting the pace. A theme emerges, almost siren-like, warning of calamity. Then a return to the calm piano and soft high hat in the final minute. The danger passed, the comet safely away again, a joyful return to the theme. A shimmering single-note organ coda brings it to an uncertain conclusion, as if a final reminder that Comet Kohoutek is still out there, speeding toward its eventual return.

"To Play Some Music," by hitmakers Rolie and Schon, superimposes a catchy tune and a simple vocal over a swinging, triumphant, danceable, organ-driven boogie-woogie to start side 2. Halfway into this conventional-length, radio-ready number is a minute-long organ solo, followed immediately by a half-minute guitar solo. "Topaz," by Tickner, meanwhile, is a six-minute instrumental that showcases the players' versatility. It begins with a soft guitar backed by a smooth, slow organ. The theme emerges quickly. Dunbar brings it into an up-tempo portion, joined gleefully by Schon, as Rolie emits a yelp. This is the jazziest number so far. Drums, piano, and bass lay out a path for the guitar to whimsically stroll. Mid-song the drums take on a character of their own, joined by a complex bass line followed by a final restatement of the theme. "In My Lonely Feeling/Conversations," by Rolie and Valory, is soulful and melancholy. The lyrics seem to cry out for understanding. The first two verses are punctuated by an insistent lead guitar, followed by a midsong guitar-piano bridge, teasing some jazz elements that commence the "Conversations" portion, an instrumental with what sounds like a funereal church bell in the distance, a "conversation" between Schon's guitar and the other instruments.

Finally, "Mystery Mountain," by Rolie, Tickner, and Diane Valory (Ross's wife at the time), has a radio-friendly length at about four minutes. It provides a danceable, hard rock tune to close out the album. Rolie again emits a whoop as the intro moves into the theme. The lyrics evoke the eruption of a previously dormant volcano, an apt metaphor for the band, as Rolie and Tickner emerge from musical dormancy to create rock music that is explosive and eerily prescient of the unexpected 1980 eruption of Mount St. Helens in Rolie's native Washington State. The song includes a complex guitar solo for Schon, while Valory's bass line is entrusted with the theme.

Back out on the road to promote the album in the summer of '75, reviews of the live show continued to be positive, singling out Dunbar for accolades. After the band's several-night shows at the Starwood, Richard Cromelin of the *Los Angeles Times* likened the drummer to "Keith Moon with jazz tastes," adding that the band "has the raw material and needs now to come up with some songs that have a bit of personality and to rid itself of the musical shackles which seem to impair its performance." After seeing them open for the glam-rock band Kiss, Mimi Smith of the *Boston Globe* chimed in, "Those who straggled in late missed some of the best music-making of the evening, provided by Journey . . . composed of Aynsley Dunbar on drums, one of the best session men in rock," adding that "their LP would seem to make a good investment."

To husband their funds to stay out on the road longer, Herbie and Bramy proposed a novel concept. They incorporated the band as Nightmare Productions, Inc., a company to be owned equally by the musicians and themselves. The new entity would collect all royalties from the records, including the advances paid by Columbia for the tours, and any receipts from the live show; it would also assume all costs related to the band's work. All five musicians signed contracts agreeing to become employees of Nightmare. Rather than collect regular salaries, they would invoice Herbie and Bramy for their needs. In return, they were offered stability: no band member could be fired except for "willful default" or breach of the contract, or unless the band broke up, in which case all the musicians' employee contracts would be terminated. The musicians in Journey understood that they were making an investment in themselves; the riches could wait.

As the band prepared to return to the studio to cut their sophomore release, George Tickner decided to leave. He was worn down by "the grueling grind" of life on the road, and it didn't look like Journey was heading toward any major success at that point. Already a registered nurse, the guitarist and creative songwriter left to attend the prestigious Stanford University School of Medicine, ultimately becoming a surgical technician. His departure marked one of the rare instances of a member of a successful musical act leaving the industry of his own accord for an entirely different professional pursuit. His music continued to reverberate with Journey in songwriting credits on the next two albums, and they all remained friendly, with Tickner turning up at occasional rehearsals for several years to come. But his bandmates—and managers—got the best of the deal: when Nightmare Productions issued its first shares, Tickner was not included, and he has never received any royalties from the one album they recorded together. "Nobody was the most honorable person in the world," he told me with a hint of bitterness, "except maybe for me."

The band returned to the Automatt in August 1975 to begin recording their second album, *Look into the Future*, which Columbia Records released in January 1976. Although it did somewhat better in the charts, rising to number 100, it garnered significantly fewer reviews than their first effort, albeit again generally positive. Evan Hosie, writing in the *Berkeley Gazette*, called their "debut album a year ago . . . a journey in the wrong direction," but found that "their second stab at success, 'Look into the Future' come[s] a lot closer," adding that Rolie's "vocals stand out as they never have before . . . their new album packs a mean punch, and Journey is obviously heading in the right direction." Kelly Hodge of the *Austin American-Statesman* noted, "The Columbia Records information sheet on Journey describes the band's music as 'heavy space.' What a concept! . . . the music is controlled and only occasionally becomes absurd . . . *Look into the Future* . . . is a sharp second effort."

In a lengthy interview with Michael Hill of the *Baltimore Sun*, Neal Schon compared the band's sound favorably with British rockers Led Zeppelin and the Who. "The people in this band have . . . been in successful groups and know how it feels and what it takes, so they speak with some authority when they say this one's going to make it," telling the reporter that Journey was "getting ready to take over the world." Gregg Rolie predicted longevity: "This group's going to have a 10-year anniversary . . . [w]e should be together for 30 or 40 years," adding that "[t]here's a lot of talent involved in this band . . . we're ready to try anything." But the real lynchpin of the group was their drummer. "Things didn't really click for Journey until Aynsley Dunbar came along," Hill averred, quoting the Brit as saying, "This is something I've been looking for for a long time. . . . I'm really getting something together with some people instead of just being used by somebody else." As for their sound, it "is definitely rock, but they seem limited in that format and extend their songs with jazz dynamics and progressions," wrote Hill. According to Dunbar, "People may come to a concert to hear somebody else, but they leave thinking about us because we've made some complex music very accessible to them." Schon's take was that "[t]here are endless possibilities. We're just finding out what they are." And they had quite the work ethic. "This group's even serious at rehearsals," claimed Dunbar. "We don't just mess around, we get down and do some work."

Columbia Records pushed hard to get airplay for the songs and sales for the album, placing an advertisement in newspapers around the country, timed for the day after each show on the band's tour. "Out of San Francisco's legendary musical past comes its spectacular future, Journey . . . they were knocking out audiences on the West Coast even before they had an album out . . . you saw and enjoyed Journey last night in concert—now get this great new album at National Record Mart."

The music itself was indeed a step forward from the first album, especially when it came to the production, which the band itself took over this time, aided by studio engineer Glen Kolotkin. "On a Saturday Night," by Rolie, is radio-friendly, danceable, and not too long, at exactly four minutes. Sporting a simple verse-chorus-guitar solo structure, it's mostly vocals over piano for the verses. "It's All Too Much" is a cover of the Beatles' song by George Harrison. Journey's take is frenetic and guitar-heavy, far less psychedelic than the original and two minutes shorter, with abbreviated lyrics, no tambourine or cymbals, and a vocal whoop in the intro. This version would have been wrong for *Yellow Submarine* but is perfect on *Look into the Future*. It concludes with the title refrain played backward, a nod to the urban legend that if one plays the final bars of the Beatles' "I'm So Tired" backward, it sounds like they are saying, "Paul is dead, miss him, miss him, miss him."

"Anyway," by Rolie, is a haunting, dark song. It has jazzy moments during the verses, and during the refrain, it seems ready to explode, pulling back each time. This track contains some interesting guitar explorations by Schon. "She Makes Me (Feel Alright)," on the other hand, with music by Schon and words by Rolie and Alex Cash, is a rollicking up-tempo with lyrics that strain to keep up with instruments seemingly racing forward like greyhounds. The drums, bass, and guitar drive this one, as if Rolie barely has time to voice the vocal, let alone play the organ. At three minutes and twelve seconds long, this is the shortest track on the album.

"You're on Your Own," with music by Tickner and Schon and words by Rolie, closes out Side 1. It begins with a mournful piano, shortly joined by drums, guitar, and bass. Schon's guitar offers the theme, and the vocals presage a brief up-tempo portion. Rolie's lyric teases "maybe will, maybe won't," mirroring a back-and-forth instrumentality. Schon provides a strong guitar line at midsong, joined soon thereafter by a powerful organ line by Rolie. Then Schon's guitar mournfully picks up the theme again, joined by Rolie's lyric "try and make up your mind" in a strangely melancholy up-tempo.

Side 2 starts with the title track, at eight minutes long, the longest on the album. With music by Schon and words by Diane Valory and Rolie, "Look into the Future" begins with a calm guitar and soft drum. Schon's guitar answers to Rolie's vocal questions are what's truly lyrical here, although the organ is also prominent. The song sports a traditional hard rock guitar solo, answered by an organ refrain, with a guitar response, and then a return to the theme. If one were looking for a slow dance, this might fit the bill. A contemplative, midsong instrumental portion moves the song into a new theme, still mostly with a slow beat, offering an opportunity for some interesting guitar statements. Rolie chants "It's right around the corner, just around the corner" to accompany Schon's guitar statements, which move into a crescendo before a definitive end. The song fills the time; it's hard to imagine it being any shorter and still accomplishing what it does.

"Midnight Dreamer," with music by Schon and words by Rolie, begins with an insistent drum, soon joined by a Schon guitar riff and powerful Rolie vocal. This is a hard rock song with strong R&B influences. In the second minute it devolves into jazz, Dunbar's drums mixing with Rolie's piano. Schon joins in with some space-age guitar stylings, devolving into classic rock soloing. The rhythm is a repetitive train. Dunbar brings it home, with "ah-ah" vocals from Rolie.

"I'm Gonna Leave You," with music by Schon, Rolie, and Tickner and words by Rolie, is a space-age, fusion rock rewrite of "Babe I'm Gonna Leave You," by Anne Bredon, with all of the hard rock guitar of the Led Zeppelin version and none of the acoustic folk sentiment of either Jimmy Page or Joan Baez. It begins without a break from the previous track. In a five-note refrain repeated throughout, the guitar dukes it out with the organ, jazzy vocals serve as referee, and bass and drums are the ropes, keeping everyone in. Although Dunbar doesn't have a writing credit here, this song would have fit on any album by his previous blues group Retaliation, with Rolie sounding almost like singer Victor Brox. Already lengthy at seven minutes, it nevertheless leaves the listener wishing it were longer.

In the 1976 tour, Journey now found themselves headliners as often as opening acts. They opened for Uriah Heep at the Vancouver Coliseum, earning the accolade "astute—while still heavy-metal-oriented . . . [t]asty and tolerable stuff." At Bill Graham's "Day on the Green" in San Francisco, "Journey . . . clearly provided the afternoon's musical highlights" in a show that included Jeff Beck, which must have made for an interesting backstage reunion with one of Dunbar's old bandmates. Unfortunately, "Sound problems marred the noon-hour performance by Journey, an offshoot of the Santana band with two albums and an increasing national reputation. Regardless of technical difficulties, the hard rock quartet earned two encores from the crowd," reported Joel Selvin. Calling Dunbar "the most prolific drummer to come out of England," Joseph Bensoua found Journey, after their performance at Hollywood's Starwood nightclub, "one of the most volatile rock groups to come out of San Francisco," calling their sound "jazz, space, funk and rock." Dunbar "has pushed the band into off-beat patterns which take it out of the standard norm without losing its rock credibility," gushed Bensoua, while "Neal Schon . . . takes command on stage with his articulate lead attacks. Sometimes haunting, often times searing, his riffs open the door to Dunbar's stylish drumming and complement Rolie's brash vocals . . . something to behold." Al Rudis of the *Chicago Sun-Times* also saw that show and agreed, crediting the talent of the musicians and the absence of Tickner. While talented, Rudis opined, Tickner lacked the extensive experience of the other members, especially Dunbar. But actually, any improvements were coincidental to the departure of the guitarist.

As before, there were negative notices. Journey made the pages of the prestigious *New York Times* for the first time—but not the last—after they "headlined a triple bill at the Palladium," a Victorian-era Broadway stage near New York's Union Square that had been converted into a rock ballroom. "Journey may be a California band, but it is hardly typical of the kind of folk-rock normally associated with that state," wrote John Rockwell, confusing both regions and decades. "It's a classic late-1970's sound, carefully constructed and quite remarkably without excitement," he inexplicably wrote. But "[w]hen toward the end of the set Mr. Schon made a few desultory lunges at his amplifiers and lay down on his back to play, it was one of the most absurd, dispiriting things this observer has seen in a long time. If Journey wants to play it safe, fine; they do it pretty well. But please, let's not pretend any real relation to violent, old-fashioned rock-and-roll."

Bad promotion for a show at Albuquerque's Tingley Coliseum led to Ike and Tina Turner being listed as headliners when in fact they opened there for Journey, and much of the crowd left before Journey started—further indication of the growing split between white and African American music fans. The reviewer stayed but was unimpressed. "The famed guitar and keyboards of ex-Santana players Neil [sic] Schon and Gregg Rolie merged into an indistinguishable buzz. Their albums indicate they are an exceptional band and their live reviews tout them as a future supergroup," whatever he meant by that, "but only a hundred or so die-hards perceived . . . something, that held them there to the bitter end." There wasn't any reported violence, soon to be the go-to excuse for concert promoters who increasingly eschewed such pairings, to the detriment of Black artists who found their bookings mostly in smaller venues.

The live show was remarkably similar to Journey's recordings. Rolie was more than a lead vocalist; he was very much a bandleader, albeit mostly hidden behind all of his keyboards, introducing songs and yelling out whoops of encouragement during the guitar solos. (When he yelled, "Aw, look out" at the start of "You're On Your Own," it was another callout to the Beatles: John Lennon emitted a similar cry on *Abbey Road* at the start of "She Came In through the Bathroom Window.") Rolie also enunciated somewhat better live than on the studio versions, indicating that their concert mixing favored the vocals.

This was ultimately a band in search of an audience. The pairings with Ike and Tina Turner, as with Bill Graham's earlier pairing of Santana with Bobby Womack, proved more amenable to the tastes of the musicians than to their listeners. Progressive rock's white teenage audience was finding much to admire in the new punk scene, with its fascist overtones. Some artists would use this as material—Pink Floyd most notably in *The Wall*, and when Electric Eels, less famously, attended a house party in American Nazi Party T-Shirts. Finally, in October 1976, opening three nights for Lynyrd Skynyrd in the Pacific Northwest, they clicked. "Everywhere we played with Skynyrd, we commanded two, three encores," reported Schon.

Without intending it, Journey's progressive rock was becoming increasingly "coded" for white audiences who also dug Skynyrd, with their unabashed white Southern rock replete with a Confederate flag onstage, while the Black concertgoers who grooved to the soulful sounds of Ike and Tina Turner found little in Journey to admire. But all too quickly, the vagaries of the tour schedule took them away, and they spent the rest of that fall playing in Europe, not opening again for the storied southern rockers until a New Year's Eve show at Oakland Coliseum and one on New Year's Day 1977 in San Diego. Tragically, a plane crash would kill several members of Lynyrd Skynyrd the following October.

Journey's lackluster sales did not impress the executives at Columbia Records, who wanted more. The label's former president, Clive Davis, had once said that to be successful, "the key question . . . is whether there is a Top 40 hit in the album." Journey had an impressive stage show and had earned critical acclaim, but the band had no hits.

Nervous that they would be dropped by the label, Herbie identified three problems: songwriting, onstage performance, and singing. To address these issues, Dunbar started writing lyrics, and the band started developing harmonies. After a series of intensive vocal lessons with soul singer (and Zappa alumna) "Lady Bianca" Thornton, they entered His Master's Wheels Studios in the summer of 1976 to record their third album.

*   *   *

Columbia Records' concerns about Journey were not unexpected, given the company's history and the trends in the industry at the time. Named for Washington, DC (District of Columbia), the city of its 1880s origins, the company initially produced graphophones, which played cylindrical audio recordings. Originally conceived as a shortcut for recording dictation, the product consisted of a hand-cranked box that turned a cylinder with recordings engraved on the outside, amplified through a brass horn. When rival Victor's "Victrola" disc player became a household name, Columbia pivoted from machinery to recording and began producing discs for the new players. The Victrola played discs at 78 rpm (revolutions per minute). Audio was encoded as microscopic bumps within a continuous groove on the disc, and a sensitive needle stylus interpreted the bumps to reproduce the sound. Initially they were single sided and short, but before long, the records developed "B sides" to increase overall playing time. Household musical entertainment, which had previously involved singing and the playing of instruments, pivoted to recordings as more and more Victrolas appeared in American and European homes. White families listened to classical, music hall, and operetta until Paul Whiteman made jazz—previously disparaged as "race" music—acceptable in white homes. During the Great Depression, jukeboxes (so named for their presence in African American "jukes," or small dance clubs) made communal listening experiences cheaper when live entertainment was unaffordable to most; they had the added effect of helping record companies like Columbia determine the most popular styles and produce more of what people wanted to hear.

Columbia was by no means the dominant label in the industry for the first half of the twentieth century, but the company's fortunes changed in the 1940s after being acquired by the Columbia Broadcasting System (CBS). They signed a young crooner from Hoboken, New Jersey, named Frank Sinatra, who quickly became a superstar, replete with swooning teenage girl fans twenty years before the Beatles set hearts aflutter at Shea Stadium. The company benefited from the war by recording their musicians on V-discs (the V standing for "victory"), distributed to military bases, when shellac—a necessary ingredient—was in short supply in the civilian market. Finally, in 1948, Columbia beat rival RCA Victor (the Radio Corporation of America had purchased Victor in 1929) in the creation of the long-playing record (LP), a twelve-inch disc with a "microgroove," played at 33⅓ rpm for more than twenty minutes on each side. Because of its length, the LP was well suited to classical symphonies, and Columbia became a major player in the classical market during the 1950s, recording multiple records with superstar conductor Leonard Bernstein. In the popular realm, Columbia cornered the market for original cast recordings of Broadway musicals, also sized to fit the new LPs.

Most African Americans at the time could not afford the new LP players, so Columbia largely shied away from "race music"—now called rhythm & blues. As a result, with the advent of rock and roll, the new racially integrated genre fell to upstart labels like Capitol Records. Rock and roll musicians typically recorded "singles," smaller discs played at 45 rpm, one song per side. Occasionally these would be collected and sold as "record albums," multileaf books of singles; albums eventually evolved into multiple-song, two-sided LPs instead.

Columbia finally started signing rock acts in earnest just as the genre was entering its post-Beatles phase. A variety of forms emerged in the mid-1960s that appealed to the growing number of teenagers born during the baby boom. A young lawyer at Columbia, Clive Davis, recognized the lucrative nature of rock; in 1967, thanks to a corporate reorganization, he became president of the label and set about signing acts like Santana, Big Brother and the Holding Company, Chicago, Billy Joel, and Bruce Springsteen. Between their stable of superstar rock acts and their dominance of the mail-order market through the Columbia Record Club, the label quickly dominated rock recording. Davis was removed from the label in 1973 over a financial scandal (he was eventually cleared of wrongdoing). His replacement was Goddard Lieberson, who had previously served in the post and was now also president of the Recording Industry Association of America (RIAA), a trade group that, among other things, measured record sales. Lieberson returned to head the label just as Herbie Herbert and Lou Bramy were negotiating Journey's first record contract.

Of course, American households did not only hear their music live and on records played at home; there was also the radio. Prior to the advent of television, radio primarily served the purpose that television later would: short story or serial in-home theater and variety shows. Rock and roll emerged just as television became popular. As TV eclipsed radio for the spoken-word market, radio stations—virtually all of which were on AM (amplitude modulation) frequencies—reprogrammed as music stations. To accommodate their regular need for new material, record companies provided the stations with 45 rpm singles, often accompanied with bribes for "disc jockeys"—on-air personalities—to play their submissions. When this "payola" scandal was uncovered, program managers took over, determining playlists based on charts covered in trade magazines like *Billboard*.

By the mid-1960s, there was a chicken-and-egg aspect to hitmaking; airplay drove sales, but sales drove airplay. As a result, much of the music on the radio was anodyne, second-generation surf music with little of the avant-garde. Songs made the Top 40 listings in the trades as much through bribery and favors—payola never went away, it just changed—as through genuine listener demand.

Cutting-edge artists like the Doors, Led Zeppelin, and Pink Floyd found no home on AM. To get their music out, they turned to a much smaller portion of the radio market: FM (frequency modulation) stations. Whereas AM had significantly further reach—the signal could bounce off the stratosphere and back down to Earth, hundreds of miles from the source—FM required a more direct signal but came through clearer, with less static. Thanks to its patents, RCA had achieved a virtual monopoly on FM household receivers during the 1930s and mostly avoided producing them, the better to drive business to the AM stations it controlled. By the early 1960s, the company's hold on radio was loosening, but FM dials were still not standard on car stereos. A 1965 Federal Communications Commission ruling required FM stations to play at least 50 percent different material than their sister AM stations, thereby creating a home for experimental music—often selected by DJs who were high on the psychotropic drug LSD. As a result, FM became synonymous with teenagers sitting in their bedrooms listening to cutting-edge progressive rock—like Journey.

And something else was different on FM. Especially in these early years, many stations adopted a free-form format, allowing the disc jockeys to choose the music once again. "Deejays have probably been even more effective than journalists in defining new genres," writes Simon Frith. One early pioneer of free-form style was San Francisco DJ Tom Donahue, who birthed a genre called "album-oriented rock" (AOR). It's not that Donahue and other AOR jocks played entire albums at a time—although sometimes they did—but that they played deeper cuts, beyond the few songs that the label released as 45 rpm singles. With DJs on FM playing deep cuts, artists and listeners alike began thinking of the album, rather than the individual song, as the work of art. And this was literal: AOR albums often had covers that displayed incredible artistry, like Santana's *Abraxas*.

It is through their FM broadcasts that Journey was able to build their initial nationwide following and get their modest sales. "FM saved us," said Journey bass player Ross Valory. But not for long: they couldn't get hits without AM airplay.

"Wheel in the Sky," 1977–1978

Steve Perry. His name's been comin' in and out of my life from the beginning of time.

—*Herbie Herbert*

The band released *Next* in the winter of 1977, just in time for a few dates opening for Electric Light Orchestra—ELO for short. Reviews were mixed. Joseph Bensoua, who had earlier reviewed Journey's appearance at the Starwood, delivered a positive one, writing that "there's nothing holding Journey back. Each new release, so far, has been astounding. Again," he stated, "we're knocked over with a beautiful blend of offbeat rock n' roll, soaring ballads and exceptional instrumentations. Gregg Rolie's vocals are as superb as ever," and "Aynsley Dunbar's drumming and Ross Valory's bass lines continue to search out creative lines of expression." He saved his best praise for last: "[S]tanding above even these masterful personalities is one man who can be considered the most exploratory and dynamic guitarist in America today—Neal Schon. His playing is incredible. His leads are hypnotizing." Robin Welles of the *Tipton County Tribune* added that "[c]onstant touring and a couple of solid albums have brought the fans running to the ticket office. Young Schon is a whiz on guitar." Rock listeners agreed, if not overwhelmingly. The album continued the band's track record of marginal improvement in the charts, peaking at number 85 on the *Billboard* 200.

On the other hand, "Journey seem[ed] to have taken a step backwards," according to the *Austin American-Statesman*'s Kelly Hodge. "The problem with 'Next' is not the ideas—Journey's intermixing of rock with jazz is usually interesting. But this time the disc doesn't gel." Hodge took specific umbrage with the songs "People" and "Nickel and Dime," finding that although they were "mildly enjoyable, they're nothing special." The critic added a crushing postmortem. "What went wrong this time is not easily determined. The vocals of Gregg Rolie . . . seem to improve with every disc as does the guitar work of Neal Schon . . . Ross Valory and drummer Aynsley Dunbar seem to uphold their ends. Perhaps the musicians are a little too conservative on this disc, causing the excitement to suffer. . . . Hopefully 'Next' will be a one-of-a-kind miss for this talented ensemble."

Actually, *Next* is a calmer, more contemplative album than the band's first two offerings. Neal Schon took over lead vocals on two songs, Aynsley Dunbar authored (or coauthored) the lyrics to most of the songs and, with Ross Valory, was enlisted on harmonies for the first time as the band began a transition to more lyrical, vocal-oriented rock intended to grow their audience and keep their contract with Columbia. "Spaceman," by Dunbar and Rolie, begins the album with piano and drums, soon joined by guitar. Rolie sings a cool, laid-back vocal on this jazz-inspired rock tune. The lyric, punctuated by a brief guitar lick between verses, is a response to critics calling the group's musical style "heavy space." There are very subtle backup vocals. The intensity of the music is teasing, building up and pulling back. Schon's guitar solo is clean and clear, and Rolie sings to the guitar in the final notes.

"People," by Dunbar, Rolie, and Schon, begins with two atonic, multi-instrument notes and then develops into a psychedelic railroad-track rhythm with some guitar statements. The chorus word "people" includes harmonies. The final guitar licks sound almost like birds chirping—or people talking. The song ends as it began, with a single note by all instruments, broken down after starting together. "I Would Find You," by Schon and his wife at the time, Tena Austin, and a lead vocal by Schon, begins with spacey guitar akin to that found at the start of Steve Miller's contemporaneous hits "Jungle Love" and "Threshold," moving smoothly into a sound reminiscent of *Caravanserai*-era Santana. "Here We Are," by Rolie, begins with a piano instrumental and includes harmonies. Toward the end he screams out the lyrics, à la late Beatles, and a rollicking boogie-woogie takes the song through the fade-out.

"Hustler," by Dunbar and Rolie, begins with an insistent guitar riff and almost a call-and-response with Rolie's vocals. Dunbar adds a cowbell (or possibly timbale) in this hard-driving, aggressively confident number.

"Next," the title track, by Dunbar, Rolie, Schon, and Heidi Cogdell, begins with an insistent beat via drums and guitar. The rest of the band joins in, and they play a hard up-tempo for about a minute before cooling down into a ballad, with Rolie singing a jazz-rock tune. There are good harmonies in the chorus. The beat picks up again for an extended hard rock gallop to the finish line. "Nickel and Dime," an instrumental by Rolie, Schon, Valory, and George Tickner, begins with a jazz section that quickly devolves into hard jazz-rock. The second minute features a change and some space-rock sentiment, with a pronounced bass reminiscent of the first two albums—unsurprising, given Tickner's writing credit. The song ends with two overdubbed guitar lines.

Dunbar's sticks count the band into "Karma," the album's final number, which he cowrote with Rolie and Schon. The guitarist, who starts scratching his strings before the band joins in with what is best described as "rhythmic cacophony," handles lead vocals on this one. The drum line at times sounds like a rattlesnake—no small feat. This is perhaps the most forward-looking, experimental track on the album. Even the coda has a brief coda of its own, a shimmering electronic half note. With a haunting fade-out, the song is geared toward a hard rock sensibility that Schon would continually attempt to infuse into the band's music in the years to come, with varied success with his bandmates and fans. But in this song, the guitarist is very much in control. Unlike their live set from the first two albums, where Rolie was clearly the bandleader, Schon ends the album with his own stab at leadership.

Journey did not lack a leader in their interpersonal dynamics and business affairs; Herbie Herbert amply filled that role. The former equipment manager for Frumious Bandersnatch, road manager for Santana, and co–general manager for Journey had built the band around Schon and Rolie, musician by musician. In 1976, at the band's request, he and Lou Bramy dissolved Spreadeagle Productions, after which he managed the band unchallenged. (Bramy took on Spreadeagle's other client, Y&T, for several years before becoming an A&R [Artists and Repertoire] executive for Atlantic Records.) Herbie did not write or perform any of the music, but he chose the musicians who did. So the band did not lack for leadership. But Herbie did not step onstage during the shows; that was where they needed a central figure around whom the other players could rally while playing. Without a focal point on the stage, it was hard to turn an appreciative audience into a fanatical one.

Indeed, leadership of the band was very much an open question as they headed out for their dates with ELO in the winter of 1977. Rolie was a veteran, a star lead singer, but he was tucked behind that immovable albatross of a Hammond B-3 organ, his showmanship increasingly limited as he made room for Schon's growing vocal skills.

Dunbar, similarly tucked away behind the drums, was nevertheless finally asserting himself. He had been a drummer for hire for so long, but after recording the first Journey album as "the new guy," he had brought his British blues sensibility to *Look into the Future* and was now seeking a more prominent role in the band as its chief songwriter. Schon and Valory, on the other hand, were the most mobile onstage, with only the wires to limit them; but Valory was content to rock out by the drum set, in musical conversation with Dunbar; and Schon's embarrassing attempts at Pete Townshend–style showmanship had already earned the dismissal of a major national newspaper.

The release of *Next* came at perhaps the worst time in the history of progressive rock. According to Van Halen chronicler Greg Renoff, in 1977 "very few people in the music industry saw a bright future for hard rock and heavy metal." But it was in the midst of this uncertainty that the band's real leader, Herbie Herbert, had yet another of his eureka moments. And this time, his big new idea would change the course of music history.

*   *   *

Robert Fleischman grew up in the suburbs of Los Angeles, where unlike Steve Perry, he was far from lonely. At age eleven a cousin brought him to see the Beatles play the Hollywood Bowl and gave him a bug for music. "I used to go in my parents' living room and plunk a record down and record it on the little tape recorder," he told me. "I sort of turned on the tape recorder and I would sing along with records and see if I could like blend in with them. And . . . I sort of developed my tone and everything so I could blend in with all these different bands I used to sing with—along with the Hollys, and the Yardbirds, and the Stones, and the Beatles."

His first band rehearsed in upscale Palos Verdes, in a house designed by Frank Lloyd Wright with a view of the Pacific. From there it was a short trip to a first brush with stardom. At age twenty-two, he was approached by the English group Genesis after their lead singer, Peter Gabriel, left to pursue a solo career. "I was gonna go to England and do *Trick of the Tale*, and . . . I had my flight and everything all arranged, and then I got a phone call saying that Phil Collins decided to go in and take a crack at the vocals. And so he did, and that was it." In consolation, the head of A&R for Columbia subsidiary Epic Records sent him to Chicago to choose from among three groups in need of a vocalist. He chose one and toured the East Coast and Midwest with them for most of 1976 before catching the attention of Barry Fey, the Denver-based promoter who had famously objected to allowing Led Zeppelin to join a bill including Vanilla Fudge and Spirit at their very first gig. Fey arranged a showcase for Fleischman in Denver, where recording executives from both coasts could attend, in early 1977. "He put me in the Hyatt Hotel there in Denver and I started writing. And then about three weeks later, I had put together a band and wrote a bunch of songs and I was doing a show for CBS Records."

Things moved quickly after that: "About two weeks later I was sitting in Los Angeles at the CBS offices . . . and they said that they have this band, Journey, and that they were looking to have a lead singer . . . because they . . . were just selling [only] so many records, and at that time I think Foreigner and Boston were coming out and they wanted to get on that whole bandwagon" with melodic rock.

Journey, meanwhile, was about to lose its record contract. Although sales of *Next* had improved on the previous two albums, after four years together, the band had not lived up to their label's "supergroup" expectations. Sales were not approaching those of Santana's *Caravanserai*, let alone the blockbuster *Abraxas*. Columbia Records president Walter Yetnikoff told manager Herbie Herbert that they were finished. But by now Herbie had a good sense of the currents in the industry and knew that CBS was trying to do something with Fleischman. He proposed they take him on, and "the head of artists' development at Columbia in New York gave us a stay of execution."

Fleischman flew to San Francisco, where he was met by Herbie and whisked directly to Studio Instrument Rentals (S.I.R.) to join the band. "I got there and met everyone and then we started jamming." They were ready for him. He faced the studio booth as if it were an audience, away from his new bandmates. And when they played that first note, "it was like having rockets in my back pockets"—the music just seemed to explode from the band toward the singer. "And they'd been together so long and they were so tight that it was great to play with people that way," Fleischman recalled. During those sessions at S.I.R., they wrote some songs—"Anytime," "Wheel in the Sky," and "Winds of March"—all of which would eventually end up on the next Journey album, with some modifications to the last one. From there it was just across the street to the Automatt, where the band had recorded *Journey* and *Look into the Future*, to lay down some tracks. Like George Tickner and Neal Schon before him, Fleischman moved into Gregg Rolie's house. And rather than have the band self-produce its recordings, as they had with *Look into the Future* and *Next*, Fleischman, conscious of the need for a good mix of vocals and instrumentals, recommended they work with Roy Thomas Baker, who had produced the first four albums by British rockers Queen and their operatic tenor, Freddie Mercury. Baker was not entirely unknown to the group; he had previously worked with drummer Aynsley Dunbar as an engineer on Frank Zappa's *Chunga's Revenge*.

"For You," which ended up in the Journey box set years later, was written by Fleischman, Schon, and Rolie. It begins with a guitar theme, electric but soft. Fleischman sings the verse and is joined by the other members in harmony during the chorus. There is an evident restraining of the instrumental talents; the band is trying with some success to check their free-form, exploratory musical tendencies—especially those of the explosive Dunbar. The guitar solo, somewhat brief by Schon's standards, is nevertheless reminiscent of his earlier work. The song is a good showcase for the talents of Fleischman's four-and-a-half octave range. Toward the end, he seems to go into falsetto, but it's actually full voice, demonstrating a talent beyond the great rock screamers of the time, like Robert Plant of Led Zeppelin and Lou Gramm of Foreigner, and proving his worth to his hypertalented bandmates.

Fleischman joined the band on their summer tour opening for Emerson, Lake, and Palmer. (They started the year with Electric Light Orchestra— ELO—and were now with ELP, almost as if Herbie was booking gigs based on the alphabet.) "Journey will never be the same again," said Al Rudis after seeing them at Soldier Field in Chicago, where they performed five new songs and got the crowd going with "Wheel in the Sky" as well as their standby "On a Saturday Night." "Fleishman [sic] belongs to the athletic, energetic school of singers . . . unlike your . . . Roger Daltreys and Rod Stewarts, he doesn't constantly strike poses . . . he's got vocal cords of steel." Philip Elwood, reviewing Journey's August 4 show at San Francisco's Cow Palace, wrote that Fleischman "has a strong, melodic voice that seems to be blending into the heavy ensemble."

But Vaughn Palmer, who caught them at Pacific Coliseum in Vancouver, British Columbia, dismissed the addition of the singer as "an attempt to 'go commercial.'" The fans were similarly nonplussed. "Journey was a cult, they . . . had a really strong fan base. So all their fans would get front row seats and start flipping me off every night," Fleischman said.

Fleischman's tenure in Journey was over almost as soon as it began. "Herbie requested that I leave my manager—this I could not do because I had a contract with Barry to fulfill," the singer recalled. Fey "had a percentage of me and Herbie also wanted a percentage. This arrangement would have made me a broke slave. The managers could not work out an agreement, and that's where it all fell apart." Indeed, Fleischman could not abide Journey's payment scheme, especially with Fey taking a cut. The original plan—wherein the musicians took income as needed—had morphed into modest annual salaries of only $17,500 (about $88,300 in 2023 dollars), and Fleischman was never offered shares in Nightmare Productions, which husbanded all royalties.

Herbie also had conflicts with Fleischman's personality—he called him "a pampered poodle." An incident in Fresno brought out the worst between the two. "[W]e were playing this huge gig, and Herbie didn't want me to sing. 'I thought you guys wanted me here, and then all of a sudden, you don't want me singing tonight, so why should I even go up on the stage? It's not like I'm playing drums, so you just want me up there to clap.'"

Herbie fired Robert Fleischman after the show at the Cow Palace. The singer moved to New York, where he recorded a solo album, *Perfect Stranger*, at John Lennon's Record Plant studio. After partying at Studio 54 with the likes of Andy Warhol, Lou Reed, and Peter Wolf, he formed a band called Channel, later joining Vinnie Vincent Invasion and the supergroup Asia.

It's possible that Herbie hired Fleischman while knowing he would fire him within weeks. By now a seasoned manager, he surely understood the complications posed by hiring a singer signed to Barry Fey. Knowing that Columbia Records was about to drop the band and that they were looking to do something with Fleischman to keep Fey happy, Herbie may have hired Fleischman as a temporary measure—a "stay of execution"—while he figured out how to save the band.

*   *   *

Regardless of any other excuses, however, Herbie needed to be rid of Fleischman because he had another singer in mind: Steve Perry. "When I first heard his tape," he told columnist Joel Selvin, "I went through the roof . . . and it's an 18-foot ceiling." (In another interview, he recalled saying simply, "Oh shit. This is the guy.") He flew Perry to Denver, where the band was opening for Emerson, Lake, and Palmer, for a songwriting session with Neal Schon in the guitarist's hotel room. Although Perry was initially very shy and had a great deal of trepidation about joining the band, including concerns about his own self-worth, the collaboration quickly produced the songs "Patiently" and "Somethin' to Hide."

Schon didn't think there was necessarily more chemistry with Perry than with Fleischman, and Gregg Rolie still wasn't totally sold on the idea of a new lead vocalist in any event, but for Herbie, it was a done deal. He arranged an elaborate subterfuge to keep Fleischman in the dark, putting Perry on the books as a vocal coach and introducing him to the crew at a Soldier Field gig as roadie John Villanueva's "Portuguese cousin." At a show in Long Beach a week after Fleischman's last show, Herbie put Perry out onstage, and the singer delivered a flawless rendition of Fleischman's "For You," so nervous that he performed with his eyes tightly shut. He got a standing ovation. Welcomed warmly into the band, he moved into Rolie's capacious house to write songs, now apparently a rite of passage.

Steve Perry walked onstage at San Francisco's Old Waldorf as Journey's official lead singer at about 10:00 p.m. on Friday, September 30, 1977, for the first of six appearances over three nights. Joel Selvin's review noted that Aynsley "Dunbar may be the single most outstanding instrumentalist in the band," while Schon "has matured remarkably over the last few years," but the "most dramatic development . . . is the band's overall vocal sound . . . a thoroughly professional and worthy vocal mix," concluding that "[w]ith Perry, the band performed two tunes including 'The Lights of the City,' which Perry helped write."

What was it about Steve Perry's voice that was so compelling? What Sam Cooke's biographer Peter Guralnick wrote about the late soul superstar was equally applicable to Perry: "[H]e *caresses* the songs with a voice that is at once smooth, insistent, and utterly beguiling." Perry had an angelic tenor range that could soar to the highest notes one moment and then come back down to the lower register reverentially, almost confidentially. He sang in a style so personal that it made the listener feel that he was singing directly to her, in the same room as her, sharing a special secret with her.

Between their sessions with Fleischman and the addition of Perry, Journey had more than enough material for a new album to exploit Perry's talents. They went into His Master's Wheels Studios in San Francisco with producer Roy Thomas Baker to record *Infinity*. Baker was quite a character. Perry remembered that the producer "just comes and goes . . . has a piece of cheese, says 'I love it' or 'I don't' and he leaves," and Herbie "didn't like the sound that he got," finding it "so damned loud," of all things—the opposite of what some critics said about the band's first album. The whole project was almost lost when Baker, "in some kind of crazed pique," sprayed the studio with a chemical fire extinguisher—which corrodes recording tape. Band members later downplayed the incident, saying that they were all fooling around after a particularly noteworthy solo by Schon, but Baker incurred thousands of dollars in cleanup fees, and the band had to move to Cherokee Studios in Hollywood to finish the job. They released the album on January 20, 1978, with a stylized cover featuring the mathematical symbol for infinity, a scarab beetle, and—for the first time on a Journey album—no band members (although a photo of the five appeared on the back, with Ross Valory adopting a comic pose).

The music itself is a strong progression from Journey's previous work. "Lights," a calm rock ballad by Perry and Schon dedicated to San Francisco, the "city by the bay," begins with soft electric guitar and bass, then drums, and then Perry's powerful tenor. Perry's original lyric had been "the sun shines on L.A.," not "the bay," but being in Journey meant being "from" San Francisco. Rolie's organ joins in for the second verse, which ends with harmonies. The third verse repeats the first, with all but the third line harmonized. Schon's guitar solo, although inspired by Jimi Hendrix, is somewhat subdued compared with his earlier work. "Feeling That Way," by Perry, Rolie, and Dunbar, another calm rock ballad, begins with piano and Rolie's vocals. After the first verse, Perry and Schon take over for the chorus, which Rolie concludes. Rolie picks up the second verse, joined by Perry in harmony with the second line. Like "Lights," the guitar solo is subdued. The harmonies are clean and clear, thanks to Baker's production. The tempo picks up in the final minute. This one was originally written for *Next* as a harmony-laden, hard rock song called "Velvet Curtain." Overall, it sounds somewhat like an up-tempo version of Thelonious Monk's 1957 hit "Monk's Mood" (also originally called "Feeling That Way"). The recording goes into the next song without a break, but it's in a different key, which forced Rolie to provide a piano note as a prompt when they performed the sequence live. Written by Rolie, Fleischman, Schon, Valory, and Roger Silver, "Anytime" begins with the harmonized refrain "Ooh, anytime that you want me/Ooh, anytime that you need me." As with "Feeling That Way," Rolie handles most of the vocal duties, with Perry (and the others) joining in for a harmonized chorus. Schon's solo is again rather controlled and brief in comparison to his prior work. Piano, guitar, and the refrain compete in the final minute, with a prominent drum line.

"Lă Do Dã," written by Perry and Schon, is the song that most closely resembles the pre-Perry Journey on the album so far, but with a lyric and melody taken from a demo Perry recorded with his previous band, the Alien Project: "Something about You Baby." It begins with a powerful driving guitar, including some string-scratching. Perry's vocals could easily have been replaced by Rolie if the song had appeared on an earlier album, perhaps in a lower key, and without the long notes at the end of each line. The chorus is instrumental: guitar, drums, and bass—then a wild, free-form, more typical Schon guitar solo. The final minute is a call-and-response between Schon's guitar and Perry's "My, my, my." Dunbar's drums, sounding like an airplane engine, end the piece. "Patiently," also by Perry and Schon, begins with a long organ note, joined by acoustic guitar and a calm Perry vocal similar to "Lights." For two verses it's a ballad, before a seemingly background electric guitar drives a switch into hard rock. This is a production trick; when the guitar line repeats, it seems closer: Roy Thomas Baker at his best. Perry sings a line and then lets Schon have a solo that's half wild, half controlled, before it returns to ballad form with acoustic guitar and soft vocal.

Side 2, with fewer radio-friendly hits but more interesting musically, starts off with "Wheel in the Sky," by Schon, Fleischman, and Diane Valory. The song begins with a soft acoustic guitar playing a refrain almost directly borrowed from Eric Clapton's "Layla" before Dunbar pulls the group into what might be best described as an "up-tempo ballad." Perry takes command in verse, with the others assisting in harmonies during the chorus. The rolling, rhythmic, repetitive tune is occasionally punctuated with the tinkling of

Rolie's piano keys. The guitar solo is the "new," subdued Schon. As for the lyrics, in a similar vein to "Look into the Future" ("Don't know where I'll be tomorrow"), the jury remains out on their meaning. Possibly inspired by the Byrds' "This Wheel's On Fire," Schon said the idea was originally "[w]heels in my head keep on turning," as in ideas—but how those "wheels" became heavenly is anyone's guess. Journey was hoping the song would break through as its "Stairway to Heaven," a megahit with similarly cryptic lyrics from Led Zeppelin's fourth album.

"Somethin' to Hide," by Perry and Schon, is contemplative, beginning with a strong drum supporting a clear organ and guitar refrain. Perry shines in the verses with long high notes at the end of each: "You've got somethin' to hide/ That you're not telling me/I know." The chorus likewise is a vocal stretch: high without resort to falsetto. Schon's solo is the "new" Neal. The song ends on a sustained organ note.

"Winds of March," by Schon, his father Matthew, Fleischman, Rolie, and Perry, has a similar structure to "Suite Madame Blue" by Styx. It begins with an acoustic guitar sea shanty, for nearly a full minute of intro. Dunbar's air-strip sonics lead to Perry's light, airy vocals. There are some neat drum effects here, and Perry adds an operatic touch. The chorus is much like the two verses it follows. Then, with a long vocal note that goes even higher at the end, Schon, with a rather subdued solo, takes us into an instrumental, hard rock portion. When Rolie joins in with organ, it feels suited to the band's prior work, as organ and electric guitar trade solos. In the final minute they come together and return to the vocals, ending with tenderness.

"Can Do," by Perry and Valory, is similarly hard rock with the feel of the previous albums. Despite Perry's vocals and the harmonized chorus, the song has much in common with "She Makes Me (Feel Alright)" from *Look into the Future*. "Opened the Door," by Perry, Rolie, and Schon, closes out the album with another calm rock ballad. It begins with a soft cymbal from Dunbar, joined by Rolie on organ. Then Perry's clean, bold lyric presents the first verse, the final line providing a nice interplay between vocals and organ, followed by a haunting Schon riff. At moments in the second half, it seems as if Schon and Dunbar are about ready to break out and play as they have in the past, but they pull back and get in line with the song's relaxed tempo.

While recording the album, the band had at least two more performances, not particularly distant from their home base in San Francisco. They headed down the bay for a November 26 show at the Santa Cruz Civic Center, which a critic found too loud; over the holidays they went up to Reno to headline a show with Eddie Money, where yet another reviewer found them too loud, adding that Valory's bass solo was boring and Dunbar's drum solo even more so. Aside from the aural sensitivity, what is striking about these reviews is that neither mentions Steve Perry. Possibly the reviewers were unfamiliar with the band and did not recognize the change the singer's presence represented. But it's also possible that Perry was not with Journey for these dates: a curious notice appeared under "Clubs" in the "What's About Town" page of the *Vancouver Sun* on December 23: "Steve Perry. To Dec. 31. Avalon Hotel, N.V."

To be fair, the members of Journey had no idea that *Infinity* was going to do for Journey what Woodstock had done for Santana. They all knew they were talented, that the songs were good, that the album was good. But they had felt the same way about *Next*. Sound engineer Joe Chicarelli said, "When we were mixing I loved the music but I never imagined it would be so successful." Under the circumstances, Steve Perry can hardly be faulted if he used his new record company connections to book himself a few gigs up in Canada. As Herbie later would say, "You gotta make hay while the sun shines."

Reviews of the album were almost overwhelmingly positive. "Perry has a powerful voice . . . but he is also a strongly controlled singer," wrote Rick Atkinson in the *Hackensack Record*, adding particular praise for the production work of Roy Thomas Baker. He felt that "La Do La" [*sic*] showcased the new lineup's strengths, but "Wheel in the Sky," which he called "Perry's best vocal of the album," would be the hit, as far as he was concerned. "If Steve Perry turns out to be half as good on stage as he is on this album," Atkinson concluded, "Journey can finally achieve the success that has always been just around the next corner." Rich Warren wrote in the *Pittsburgh Press* that "Journey's time might finally have come . . . with an album that might well be the left-field hit of the winter," adding brief kudos for Baker's production work. Ace Adams of the *New York Daily News* wrote that "'Lights in the City,' 'Winds of March' and 'Feeling That Way' should carve an additional image of Journey as a band composed of experienced musicians whose future is only now beginning to take shape." And Dale Kawashima wrote in the *Los Angeles Times* that "Journey's compact arrangements still are overly shaped by ex-Santana members Gregg Rolie and Neal Schon's cosmic, psychedelic inclinations," but "the anguished and prophesizing overtones characterizing the group's earlier works generally have disappeared in favor of refined but dynamic execution plus simple, earnest lyrics." Steve Soltis and Jeff Brown, writing in the *Plano Daily Star-Courier*, called the album "original," with "material ranging from good to excellent," even as they strangely (and incorrectly) labeled Perry a "British chorister."

As always, and as expected, there were a few detractors. While Pete Bishop of the *Pittsburgh Press* liked "the addition of singer Steve Perry" and Bill Bleyer of the *Bridgewater Courier-News* allowed that "the material is finally up to par with the sound of the band," noting that "there is not a bad cut on the entire disc," both reviewers took issue with its "annoyingly simplistic" lyrics. They had a point. "Give me all of your sunshine . . . /Well what more can I say," from "Anytime," is hardly Ralph Waldo Emerson.

Susan Ahrens wrote the most thoughtful review of the album, in *Circus* magazine: "Journey had a hard time breaking free of their past and creating a solid new identity," she averred, calling them "a firmly entrenched sixties band" that only with a new lead singer could move into the '70s. As for Roy Thomas Baker, "one of his real strengths lies in tightening a band's usually scattered energies into one explosive package," which she heard clearly in "Opened the Door." Ahrens found that Ross Valory shone in "Can Do," which "truly embodies the sensation of being 14 and hot for the very first time." On Steve Perry, she noted, correctly, "The sweetness in his voice 'comes from listening to a lot of Sam Cooke.'" The scarab album cover gave "Journey an instantly recognizable logo," she wrote, concluding that "with a new singer, a new producer and an entirely new sound," Journey "yields a brand of honeyed heavy metal uniquely their own."

Within days of the album's release, the band was back on the road. There was no question now where Steve Perry would be. Journey "featuring Steve Perry" played two shows on February 18 at the Community Center Theater in Salinas, on Monterey Bay. On February 21 they headlined a show with guitarist Ronnie Montrose and his band at the Stockton Civic Auditorium. And on February 26 it was back into the Central Valley to open for Santana, with reporting by Steve Perry's hometown paper, the *Hanford Sentinel*.

Journey then embarked on a national tour supported by Montrose and an up-and-coming Los Angeles band called Van Halen (whose flamboyant lead singer, David Lee Roth, like Steve Perry, was steeped in African American musical traditions). After the opening acts, Journey played one quick set of their previous music, and Rolie plinked out the piano notes of "Feeling That Way" and sang the first lyrics. Then Perry burst onstage and started singing, "When the summer's gone, she'll be there, standing by the light," to uproarious applause each time.

Life on the road for the still-struggling band was hard. "We never stopped," Perry recalled. "A day off wasn't a day off . . . it was a travel day." They could not afford to sleep in hotels, so they would get "day rooms"—shared rooms for a shower before a show, without enough towels. "It was like running for public office. You really had to travel every single day and perform every night." So used to the grind did he become, in fact, that when he finally got a break, and was at his mom's house for a few days, Perry said, "I was sleeping down the hall and the phone rang. And I jumped out of bed buck naked [and ran] down the hall . . . thinking I was late for the bus."

Despite all the hard work, the band's status as headliners was hardly secure. After an appearance at the Orpheum in Madison, Wisconsin, on March 8, Rob Fixmer of the *Capital Times* openly mused that perhaps Journey should be opening for Montrose, who had played with the Edgar Winter Group until Bill Graham started putting him out on his own. After seeing their show on April 1 at Kiel Opera House in St. Louis, critic John Cullinane of the *Post-Dispatch* said that Montrose "was the highlight of the evening," while Journey and Van Halen "blasted their way into mediocrity," allowing that "Steve Perry was impressive but his vocals, like everything else, came through the sound system distorted because of the excessive volume." Steve Wingfield, who caught them in Murray, Kentucky, on April 8, said simply that Montrose "stole the show." But the *Kansas City Star* logged a generally positive review of Journey, especially for their performances of "Winds of March" and "Wheel in the Sky." That reviewer appreciated the vocal interplay between Rolie and Perry on lead and Valory's harmonies, calling the group "not just a hard-rock heavy metal band." Van Halen guitar tech Rudy Leiren's take, unsurprisingly, was that his employers outplayed Journey and Montrose, arguing that "it became very apparent that the majority of the people were coming to see Van Halen." The musicians themselves engaged in friendly competition, notwithstanding the accidental dousing of Steve Perry's hair with guacamole during a backstage Van Halen food fight one evening. Van Halen even taught Journey how to be bad boys, throwing television sets into hotel swimming pools and overturning catering tables.

Questions of relative prominence were not altogether unexpected given Journey's previously lackluster sales, but as the tour made its way around the nation—at such venues as Morris Civic Auditorium in South Bend, Indiana; the Tower Theater in Upper Darby, Pennsylvania; the St. Paul Civic Center in Minnesota; and War Memorial Auditorium in Nashville, Tennessee— reviewers began to take more positive notice. "The addition of Perry was the discovery of the proverbial missing link . . . Journey has never sounded better," said one. "Journey . . . has improved with the recent addition of lead singer Steve Perry," said another. And one predicted that Perry, although somewhat inexperienced, could prove the "focal point" necessary to bring the band success.

And something else began to change. As the three bands performed and traveled through the late winter and into the spring, Journey's music was turning up more and more on the radio, and the shows started selling out. By the time they played their April 23 date at the Fox Theater in Atlanta, *Infinity* had moved up the charts "into the national Top 20," according to Scott Cain of the *Atlanta Constitution,* and was poised to attain gold status—five hundred thousand copies sold, and at least $1 million in wholesale revenue. The album hit that mark on May 3 (although the writer was slightly off; the album peaked at a nevertheless impressive number 21 on May 5).

This success did not happen easily. In 1978 it was very difficult to get new rock on the radio, given the immense popularity of disco music. Some established rock artists, most famously the Bee Gees, converted to disco. Herbie made alliances with FM radio stations (rather than follow the traditional route for rock acts of seeking AM airplay). Watching sales at the Tower Records store on Columbus Avenue and Bay Street, directly across from his office, gave him the idea to market the album at the point of purchase, paying record stores like Tower to play Journey's latest music in rotation and supplying the cashiers with Journey T-shirts to wear on duty. "[O]bserving how people browsed really taught me a lot. . . . You had a captive target demographic. I went crazy spending money on point-of-purchase materials. It was very, very effective." The strategy made being a Journey listener "cool" and an "insider thing"—a marketing trick not unlike when Led Zeppelin released the album *In through the Out Door,* with six different collectible album covers, later that year. (The album was sold in a brown paper bag so buyers would not know which cover they were getting, like collectible baseball cards.)

Herbie's point-of-purchase marketing also took advantage of a developing backlash against disco. Rooted in racism, the backlash by rock fans would famously culminate in 1980's "disco demolition night," a planned immolation of hundreds of disco records at Chicago's Comiskey Park that led to a riot. It was, of course, neither the intention of Journey nor their manager to burn disco records; they only wanted to sell their own. But it was the growing backlash that fed the sudden hunger for new, innovative rock, and it was that hunger that sold *Infinity* and led to the band's growing popularity.

Stardom tends to snowball, and on April 28 Journey flew to Burbank, California, to host *Burt Sugarman's Midnight Special*, a weekly rock television program broadcast on Friday nights on NBC after *The Tonight Show Starring Johnny Carson* from 1973 to 1981. They performed "Wheel in the Sky," "Feeling That Way," "Anytime," "Patiently," and "Lǎ Do Dā"—all from *Infinity*. Popular disc jockey Wolfman Jack introduced the show, and a wisecracking Valory introduced his bandmates, joking about cannabis (but mimicking inhaling a joint with his forehead rather than his lips, to satisfy network censors). Rolie played a white grand piano with a synthesizer on the side, while Dunbar played behind a plastic shield baffle with Swiss-cheese holes. Perry did not interact much with the studio audience and missed his key a few times. It was not Journey at their best, by any stretch of the imagination—but it was an opportunity to promote the new album on national television and cement their status as headliners.

The next part of their tour was indeed as bona fide rock stars. Sold-out shows. Limousines and airplanes. Stomping fans demanding encores. Panties thrown at the stage. Press interviews with individual band members. An exhausting jaunt across the ocean to play a festival in Amsterdam. A gig opening for the Rolling Stones at Chicago's Soldier Field. After a tour of upstate New York, they played Philadelphia and triumphantly returned to the Palladium in New York City, where they eclipsed the previous year's negative review in the *New York Times* with a positive one in *Rolling Stone*. They played Cobo Hall in Detroit, opened for Foreigner at Market Square Arena in Indianapolis, and joined Ted Nugent and Aerosmith at Giants Stadium in New Jersey. By mid-May the band had "appeared before more than a quarter-million" fans and was "flirting with capturing its first platinum record award"—one million units sold. Ed Kociela of the *Los Angeles*

Herald-Examiner predicted that Journey "will most probably be the success story of the year."

*   *   *

Most discussion of the change that took place with the addition of Steve Perry has been written from the perspective of 1981 and later, which is to say from the perspective of Journey as a superstar rock group that headlined stadiums. This has led to the impression that Perry's arrival brought a sudden revolutionary change to the music. In fact, from the perspective of 1978, there were some shifts in the band's music, and significantly greater album sales, but Perry's presence was not revolutionary so much as *evolutionary*. This is best demonstrated by their live show, in which they continued to play songs from the first three albums and in which Perry hardly overshadowed the other members of the band. Furthermore, the music of *Infinity*, while including Perry's soaring, angelic high tenor, is no more different from *Next* than *Next* was from *Look into the Future*.

An examination of one of their 1978 performances demonstrates this point. On June 10, the band performed at the Capitol Theater in Passaic, New Jersey, recorded live by New York radio station WNEW-FM. They started off with "Lǎ Do Dā," from *Infinity*, followed by "Next," with Perry hitting a cowbell and singing the vocal originally recorded by Schon. Then they launched into "Feeling That Way" and "Anytime," with Rolie having some difficulty on vocals. During "On a Saturday Night," from *Look into the Future*, Perry ad-libbed some additional vocal lines and joined Rolie on the melody. As they moved into "Winds of March," from *Infinity*, Perry ran out of breath on the long note before the transition, at which point Rolie stood up on his bench (in a silver jumpsuit) to dance and lead the crowd clapping to the beat. "Wheel in the Sky" was next, with the opening guitar chords getting audience recognition and applause. After that, Dunbar performed a drum solo, including a light show and more than demonstrating the technical proficiency he had honed with Frank Zappa, David Bowie, and his own blues band; in fact, in the final moments, he seemed to have twelve arms. Schon followed with a guitar solo featuring his lighter side, accompanied by Rolie on piano. Perry did not do much during "You're on Your Own," from *Look into the Future*, the final song of the set, but he did join Rolie during the eponymous one-line chorus, while Schon spent some time grinding on the floor as the song moved into space-age electronics. The band ultimately came out for an astonishing three encores. "She Makes Me (Feel Alright)," also from *Look into the Future*, saw Rolie out front with Perry, Schon, and Valory, dancing and singing. Then it was off again while a row of young men pounded their fists on the stage. After a few minutes the band came back to play "Patiently" from *Infinity*, introduced by Rolie, now back behind the organ. Then they played "Opened the Door" from *Infinity* and left the stage again, returning to play "Lights" for a third and final encore. All told, they played eight songs from *Infinity* and four from the previous albums; Perry was clearly the lead singer but hardly a bandleader.

Journey's success also represented the culmination of popular music's resegregation. In 1978 white rock listeners tended to embrace rock bands like the Ramones and Lynyrd Skynyrd (who overtly eschewed the folk sensibility of Crosby, Stills, Nash, and Young), while Black fans tended to gravitate toward Motown acts like the Jackson 5 and Rick James. With Jimi Hendrix dead and Lenny Kravitz not yet in high school, rock music was decidedly a white-oriented genre—if not actually racist, still largely exclusive.

If there was a style that perpetuated the integrationist ethos, it was disco, popularized (and made briefly acceptable to macho white youth) with the release of the major motion picture *Saturday Night Fever*, which saw commercial success during Journey's *Infinity* tour. Those kids in Passaic who saw Journey at the Capitol Theater on June 10 may have seen *Saturday Night Fever* the night before, just up the street at the Central Theater. But the disco craze, as we have seen, was short-lived.

Meanwhile, nostalgia, a yearning for a mythical past, was taking root in white American households, especially among the late–baby boom teenagers and young adults. For them, popular television shows like *Happy Days* spoke to a time in their lives (or more often those of their siblings, aunts, and uncles) when things were supposedly simple and carefree. For many white youngsters, this also equated to a time when Black people were largely invisible to whites, as they were excluded from the industrial jobs and suburbs so typical of postwar life, or relegated in popular culture to roles ranging from subservient to silly. While acts like Johnny Thunders & the Heartbreakers and the Ramones repurposed the music of early rock and roll for a growing punk audience, in *Infinity*, Journey had started to do the same with soul and blues—but without any actual African Americans onstage.

One Journey gig was the exception that proved the rule. After the Soldier Field concert in Chicago, they recorded a show for the program *Soundstage*, broadcast by Chicago's PBS affiliate WTTW. It being Chicago, they could not resist inviting some local blues players onstage—a treat for Aynsley Dunbar, no stranger to the blues, and Neal Schon, who cut his teeth listening to Eric Clapton. One at a time, Steve Perry welcomed onstage four Chicago Blues legends: Jerry Portnoy on harmonica; Luther Allison and Albert King on guitar; and Pinetop Perkins on piano. All but Portnoy were African American. As Allison, King, and Schon took turns playing guitar solos, followed by Gregg Rolie trading keyboard solos with Perkins, the all-white audience seemed to realize that they were witnessing blues history. Allison, King, and Perkins had learned the blues in the juke joints of the Mississippi Delta (Allison was from nearby Arkansas), were literally born on cotton plantations in the sharecropping South, and had been part of the Great Migration to Chicago. They knew the blues because they had lived the blues—the original blues. They were trotted out not because Journey had suddenly decided to become an interracial blues band but because they lent credibility to Journey's claim to the *evolution* of the blues—an evolution available, for the most part, only to white artists. Appropriately reverential, Perry, Schon, Rolie, Dunbar, and Valory gave them their turn. But when their turn was over, it was back to rock.

It is worth considering exactly what the appeal was of this band, who had no bona fide top-20 hits, to the young men pounding their hands on the stage for more and the transfixed young women who threw moist underwear on that same stage. "People create their sense of identity through their musical choices," writes music historian Dewar MacLeod, "choosing social groups and gathering together in audiences of collective identity." Journey simultaneously provided a muscular, bass-driven rock that appealed to macho types in the audience and very sexy musicians whose onstage behavior set girls' hearts aflutter. The *Infinity* tour occurred at the height of a conversion of the United States from a production economy to a service economy; not exactly a recession, but a displacement, especially in factory towns like Passaic. Those young men in the audience sought release from their daily fears as the opportunities that had brought their parents a middle-class lifestyle seemed to be moving elsewhere. Journey provided it, building in them what music scholar Ted Gioia has called a "tribal allegiance" for the band. As for the girls, popular culture scholar Katie Kapurch notes that screaming, crying fangirls are using their emotions, tears, and other fluids to retake control of their bodies from fathers, brothers, and boyfriends. Journey, like the Beatles and Frank Sinatra, gave them that release.

When it came to onstage sex appeal, all five band members had something to offer. Schon's muscular guitar work was phallic, joining an already long tradition in rock and roll of making the electric guitar an extension of his penis. Like Rolie and Perry, Schon had a penchant for unbuttoned shirts and open kimonos, the better to show off pectoral muscles and chest hair. Rolie and Valory favored shiny clothes, and Rolie especially liked tight pants that showed off the bulge in his crotch when he stood atop his stool during the fast portion of "Winds of March," shaking his hips to the beat, and when he came out from behind the organ altogether for "She Makes Me (Feel Alright)" during the encore. Dunbar, as a drummer engaged in the most athletic of onstage rock activities, often wore sleeveless T-shirts to best show off his muscular arms, shiny with sweat, like a horse at full gallop. And horses also play a significant role in female sexual desire.

Steve Perry had a more complicated sexiness. With his high, prominent cheekbones and a body so skinny it bordered on emaciation—not to mention a voice that ranged well into alto—Perry's sexuality was almost like a shared secret, innocent. Unlike his bandmates, whose long hair bespoke a Samson-like strength, Perry's washed and conditioned jet-black hair fell straight past his bony shoulders, often covering the sideburns that would undo the feminine effect. While he, too, preferred unbuttoned shirts, he tended to tie them in a knot at the bottom, which left his nipples covered like an evening gown with a plunging neckline; unlike Rolie, his chest was mostly hairless. And the crooning style that Perry favored had long been sexually problematic. Indeed, according to Simon Frith, "crooners were initially heard as 'effeminate' and unmanly," even "freakish."

For the young men who liked Journey, much of their "macho" attitude was rooted in homophobia. Many overcompensated with outward masculinity, afraid that they would become—or be exposed as—gay. Intentional or not, Perry's onstage androgyny was of a piece with the gender-bending trend of the 1970s represented by David Bowie's Ziggy Stardust character, Elton John's penchant for feminine outfits (including that of a Disney princess), and fringe groups like the New York Dolls. Perry's softness also made him attractive to some of the female fans, for whom he represented a safer sexuality.

But Journey shed one of their most masculine members before the tour was over. In a move most Journey fans did not understand, Herbie fired Aynsley Dunbar. The drummer performed his last date with the group on September 2, 1978.

While it was not mentioned by any of the principals at the time, the firing of Dunbar started a pattern that would recur at several key moments in the history of the band. Journey at various times defined "membership" as being one of the four or five musicians, or a holder of common shares, in their company, Nightmare Productions, Inc. In 1974, after Dunbar joined the band, Nightmare had seven directors, including the five musicians and two comanagers. But the band also claimed that it "functions as a democracy." Presumably, that would mean that no individual in the band (or its management) could fire another member of the band. But in addition to being owners, the musicians were employees of Nightmare Productions and could be fired for cause by a majority vote of the board of directors. With the hiring of Steve Perry and the firing of Aynsley Dunbar, the band's metamorphosis was in full swing.

But why had he been fired?

Drum Solo
Aynsley Dunbar

I can play the technical stuff like I did with Frank Zappa, and I can play the simple stuff like I did with Journey.

—*Aynsley Dunbar*

When the Beatles arrived at New York's recently renamed John F. Kennedy International Airport and started the "British Invasion," American music had already launched a musical counterinvasion of the old country. The blues, a product of the Jim Crow South and the Negro spiritual tradition, quickly took root in the mining and factory towns of the English Midlands, resulting in a new subgenre known as the British blues. Aynsley Dunbar was determined to be part of it.

Born in 1946 in Liverpool, Dunbar spent his teen years watching the Beatles rise in popularity in their shared hometown. He abandoned the violin after two years of lessons, rejected the guitar because "[m]y sister started playing and I didn't want to be in competition with her," and ultimately picked up the sticks after seeing a drum trio on television. "What I saw in drums was power, being able to powerhouse a band." Starting on tin cans, he built up his kit one piece at a time, learning each drum. At thirteen he started lessons, but "[b]y that time I was playing rudiments better than my teacher, so all he could do was help me read music and understand it." At fifteen he quit school and started playing Dixieland jazz and blues in local clubs, joining a number of acts, including one called the "Merseysippi Jazz Band," a name that combined Liverpool's River Mersey with the storied waterway of New Orleans, birthplace of the genre. At eighteen he was recruited by the beat group the Mojos and spent the next two years touring and learning the yeoman's technique of rock and roll drumming as they performed their popular single "Everything's Alright" in and around London.

One of the most important early practitioners of the British blues was a multi-instrumentalist named John Mayall, who founded the Bluesbreakers in the same year the Beatles crossed the pond and Dunbar joined the Mojos. "John Mayall & the Bluesbreakers" proved a crucible for the British blues, launching the careers of John McVie, Peter Green, and Mick Fleetwood, who would together form Fleetwood Mac in 1967; Jack Bruce and Eric Clapton, who would form Cream in 1966, the latter founding Derek and the Dominos in 1970 and then enjoying a long and fruitful solo career; Mick Taylor of the Rolling Stones; and many, many others—including Aynsley Dunbar. Not long after the Mojos broke up in the autumn of 1966, Mayall gave Dunbar his first big break to help record the group's second album *A Hard Road*.

While with Mayall, Dunbar often performed Otis Redding's "All Your Love (I Miss Loving)." Guitarist Peter Green, inspired by that tune, wrote "Black Magic Woman," which he later recorded with Fleetwood Mac—and which Gregg Rolie and Carlos Santana recorded with Santana. And so in some sense, when Dunbar got to work with Rolie in Journey, he had come full circle.

Unfortunately, the big break with Mayall's Bluesbreakers didn't last long. Dunbar played with the band for barely six months before being replaced by Mick Fleetwood. Although usually referred to as a "firing," the separation seems to have been the result of Mayall's constant tinkering with the lineup rather than any cause on Dunbar's part. And the young drummer was quickly snapped up by another influential British blues band, the Jeff Beck Group.

Although his tenure with Beck was even shorter, it was notable in that he got to work with future Rolling Stones guitarist Ronnie Wood and future rock superstar Rod Stewart (as well as future guitar legend Jeff Beck). Because Beck booked fewer gigs than Mayall, Dunbar picked up side gigs in and around London, a habit that would keep him fully employed for decades. He recorded with African American bluesman Eddie Boyd and his Bluesbreaker friend Peter Green on *Eddie Boyd and His Blues Band Featuring Peter Green* in 1967, and in early 1968 went into the studio with Joe Cocker for his forthcoming album *With a Little Help from My Friends* (although the tracks he recorded were not included on the release).

By the spring of 1968 Dunbar had made enough friends in the British blues scene, and earned a strong enough reputation among recording executives, that he felt comfortable putting together his own band. He called it the Aynsley Dunbar Retaliation as a tongue-in-cheek nod to being fired by Mayall the previous year; his success would "retaliate" against Mayall. The band included John Morsehead on lead guitar and vocals; future Bluesbreaker Alex Dmochowski on bass; and soulful Lancashire native Victor Brox, "described by Jimi Hendrix and Tina Turner as their favourite white blues singer," on lead vocals, organ, and trumpet. Because Morsehead was born in India and Dmochowski in Israel, press releases described the band as "international" (even though both of those "foreign" locations were actually part of the British Empire when the two men were born). The group signed with the London branch office of Liberty Records, a New York–based recording company, just before the label was sold to San Francisco's Transamerica Corporation and merged with their United Artists subsidiary. This acquisition by UA proved fortunate, as it gave the group the opportunity to tour the United States in support of their first album, *Retaliation*. Although mostly a vehicle for Dunbar, the album showcased Brox on their cover of "Whiskey Head Woman" by African American bluesmen Freddie King and Sonny Thompson, and concluded with "Mutiny," a seven-minute, up-tempo instrumental by Dunbar and Morsehead consisting mainly of solo drums.

Forming his own band meant turning down lucrative offers and, in retrospect, close brushes with superstardom. Beck and Jimmy Page offered him a seat with the Yardbirds, and after a few London jam sessions with Jimi Hendrix, he garnered an offer to join that rock pioneer as well. But Dunbar was loyal to his own group. "I couldn't leave the people in my band just to do some wandering around the country, although it would have led to the Led Zeppelin gig, which was offered to me as well," he told *Modern Drummer* magazine. Indeed, Led Zeppelin's manager confirmed that the Liverpudlian was the first choice, before they settled on Birmingham's John Bonham: "We definitely approached Aynsley Dunbar."

Released in early 1968, *Retaliation* did not bring the group superstardom, but it sold some stacks and made the group a headliner in midsize venues throughout England, like one on Eel Pie Island in Twickenham-on-Thames, a storied blues spot. Eager to produce and to keep the record company satisfied, they went back into the studio later that same year to record *Doctor Dunbar's Prescription*. Released in the United Kingdom in 1968 and in the states early the next year, this one included their take on the T-Bone Walker classic "Mean Old World." In January 1969 Blue Thumb Records released the group's first album in the United States, and in February they "crossed the pond," opening for Country Joe and the Fish, the Everly Brothers, and old friend Jeff Beck at such venues as San Francisco's Fillmore West and Chicago's Kinetic Playground—the same ballrooms that hosted Santana. Then it was back to the studio for a third offering, *To Mum, from Aynsley and the Boys*. Featuring Tommy Eyre on keys, this one was produced by none other than John Mayall; clearly there was no bad blood over either his firing of Dunbar from the Bluesbreakers or the meaning of the band's name. Although still produced by Liberty, *To Mum* was distributed by Sonet Records, the Swedish subsidiary of Universal; the album cover featured the members of the band ironically dressed as Teddy Boys, a style of clothing popular among 1950s British youth emulating the turn-of-the-century Edwardian era.

After releasing *To Mum*, Dunbar discontinued the band because they were already resting on their laurels, and he knew they had a lot more learning to do. "[W]e were doing very well in England and everybody got a big ego. It was like the first step and they thought they were halfway up the ladder." Morsehead and Dmochowski joined Jackie Lomax in his short-lived British version of Heavy Jelly. Singer-organist Brox, at the label's urging, assembled a fourth Retaliation album with three outtakes from *To Mum* and additional tracks he recorded with his wife Annette, released in 1970 as *Remains to Be Heard*. He then sang the role of Caiaphas for the original cast recording of *Jesus Christ Superstar*.

Bringing back Tommy Eyre, the young keyboardist who had joined Retaliation for *To Mum*, Dunbar put together an eight-piece progressive rock group, Blue Whale, and recorded an album at Marquee Studios in London. Ranging from bossa nova–inflected jazz to up-tempo, jazzy blues, the album was a clear departure from the British blues of Retaliation. It even included a cover of Frank Zappa's "Willie the Pimp," a fifteen-minute extravaganza with typical phallic allusion. But Blue Whale had structural problems. "I could never get the same brass section to stay in the band. They'd get a gig somewhere else paying a couple of pounds more, so they would send a substitute [who] would not be able to solo or ad lib or anything else."

Dunbar first met Frank Zappa when the American avant-garde composer jammed with Retaliation at a festival in Belgium in October 1969. "I look around and see Frank standing there with the producer. We'd done a half dozen songs, and the guy waves to me to say, 'Frank would like to sit in, but he has no guitar.' So our guitar player, John Morsehead, lent him his, and we played three songs." After he also did a few numbers with Pink Floyd, "he and I sat in my car for about an hour and he talked about how it could be so great for me in America. I was thinking it sounded great . . . and then he said, 'Think about it.'" When the convicted pornographer came to London to record portions of what would become *Chunga's Revenge*, he needed a dependable, versatile drummer, and Dunbar was available. "About six months later I got this urge to go down to this club where the band played quite often," the drummer recalled. "I went in and the girl at the desk said, 'Frank Zappa is waiting for you in the restaurant.' I said, 'What!' So I went there, and that's when Frank asked me to come over to America and join him."

Zappa's musical tastes ran the spectrum from classical through jazz, blues, doo-wop, and heavy metal with lyrical themes that ranged from overtly scatological to simply oedipal. Having recently disbanded his group the Mothers of Invention, in 1970 he assembled a new version of the Mothers including jazz keyboardist George Duke and three former members of the pop group the Turtles, known for their hit "Happy Together": Jim Pons on bass and Mark Volman and Howard Kaylan on vocals. The latter two could not record under their real names because of a stipulation in their record contract from their time with the Turtles; Zappa, never short of zany ideas, rechristened them "the Phlorescent Leech & Eddie."

But he still needed a drummer. Dunbar, despite his frustrations with Blue Whale, had no shortage of work. He contributed drums on expatriate African American blues artist (and Zappa intimate) Shuggie Otis's *Freedom Flight* and then teamed up with guitarist Jon Mark and saxophonist Johnny Almond for their second collaboration *Mark-Almond II*. The two were fellow alumni of John Mayall's Bluesbreakers, and they had initially planned to do without a drummer, but their band included Tommy Eyre, formerly of Blue Whale and Retaliation, and when they decided they needed cymbals and skins, they knew who they wanted to hire.

After hesitating for two weeks, Dunbar agreed to join the new Mothers, and they went into the studio to record the soundtrack to a film Zappa had written, *200 Motels*, as well as the film itself. Zappa flew Dunbar to Los Angeles, where "his wife picked me up at the airport and took me to his house, where I lived for nine months." Then it was off to New York City to record a live concept album during a gig at Bill Graham's Fillmore East. Released in August, *Fillmore East—June 1971* includes lots of vocals, spoken word, and dialogue, and the voice of every member of the band except Dunbar. The concept is an overly simplistic story revolving around a musician's encounter with a potential groupie, arguably humorous when it explains how a "top ten radio hit" is a requirement for sex. It often turns graphic, as in the song "Mud Shark," which recounts a story Zappa was told by members of Led Zeppelin involving the penetration of a groupie's buttered vagina with various fish at the Edgewater Hotel in Seattle. Following this unorthodox climax, the performance incongruously moves into a storybook ending as the band performs the Turtles' hit "Happy Together."

That fall, with the Mothers appearing at New York's storied classical concert venue Carnegie Hall, United Artists released *200 Motels*, the band's psychedelic movie with a concept-album score in line with the Beatles' *Yellow Submarine*—with less plot and more Ringo. Such as it is, the story is roughly identical to that of *Fillmore East*. Dunbar appears, both playing drums and participating in scenes where he creepily scopes out potential groupies with binoculars, in a club with those same groupies and with members of the band discussing groupies and their own penises. The onscreen conversations among the band members include meditations on whether involvement with Zappa was actually good for any of their careers—a postmodern twist on what was, in retrospect, a legitimate concern. Beatles drummer Ringo Starr, actor Theodore Bikel, the Who's Keith Moon, and the Mothers' singers Kaylan and Volman dominate the action. Zubin Mehta conducts an almost incidental London Philharmonic Orchestra, both onscreen and for the soundtrack.

While touring Europe in support of *Fillmore East* and *200 Motels*, they suffered an equipment loss in a fire, and shortly thereafter Zappa was attacked by a jealous fan and hospitalized with life-threatening injuries. Although he would fully recover, the band—including Dunbar—moved on with Zappa's blessing as "Flo & Eddie" (after Kaylan and Volman's stage names), releasing two albums (1972's *Phlorescent Leech & Eddie* and 1973's *Flo & Eddie*) as well as the soundtrack for an animated soft-core pornographic film written by and starring Kaylan and Volman, *Dirty Duck* (1974). This best-forgotten film, replete with racial and ethnic stereotypes, near-constant objectification of women, and gratuitous violence, centers on a "mild-mannered" insurance adjuster who has a meaningless adventure with a penis-obsessed anthropomorphized duck. Kaylan and Volman were zany hit-writers, but as Flo & Eddie they lacked most of Zappa's artistry. As for Dunbar, who had gone so far as to have his own penis cast by the groupie Cynthia Albritton—known as "Cynthia Plaster Caster"—around the same time, it would be harsh to say his talents were being wasted any more than any of them. Every member of the band was fantastically proficient, but it is evident from these albums (and those he did with the Mothers) that after nearly a decade as a professional drummer Dunbar had developed an artistry but still hadn't quite found his niche.

At least some London-based rockers agreed. Guitarist Mick Ronson and rock superstar David Bowie—himself no less avant-garde than Zappa, if more commercially successful—availed themselves of his talents in the summer of 1973, inviting Dunbar to record Ronson's *Slaughter on 10th Avenue* and Bowie's *Pin Ups* at Château d'Hérouville in France; once he had recorded the drum part, he stuck around to help with production. When the journalist Charles Shaar Murray descended on the Château, he described Dunbar as "wearing a magnificently studded and rhinestoned denim jacket with his name emblazoned on the back, and so many rings and bracelets that he clanks when you shake hands with him." In his leisure time he played a "football machine" (probably a foosball table); either the reporter was leaving out the good parts, or—less likely—Dunbar lived a tamer life with Bowie and Ronson than he had with Zappa and Flo & Eddie. Then it was back to London to work on Lou Reed's *Berlin*, Herbie Mann's *London Underground*, and the album *People from Bad Homes* with Bowie's lover Ava Cherry and her band the Astronettes. Ronson and Bowie must have especially liked his licks, because they brought him back in early 1974 for Ronson's *Play Don't Worry* and Bowie's *Diamond Dogs*. There might have even been more work with Lou Reed, for whom Dunbar had been recruited by Canadian producer Bob Ezrin, except for an apparent tiff between Reed and Bowie: "I think [Reed] disliked Bowie so he was giving him a hard time, and me too," the drummer said. So he went with the British glam-rocker just as Bowie was retiring his

Ziggy Stardust character. But after a negative run-in with a Bowie manager, who pushed him to sign a handwritten contract without benefit of counsel, Dunbar found himself out on the market again.

Diamond Dogs produced two smash hits, including "Rebel Rebel," still very much a mainstay on classic rock playlists. The album reached number one in the United Kingdom and Canada and number five on the US *Billboard* 200. Aynsley Dunbar had reached the pinnacle of rock stardom. But he still needed a musical home to showcase his developing sound, now significantly evolved from the blues of Retaliation and the progressive tone of Blue Whale. Little did he know that the best was yet to come. Within months, he had been offered the gig in Journey—and a chance to really shine as an equal partner of a supergroup. Until, of course, Herbie Herbert fired him.

*   *   *

Many of the band's statements on the firing of Aynsley Dunbar seem guided more by hindsight and self-justification than historical perspective, but they coalesce around Dunbar's supposed failure to adapt to the band's new sound, arguing that he was the one member of the group most committed to the instrumental-dominant style of the first three albums. Neal Schon said that Dunbar "was playing way too much for the simplicity of the songs. He used to warm up during our songs for his drum solos," later adding that he was "just gritting his teeth and doing it." Steve Perry called it "a touchy situation . . . there's swing drumming, and there's beefy drumming. He gave us swing when we wanted more beef," adding, with less strained analogy, that "there's a certain kind of music coming from [Schon] and me, and it was different from what he was doing." Rolie agreed. "The way I looked at it," he said, "Aynsley wanted to play a different kind of drums." As for Ross Valory, his take was that "Aynsley was able to play straight ahead and according to format when we were in the studio, but he got bored on the road and was unable to hold himself back in concert. He'd fill up all of the vocal space with drum sounds."

Indeed, Dunbar himself experienced some frustration. "My art is being able to produce things on stage which nobody else basically likes to even have a go at," the drummer said. Journey "didn't want that. They wanted it to conform to a set pattern so that you wouldn't be playing anything they couldn't understand." One journalist said Dunbar was "[u]ninspired by the band's new emphasis"; another said he was "disgusted by the lack of a clear-cut musical direction." Dunbar put a finer point on it, concluding that "what they tend to do is copy themselves. There was no ad lib with them. . . . They wanted me to play note for note behind them, and I wouldn't do it." He later said, "It bored the shit out of me. They could never understand my freedom. They don't understand my playing. They thought I was trying to prove I have technique. Getting out of it was the best thing that ever happened to me."

Herbie also pointed to musical incompatibility, on the one hand claiming that Dunbar "had started playing erratically, if I take the band's word for it," and then arguing that Perry "was afraid of Aynsley Dunbar not having a groove, being too white, a British drummer with very minimal exposure to soul or R&B and not strong on the backbeat." While it's possible that Perry had initially had this impression of Dunbar, it would be unlikely for him to have kept it after months on the road with the drummer, since it was so obviously untrue, given Dunbar's background in the blues. It is also highly unlikely that Perry would have said this, considering the singer's own thorough knowledge of rock history, including the British blues. What's more, since all sources point to Herbie being fully in charge of personnel, it seems odd that he would place the blame for the termination on Dunbar's fellow musicians, rather than own it himself.

But this explanation is incomplete. As we have seen, the style change had hardly been either sudden or overwhelming, and *Infinity* included plenty of exciting music to keep Dunbar interested. Further, he was hardly the band member most threatened by the change; Schon and Rolie had long been dominant members, leading the crowd during the stage show and handling much of the songwriting. While Schon's role continued at roughly the same level after the arrival of Perry, the band member in greatest need of adapting was Rolie, not Dunbar.

Dunbar spoke on several occasions of how he had adapted to the new style, comparing his work with Journey to that of Mick Fleetwood with Fleetwood Mac, another group that had changed its style toward a more commercial pop sound. Of course, Mick Fleetwood was a drummer whose very name was integral to his band: Fleetwood Mac could hardly be Fleetwood Mac without its named founders, Mick Fleetwood and John McVie ("Mac"). Dunbar did not enjoy a similar status in Journey. Although George Tickner considered

Dunbar the original drummer, he had joined the group after their first
choice—Prairie Prince—had chosen to stick with his other band, the Tubes.

At least one reviewer thought Dunbar had been carrying Journey. After a
show in Wisconsin, the drummer "claimed that his playing is getting simpler.
But his improvisational solo during 'Wheel in the Sky' was a technical masterpiece and one of the highlights of the concert," reported Rob Fixmer of the
Madison Capital Times. "Though the sound crew initially had some problems
with the 18 mike's [*sic*] surrounding him, Dunbar's double bass drum work
and punchy accents drove Journey from beginning to end."

Perry later said that Dunbar was actually fired because he lacked versatility—the opposite of the claim that he was too versatile and unhappy playing
the same as on the albums, note-for-note. It's a patently false claim: what does
it take, if not versatility, to move from the blues of Mayall and Brox to the
jazz of Blue Whale to the avant-garde of Zappa and Bowie to the progressive
rock of Journey? Howie Klein of *Bay Area Music* called his versatility "unsur-
passed" and compared him favorably with Cream's legendary drummer Ginger Baker. When singer-guitarist Sammy Hagar, the Montrose veteran who
would later front Van Halen, invited him to play on his 1976 solo album, *Nine
on a Ten Scale*, he was impressed by how quickly and thoroughly Dunbar
wrote his part without even listening to the demo, and that despite charging
triple the going rate, he worked so fast that it was more than worth it.

Other sources claim that Dunbar separated from the band because he
couldn't get along with the new singer. "There were personality conflicts,"
Perry admitted. And Perry was looking at Steve Smith, the drummer for one
of the band's opening acts, Montrose. "[W]e saw him play every night and I
turned to Neal and said 'this is the guy we should have in our band. This is
what we need.' I admit I was making trouble, but I had a gut level . . . that we
had to look at making a change." Rolie later placed the decision squarely at
the singer's feet, claiming that "it was really Perry's call." But that too seems
a limited explanation since, according to Herbie, "Perry didn't get along with
anybody."

Herbie later complained that Dunbar was something of a showboat: "The
problem with Aynsley was that he was anything but a team player. He was
doing anything and everything to look great." He said the band would "walk
into bars after a big stadium show, and he's like, 'I'm the band leader, and
I can't get these guys to play right.'" This explanation makes sense in terms

of Dunbar's relationship with the band and its manager, but that sort of showboating was common in the industry and in this case seemed to doom only the drummer. Perry was also very much the showboat, but, of course, that is what he had been hired to be. Valory was a jokester on and offstage, but that did not get him fired. Schon and Rolie, at times, took center stage and grabbed the attention of the audience. But the drummer, despite a proficiency at his craft that easily equaled any of the others, had fallen into a second-class status within the group. Despite his prolific writing on *Next*, he was allowed to cowrite only one song on *Infinity* ("Feeling That Way"), whereas Schon and Perry were rapidly emerging as the band's songwriting duo.

Still other sources claim that Dunbar had complained too often that he was losing lucrative session work to attend low-paying Journey dates. "He complained constantly," Schon said. "He didn't want to be in that situation." Indeed, as the drummer later told Robyn Flans, "they stopped me from doing a lot of sessions when I was with them by putting what I would term bullshit gigs in the schedule . . . something which must have gotten the band $2,000, whereas I was losing about $6,000 from a week's session work." Certainly, Dunbar could earn a tremendous amount as a session player, but by the time he left, the band was earning significantly more per show. And after he left Journey, rather than go on the market for session work, Dunbar immediately joined another touring band with commercial rock hits, Jefferson Starship. So this explanation, too, has its flaws.

Herbie also justified firing Dunbar because of his seemingly unmanageable extracurricular behavior. It "was constantly like the road manager would wake the band up, and say 'we gotta get out of the hotel. Some general, or some sergeant, or some police officer is looking for his underage daughter, and she's with Aynsley' . . . that happened several times," the manager recounted. "What they called 'Pampers and platforms'—you could tell the Aynsley groupies 'cause they were so young they were still in Pampers but they were wearing platform shoes and makeup so they'd appear to be older than fifteen." While hardly out of place for a rock star, Journey was already building a reputation for eschewing the sort of "bad boy" behavior for which Led Zeppelin had become infamous. In retrospect, that group might have been a better fit for him (and they considered him again after John Bonham's death in 1980, but they broke up instead).

The band also accused Dunbar of other "bad boy" behavior for which there is no evidence and which seems simply spiteful. They told Jefferson Starship's Paul Kantner not to hire him because "he was a drunk who couldn't keep time." Fortunately for the Starship, Kantner saw through the pettiness and never had any complaints of that sort.

The fact is that Dunbar had been moving into a leadership role before *and after* Perry joined Journey. In 1978, when two limos carrying the band to a TV interview in Detroit collided fender-to-bumper, it was Dunbar who had the presence of mind to ensure that his bandmates were uninjured and find the nearest pay phone to seek help, engaging the leadership skills he had developed in his years with Retaliation, while the other band members spent the minutes after the crash kicking and jumping on the limos and arguing with passing motorists.

In fact, contrary to the idea that Dunbar could not adapt to the band's new musical direction, the hiring of Perry gave him something he could work with. Drawing from another part of his résumé, his year with David Bowie, he saw Perry's potential as the androgynous pixie, akin to Bowie's gender-bending Ziggy Stardust character. Dunbar knew how to support center-stage androgyny: he provided a drum set masculinity to assuage the complicated sexual feelings of the men in the audience who did not understand, could not explain, or were unwilling to confront their attraction to the "fairy" at center stage. It might have worked. In the mid-'70s, androgyny, glam, and makeup were all the rage, from Lou Reed to the New York Dolls to Kiss, and Dunbar imagined a Journey superstardom in this vein.

But the drummer's vision for Journey clashed with the manager's. By 1978 glam rock had split into disco and punk, neither of which appealed to Herbie. On the other hand, Herbie had observed the rise of country rock with the success of such groups as the Allman Brothers, Lynyrd Skynyrd, the Eagles, Fleetwood Mac, and old friend Steve Miller, and felt that rock listeners were asking for something more "wholesome" than the open bisexuality of Bowie and Elton John. That was the model Journey needed to follow: Perry would play down the femininity, and they would hire a soft-spoken jazz drummer who would not provide too much contrast. Plus, Herbie needed to be in charge.

*   *   *

Beyond *why* Dunbar was fired, the question of *how* matters, especially for its future implications for the band. Like the other members, including Steve Perry, Dunbar not only had a permanently-renewable annual contract with Journey as an employee-musician but was also an equal shareholder in Nightmare Productions, the band's parent company.

For most of his tenure in the band, the musicians had been paid according to immediate personal need, agreeing to leave all profits with their corporate entity, including the royalties they earned from their albums. In 1978 they were earning $17,500 per year (about $81,000 in 2023)—not exactly "rock star" pay, but they spent so much time on the road or in the studio, they had little time to spend much money. Perry didn't even own a home; during the brief breaks, he stayed with his mother back in Lemoore.

The employment contract allowed the manager to terminate an individual musician "for willful default or breach of the obligations" of the contract. None of the stated reasons for firing Dunbar—not even purported dalliances with underage groupies—rose to this level; he continued to perform in the studio and on the road, his only obligations (although if he had been incarcerated for statutory rape, that would have been sufficient grounds, but he never was). So technically, legally, he wasn't fired.

The employment contract did allow the manager to choose not to renew the contracts of all of the band members at the same time. So Herbie concocted a scheme to fire Dunbar without actually firing Dunbar: he did not renew any of the five musicians' contracts, but then he hired four of them back. This itself was a breach of the contract, as it could only be done in the event of a band breakup. Dunbar later accused all of them—including his replacement Steve Smith, who was in the opening act, Montrose—of engaging in a conspiracy to remove him as early as June 1978, when they were only midway through the *Infinity* tour, although there is no corroboration for this.

Even if Herbie had been within his rights to fire Dunbar, there was also the matter of the drummer's share of Nightmare. Dunbar owned one-sixth of the company and was entitled either to a buyout (if he was willing to sell) or continuing ownership.

Herbie (and—if we believe Dunbar—Jeanne Herbert, Gregg Rolie and his wife Garnett, Neal and Tena Schon, Ross and Diane Valory, Steve Perry, and

Steve Smith) found a variety of ways to dilute the value of Dunbar's shares. First, they issued five hundred shares—the same amount Dunbar owned—to Steve Smith, as an equal partner. Then they transferred the band's trucking and lighting operations to a new company, Nocturne, Inc., and the album royalties from Columbia Records to another new company, Daydream, Inc. Dunbar owned no shares in either of these new entities. Daydream purchased a house in San Francisco, which it rented to Nightmare well above market rates: that meant yet another transfer of wealth from Nightmare—which Dunbar co-owned—to a company that his former bandmates and manager owned on their own.

When Dunbar learned of all this, he threatened to sue, and Herbie later claimed to have offered Dunbar a one-time payout of $70,000 (more than $250,000 in 2023), but Dunbar's lawyer staunchly refuted this; it wouldn't have been enough, in any case.

The drummer sued for just under $6 million (nearly $22 million in 2023), which he calculated from the loss of earned and future royalties, interest, and punitive and exemplary damages (legal terms meaning to punish and set an example). He also demanded the conversion of Nocturne and Daydream into wholly owned subsidiaries of Nightmare and a full accounting of the three companies' assets. He did not contest the awarding of shares to Steve Smith, but he did sue to prevent Nightmare from further stock issues.

The parties settled for $250,000 (about $915,000 in 2023), "plus royalties on past albums." Unlike George Tickner, who never received any royalties for Journey's first album (and told me he couldn't afford a lawyer in any case), Dunbar not only received royalties from Journey's first three albums but also *Infinity*, which has since gone triple platinum. More important for the band, Dunbar gave up his shares in Nightmare, so that Journey's corporate entity could legally continue without him.

*   *   *

Aynsley Dunbar played with Jefferson Starship until 1982, after which he joined David Coverdale's band Whitesnake. He later played with legendary British Invasion singer Eric Burdon in a band Burdon called the New Animals, playing Animals' classics "The House of the Rising Sun," "It's My Life," and "We Gotta Get Out of This Place," among others. Tragically, in

1999 Dunbar's four-year-old son, Dash, was diagnosed with pontine glioma, "a rare form of an inoperable tumor that attacks the brain stem," and ex-wife Karen took to organizing benefit concerts to pay the child's enormous medical bills. Dash did not recover. In 2003, Dunbar joined Steppenwolf's Nick St. Nicholas in a supergroup called World Classic Rockers, which performed a variety of classic rock songs on tour.

"Someday Soon," 1978-1980

Since we're sleeping in the same bed you think they'd at least fuck us.

—*Steve Perry*

Journey hardly skipped a beat after the replacement of their first long-term drummer by Boston native Steve Smith. Invited into the studio to record "SuperJam II" for the *King Biscuit Flower Hour* radio show, they asked Annie Sampson and Jo Baker of Stoneground and Tom Johnston of the Doobie Brothers to join in on vocals, with the Tower of Power horn section providing a brassy backup. They performed five songs from *Infinity*, including a version of "Wheel in the Sky" with a haunting intro they would later repurpose on the soundtrack to the 1980 experimental Japanese motion picture *Dream, After Dream*.

But they took it more than a step further, showing off their versatility with eight Motown and blues classics. After Junior Walker's "Roadrunner," Sampson and Baker brought in the Everly Brothers' oft-covered "Love Hurts," with Steve Perry adding a verse from the Righteous Brothers' "Unchained Melody" to the song's middle—and almost made it fit. Then they performed the exciting "Hold On I'm Coming" by Sam and Dave, and the Impressions' inspiring gospel number "People Get Ready." At Johnston's suggestion, they added "Show Me," by Joe Tex, and the Robert Johnson blues classic "Crossroads," with vocal duties shared by Johnston, Gregg Rolie, and

Perry, and a downright gleeful guitar line, Neal Schon emulating Eric Clapton. Rolie enjoyed singing Albert King's "Born under a Bad Sign," with its resemblance to his Santana hit "Black Magic Woman;" and Perry soared in his take on his childhood idol Sam Cooke's hit "Good Times." Recorded in October 1978 at San Francisco's Automatt Studios for anticipated use during the Christmas season, the episode, sadly, was never aired. And although "Good Times" later made it into the band's 1992 box set, Journey fans would have to wait until the advent of YouTube before they could hear the show in its entirety, replete with thoughtful introductions by Ross Valory and Perry. But the fact that it went unaired demonstrates—yet again—the depth of the resegregation of popular music by the end of the 1970s. Here we have a perfect example of the multiracial musical roots of the band, especially in "Hold On I'm Coming," "Crossroads," and "Born under a Bad Sign." But someone—probably manager Herbie Herbert—decided that allowing the episode to air would cut into Journey's developing—and almost exclusively white—fan base.

In November they returned to Cherokee Studios in Los Angeles to record *Evolution*, Roy Thomas Baker again in the booth. Overall, this first Journey album without Aynsley Dunbar has a cleaner sound than *Infinity*. Steve Perry is clearly asserting his status, sharing vocals with Rolie on only one song, while he and Schon affirm their position as the band's dominant songwriters.

The album begins with "Majestic," a mostly instrumental number written by Perry and Schon that starts with acoustic guitar, joined with bass and organ, and then an electric guitar with the theme. The band members harmonize "ah, ah, ah" three times. "Too Late," also by Perry and Schon, similarly begins with a brief acoustic guitar intro, quickly joined by Perry's clear vocals in a ballad. The lyrics speak of a change. Perry's final verse is sung an octave higher than the first two, further demonstrating his astonishing range.

"Lovin', Touchin', Squeezin'," a blues tune by Perry destined to be the group's first bona fide top-20 hit, begins with a strong bass line, joined by piano at just the right moments. The lyrics, inspired by Sam Cooke's "Nothin' Can Change This Love," develop a story about a jilted lover who predicts that the former partner will soon likewise be jilted. The final minute is a harmonized wagging finger: "Na na na na na," repeated ad nauseam—either the most obtuse or the most brilliant creation in Journey's musical development. Whatever. The song rose to number 16 on the *Billboard* Hot 100.

"City of the Angels," by Perry, Schon, and Rolie, is a harmonized attempt to capture the frenetic, disjointed, yet strangely appealing spirit of Los Angeles that first lured Steve Perry—and so many others—seeking fame and fortune. "I've got this feeling that things will work out." The song also serves as something of a response to the previous album's "Lights," which lionized San Francisco (and which Perry had originally also conceived for LA). After a harmonized vocal intro, Schon delivers a brief solo; then Perry comes in with the lyrics, borrowing elements from his Alien Project number "If You Need Me, Call Me." Next up is "When You're Alone (It Ain't Easy)," another pining love song by Perry and Schon, with a rather simple composition that begins with an insistent guitar theme. Perry covers the verses with the high notes, joined by the band on the harmonized chorus at a lower register. Like "City of the Angels," the song borrows from Perry's work with the Alien Project, specifically the song "My My My."

"Sweet and Simple," by Perry, is just that. It begins with Rolie's piano, backed by Schon with a repetitive guitar lick. The verse lyrics are indeed simple and sweet, while the chorus is a controlled vocal explosion. Schon delivers a haunting guitar solo. Perry's final line in the chorus features one of the highest male vocal notes in rock music. The band closes the song with a harmonized "It's what I like to do" over Schon's guitar explorations and Perry's angelic stylings. Surprisingly, for such a simple song, it's the second-longest on the album, closing out side 1 with over four minutes of material.

"Lovin' You Is Easy," by Perry, Schon, and Greg Errico of Sly and the Family Stone—Schon's old bandmate from the interval between Santana and Journey—is a rollicking up-tempo start to side 2, with a commanding bass and drum beat, solid vocals, occasional piano, and a funky guitar solo. It leads directly into "Just the Same Way," by Rolie, Schon, and Valory, another up-tempo, the only song on the album not written or cowritten by Perry—and the only one to feature a shared Rolie lead vocal. It starts out strong with piano, joined by drums and bass and then a strummed guitar line. The song includes an interesting triplet. The chorus is not unlike how Perry joined in on the material from the first three albums: a subdued backup singer. Only at one brief juncture, during the bridge, does Perry take charge. Schon's guitar solo brings the song into a fade-out.

"Do You Recall" follows with a mid-tempo by Perry and Rolie, beginning with organ, guitar, and an insistent vocal. Rolie's voice joins Perry's in the

chorus melody. In the middle, the song breaks into a brief jazzy portion, featuring new drummer Steve Smith, punctuated by Schon's electric guitar. It is
followed by "Daydream," a nod to the musical style of *Next*, by Perry, Rolie,
Schon, and Valory. This stylized ballad includes some spacey effects punctuated by a hard rock chorus.

The album concludes with "Lady Luck," by Perry, Schon, and Valory. The
song begins with a guitar-and-drum theme, joined very quickly by Rolie's
organ in a sequence reminiscent of the first two Journey albums; Perry delivers a searing vocal. This is most definitely *not* a take on "Luck Be a Lady," the
standard most famously recorded by Frank Sinatra, although it shares the
theme of an unsuccessful casino sojourn. A repeat of the guitar-and-drum
sequence gives way to a Schon solo that mimics the vocal theme.

Reviews of *Evolution* were mostly—but not overwhelmingly—positive.
Joseph Bensoua called it, without a hint of irony, "a marvelous extension
of 'Infinity.'" John Howard of the *Jackson Clarion-Ledger* compared Ross
Valory's thumping bass on "Lovin', Touchin', Squeezin'" to a beating heart
and heaped praise on the song "Daydream." New York's *Glens Falls Post-Star*
noted that "[t]here is little of the group's former penchant for electronic effects
here, and the strength of the music completely overrides any fond memories
you have for it," with trusty Joel Selvin adding that "Journey is toning down
its stance as a hard rock machine and developing a rock and roll style of its
own." Ernie Welch went even further, writing that "'Evolution' may be the
band's strongest effort to date" in Smith's hometown *Boston Globe*. "Perry,
a fifth wheel . . . last spring, now plays an important role" adding that "Journey's rock 'n' roll may be grandiose and out of vogue, but for those willing to
ignore the trends, 'Evolution' should be an inspiring musical trip."

Other reviewers expressed concern, either with the loss of Aynsley Dunbar
or the continued move away from the progressive rock of the band's early
years. While celebrating the album's "harmonies, lush electric arrangements
and seductive transitions [that] are all commissioned for their optimum
value," Mark Lundahl of the *San Bernardino County Sun* still found it "a bit
unsettling due to the band's waste of instrumental talent." Jim Healey of the
Des Moines Register agreed: "The songs begin attractively, perhaps with an
unusual vocal or clever instrumental, build nicely, then crumble to creative
dust as Neal Schon throws out a handful of the same tired electric guitar leads
every rock 'n' roll fan over age 3 has heard too often." Robert Chamberlain of

the *Calgary Herald* liked *Evolution* but felt that Perry was not using his vocals enough now that Dunbar was no longer around to challenge him. Eric Hegedus was likewise cool to the latest Journey effort. "The onslaught of guitars unleashed by this soulless Bay Area rock outfit begs for mitigation that never comes," he wrote in the *Allentown Morning Call*, adding that "by the end of this LP I was absolutely bored with Steve Perry's callous vocals . . . perhaps he should follow Dunbar's lead and split." Calling the band a "soulless Bay Area rock outfit" was also ironic, given the actual, demonstrated "soul" evident in the band's *King Biscuit* recording, of which Hegedus was no doubt ignorant.

The negative reviews didn't stop the album's rise on the charts, however. It peaked at number 20 on the *Billboard* 200 and by the end of May, after barely two months, it had already sold more than five hundred thousand copies, qualifying for gold status despite cratering overall sales in the industry due to a serious economic downturn; it made platinum the following October. In San Francisco, where the band could do no wrong, *Evolution* peaked at number 1 on the *Bay Area Music* California charts, earning "Bammie" nominations for Best Album, Best Male Vocalist, and—critics of Dunbar's firing be damned—Best Drummer. As it happened, the album and its vocalist won two of the three, with Perry inviting Eddie Money and even audience members to join him onstage for his acceptance rendition of "Lovin', Touchin', Squeezin'." But the critics got the last laugh, bestowing the best drummer award on the grinning Liverpudlian for his work with Jefferson Starship on their album *Freedom at Point Zero*.

After the recording of *Evolution* and an appearance on a New Year's bill at the Winterland with Blondie, REO Speedwagon, and Stoneground, the band had only the briefest of breaks before they were back out on the road to promote the album. Schon and Ross Valory proved no hard feelings when, among other activities, they appeared with Aynsley Dunbar (as well as old friends Pete Sears and Prairie Prince) at a February 4 benefit for Greenpeace at the Old Waldorf. The band's vocalists, on the other hand, played around in a different way. Having learned all the wrong lessons from Van Halen during the previous year's tour, Rolie and Perry checked into a hotel with several dozen yards of extension cords, plugged their room TV into them, and brought the set through the lobby, dumping it into the swimming pool. "It was a wonderful sight," Perry related. "I'm telling you man, it goes up in a beautiful color. It explodes. It's great!" Kids, please don't try this at home.

The group also triumphantly returned to host *Burt Sugarman's Midnight Special with Wolfman Jack*, playing "Lovin', Touchin', Squeezin'" and "City of the Angels." This time they were rock stars, and Perry was supremely confident, jumping into the audience to serenade one particular young woman who had caught his eye, with the somewhat awkward lyric, "It won't be long, yes/'Til you're alone with your lover . . . /'Cause he's 'lovin', touchin', he's squeezin' another." This time was also different because he lip-synched (and the band hand-synched) to the prerecorded album tracks.

But all too soon it was back to business. Joined by the Pat Travers Band, Journey crossed the Atlantic in March for a tour of Europe, including appearances in Paris and London. Then it was a quick stop at the California World Music Festival at Los Angeles Memorial Coliseum, followed by an April tour of Japan, including multiple dates in Nagoya, Osaka, and Tokyo. While in Japan, they met noted designer Kenzo Takada and agreed to return in October, after the US tour, to record the soundtrack to his forthcoming film *Yume, Yume No Ato (Dream, After Dream)*. They returned to the states for two full circuits between May and August, ninety-four separate appearances, most of them headlining over Thin Lizzy. They played New York City three times, including one date at the Palladium and two in Central Park; twice again they played Comiskey Park in Chicago. "The band set a new attendance record in Detroit," according to Joel Selvin, "where 48,000 fans attended four sold out shows over one weekend at Cobo Hall." Their days as opening act at small venues were over.

Reviews of the tour were mostly positive, but as with the album, there were some noteworthy concerns. "The focal point was Perry's other-worldly vocals and emerging stage presence," wrote the *Kansas City Star*'s Nancy Ball of the band's May 12 show, despite the sound problems she felt continued to plague the band. "Journey demonstrated just why they've become a major concert attraction," gushed Roger Kaye of the *Fort Worth Star-Telegram*, "as the five-man group unleashed a fine 100-minute lesson in how to play rock 'n' roll" in their appearance at the Tarrant County Convention Center. "Hirsch Coliseum met its match last night," wrote John Andrew Prime of the *Shreveport Times* after a July 19 show there, adding that when it came to the transition from "Feeling That Way" to "Anytime," "few bands can suddenly lose instrumental backup and still maintain the same energy level as before. Journey did." But Mark Lundahl of the *San Bernardino County*

Sun griped that "drummer Steve Smith just did not match the finesse of his predecessor Aynsley Dunbar" in his otherwise positive review of the June 30 show at Swing Auditorium, the band's first appearance there as headliners, while Terry Atkinson called the band "palatably mediocre" and Perry's songs "cliché-ridden" in his review of the shows at Long Beach Arena on June 30 and July 1 for the *Los Angeles Times*.

Whatever the tenor of the reviews, there was no shortage of drama. In San Bernardino, someone in the audience threw an M-80 explosive at Schon. A quick-thinking roadie kicked it off to the side, where it fortunately exploded without harming anything (or anyone). That same show, the town suffered two earthquakes registering 3.2 and 3.7 on the Richter scale. "No one seemed to notice, though," so into the music were they. And in Florida, while still on a runway and approaching takeoff speed, the plane carrying the band lost an engine. "We veered to the side and came to a screeching halt," recalled Perry. "We got off and left an hour later with a different plane, but we were still shaken." Understandable, since they had grown up with the story of how Buddy Holly, Richie Valens, and the Big Bopper died in a plane crash between rock shows in 1959; more recently, as they knew all too well, Lynyrd Skynyrd lost its lead vocalist Ronnie Van Zant, guitarist Steve Gaines, and backup singer Cassie Gaines in a 1977 crash.

*   *   *

While out on tour for *Evolution*, the band agreed to another personnel change, most likely at Perry's request, but with Herbie Herbert's explicit approval. This time they decided to jettison producer Roy Thomas Baker in favor of his engineer, Geoffrey Workman, and their sound engineer from their live shows, Kevin Elson, an industry veteran who had worked on Lynyrd Skynyrd's 1977 album *Street Survivors*. Baker had always been volatile, most notably when he destroyed the studio during the 1977 *Infinity* sessions, but the results, with both that album and *Evolution*, were solid. When Liz Lufkin of *BAM* magazine came to visit during their work on *Evolution*, she was impressed by Baker's hands-on work and rapport with the group. "Roy has enabled us to pull off some ideas we really wanted to do, like multi-track vocals," Perry told Pete Bishop of the *Pittsburgh Press*. "It gives us the strength and width of when we're playing live." Rolie, for his part, told Lisa Robinson of the *Green Bay Press-Gazette* in 1978 that it had been "tedious" when the band had produced its own albums, and he was glad Baker had stepped in. Valory, who could find humor in virtually anything, found Baker's style "hilarious" but complained—possibly in jest—that "all he wanted to do was talk on his . . . phone with Freddy Mercury," the lead singer of Queen.

Yet even while praising Baker, Perry was always quick to credit his number two, whom he called Baker's "right-hand engineer." "This is the honest-to-God truth, Roy was out driving his Rolls-Royce or doing shopping half the time we were recording *Evolution*. It's really just produced by us and Geoffrey Workman." And he knew whereof he spoke, having worked as a second fiddle in the booths at Crystal Studios during his lean years. This led to an obvious choice when Perry had had enough of Baker's shenanigans. "We decided on 'Evolution' that since his engineer, Geoff Workman, did all the work and [Baker] wasn't even around, we'd do it ourselves," he said. "So we grabbed his engineer and did it ourselves." In the aftermath, Perry couldn't even say Baker's name in an interview with *Voice Magazine*. "The reason the job 'producer' ever comes into play is, lots of the groups are flakes, or else can't organize their time correctly in the studio . . . the guy sits there and says, 'That sounds good, sing a little harder, sing a little softer' . . . producers are record companies' insurance policies that a record will be turned in on budget, and on time," concluding, "It is sickening." As for Herbie, he "just thought he did a piss poor job," faulting Baker for "almost kind of a medieval recording style."

The fact is, Roy Thomas Baker was a fantastically talented producer, and the choice of the sound engineer from their live show—repeatedly faulted for being too loud—as one of the replacements indicates that the decision to fire Baker was the result of a personality clash more than anything else. Soon after he parted ways with the band, someone in Journey called him "an asshole."

Life in the studio can be as intense as life on the road. In his book about the recording sessions for Fleetwood Mac's blockbuster 1977 album *Rumours*, Ken Caillat describes months of incredibly long hours at the Record Plant in Sausalito and later at Wally Heider Studios in Hollywood. While some acts record "live"—meaning the entire band performs each song together in the studio until they get it right—more often individual members record their parts separately, at first with only a demonstration version ("demo") in the headsets, helping them keep time, and then with something closer to a finished product as the work progresses. Even when musicians record together, good sound engineers work hard to ensure that each instrument is recorded onto its own track with a separate microphone, and they use sound baffles to keep them from leaking into the others. Later, the tracks are mixed onto a master tape, and it is from the master that the retail copies are cut—in that era, mostly onto LPs. Having a good working relationship with the producer matters, therefore, not simply because the band needs to ensure that its music is recorded well but also because they're spending so much time together in small, windowless rooms. Tempers flare; nerves get rubbed raw.

Steve Perry took his job very, very seriously and was not always the easiest person to get along with in the studio. He held himself to a standard he often could not meet, finding fault in every slight mistake in his own performance. This led to multiple retakes of line after line. He chafed at Baker's direction, especially when the producer could not stay on task, but as the "new guy," at first there was little he could do about it. Journey's newfound popularity and the growing association of the band with Perry's voice gave him the power to make the switch.

*   *   *

The first work Journey recorded after their dismissal of Baker was to fulfill their promise to Kenzo Takada in Japan. Together with Matthew Schon, father of the guitarist and an accomplished musician in his own right, the band went into Shinanomachi Studios in Tokyo to record *Dream, After Dream*. The decision was a no-brainer for Herbie Herbert: "I knew how tremendously popular Takada was in Japan and I knew we would benefit from any association with him."

The album seems like Journey's answer to Santana's *Caravanserai*: eclectic, progressive, exotic. Produced by Journey and Kevin Elson, five local musicians complemented the band with strings and horns arranged and conducted by Matthew Schon. "Destiny," by Schon and Perry, begins sweet and soft but is not exactly a catchy tune. Midway through this eight-minute number, it moves into an up-tempo portion that feels like a chase scene. A spacey transition seems to return the song to its sweet and soft theme but instead offers Schon an opportunity for a satisfying electric guitar solo. "Snow Theme," an instrumental by Valory, doesn't seem to involve any members of Journey beyond the writing credit, relying instead on the five Japanese string and horn musicians. "Sand Castles," written by Perry and Rolie, is a jazz number with long vocal notes, a lyric that speaks to life's impermanence, prominent horns, organ, and the jazz drums that are Smith's specialty. "A Few Coins," by all five members of Journey, is little more than a few instrumental notes and only forty seconds long. Schon's skills come out at the start of "Moon Theme," another instrumental with acoustic guitars. After a minute, this gives way to his more typical electric guitar rock licks but quickly returns to the soft acoustic theme. This routine repeats before transitioning to a harp solo. "When the Love Has Gone," a melancholy jazz instrumental by Schon, has an electric guitar theme and a prominent organ. "Festival Dance" is a brief instrumental up-tempo by all five members of Journey, less than a minute in length, a snippet of Middle Eastern music suitable for a belly dancer, ending with the sound of a creaky door opening. "The Rape," an instrumental by Valory, begins with a score reminiscent of a show tune, and a guitar line borrowed from "Conversations" (the second half of a song cowritten by Valory for the album *Journey*), followed by the tolling of a church bell over a theme in a different time signature. A train horn sounds in the distance. Finally, "Little Girl," by Schon, Perry, and Rolie, is the most "Journey-sounding" song on the album. Perry sings a mournful lyric ("I told you from the start/That love could break your heart/Girl I'm so sorry") over acoustic guitar and bass, and some of the Japanese string instruments. Schon and Rolie provide backup vocals in the repeated one-line chorus: "Ooh, little girl." Schon's guitar solo is a mournful complement to the lyrics. The song and the album end with Rolie's harmonica—a new addition to his repertoire—in a fade-out.

The film includes the entire album, and is visually stunning, although the plot is ridiculous. An elderly vagabond recalls an episode from his youth in which he crosses a desert and encounters two princesses who take him in, seduce him, and threaten his life before metamorphosing into birds that fly away.

Journey returned to the United States with their popularity at an all-time high. To capitalize on this, Columbia Records put out a double-length compilation album consisting of fourteen songs from the first three albums. This was ironic, of course, because Columbia had been ready to drop the band when these songs constituted their oeuvre. But as they approached the final days of the decade and returned to Automatt Studios in San Francisco with

Geoff Workman and Kevin Elson to record their next regular studio album, *Departure*, anything seemed possible for Journey.

Departure begins with "Any Way You Want It," by Perry and Schon. The song itself is a real departure from their previous work, no pun intended, setting the stage for the album. It begins with confident a cappella harmonies singing the theme "Any way you want it/That's the way you need it/Any way you want it." No longer writing about unrequited love—so often the theme of the previous studio album, *Evolution*—this is a celebration of a consummated marriage between Perry's soulful brand of rock with the progressive power of the original Journey, replete with African American spiritual call-and-response: "All night (all night) every night/Hold tight (hold tight) baby hold tight." With a vocal-guitar give-and-take inspired by Phil Lynott of Thin Lizzy, with whom the band had previously shared a bill, the second guitar solo, played behind the repeated harmonized theme, leads to the fade-out. The song peaked at number 23 on the *Billboard* Hot 100.

"Walks Like a Lady," by Perry, is a jazz-blues take on Bob Dylan's "Just Like a Woman"—also possibly inspired by Carlos Santana: "When a guitar player wants to get sassy and nasty, he just has to copy the way women walk and talk by bending the notes on the electric guitar." Rolie's organ pairs with Valory's bass, and Schon's guitar pairs with Smith's brushes for a satisfying jazz club number. When he performed the song live, Perry inserted a typical African American schoolyard chant that had become part of R&B: "Put your hand on your hip/Let your backbone slip." "Someday Soon," by Perry, Rolie, and Schon, sees the return of Rolie to lead singer duties, with Perry handling the high notes. The verses feature a call-and-response between Rolie and Perry.

"People and Places," by Perry, Schon, and Valory, a ballad with brief hard rock choruses, features Schon's first lead vocal since recording *Next*. It begins with a spacey organ followed by multiple voices repeating individual words in the line, "Do you feel me?" "Precious Time," by Perry and Schon, closes out side 1 with an up-tempo, rollicking acoustic guitar, Rolie's return to the harmonica, and a strong marching beat by Smith.

Side 2 includes three hard-driving, up-tempo rock songs at the beginning, middle, and end. The first is "Where Were You," by Perry and Schon, now clearly the dominant songwriting duo, continuing a partnership that began in that Denver hotel room back in 1977, when they wrote "Patiently." Schon

starts the song with a decisive lick. After Smith joins in with the beat, Perry
sings his way in with "Yeah, yeah" and then moves into a fully realized lyric
that speaks to unmet expectations and serious consequences: "I don't mind,
little lady, 'cause your sister's lookin' real good to me!" Schon's solo indicates
he's learned how to give a full, satisfying performance within the confines of
radio-friendly rock. The song ends abruptly and is answered by "I'm Cryin',"
a sad organ- and electric guitar–heavy rock ballad by Perry and Rolie in which
Schon's guitar licks sound like tears—and raindrops—each series following a
line by Perry. But as with many a rainstorm, the song ends with a rainbow,
represented by a few piano keys.

   "Line of Fire," by Perry and Schon, is a hard rocker about a violent love tri-
angle involving "Frankie," "Suzie," and "Stevie," inspired by Sam Cooke's take
on the traditional Negro blues number "Frankie and Johnny." This one, too,
involves a gunshot, in this case with a sound effect provided by Smith. It's followed by the title track, by Schon, a very brief guitar exploration and the only
song on the album not written or cowritten by Perry. Next up, as if telling a
story of redemption following the violence, is "Good Morning Girl," by Perry
and Schon, a soft, mostly acoustic, stripped-down version of "Patiently."

   "Stay Awhile," a ballad by Perry and Schon, works well following "Good
Morning Girl," which shares the theme. The song has long vocal notes and
a soft acoustic guitar and piano. "Homemade Love," by Perry, Schon, and
Smith, on the other hand, is an up-tempo rocker to close the album with lyrics evoking sex and dessert ("I need a jelly roll, sweetie/Now spread it on me,
babe").

   With *Departure* hitting the record stacks, *Rolling Stone* took the opportunity to weigh in on the band's road to success. Calling Journey the best in
"the Seventies hard-rock genre," John Swenson noted that the "addition of
megalomaniac producer Roy Thomas Baker and lead vocalist Steve Perry
further confused the issue," resulting in the loss of Dunbar, "disgusted by the
lack of a clear-cut musical direction." But with Baker out, Perry had emerged
as a leader. Swenson felt that Smith lacked Dunbar's talents, but he saw that
as a positive, arguing that "Journey works best as a band. And they've never
rocked harder." Pete Bishop of the *Pittsburgh Press* posted a moderate review,
finding *Departure* little different from the previous two albums; but he was
impressed by rockers "Any Way You Want It," "Where Were You," and
"Line of Fire." Herbie covered all bases, calling the album "a pivotal career

masterpiece stepping-stone," noting in an interview with Joel Selvin that *Infinity* and *Evolution* were still on the charts.

Selvin, for his part, summed up the album succinctly: "After three years with the band, vocalist Steve Perry holds down ... a command and confidence nothing short of amazing," but "Journey's music is to rock something like daytime soap operas are to television," producing music "that doesn't require great intellectual or deep emotional content. It is, in a sense, superficial gloss. But the shine is brilliant." And the album soared up the *Billboard* 200 chart, peaking at number eight on April 25, 1980, earning RIAA gold certification in May and platinum in July.

As the band prepared for another international tour, Herbie shifted the company into high gear. He bought four tractor trailers to haul the group's equipment, and he ordered "martial arts training ... to build up stamina for almost continuous touring."

Herbie had a number of novel ideas for running the band as a business. From Nightmare's Union Street headquarters in San Francisco's tony Marina Heights neighborhood, where his back office had an impressive view of the Golden Gate Bridge, he managed Nocturne, Inc., the spinoff production company that handled the band's impressive lighting sequences, choreographed trucking operations, and could be rented out for use by other bands whenever Journey wasn't using them. He decreed that every member of the road crew would be a full-time, year-round employee with full benefits including health insurance—a rarity in an industry that relied on seasonal help, and far different from his own early experiences working with Santana and Steve Miller (let alone the threadbare budget of Frumious Bandersnatch). Perhaps most controversially (as the average age of the Journey fan fell below the drinking age), he forged a sponsorship deal with Budweiser beer. This allowed the band to tour longer into the year, after the record label's promotional money ran out, which in turn contributed to album sales months—even years—after the initial release. With the recession continuing, band members were instructed to drink the cheaper Budweiser rather than their preferred Heineken, a more expensive import—and even to talk about it in the press. "We don't drink Heineken anymore," Gregg Rolie told *People* magazine. "We drink Budweiser." This reached a peak in absurdity "at a St. Louis gig," near Budweiser's main bottling plant, when they arrived "in a carriage pulled by the brewer's iconic team of Clydesdales."

The band members also contributed to efforts to keep themselves business-minded, jokingly establishing the "Prima" award for the band's biggest prima donna—awarded each year by the previous year's recipient. Perry "won" it in 1980.

As with the year before, Journey found themselves with a hit that helped fill larger and larger arenas and sell the new album. "Any Way You Want It" propelled *Departure* into the top 10 on the album charts and drove fans into the stadiums. Although they were still plagued by sound and electrical problems despite the best efforts of Kevin Elson and the professionalism of the road crew, the *Departure* tour proved that Journey's increasing popularity was actually more like an arrival. And Perry predicted even more to come, assuring reporter Pete Bishop of the *Pittsburgh Press* that Journey would not become "a one-album-and-one-tour-every-three-years, no-interview band," a comment he likely regretted in retrospect.

Ross Valory and Steve Smith took the opportunity to bond by filming scenes for a home video directed by Valory, *The New Avocado Revue*. Ironically, they based the film on Frank Zappa's *200 Motels*, which starred Aynsley Dunbar. In one scene that catches the spirit of Valory's role as the band's jokester, a groupie (played by Susan Gurnack, Smith's fiancée) knocks on Smith's door and invites herself in for a tryst, only to interrupt the proceedings when she has a sudden realization, turns to him, and blurts out, "You're not Steve Perry?"

The 1980 *Departure* tour proved yet another grueling seven months on the road, circling North America twice from late March through August, jetting over to Europe in September for an extended tour of Germany (as well as dates in Switzerland and England), and then making still another jaunt over to Japan in October. They played more than ninety concerts in thirty-four states, six countries, and three continents. Where this particular tour differed from the previous year's *Evolution* tour was that with Kevin Elson's assistance, the band recorded a live album, *Captured*, including songs from *Infinity*, *Evolution*, and *Departure* in three different locations: August 4 and 5 at Cobo Hall in Detroit, August 8 in Montreal, and October 13 in Tokyo. The result is a two-disc live album featuring a band that is very tight, with vocals that blend well and strong mixing. Most of the arrangements are fairly close renditions of the studio versions and show how Perry had definitively taken control of Journey's stage act, unabashedly working the crowd.

The album begins with "Majestic," the studio version, played over the speakers as a warm-up for the show at the Forum in Montreal. Perry calls out "Bon soir, Montreal" ("Good evening, Montreal") as the band takes the stage with the hard-driving "Where Were You," "Just the Same Way," and "Line of Fire." The ballads "Lights" and "Stay Awhile," smoothly connected with a brief electric guitar solo introduced by Perry at Koseinenkin Hall in Tokyo, close out side 1. These softer songs were an apt choice to record in Japan, where fans were expected to remain seated and stay out of the aisles, a decorum politely but firmly enforced by white-gloved ushers. Perry had often felt that "Lights" worked better live than in the studio, and the recording for *Captured* proves it.

The rest of the album's live numbers were recorded at Detroit's Cobo Hall. Side 2 begins with Perry telling the crowd that they're "recording a live album tonight" to cheers. They play the ballad "Too Late," followed by the previously unreleased up-tempo "Dixie Highway" by Perry and Schon. Perry introduces this one by pointing out that it is "about a highway that runs from the [*sic*] Detroit all the way down to Florida." It's a rock tune with jazz elements, a strong organ line, and simplistic lyrics about a liaison with a groupie, presumably doubling as an invitation to the women in the crowd to join the band the next day when they got back on the road. Then they perform "Feeling That Way" and "Anytime," proving they have mastered the transition between these two—Rolie no longer needs to play a chord to help his bandmates sing the key change, as he had during the *Infinity* tour. Perry fills in with some ad libs during the final lines and then adds a couple of minutes of funk, inspired, of all things, by Ike and Tina Turner's version of "Proud Mary."

Side 3 begins with performances of "Do You Recall," "Walks Like a Lady," and "Lă Do Dā." The mid-tempo "Do You Recall," which starts with a strong bass drum, is just the right song to get the crowd ready for the blues of "Walks Like a Lady," although there's a break in the recording between the two, as there were more songs in the setlist, including some from the first three albums. The grouping on the album makes sense. Perry introduces the second of these by asking if the audience wants "to hear some blues," noting, not for the first time in concert, that "[w]e've got two of the best blues players in the whole world here tonight . . . Mr. Gregg Rolie on the Hammond B-3 and Mr. Neal Schon on the Stratocaster B." There follows a lengthy, free-form organ intro before Perry's vocals, with Rolie's voice audible in the choruses. The next is a one-minute Schon solo without any melodic logic, little more than an excuse to show his talent (humorously reminiscent of a scene in *This Is Spinal Tap*, when the lead guitarist made use of his solo time by tossing horseshoes at an electric guitar during a long sustain). If this has put any in the crowd to sleep, Schon jolts them awake with a rendition of "Lǎ Do Dā," at a slightly faster meter than the studio version, and a long, midsong instrumental exploration between Valory and Smith leading into the drum solo. ("The one, the only Steve 'Machine gun' Smith," gushes Perry as the band returns to the stage.) Side 4 includes the crowd-pleasing hits "Lovin', Touchin', Squeezin'," "Wheel in the Sky," and "Any Way You Want It," each the biggest hit of their respective albums, and concludes with a studio track, "The Party's Over (Hopelessly in Love)," a mid-tempo ballad by Perry. The album was a smash success, peaking at number nine on the *Billboard* 200 chart on March 13, 1981, and earning gold certification from RIAA the following month (and platinum by the end of the year).

Notwithstanding the high energy of the band's performance on *Captured*, life on the road was proving difficult to sustain. Schon, an admitted "workaholic," had become the band's "ambassador" to Japan and Australia, making the connections that resulted in *Dream, After Dream*, but his marriage was falling apart, and at one point he forgot to call his mother for six months. Perry said, "It's difficult family-wise, you miss your friends, you miss a day-to-day . . . normal routine, that everybody [else] might take for granted." The singer was diagnosed with walking pneumonia after several nights running a fever and having some minor voice problems; his doctor told him that if he were older, he might have collapsed onstage and died. Even the normally happy-go-lucky Valory, always seemingly on a natural high, needed a break, and took his first vacation "in five or six years" that August, between the US dates and the European jaunt.

Yet neither Schon nor Perry nor Valory would prove the band's next casualty. In December 1980, the same month that rock and roll superstar John Lennon was gunned down in front of his New York apartment building, none other than Gregg Rolie announced that he was leaving Journey. "Basically, I just don't want to be on the road anymore," the expectant father told *Rolling Stone*'s Kurt Loder. Over the years, as with Aynsley Dunbar, Rolie has fielded many questions about why he would leave a successful band, why he left all that "money on the table." Like Dunbar (and, for that matter, George Tickner),

Rolie could not have predicted the band's later success. And like Dunbar, there were persistent rumors that he was either pushed out by Steve Perry or that he left because he didn't like the direction Steve Perry was taking the band.

In fact, Rolie and Perry did not share a vision for the group's musical direction. Rolie was progressive rock; Perry was Motown, so "it was never going to mesh. We came from different styles and a totally different place." For instance, "[o]n the song 'I'm Crying' I play organ the way that I would play it for myself and it just doesn't match his vocal very well."

There was also the question of band leadership. By December 1980—unlike two years earlier, when Dunbar was fired—Steve Perry truly was leading Journey. Whereas in 1978 Perry was almost hesitant onstage, avoiding eye contact with the audience and deferentially stepping back during Rolie's numbers and Schon's guitar explorations, in 1980 Joel Selvin referred to his "centerstage . . . command and confidence," and Valory and Smith jokingly chided in their film that the groupies only had eyes for him. (In fact this may have been an issue; by late 1979 one British journalist was reporting that some of Rolie's longtime women fans were pushing their twelve-year-old daughters on him at Journey shows, which could not have been comfortable for Rolie's fiancée, Lori.)

The songwriting credits provide less anecdotal evidence that Rolie's star was in eclipse, because for *Infinity*, Rolie was still very much part of the songwriting team, even as Perry and Schon wrote some of the numbers by themselves. But by *Departure*, Perry and Schon had emerged as the main songwriting duo. For the man who was out front with Santana at Woodstock and who had been a coleader of Journey for so long, it is hard to imagine that his rock star ego played no role in his decision to leave. And there was a practical aspect to Perry's newfound leadership role that Rolie resented: Perry "was always saying 'we've got to have a band meeting about this, about that, about this, about that,' where you didn't have to have one at all." Herbie was competently managing operations, as far as Rolie was concerned, and "it was unnecessary" to call so many band meetings. "[N]o one got along too well with Steve," Rolie later admitted.

Rolie already knew how it felt to overstay his welcome in a successful band; he had done so with Santana. After Michael Carabello, Coke Escovedo, and Stan Marcum left that group, Carlos's leadership and musical choices had become dominant. Now with Journey and rising star Steve Perry, Rolie saw the writing on the wall.

On the other hand, Rolie long maintained that he left Journey because he was exhausted with touring, and there's an obvious truth to that as well; after all, the thirty-three-year-old had "spent the last 12 years of his life traveling." Although the news reports of his announcement indicated that he would be producing another band or developing some sort of a solo career, to watch him live in 1980 with Journey was to see a man on the brink of exhaustion. Close-up video shows a face without laughter, a trooper going through the motions—a far cry from his 1978 performances, where he stood atop his piano bench to shake his hips to the rhythm. Now, only during "Precious Time," when he went downstage for his harmonica part, did some of the spark of the previous Rolie shine through. He was also finding it difficult to maintain the change in musical genre from the early years with the band. "I had to rethink the way I did music . . . when it got into all vocals and less solos. When Journey started it was a lot easier to comprehend for me but then it got more difficult." What's more, he recognized that he was picking up some dangerous behaviors. "I've gotta cool out here. I drink too much—this is not cool." He needed a break longer than a month or two between the tour and the studio, and Journey wasn't about to stop, so he did. Session player Steve Roseman sat in on piano for the lone studio track on the *Captured* live album, "The Party's Over." Rolie got a generous severance, including a portion of the band's future earnings, to decrease over several years. And he kept his publishing rights, allowing him to continue to profit from the band's popularity when his songs are performed, even to this day.

*   *   *

In December 1980 Journey was a successful rock group. The band toured every summer to support albums they released each winter. In "Lovin', Touchin', Squeezin'" and "Any Way You Want It," they had top-40 hits with steady radio airplay. They were supporting themselves, their management, and their employees, and making good money for Columbia Records as a middling act, their albums easily selling single platinum. As for the loss of Gregg Rolie, rock columnist Ed Ward predicted that "Journey, surely the dullest of the '70s pre-fab bands, will limp on without him."

Actually, something very different was just around the corner.

"Escape," 1981–1982

You start a business in America and America will work with you.

—*Steve Perry*

Four chords—that's all it took. A first, a fifth, a minor sixth, and a fourth (I-V-vi-IV, for those readers so inclined), in the key of E major. It happened to be the same four chords the Beatles used for "Let It Be" in 1970. Phil Spector used them for the Teddy Bears' 1958 hit "To Know Him Is to Love Him"; Bob Marley used them for "No Woman, No Cry" in 1973. The Rolling Stones used them for "Beast of Burden" in 1978. Four chords, layered with a passionate, plaintive guitar track by Neal Schon, a surprisingly intricate drumline by Steve Smith, the flawless tenor vocal of Steve Perry, and a lyric, designed to capture the zeitgeist of an era, by a Chicago pianist named Jonathan Cain. From those four chords, Journey produced one of the most memorable hits in rock history: "Don't Stop Believin'."

*   *   *

Few musicians available could match Gregg Rolie's talent on the Hammond organ, but Steve Perry and Neal Schon saw in the cofounder's departure an opportunity for musical evolution. Schon wanted a keyboardist who could also play rhythm guitar, which the live show had lacked since the departure of George Tickner, and Perry was looking for the jazzier sound of a piano—less prog rock, more Motown. Jonathan Cain, keyboardist for Journey's 1980 opening act, the Babys, got the job because he had those skills and because he got along well with Journey and their management team. He was a nice enough guy with the good fortune to have been in the right place at the right time. Little did the existing members know then that the most important thing Cain brought to Journey in 1981 was his songwriting, which reinvigorated the band and moved them in an entirely new—and significantly more successful—direction. Years of sensitivity and heartache and struggle, combined with years of eating, sleeping, and breathing rock and roll, poured into his songwriting efforts.

Whereas in *Evolution* and *Departure* the emerging songwriting team—the musical direction of the band—was Perry and Schon, with Rolie's contributions decreasing with each album, the addition of Cain instantly changed the band's magnetic north. From the moment of his hiring, Cain wrote or cowrote every song the band released. When he cowrote, he always did so with Perry, often with Schon, and occasionally with Steve Smith. With Cain now in the lead writer's chair, Journey songs included heartfelt, earnest ballads—and hit after hit after hit.

Journey recorded *Escape* at Fantasy Studios in Berkeley from April to June 1981. Produced by Mike Stone (an acolyte of Roy Thomas Baker's who had taken over for him with Queen), longtime Journey coproducer and soundman Kevin Elson, and Perry, *Escape*, according to Cain, was about "permission to dream . . . to give hope on every song and make it about, you know, blue collar people, the everyday people that have a job that want to make their life better and have prosperity."

The album begins strong, with "Don't Stop Believin'," by Cain, Perry, and Schon, one of the best-known songs in rock history. The song opens with a dominant piano, joined soon by Perry's crooning, lullaby lyric that Cain wrote to speak to the fans, to their concerns and joys in life. Because the band had been so successful with their live album recorded mostly in Detroit, the song singled out those fans with the line "Just a city boy, born and raised in South Detroit" (although no such neighborhood exists; downtown Detroit abuts the Detroit River to the south, beyond which is Canada). After a verse, Schon's guitar slowly builds to a crash. The piano stays constant until the chorus, when the bass joins in with verve. A very brief guitar solo moves the song into the final verse. The lyrics, with some odd inclusions, speak of longing, loneliness, and despair. Another guitar solo expresses the theme, followed by the harmonized, repetitive "Don't stop believin'/Hold on to that feeling/ Streetlight people," inspired not—Cain maintained—by streetwalking prostitutes, but rather by the folks often found hanging out in LA after late-night club shows, looking for a chance at the big time. For Perry, it was the people he saw hanging out after the Detroit show where the band recorded most of *Captured*, overcome by the emotion of the show, livin' just to find some more.

"Stone in Love," by Cain, Perry, and Schon, is a bluesy number that begins with an insistent guitar and bass, not unlike "Too Far Gone" by Cain's previous band, the Babys. The lyric speaks to the loss of innocence and harkens back to teen love, specifically an unrequited liaison from Perry's teen years. There is also a well-harmonized chorus: "Those summer nights are callin' . . . /Can't help myself, I'm fallin' stone in love." The guitar solo again provides the fade-out, with the band members harmonizing "stone in love."

The next song, "Who's Crying Now," by Cain and Perry, was inspired by a rainy day in Marin County, where Cain had moved when he joined the band. It begins with a light, background synthesizer note, joined by piano, then a soulful, mournful vocal, with a lyric that speaks to a devolving marriage. Bass and drums drive the changes, with guitar providing interesting arrangements. Drummer "Steve Smith was just awesome" on that one, said Perry. As with "Stone in Love," the band harmonizes the chorus: "One love feeds the fire/ One heart burns desire/Wonder who's crying now?" Perry also saw it as an extension of the theme of "Lovin', Touchin', Squeezin'," with an intriguing vocal for the bridge. Again, the guitar solo provides the fade-out, this time without vocals. "The record label came to us and said 'as soon as the solo starts you'll have to fade it or radio won't play it,'" Perry recalled. "I said . . . 'look—Neal played the most beautiful solo on this thing. It's simple, heartfelt and feels timeless; the melodics are timeless and I do not want to kill that solo. So [I] fought for it, the song becomes a hit and the stations never pulled out of the solo."

"Keep on Runnin'," by Cain, Perry, and Schon, is a fast, hard-driving, up-tempo rock tune. Schon's lead guitar starts it and drives it, with Cain's rhythm guitar, Ross Valory's bass and Smith's drums straining to keep up. Like so many of the songs on this album, this one speaks to the experience of the fans: "They get me by the hour/By my blue collar/You're squeezin' me too tight."

"Still They Ride," by Cain, Perry, and Schon, is another soulful song to end side 1. With a lyric that begins "Jesse rides through the night under the main street light," one reviewer thought the band was imagining a long-dead Jesse James returning to ride a horse through a modern main street, but it's actually about a modern, small-town kid with a penchant for drag racing, who returns after a few years to find that "[t]his old town ain't the same." This song gives Cain the opportunity to really explore the piano, even during the haunting guitar solo. And Schon is not merely reprising his solos of yore here. He distills his sound down to twenty to thirty seconds of pure emotion. Perry, for his part, takes a very light touch with the vocals, even on a sustained high note, providing an incredible tenderness.

"Escape," by Cain, Perry, and Schon, starts side 2 with a driving guitar, an anthemic lyric reminiscent of the Babys' "Jesus Are You There?" and a rockabilly reminiscent of that group's "Rock and Roll Is (Alive and Well)." Smith adds some complicated, jazzy touches to the transition, and the song also really uses Valory's bass well. Cain writes for all five instruments, not just a melody and a harmony (which characterized much of the Perry-Schon compositions of the previous three albums). The guitar solo is midsong for once, with the band members harmonizing competing lyrics in the final chorus.

"Lay It Down," by Cain, Perry, and Schon, is a bluesy rocker not unlike some of the material on the previous albums, with a lyric that speaks to an evening on the prowl, a midsong guitar solo, Cain on rhythm guitar, and some truly incredible high notes, including the line "Higher, higher, higher, then I heard her say . . . /Lay it down." "Dead or Alive," by Cain, Perry, and Schon, is a guitar-driven, up-tempo rocker with a lyric reminiscent of "Line of Fire," in this case depicting an assassin for hire. The song includes rockabilly piano à la Jerry Lee Lewis, and some fancy, fast drum work by Smith. It has no fade-out but seems to end with the exhaustion of the musicians. "I brought [the] music in," Schon told me, "and Jon and Steve finished it out. The guitar lines are actually swing big band jazz for the most part. Then [we] punked out!"

"Mother, Father," by Cain, Perry, Schon, and the guitarist's father, Matthew Schon, is a classical-inspired acoustic guitar ballad with a very strong vocal, not unlike the band's work on *Dream, After Dream*, which had also involved the elder Schon, and a lyric that speaks to the disintegration of a family through alcohol and redeemed only by faith—the start of a recurring Cain theme.

Finally, "Open Arms," by Cain, Perry, and Schon, their highest-charting hit of all time and destined to become a 1980s wave-the-lighter anthem, is a piano-and-vocal lullaby that "fit with another key factor in Journey's music—the persona that Steve Perry had built as a singer," according to Cain. Perry "was the boy next door with a broken heart who never got the girl." Originally penned by Cain as a wedding gift to his bride, Tané McClure, the reworked lyrics posit a love questioned: "Lying beside you here in the dark . . . /How could our love be so blind?" However, the love is redeemed and restored: "But now that you've come back, turned night into day . . . /Nothing to hide, believe what I say." Initially Perry, like John Waite of the Babys, had thought this song did not fit with the group's vibe, that the band did not need any more ballads, and he suggested they use it for an eventual solo project. But he came around and added a verse. Then Schon had to be convinced, because, the guitarist asked, "What are we supposed to play on that song?" He could see no space for a guitar solo. At that point Perry insisted, and Schon contributed to the arrangements. Perry had to request that the smirking axe man leave the studio while the singer recorded the track, as he was too much of a distraction. The result, however, is breathtaking—and the fans agreed. Although not given a writing credit, Smith added a drum line inspired by Bruce Rowland's performance of "With a Little Help from My Friends" with Joe Cocker at Woodstock. "It's not like I copied that note-for-note or anything," Smith said, "but just somehow the way he played that three-four kind of feel." The song also, somewhat strangely, ended up on the soundtrack to the major motion picture *Heavy Metal*.

Herbie Herbert, as usual, predicted that the new project "will be our biggest album because it will be our best." For once reality matched hyperbole. Four of the songs on the album charted in the top 20, and Herbie wisely convinced the label to release the singles months apart, minimizing self-competition. "Who's Crying Now," released in July 1981, rose to number 4 on the *Billboard* Hot 100 after 12 weeks, spending a total of 21 weeks on the chart. "Don't Stop Believin'," released in October, rose to number 9 after eight of a total 16 weeks on the chart. "Open Arms," released in January 1982, spent 6 of 18 total weeks on the chart at number 2 (bested for the top spot by the J. Geils Band's "Centerfold" for the first 3 weeks and then by "I Love Rock 'n

Roll" by Joan Jett & the Blackhearts). "Still They Ride," released in May 1982, peaked at number 19 on *Billboard* after 9 of a total 14 weeks on the chart. Finally, "Stone in Love," released in October 1982, made it to number 14 after 2 weeks on *Billboard*'s Mainstream Rock chart. For nearly two years, there was not a week in which at least one song from *Escape* was not receiving significant radio airplay all over the country. The album itself rose to number 1 on the *Billboard* 200 on September 11, 1981, spending a total of 152 weeks on the chart; it was certified gold and platinum simultaneously on September 18.

To put these numbers in perspective, one need only look at similar numbers for the three previous studio albums and the live album. *Infinity*, which brought the band their first real success, made it to number 21 after 15 weeks, with three singles, the most successful of them ("Wheel in the Sky") topping out at number 57. *Evolution* made it to number 20 after 6 weeks along with three singles, one in the top 20 ("Lovin', Touchin', Squeezin'," which hit number 16). *Departure* reached number 8 after 8 weeks, likewise with three singles, none doing better than number 23 ("Any Way You Want It"). *Captured* made it to number 9 after 6 weeks, with "Dixie Highway" topping out at number 30 and "The Party's Over (Hopelessly in Love)" reaching number 34 on the Hot 100 (number 2 on the Mainstream Rock chart).

So from 1978 to 1980 this very successful band, which gave their label no reason to complain and earned millions of dollars per year, had produced exactly zero top-10 hits on the *Billboard* Hot 100 and only one song that made it into the top 20. By the end of 1982, on the other hand, *Escape* had sold more units than all four combined, and produced three top-10 *Billboard* Hot 100 hits and one more in the top 20. Most Journey fans became devotees of the group because of the music on *Escape*. I did. You probably did too.

*   *   *

The unprecedented success of *Escape* in the summer of 1981 changed just about everything for the band members. Now, in addition to coverage in industry periodicals, local *San Francisco* papers, and concert and album reviews in the national press, the band found themselves the subject of profiles in such magazines as *Tiger Beat*, *Hit Parader*, and *16 Magazine*—publications that, aimed largely at teen (and preteen) girls, covered the band as much for their sex appeal as their music. Steve Perry was "hot, sexy, and downright incredible," gushed *Tiger Beat*, a monthly devoted to a Caucasian standard of male beauty typified by Scott Baio, Ralph Macchio, John Stamos, and the stars of the television show *The Dukes of Hazzard*. (The Portuguese Perry and half Italian Neal Schon fit neatly into the Mediterranean category of the first three.) "Of course he's not the only thing which makes Journey such a great group," the magazine allowed in a piece between advertisements for nail polish and Dr. Pepper-flavored lip gloss, "but when you see this guy on stage shaking his stuff and throwing his mane of brown locks around, you can't help but become his biggest fan (and fall in love at the same time!)." Months later, the same magazine printed letters from ostensible fans, including one Dawn Thibodeaux, who wrote that she had "'Open Arms' for all the group and 'My, Oh My,' is Neal Schon cute," and a certain Marla Watson, who wrote suggestively that she "wouldn't mind being stuck on the North Pole if Steve [Perry] were there to cuddle up next to me!" The pages of *16 Magazine* helped slake their thirst, offering tidbits about how Perry was "tickled pink with the love and loyalty he gets from Journey's admirers" but also humanizing the rock star, noting that "[w]hether it's an hour alone in his hotel room or a chance to putter around his home making minor repairs, those tiny pockets of time are the stuff that Steve Perry's creativity is made of." Rarely, however, was Jonathan Cain similarly idolized, despite his own boyish good looks and the importance of his writing to the band's newfound superstardom.

All told, the band played 143 concerts in a little over a year promoting *Escape*. Most of the dates featured the Greg Kihn Band or Loverboy as opening acts; most of the dates sold out. After kicking off the tour in June 1981 with 2 shows at the Mountain Aire Festival in Angels Camp Fairgrounds, Journey crossed the Pacific for 6 dates in Japan. Then it was off to Canada for 3 shows in Toronto, Montreal, and Ottawa in mid-August, followed by 4 dates in the northeastern United States. The first week of September, as *Escape* approached number one, Journey played 2 concerts each in Cleveland, Chicago, and Milwaukee before an extended 6-night stint in Detroit at Pine Knob Music Theater, where they celebrated the album's success, and where screaming fans reveled in the locally sourced lyric to "Don't Stop Believin'." After another swing through the Midwest, the band headed east to open for the Rolling Stones for 3 shows at JFK Stadium in Philadelphia. Then it was another series of dates in the Northeast, including an appearance on Tom Snyder's *The Tomorrow Show* in New York City. They spent the second half of October and the first half of November touring the South before moving through the Southwest back to California for a 4-night stand at the Los Angeles Forum on Thanksgiving week, and a triumphant return to San Francisco to appear at the Cow Palace for three nights, including one fundraiser to benefit the San Francisco cable cars, an iconic transportation mode in danger of permanent removal. Steve Perry briefly took sick, resulting in cancellations in Salt Lake City and Denver. But by December they were back in the saddle, performing 3 nights in Seattle, 3 in Portland, and 3 more in the Bay Area, culminating in 2 nights during Christmas week in Hawaii.

Life on the road for the newly christened rock superstars was an exhausting series of airplane, bus, and limousine rides punctuated every night by ninety minutes of adrenaline-fueled performance. Now that they could afford a plane even for domestic dates, the band members could return home periodically during the tour, but the road became monotonous. A limousine from the airport straight to the show; a performance and an encore in front of several thousand screaming fans; a limo ride to a hotel; and then, in the morning, another limo ride back to the airport. At each stop, Perry would personalize "Don't Stop Believin'" ("Just a city boy, born and raised in *Tampa Bay! . . . Salt Lake City! . . . South Bend, Indiana!*"). After once confusing Toledo with Cleveland, resulting in rare boos from the crowd, a roadie started placing a small sign with the name of the town between the two bass drums for him to read. But even that system was vulnerable: singer-guitarist Greg Kihn, of the opening act, sometimes switched the roadies' trip sheet as a prank when he learned that Perry was relying on this. Fortunately they always caught it in time.

Perry often claimed that pizza and beer were among his favorite vices. At the same time, he had to be very careful with his health, which was difficult on the road. Beer dehydrates the throat and pizza is high in dairy, which creates phlegm. Both are concerns to a serious singer. Hot herbal tea was his usual drink. While Gregg Rolie had sipped beer to relax and get in the groove with his music, he wasn't so much a serious vocalist as a serious organist who sang well. Perry probably kept his pizza-and-beer habit to his exceedingly few days off back home at his mother's house in Lemoore. He may not have had such a habit at all; it's equally likely he told this to the press in an attempt to build an "everyman" persona and promote a masculinity otherwise lacking in his performances. Tea drinking, while helpful for his voice, did not help in this regard. It also, thanks to some tea leaves' resemblance to cannabis, caused him to get stopped at customs in Japan, leading the roadies to order joke T-shirts reading, "I survived the Yokohama Tea Party."

Drummer Steve Smith responded to the stress by bringing his new bride, Susan, on tour with the band; before long they were expecting their first child. Perry, who pushed through jet lag for the Japanese dates and was finally showing good muscle tone from an improved diet, began a serious relationship with model Sherrie Swafford, who (at first) seemed able to handle the pressures of a relationship with a superstar. Schon and Ross Valory, on the other hand, found their luck in that area had run out: both were getting divorced, Valory from Diane, his wife of eleven years, who had coauthored some early Journey songs, including "Wheel in the Sky." Schon became estranged from his wife of five years, Tena Austin, and started dating Rose Montanaro, age twenty-three, with whom he appeared in a *People* magazine spread. (Schon himself was only twenty-seven.)

As for Cain, the band's bard channeled his loneliness for his wife, Tané, into his songwriting. Feeling constant pressure to seek solace with any one of the hundreds of potential groupies available at every stop on the tour but dedicated to his marriage, "in the hum and steady rocking on a tour bus heading to Saratoga Springs, I heard a tune in my dreams and thought of lyrics that woke me up." In the minutes and hours that followed, the lyrics "flowed out of me, and I wrote them down almost frantically, as though I was struggling to keep up with the sentiments of my soul." This produced the song "Faithfully," which one critic dubbed "the greatest power ballad of all time." As with "Open Arms," Cain "wrote the song, and presented it to my lady." But this time, confident that he had a timeless hit on his hands, he did not approach Perry to finish it. He simply presented it to Perry and the rest of the band as a complete song, and that is how it stayed. Perry merely added his iconic "Whoa-whoa-whoa," modeled after Sam Cooke's style, to the end.

Subsequent statements by band members give the impression that the critics were uniformly harsh in their assessments of *Escape*. While there were some negative reports, including one in *Rolling Stone*, which found the songs "derivative" and predicted Journey's "streetlight people . . . would soon glow out of it" (har har har), most reviews of the album were positive. These included those of Bruce Britt of the *Detroit Free Press*, Pete Bishop of the *Pittsburgh Press*, Ben Lass of the *Utah Statesman*, and stalwart Journey supporter Joel Selvin of the *San Francisco Chronicle*. These reviewers largely applauded Journey for the very same things Deborah Frost at *Rolling Stone* decried; what she called derivative, they saw as a tried-and-true method of tapping the talent of yesteryear.

Some of the retrospective sense of negative treatment by the critics seems to have been more the result of concert reviews than those for the album. When the band started their *Escape* tour in June 1981, they initially played mostly material from *Infinity, Evolution,* and *Departure*—the songs that had made *Captured* such a big hit. But as *Escape* and its singles rose through the charts, the setlist changed to encompass nearly the entire new album, as sellout crowds forced additional dates in many cities and a strained tour schedule. Here the criticism was full force. Writing in the *New York Times*, Stephen Holden said that although Perry "sometimes recalls Steve Winwood and at other times Sam Cooke" with a "real anthemic power," he also looks like "a flabbier, seedier Rod Stewart" (naming the only singer who could possible make Steve Perry appear flabby). "Journey's many hard-rock numbers never rose above the mundane, partly because of . . . Steve Smith's sledge-hammer support and partly because the material was so banal." Journey "are heavy-handed purveyors of a style so hackneyed that only a massive infusion of passion and energy could revitalize it," he concluded. Deborah Deasy of the *Pittsburgh Press*, for her part, took aim at Schon, calling him "boring," saying that he "often plays like a distempered dog, attacking his guitar, rather than courting it," and complaining that the band's "uninspired songwriting" meant they would "make better music playing other people's hits."

But now that the Journey fan base had increased exponentially, more than a few were ready to correct the record. "Steve Perry does not have a harsh voice," wrote Michael Wolff of Squirrel Hill, Pennsylvania, adding that "Nel [*sic*] Schon does not play his guitar like a distempered dog. He plays it like it's supposed to be played. . . . If Miss Deasy is wondering how it is possible for Journey to be the No. 1 rock group in America . . . it is because everyone loves them and the way they play their music." Another Pennsylvania writer, Karen Rinald of Mt. Lebanon, found that "far from being monotonous," the concert "was incredibly moving. Steve Perry's voice saturated the civic arena with emotion." And Stephen S. Pruzhynski of Level Green said that "[i]f going against the grain by playing non-danceable music is monotonous, somebody should mention it to the Rolling Stones and Bruce Springsteen, two of the more successful rock acts today."

Yet the fans' responses to the negative reviews only added to the overall tone of the professional critics. Bruce Britt followed up his positive review of the album with one of their live show, calling Journey's appearance at Pine Knob in Detroit "the right time and the right place," while Ed Westarp of the *Charlotte News* bestowed praise on Cain for his "haunting piano solo in 'Who's Crying Now' and Smith for his 'strong, but not overpowering, backup.'"

*   *   *

By the end of 1981, with their final performances in Hawaii, the band was understandably exhausted—and embarrassingly rich. They wanted a break, and manager Herbie Herbert would hear none of it. "You gotta make hay while the sun shines," he said. But after several attempts, he failed to get the band to agree to the arena tour he had scheduled for 1982. "We've worked all these years so hard," they told him, not unreasonably. "We want to sit by the pool and enjoy our success." Finally, Herbie called in legendary promoter Bill Graham, who stood to lose if Journey failed to perform at several high-profile events he had set up in the Bay Area that summer. According to Herbie, Graham literally begged Perry to agree to the tour. The tough-as-nails businessman who had famously challenged the thugs employed as security by Led Zeppelin at his Day on the Green festival in 1977 "[dropped] to his knees . . . at which point Steve Perry cracked like an ice cube," extracting only a promise that "Herbie can make a stadium intimate."

To keep that promise, Herbie's Nightmare, Inc., inaugurated a practice that would soon become de rigueur for arena concerts: the big screen. The company assembled a pair of jumbo screens that would simultaneously carry a close-up of the action onstage, at a cost of $35,000 per show (almost $110,000 in 2023 dollars). From that point on, every seat in the house could see what the front-row ticketholders could see. In fact, they could see more: three camera operators provided close-up shots of each of the musicians from various perspectives, including above the piano and behind the drum set. The idea quickly caught on industry-wide, and before long Nightmare was providing screens and camera operators for other acts, including Simon & Garfunkel and David Bowie, who were enjoying a resurgence in popularity.

And so, after a three-month break, the band was back in Japan again for seven shows to kick off a 1982 spring tour. Premiering a new song by Cain and Perry, "Separate Ways (Worlds Apart)," they moved across Canada from west to east in late April, then through the northeastern United States again, the Midwest again, including four nights in Chicago in May, across the Rockies by way of Denver and Salt Lake City—to keep the dates they had rescheduled due to Perry's post-Thanksgiving illness—to another three nights in Portland, then a few dates in Texas, and a few more back in California before concluding—again—in Hawaii.

"Separate Ways" and giant screens were not the only things Journey premiered on their 1982 *Escape* encore tour. Steve Smith enjoyed arcade games and claimed to have set a world record on *Defender*. Collaborating with the San Jose company Data Age, the band released *Journey Escape*, a video game designed for the Atari 2600 home video console, which eager players connected to their televisions; another version appeared in a coin-operated machine by Bally/Midway. The game served to further connect the fans to their beloved band. According to its manual,

> You're on the road with JOURNEY, one of the world's hottest rock groups. A spectacular performance has just ended. Now it's up to you to guide each JOURNEY Band Member past hordes of Love-Crazed Groupies, Sneaky Photographers, and Shifty-eyed Promoters to the safety of the JOURNEY Escape Vehicle in time to make the next concert. Your mighty manager and loyal roadies are there to help, but the escape is up to you!

Steve Perry opposed the creation of the video game but was outvoted. "Everybody went against me on that issue," he said. "I personally thought it was dumb . . . I thought that we were big already, that we didn't need a video game."

Overall, the two halves of the *Escape* tour netted the band about $2 million in concert tickets, plus about $6 million in merchandise sold at venues, especially after Herbie renegotiated that aspect of the business. So talented did he prove at this, even the Rolling Stones' Mick Jagger "brought his staff to our corporate offices in San Francisco . . . and spent several days visiting with Herbie Herbert to learn from him how one runs a rock band smoothly," reported Ross Valory.

From the Budweiser sponsorship to T-shirt sales to the video game, Journey gave its critics much to decry in the vein of "corporate" rock, as if they were expected to have a monastic lifestyle and produce art for free. The argument was not a new one, and it crossed genre lines. In 1963, Malcolm X had criticized Sam Cooke for writing too many dance songs like "Good Times" (which Journey had covered on their unaired episode of the *King Biscuit Flower Hour*) and not enough "meaningful" protest songs like "Change Is Gonna Come." Worse, the critics often failed to mention the collateral success that Journey's management engendered for the band's employees, including medical insurance and year-round employment.

With the unmitigated success of *Escape*, Journey's showing at the 1982 Bay Area Music Awards, hosted by champion San Francisco 49ers' quarterback Joe Montana, was almost an afterthought. As usual they were nominated for a slew of "Bammies," including for Best Group, Best Album, Best Male Vocalist, Best Guitarist, Best Keyboardist, and Best Drummer. They took two at the event, Best Album and Best Keyboardist, losing out to Jefferson Starship for Best Group and Best Male Vocalist (and Best Drummer: Aynsley Dunbar again). Neal Schon lost out to Carlos Santana for Best Guitarist but took home something of a consolation prize in the Best Debut Album category, which he won with keyboardist Jan Hammer for their collaboration *Untold Passion*. He also won the satisfaction of knowing his guitar stylings had contributed to the band's victory in the "Best Album" category—and all the proceeds that came from a number-one national album and nearly sold-out international tour.

*   *   *

From 1978 to 1980, when Journey released *Infinity, Evolution, Departure,* and *Captured*, many rock reviewers categorized the band's music as "heavy metal." While in retrospect it may seem as if one can draw a straight line from the progressive rock of the early 1970s to the heavy metal of the mid-1980s, in the United States of 1980, the term "heavy metal" was interchangeable with "hard rock"—which included the punk rock of Sid Vicious, the progressive rock of early Journey, the lyrical rock of Journey's *Infinity, Evolution,* and *Departure,* the anthemic rock of the Babys, the heavy rock of Led Zeppelin and Deep Purple, and the actual British heavy metal of Black Sabbath. Indeed, even in reviews of *Escape* and *Frontiers*, some reviewers still used the unlikely phrase to describe the Journey sound, and "Open Arms" even made the soundtrack to the movie *Heavy Metal*, as described above.

But the evolution of the descriptor "heavy metal" from the sort of hard rock that included Journey into the even harder rock that categorized Ozzy Osbourne, Quiet Riot, and Anthrax took place as much because of Journey's evolution as despite it. When Jonathan Cain joined Journey and merged his songwriting inclinations with Steve Perry's desire to move toward a more soulful sentimentality, the band became known for hits like "Open Arms" and "Faithfully." Even though Journey continued to record hard rock—"Keep on Running," "Escape," "Lay it Down," and "Dead or Alive" are certainly hard rock songs—and continued to include earlier hard rock in their live shows—the setlist from their April 20, 1983, show in Atlanta, for instance, included "Wheel in the Sky," "Line of Fire," and several hard rock tunes from *Escape* and their subsequent album *Frontiers*—their reputation on radio told a different story and attracted a different sort of listener. In this manner, hard rock branched off into the niche, macho, heavy metal, on the one hand, and more popular, teenage-girl-oriented, commercial rock music of the 1980s, on the other.

"The taste of the average audience is about . . . it must be 13 [years old] now. And so, you produce songs that [appeal] to the twelve, thirteen, fourteen-year-old mind," said E. Y. Harburg, lyricist of such Depression-era hits as "Brother Can You Spare a Dime" and "Somewhere Over the Rainbow." This was borne out by a 2008 study in the *New York Times* using data from Spotify. "The most important period for men in forming their adult tastes," wrote Seth Stephens-Davidowitz, "were the ages 13 to 16," while "[t]he most important period for women were the ages 11 to 14."

The explosive success of *Escape* was fueled by teenagers, who one reviewer said "all look like Leif Garrett . . . symphonies in brown and blonde." Another, noting that 90 percent of the audience consisted of "disgustingly fit teenage California girls," labeled the rest "unpimpled males." In 1981, these were the very youngest of the baby boomers and the oldest members of Generation X, born between 1962 and 1970. They knew what they liked, and what they liked was Journey.

But the critics were mostly male, older boomers born between 1945 and 1955 who were then in their late twenties and early thirties. For them, *Escape* compared poorly to the music of their youth—Jimi Hendrix, Janis Joplin, the Doors, Jefferson Airplane, Frank Zappa, Santana, David Bowie. To add insult to injury, by the time Journey released *Escape*, they had purged their two members most closely associated with that "classic" era of rock—Aynsley Dunbar, who had played with Zappa and Bowie, and Gregg Rolie, an original member of the Santana Blues Band. For this cardinal sin—and the propensity of the band and its management to actually turn a profit—some critics labeled Journey "corporate rock," "immature," and other unhappy monikers. They were neither right nor wrong; they just had a different perspective from the fans. Culture is subjective.

These critics had applauded Journey as an unpopular progressive fusion act because they expected that their musical flights of fancy might lead to a new type of music. The original members of Journey were exploring and combining genres much as their predecessors had in the 1950s and 1960s—predecessors who had created rock and roll out of country, jazz, ragtime, and the blues and had gone on to develop surf rock and psychedelia. The problem was that neither Journey nor any other rock act developed anything truly new and groundbreaking in the late 1970s. There were some new subgenres of rock—punk, new wave, and eventually grunge—but after Black musicians and Black listeners went their own way, rock lost its soul. It became corporate. Mainstream. *Acceptable.*

The expectation that Journey's music remain progressive and its members remain poor was unfair and ahistorical. As Harburg noted, "Songwriting is a part of capitalism ... people are in it mostly to make money." Goddard Lieberson, the former president of Columbia Records, added that "the best artists are good businessmen."

As music scholars Steve Chapple and Reebee Garofalo have written, the nature of the capitalist system is to commodify everything, including the escape from the capitalist system through pastimes like popular music. The members of the counterculture that produced critical rock publications like *Rolling Stone* and *Creem* in the 1960s believed they were undermining the system, but they ended up reinforcing it by making profits for corporations like Columbia and RCA, who had ties to the same military-industrial complex that was sending music fans to fight in Vietnam to perpetuate the system. Similarly, by fostering the resegregation of popular music, these companies were co-opting the art that proposed a racially equitable society. And after the

decline of glam, rock's glorification of the guitarist's phallic instrument perpetuated the social order that confined men and women to traditional roles.

Rock music, at least after Bob Dylan famously switched to an electric
guitar at the 1965 Newport Folk Festival, has been considered "authentic"
primarily because its artists write their own material. Performing the material of others—as was common with the crooners of the 1940s and 1950s and
remained common in country music—has been considered inauthentic and
commercial. The argument that Journey was commercial in this sense was off
base because, with very few exceptions, the music of Journey was written by
the members of Journey.

The replacement of Rolie by Cain, and the success that it generated for
Journey, was based on far more than Cain's songwriting skills. When Herbie
Herbert hired Jonathan Cain, he thought he was getting Bruce Springsteen.
And to some extent he was. Cain combined the folk songwriting tradition he
had inherited from his Arkansas-born father with an urbane darkness from
Chicago—not altogether different from the Boss's postindustrial, suburban
New Jersey Blues. And yes, this was reflected in the music he made with Journey. But the act of replacing a founding member also resulted in the further
solidification of Steve Perry's control of the band. As long as Rolie had been
in Journey, Perry was still the "new guy," even though it was him at center
stage every night and even though he and Neal Schon wrote most of the
songs. After Rolie left, Perry's leadership of the band's musical direction was
unquestioned. Furthermore, Cain mostly wrote with Perry—and not on his
own—creating a dynamic where Schon, one of the two remaining founders,
became something of a second (or third) fiddle.

Although in theory the band had come closer to the style of music that
had brought success to groups like Fleetwood Mac and the Eagles, the choices
that Perry made were steeped in a different tradition: Motown. This is what
led directly to Journey's superstardom with *Escape*. In the late 1970s, white
rock listeners, as part of a racial backlash against the achievements of the civil
rights movement, hungered for the country rock that groups like Lynyrd
Skynyrd, the Allman Brothers, and even Bruce Springsteen delivered. By the
1980s, without realizing it, what they wanted was no longer backlash rock but
appropriation rock. White fans again wanted what they had always wanted
before the integration of rock and roll: Black music performed by white artists. Journey, with its soulful groove and Motown influences layered atop

muscular, white hard rock, gave the fans exactly that. It was the same formula that Elvis Presley, Bob Dylan, and the Beatles had used—whether they knew it or not.

Journey's musical success also came at a time when the nation—or at least many whites in it—began looking back at the 1950s as something of a golden age. With inflation, unemployment, and crime at unusually high levels, the fans who idolized Journey yearned for a mythical past, ignoring (or unaware of) the fact that the 1950s was really only a golden age for nonethnic, white, suburban men. They elected a grandfatherly Hollywood actor to the American presidency and rewarded a nostalgia-driven resurgence of 1950s-style rock and roll epitomized by the Stray Cats and, from Journey's own formerly cutting-edge San Francisco, Huey Lewis and the News. Other artists dabbled successfully in the concept: Bryan Adams had a hit in 1985 with "Summer of '69"; Billy Joel recorded a doo-wop album in 1983, *An Innocent Man*, which earned him a Grammy nomination. Even actual 1950s acts had new music on the radio: the Five Satins, famous for their 1956 hit "In the Still of the Night," had a 1982 hit with "Memories of Days Gone By." In 1985 the top-grossing film in the United States was *Back to the Future*, where a teenager from a postindustrial California town travels to a cleaner, sunnier version of the same place—in 1955. (The town is based on Mill Valley, which is in the Bay Area's Marin County, then home to Jonathan Cain.) Individual acts like Jackson Browne might still write protest songs decrying the Reagan administration's depredations in Central America, but for the most part, musicians refocused on what their listeners demanded. Journey's superstardom was part and parcel of that nostalgic trend; even Steve Perry's onstage costume—topcoat and tails—spoke to nostalgia for an earlier time. Put yet another way: popular music was always about rebellion, and the rebellion of the white youth of the early 1980s was a rebellion against liberalism. A conservative rebellion.

Whatever the reasons, the fans wanted more, and Herbie was ready to capitalize on that. He booked space at Fantasy Studios in the fall of 1982 for Journey to record another album.

Keyboard Solo
Jonathan Cain

So I wrote the song, and presented it to my lady.

—*Jonathan Cain*

Jonathan Cain was born Jonathan Leonard Friga in Chicago, Illinois, in 1950, to a devout Catholic family that enrolled him in the local parish elementary school of their Humboldt Park neighborhood. Called Our Lady of the Angels, the school tragically lived up to its name when Cain was in third grade. A fire broke out in a basement stairwell and rapidly swept the building, taking the lives of dozens of children and a handful of teaching nuns. Trapped between burning hallways and locked fire escapes, entire classrooms died knelt in prayer. Cain was assigned to classroom 101, next to an exit stairwell and some distance from the fire's origin; his quick-thinking substitute teacher, Sister Mary St. Florence Casey, quickly ushered her frightened wards out to the street, saving their lives. Although Cain and his closest friends survived the inferno, his faith was shaken; he turned to music for consolation.

The great-grandson of European immigrants, Cain also had a lineage in the American South. His father, like so many of that generation, had moved north to Chicago for work in the town's exploding wartime industries. Cain later attributed his early musical inclinations to a visit to tiny Paris, Arkansas, where he saw his grandfather and other relatives playing guitar, fiddle, and harmonica. "I got lost in the whirling musical conversation as the melody and rhythms were traded back and forth," the Journey songwriter and pianist later wrote in a memoir. "I . . . began to clap and stomp my feet with the others. When I looked over and saw my father, I was surprised by the expression on his face. It mirrored the joy I saw in the other musicians." Back home in Chicago, Cain undertook years of training—on the accordion. By his teen years he had assembled a band with his younger brother that played weddings and confirmations around his home in suburban Franklin Park, where the family had moved after the fire.

Influenced by rock and roll, including the hit bands of the '50s and '60s, Cain determined to make a career in the industry. After a tiff with his mother over a girlfriend, he moved into a small apartment near Roosevelt University, where he attended the Chicago Musical College thanks to his wedding-circuit earnings and his father's help. There he deepened his understanding of classical music and music theory and developed a talent for the piano and guitar, dropping out after two years when he felt he had learned all he needed. He began playing club gigs, expanding his zone with an old carpet van to store the instruments and slowly building a songwriting voice and a style of playing increasingly at odds with the type of events he had once played with his accordion.

Cain saw a major turning point when he was "discovered" in 1969 by Jerry Milam, a record producer who operated Golden Voice Recording in Pekin, Illinois, a studio in the cornfields that listed Dan Fogelberg among its credits. Milam liked what he heard and sent a tape to Buddy Killen, owner of Tree International Publishing, a major Nashville label. Once credited with having "discovered" Elvis Presley, Killen now flew the excited, starstruck youth to Tennessee to record an original single, "Song of the City," under the stage name Johnny Lee, a contraction of his first and middle names with a nod to Jerry Lee Lewis. He was supported in the studio by the Muscle Shoals Rhythm Section, the hypertalented folks who served as a backup band on recordings by such artists as Wilson Pickett and Aretha Franklin and who inspired the Bay Area version eventually renamed Journey. The song was distributed to radio stations in Memphis and Chicago—and was completely ignored. So much for the big break. But the episode underscored the possibilities for the budding songwriter. In the summer of 1972, he resolved to try his luck in Los Angeles. "My parents thought I was a crazy fool, but I said no, it's out there, believe me." *Believe* me.

The move to LA was assisted by Cain's again being "discovered" by yet another industry insider: Nick Papas, who ran public relations for celebrity deejay Wolfman Jack. Papas had heard Cain play at one of the many bars near Chicago's O'Hare International Airport that catered to bored and randy flight attendants and urged him to bring his band out to the Golden State. But here again, the results were mixed. Set up in a sumptuous house in tony Laurel Canyon, Cain learned the dangers of the rock and roll lifestyle up close when Papas sank into a deep depression and became addicted to cocaine after the death of a girlfriend in a boating accident off Catalina Island, and subsequent charges of manslaughter (from which he was ultimately cleared). But Papas did provide a connection with the Wolfman's manager, Don Kelley—who also agreed to manage Cain. After booking him time in Quantum Recording Studios, Kelley got him a coveted spot on Dick Clark's *American Bandstand* to chat and perform one of his songs, "'Til It's Time to Say Goodbye." The song then got some airplay but, like "Song of the City" before it, was soon forgotten. Next, Papas and Kelley arranged an introduction to Bob Dylan's manager Albert Grossman, a founder of folk trio Peter, Paul and Mary who was noted for his work managing the likes of Janis Joplin, John Lee Hooker, and the Band (and a fellow alumnus of Roosevelt University). If anyone could turn an introspective songwriter into a rock star, it was Grossman.

Intrigued by his sound, Grossman brought Cain and his band to his Bearsville Studios in Woodstock, New York—famous as Bob Dylan's latter-day haunt—to record an album of original material. Bearsville had recently seen Meat Loaf record parts of his album *Bat Out of Hell*, including the hit "Paradise by the Dashboard Light." This latest "big break" for Cain resulted in another name change. "Johnny Lee" was already taken—by a country singer—and "the Jonathan Friga Band" did not exactly slip off the tongue. After brainstorming a few ideas, he and younger brother Tommy took the edgy, biblical stage name "Cain," and "the Jonathan Cain Band" headed off to Woodstock to record *Windy City Breakdown* in 1977.

Cain's first full-length effort employed elements of the blues, rockabilly, jazz, and even punk in a dark, urban style inspired by such varied musicians as Chuck Berry, Van Morrison, the Allman Brothers, Meat Loaf, Steely Dan, and more than a little Bruce Springsteen, especially the postmodern cynicism and angst of the Boss's "Promised Land" and "Backstreets"—a darkness Cain would continue to tap when writing the lyrics to "Don't Stop Believin'" and

"Escape." Three songs were coauthored with J. C. Phillips, another Wolfman Jack intimate with whom Cain coproduced the album; four songs were by Cain himself; and one is a cover of the Moody Blues tune "Go Now." The title track, "Windy City Breakdown," has elements of the theme to the television show *Welcome Back, Kotter*, while "Lay Down Joe (Holiday on Ice)" is reminiscent of "Mack the Knife." "Rollercoaster Baby" employs carnival sound effects, while the lighthearted "Rock It Down" includes regional references such as "reminds me of a girl I met down in Kankakee," a city about an hour south of Chicago. All told, the album is a statement about rock music in the 1970s; Cain had clearly captured the zeitgeist of the era.

But here again, his music went nowhere—in this case because the impresario refused to push it. Cain stopped by Grossman's LA headquarters, at the Chateau Marmont hotel on Sunset Boulevard, to ask why. Chateau Marmont was long famous for the debauchery of Led Zeppelin, who also used it as their West Coast home base. After getting the producer high on cannabis to loosen him up, Cain got his answer. "It lacks the urgency and passion I saw when I first signed you," Grossman said, adding, "No one will buy your wretched album, I promise you!" Nick Papas stepped in, forcing the label to master the record and print five thousand copies, and promoting some airplay for its cover of "Go Now," which earned Cain a trip to San Francisco to play the Warfield. Back in LA, he got a gig at the Starwood, a frequent Journey haunt and "L.A.'s premier rock nightclub," according to Van Halen chronicler Greg Renoff. But that was it. The Jonathan Cain Band's last gig, a two-hour drive away, earned only a bounced check. Summarily removed from the Laurel Canyon house, Cain found himself in a tiny North Hollywood apartment, virtually destitute, watching the "streetlight people" below his window. Like so many others before and since, his Los Angeles dream had become just another nightmare.

After spending the winter months of 1977–1978 cleaning toilets and selling overpriced speakers at Cal Stereo, subsisting on occasional handouts from his steadfast father, Cain got another call from Albert Grossman. Oblivious to any bad blood, Grossman wanted to see Cain work with English songwriter Robbie Patton, who had recently written songs for Fleetwood Mac singer/pianist Christine McVie. Patton had liked *Windy City Breakdown* and wanted to explore writing with Cain. Once they had written a few songs together, Patton alerted Cain to a new vacancy in the local rock scene. The Babys were looking to replace their keyboardist, and Patton arranged an audition.

The unfortunately named British rockers the Babys, featuring John Waite on lead vocals and bass, Wally Stocker on guitars, and Tony Brock on drums, had already cut two moderate-selling albums and earned solid airplay with their top-40 hit "Isn't It Time." After keyboardist Michael Corby left, they recorded a third album, *Head First*, with session players on piano and synthesizer, yielding a second hit, "Every Time I Think of You." That's when the band and its management realized they needed a permanent replacement for Corby if they were going to manage a tour. "I arrived at [Studio Instrument Rentals] with my complete setup [and the] English roadies were eager to help me get my stuff ready, something I'd never had the privilege of experiencing," Cain recalled in his memoir. When the band came in, they played five songs together, including "Isn't It Time," and they gelled. After Waite asked Cain to play something original, he played "Stick to Your Guns," a song inspired by his father's constant advice about—and support for—his musical career. "By the time I got to the second chorus, John Waite began singing a harmony part that gave me chills." Founding member Tony Brock called Cain "a Christmas present." And just like that, after all his years of disappointment, Cain was a rock star. The Babys had found their new keyboardist.

In the winter of 1979, the Babys—with Jonathan Cain on keyboards and another American addition, Ricky Phillips, on bass—did several appearances in Europe and then returned to the United States in support of Alice Cooper. After appearances on programs including *Burt Sugarman's Midnight Special*, the *King Biscuit Flower Hour*, the Nickelodeon children's talk show *Livewire*, and *Dinah!* (Dinah Shore's 1970s talk show), they spent the summer headlining midsize venues. Then it was back to the larger venues, this time opening for Styx at such places as San Francisco's Cow Palace and the Pittsburgh Civic Arena—with Anne Marie Leclerc providing backup vocals (and the high notes that John Waite avoided). By early 1980 they were headliners again—including in some larger venues like the Santa Monica Civic Center and Sacramento's Memorial Auditorium. After appearances at the Bottom Line and the Palladium in New York, Cain sat for an interview with music columnist Steve Wosahla in that city's storied Gramercy Park Hotel. "The Babys are an established act and established music," Cain said. "It's strange when you jump into a band that's already been established. There's certain things you have to play that have been put down." But he looked forward to being in the studio again, noting that "there's this thing inside me. I know I'm thinking about the next album and the one after that. We are doing some new stuff but I'm gonna save my horn blowing for the next album."

The fans did not have long to wait. In the fall of 1979, the Babys went into the studio to record *Union Jacks*. Released early in 1980, the album launched three singles, including "Back on My Feet Again," a top-40 *Billboard* hit by John Waite, Dominic Bugatti, and Frank Musker. Cain cowrote four of the album's nine tracks, including the other two hits, "True Love, True Confession," which featured a backing vocal by Leclerc, and "Midnight Rendezvous." Also noteworthy was "Jesus, Are You There?" by Waite, Stocker, and Cain. Starting with a church organ introduction by Cain, the song blends into a radio-friendly hard rock up-tempo anthem with a lyric that seems partly inspired by Cain's childhood brush with death at Our Lady of the Angels as well as a critique of the rock and roll lifestyle of copious drugs and sex. And Cain wrote "Turn Around in Tokyo" by himself, providing lead vocals on that one. Reviews were generally positive, if not glowing. Calling *Union Jacks* "the best the Babys have ever sounded," Pete Bishop of the *Pittsburgh Press* said their "copy-catting . . . might well earn them the sobriquet 'Foreigner Jr.'"

The Babys had high hopes for their 1980 tour: they would be performing in large arenas as the opening act for . . . none other than Journey. On the afternoon before the first show, Cain found himself roller skating around Oakland Coliseum while the roadies started coming in and setting up equipment. He had developed a ritual during the previous year's tour, scoping out the venue from the perspective of the audience and forcing himself to think about what they wanted from his performance so that he could be sure to give it his all. According to his memoir, on this particular day, March 28, 1980, he stopped skating and watched as, one by one, the members of Journey came in for a sound check. Neal Schon's guitar let out a lonely peal across the arena. Then came *tap-tap-tap-smash!* as Steve Smith started checking his drums. Ross Valory joined them soon after, adding his *thrum-thrum-thrum* on the bass. Finally, out came Steve Perry, whom Cain recalled as "clearly in charge." Conspicuously absent from this account was organist Gregg Rolie, almost as if Cain in his recollection was already erasing the Journey founder from the band, much as he would soon eclipse him as not only Journey's keyboardist but also their most prolific songwriter. Indeed, just a few weeks later, after Cain had gotten to know the members of Journey over many a postshow dinner, he found himself in a limousine riding back to a hotel with Schon,

Herbie Herbert, and road boss Pat Morrow, sitting up front while the three in the back were getting high on pot, laughing. "What's it gonna feel like to be the next keyboard player in Journey, Caino?" asked Herbie. Cain recalls being unsure "what my ears clearly heard. I put my face in the barricade and squinted as my eyes burned from the reefer. 'What'd you say?'

"Herbie just looked at me and rolled his eyes. 'Oh, nothing.'"

For now, though, with Gregg Rolie still in Journey, it was back into the studio for the Babys' fifth album, *On the Edge*. Released late in 1980, this one enjoyed even more of Cain's influence than did *Union Jacks*. He cowrote seven of the nine tracks of the moody album, inspired by Bruce Springsteen's *Darkness on the Edge of Town*, including the hit "Turn and Walk Away," which flirted with the top 40 (but ultimately topped out at number 42), and "Love Won't Wait," for which he again provided lead vocals. But Steve Wosahla's not-unfriendly review lamented that the band was still failing to meet expectations. "Just like Bad Company woke up the world in '74, the Babys have the potential to put their stripped-down rock basics in overdrive and wet an insatiable rock thirst."

Despite their talent, popularity, and potential, however, the Babys were plagued with financial problems. Years of mismanagement had left the band deep in debt. Ticket sales marked a consistent shortfall and did not significantly boost album sales. Indeed, when Jonathan Cain joined the band in December 1978, he was only offered a salary of $250 per week—enough to maintain his small apartment in LA and keep him fed and clothed but hardly "rock star" pay. By the end of the year, John Waite confided in him that he was leaving the group to pursue a solo career. And when road manager Pat Morrow made the official offer for Cain to join Journey in December, informing him that after a year on tour with their opening act there was no need to audition, that spelled the end of the Babys. Their label, Chrysalis, released the compilation album *Anthology*, which sold moderately well and helped recoup some of the sunk costs, but not all of them: twenty years later, the band still owed the label "something like half a million dollars," according to Waite.

"Separate Ways," 1983–1987

It's not so much what you play . . . it's what you don't play. The spaces count.

—*Gregg Rolie*

In the fall of 1982, Journey returned to Fantasy Studios in Berkeley to record their next album, *Frontiers*, again produced by Mike Stone and Kevin Elson. Steve Perry delivered a raspier vocal than he gave for *Escape* and explored some of his lower register. As with that previous effort, the songwriting team was primarily Perry and Jonathan Cain, with Neal Schon joining for half the numbers and Steve Smith for two—the drummer's first songwriting credits since joining the band, despite his authorship of the drum fills that gave their previous material so much flair.

Frontiers starts off with "Separate Ways (Worlds Apart)," a hard rock tune penned by Perry and Cain during the *Escape* tour and inspired by the troubles band members had been having in their marriages. Beginning with a crystal-clear synthesizer theme, soon joined by hard rock guitar and bass, the song has a lyric urgency that speaks to the impending end of a relationship and a promise that "If he ever hurts you . . . /You know I still love you/'Though we touched and went our separate ways." The guitar solo presages a restatement of the keyboard theme, then a final chorus, and a definitive ending.

Continuing the lyrical theme of love lost and marriages cut short by the pressures of life on the road, "Send Her My Love" is next, a haunting ballad by Perry and Cain with a strong drum rhythm and some interesting guitar and keyboard arrangements. "I sat down with Jonathan Cain and that song just slowly started coming together," said Perry, adding that "it was sort of a goodbye song, you know . . . if you see her, send her my love, even though it's over with . . . I hope she's doing well."

Cain concurred:

> I met this person that knew this girl that I had not seen in years and I was just kinda choked up 'cause I guess I wasn't expecting it—it caught me off guard. So I just said, you know, "send her my love." And it just keyed up one of those things. I know it happens to everybody and I just—it was too irresistible, you know, so it just happened. It was one of those things that kept haunting me and that's what I wanted it to be and I think we captured it.

Although not a coauthor of the song, it mattered to Schon, who had recently broken up with his girlfriend. And unbeknown to the rest of the band, Schon recorded the guitar track while recovering from a motorcycle accident that fortunately left his hands largely unscathed. "I just dragged the bike home and cleaned the cuts out in my pool. I didn't even see a doctor. Hell . . . I didn't even tell the band. It wasn't gonna affect my playing so I figured, 'What the hell, it's my business, not theirs.'"

After that, it was time to rock out. "Chain Reaction," by Perry, Schon, and Cain, is a jumpy, rhythmic, and explosive number—as the title suggests. Perry shares lead vocals with Schon. An extended guitar exploration brings the song to a fade-out, but the theme of the album continues with "After the Fall," a moody ballad by Perry and Cain with a standard composition and harmonies in a chorus that simplistically restates the problem: "Can't stop falling/Heartache's calling," ultimately asking, "What's left after you fall?"

As if in answer, side 1 concludes with "Faithfully," a crooner's dream ballad by Cain. It begins with a clean piano theme and potent lyrical imagery: "Highway run into the midnight sun . . . /Sending all my love along the wire." Separated by the road, connected by the phone. A haunting guitar joins in after the first chorus. Although Cain wrote it pining for his wife,

Tané, at least he got "the joy of rediscovering you," resulting in the vow that "I'm forever yours, faithfully." Ross Valory, the band's jokester—who once told an interviewer that "in my spare time I like to hitchhike through Venice" (California)—inspired the line, "We all need the clowns to make us smile." The song sets the tone for the eighties hard rock ballad, demonstrating how a piercing electric guitar, which Schon delivers in the final moments to support Perry's extended high notes, can provide sweetness, depth, and subtlety, not just raw power. When the soul rocker Prince, preparing to release *Purple Rain*, realized that his title track sounded remarkably like the chord changes in "Faithfully," he contacted Cain through Columbia Records, worried that Journey would sue him. But all agreed there was no conflict.

Side 2 begins with "Edge of the Blade," a guitar- and drum-heavy rocker by Perry, Schon, and Cain, with a subtle synthesizer line and an overtly violent lyric: "If it's sharp, and if it cuts, enjoy yourself." One reviewer suggested that Schon wrote those lines in retaliation for former Journey drummer Aynsley Dunbar's lawsuit against the band, calling the song "a blast at a former band member"; given the continued friendship with George Tickner and Gregg Rolie (the latter then still drawing a Journey paycheck), the only other candidate would have been Robert Fleischman, who was not challenging his dismissal in the courts, whatever sour grapes he may have harbored for Journey's success. That said, neither Schon nor either of the other songwriters ever confirmed that it was directed at Dunbar or any former band member.

"Troubled Child," by Perry, Schon, and Cain, is a synthesizer and (mostly) acoustic guitar–driven elegy to misspent youth. Vocals, guitar, and keyboards provide the verses, with bass and drums joining in during the choruses and bridge. It is followed up neatly by "Back Talk," a drum-heavy, guitar-driven up-tempo by Perry, Cain, and Smith, with Schon's guitar solo providing the titular "back talk" as a call-and-response. These two songs were not originally slated for the album. As always, the band recorded more tracks than they needed and decided which ones to include as a final step before release. These last-minute substitutions gave the album a darker, rougher edge than in *Escape*, which used the final four songs of its side 2 to bring listeners down gradually from the excitement of "Escape" to the lullaby of "Open Arms." Not so here.

Next up is the title track, "Frontiers," a futuristic, synthesizer-heavy mid-tempo by Perry, Schon, Cain, and Smith, with a lyric that speaks to the rise of modern technology in a rapidly computerizing world. "We're on the verge of a changing skyline . . . /We all need new frontiers," even if, as Perry reminded listeners, "Barbarians play." Had it not been the title track, the song might have been better suited to the soundtrack to the motion picture *Tron*, about people trapped as programs in a computer, and the Journey song "Only Solutions," which actually was in the movie, could have taken its place on the album.

Frontiers concludes with "Rubicon," a guitar-heavy mid-tempo by Perry, Schon, and Cain, with long-sustained vocal notes and a lyric that likens the fans' (and the songwriters') life-changing decisions to Caesar's fateful choice to cross the Rubicon River and invade Rome. "It's basically a statement about committing yourself to whatever it is you do or believe in, and the whole world has to do this because time is not on our side anymore," said Perry of the track. "Burning youth won't wait, people just will not put up with much anymore." As for Cain, "I've always been fascinated with the idea of a river, and Rubicon's a famous river that Julius Caesar dared to cross . . . but he had to make the decision to his armies . . . whether or not to go across the Rubicon." The lyrics bear out the sentiment, prophetically closing out the album with "Take your time and choose the road you want/Opportunity is yours."

The cover art is a departure from the theme of the preceding albums, which had featured the work of Stanley Mouse and Alton Kelley of Grateful Dead and Jimi Hendrix fame. No more planets, no more flying scarab beetles. The back had a picture of the five band members performing a sky-diving stunt in freefall, holding hands to form a circle. The front, perhaps inspired by the album's title song, depicted the head of "Elmo"—some sort of a robot or helmeted space alien. Valory, who called the figure a "space spook" in a choice of words that has become less appropriate over time, ducked questions on the choice, attributing it to Herbie Herbert. But the manager disclaimed this, blaming Perry for deviating from a game plan he claimed to have put together for six album covers and titles, from *Infinity* to *Freedom*, the title he had scheduled to follow *Frontiers*. "Steve really wanted to interrupt that, and he fought like hell to change the art and the imagery. And we did—to that Elmo space-guy. . . . I prevailed on the name, and he prevailed on changing the art."

Journey, of course, had high hopes for the success of their latest album. "I'd like to think that Frontiers is really the beginning of a whole new era for the band," Schon told Andy Secher of *Hit Parader*.

Any hopes for positive reviews, however, were soon dashed. This time the press was nearly unanimous in their disdain for the effort. Rich Shefchik of the *York Daily Record* said *Frontiers* was "not rock 'n' roll [but] middlebrow pap just as sure as Bing Crosby and Petula Clark were born," referencing two easy listening crooners whose hits defined midcentury "middlebrow" music. Ken Maffitt of the *Spokane Spokesman-Review* likened *Frontiers* to a math equation, stating that "it would be even more pointless to rate this record than review it" but correctly predicting it would quickly go platinum. Most reviewers liked Schon's additions to the album but saw his creative freedom being squelched by the softer, "corporate" sound produced by Perry and Cain. "Melodic rockers, piano-flavored ballads, heavy-metal thumpers—this well-crafted collection of mainstream pop-rock is a marketing man's dream," wrote the *Los Angeles Times*. Gary Graff of the *Detroit Free Press* also saw a clear divide between the rockers cowritten by Schon and the ballads credited solely to Perry and Cain, and reviewers from both *Rolling Stone* and the *Morristown Daily Record* preferred *Here to Stay*, Schon's second effort with keyboardist Jam Hammer.

The tour met with a similar blasé reception from the critics despite, or rather because of, the band's continued ability to sell tickets. Journey played 108 dates in 1983, starting at Japan's storied Budokan martial arts arena on February 22—the date *Frontiers* was released—and ending in Hawaii on September 6, with multiple sold-out arenas in major stateside markets, this time supported by Bryan Adams. Herbie depicted the stateside path as resembling "kind of a figure-8"—to the delight of fans of the logo from the *Infinity* album cover—"from Seattle through the Salt Lake area, Denver, St. Louis, straight on down . . . through Atlanta, into Florida, the Eastern Seaboard, in through the Midwest, down through the Southwest and Kansas City, through Texas." Yet the critics spent their time decrying the video screens, which allowed the band to do a low-energy job onstage, according to John Spitzer of the *Pittsburgh Post-Gazette*. The best that John Christensen of the *Honolulu Star-Bulletin* could muster, after seeing Journey at Blaisdell Arena, one of the last shows on the tour, was that they were commercial yet satisfying, noting that the T-shirts sold out quickly but the sound system was lacking.

As with *Escape*, however, the fans passed their own judgment—by buying records and tickets. On March 11—little more than two weeks after its release—the album dislodged the Stray Cats' *Built for Speed* for the number-2 spot on the *Billboard* 200 and stayed there for ten weeks, holding off a challenge from *Kilroy Was Here* by Styx but ultimately failing to dislodge Michael Jackson's *Thriller* from the top spot (although it did take number 1 on the rock album chart, holding the position for several weeks). It was certified gold and platinum by RIAA on April 4. During the weeks the album was at number 2, "Separate Ways (Worlds Apart)" peaked at number 8 on the Hot 100 and "Faithfully" at number 12, while "Billie Jean" and "Beat It" from Jackson's *Thriller* each made it to number 1.

Those two hits from *Thriller* were accompanied by lavish, big-budget, highly choreographed videos in heavy rotation on MTV that spring. Launched in 1981 in a single region in northern New Jersey, the Music Television cable channel grew quickly into a nationwide phenomenon as households abandoned rabbit-ear antennae for the clearer cable signal. Initially focused on rock music to the point of being accused of excluding Black artists, by early 1983 the network was something of a televised top-40 format radio station, playing the latest hits—so long as they filmed videos. The station even launched the careers of "veejays," the video equivalent of DJs.

The lesson of *Thriller* was not lost on Herbie. He arranged for Journey to film stylized videos for three songs from *Frontiers*, sending the group down to New Orleans for the shoot. The "After the Fall" video features Steve Perry in a plain square room, alternately furnished with a chair, a bed, or a table, occasionally joined by other members of the band, sometimes playing instruments or singing, sometimes inexplicably sitting around drinking from coffee cups, striking poses in conversation with Perry. During one chorus, the band members are seen falling one at a time, in slow motion, outside a glassless open window. The "Chain Reaction" video, in which Schon shares lip-synched lead vocals with Perry, begins with Schon and Perry in tuxedos, arguing over a female mannequin, tossing martinis, and then joining the rest of the band in a checkerboard-themed room reminiscent of *Alice in Wonderland*. At least they seem aware of how ridiculous this all was. There is much less self-awareness in the even more ridiculous video for "Separate Ways (Worlds Apart)." Filmed at the Louisa Street Wharf on the Mississippi River, this one features the band playing "air instruments"—that is, pretending to play nonexistent instruments—while an oblivious model walks by. The actual instruments eventually appear, and at one point, Cain seems to be playing a synthesizer glued to the wall of a warehouse. Although the band members were asked to leave their wives and girlfriends at home for the shoot, Perry brought his girlfriend, Sherrie Swafford, who got into an argument with the singer when she learned that Margaret Oldsted, a local model—rather than Swafford herself—would star in the video. The filming was also arduous because of a wintry breeze coming off the river, which forced Perry—who is actually singing, rather than lip-synching, in an attempt to add a touch of reality to his performance—to flee for his trailer between takes to rest and warm his throat. The band also showed up to the set late and hungover—they had been out drinking in the adjacent French Quarter the night before without realizing there is no such thing as "last call" in New Orleans. The singer, and the rest of the band, ultimately found the finished product so atrocious that they resolved to avoid such stylized videos; going forward, their videos would center on footage of the band on the road or in the studio and leave the interpretation of the music to the listener.

Notwithstanding the silliness of their music videos, Journey doubled down on the overall concept of film. After Herbie met a cameraman from NFL Films at a San Francisco 49ers game, he arranged for a crew from the fledgling video company to follow the band on tour, resulting in a documentary about life on the road, *Frontiers and Beyond*. The work also yielded footage for several more music videos, including one for "Faithfully." The documentary, which features profiles of several of the roadies, including road manager Pat Morrow, as well as the band members and Herbie, builds momentum to culminate in the band's June 4, 1983, return to JFK Stadium in Philadelphia, where rain and high winds almost cancel the show, but the can-do spirit of the road crew keeps the screens and the lighting trusses and the "spine," made of multiple power cords, functioning at peak performance.

Herbie had one more innovation in store for the rock world that year. Building on the band's earlier sponsorship by Budweiser beer, which he had abandoned amid concerns that he was promoting alcohol to Journey's underage fan base, he took out an ad in *Advertising Age* that offered up Journey fans' pocketbooks in exchange for corporate sponsorship of the tour. More than two decades before the rise of Facebook and Gmail, which provide "free" services that ultimately make the *user* the product, Herbie attempted to sell the fans of Journey to the highest bidder. By the conclusion of the *Frontiers* tour, Journey had sold two million T-shirts and 5.3 million copies of the album but still had not pulled the trigger on a new lucrative corporate sponsorship, refusing offers as high as $1 million. "We are going to gross $30 million in ticket sales alone in 1983 and $10 million more in record sales," Herbie told Michael Specter of the *New York Times*. "So why go out there and sell our souls for a lousy million bucks?"

*   *   *

With the conclusion of the *Frontiers* tour, the band finally got the extended break they had sought in 1982. No entreaties from Herbie nor begging by Bill Graham could change that fact. But they hardly stayed fallow, finding other projects to occupy their time. Even before the end of the tour, Steve Perry teamed up with singer/guitarist Kenny Loggins of the Nitty Gritty Dirt Band and Loggins and Messina to write and record the song "Don't Fight It" for Loggins's solo album *High Adventure*. Neal Schon teamed up with Sammy Hagar, and Steve Smith formed a jazz band. Jonathan Cain threw himself into his wife's singing career, writing and producing a record for her, *Tané Cain*, and booking her at a few clubs around San Francisco. That album, which also featured her husband on keyboards and Schon on guitars, won Tané a 1983 Bammie nomination for Best Female Lead Vocalist, although she lost out to Grace Slick of Jefferson Starship; unsurprising, given Tané's poor tonality and vapid delivery.

And there was a little new music from Journey to slake fans' thirst. A mid-tempo, synthesizer-heavy rocker by Perry and Cain, "Ask the Lonely" was—like "Only the Young"—originally slated for inclusion on *Frontiers*. The song has a powerful harmonized chorus: "When you're feeling love's unfair . . . / When you're lost in deep despair, you just ask the lonely." While the lyric is reminiscent of Roy Orbison's "Only the Lonely," the music has more in common with the Motels' 1982 hit of the same name. It was originally released on the soundtrack to the movie *Two of a Kind*, a failed attempt to recapture the magic of *Grease* by reuniting John Travolta with Olivia Newton-John. That magic being a product of nostalgia rather than onscreen chemistry, the song did far better than the film, rising to number three on *Billboard*'s Mainstream Rock chart on January 21, 1984.

Nightmare's growing stable also included Eric Martin, a vocalist who had recently made the finals in Toto's auditions to replace Bobby Kimball. Martin had fronted a band called 415—after the San Francisco telephone area code—that Gregg Rolie managed in the months after leaving Journey. Herbie convinced him to rename it the Eric Martin Band. After that group broke up in early 1984, Martin teamed up with Schon and Smith for the song "I Can't Stop the Fire" on the soundtrack for the movie *Teachers*. Then Schon and Martin took a trip to England to work with John Entwistle, legendary bass player for the Who. Martin later fronted the Nightmare-managed supergroup Mr. Big, whose hit "To Be with You" made it all the way to number one on the *Billboard* Hot 100 chart in 1992.

Even Herbie had side projects. In addition to managing Schon's collaborations with Jan Hammer and Sammy Hagar, Tané Cain (at her husband's insistence), and Eric Martin, he teamed up with KJAZ-Radio San Francisco to put together the "Big Band Bonanza," a "Historic Blues-Jazz Reunion" featuring jazz pianist Jay McShann, jump blues singer Jimmy Witherspoon, and jazz saxophonist John Handy. But he also knew how to take a break, enjoying a box at the fifty-yard-line for 49ers home games.

Of all the Journey members' solo efforts, Perry's was the most successful. Just as the videos from Michael Jackson's *Thriller* had inspired Herbie to push Journey to film their own, the pop singer's hold on the album chart's top spot inspired Perry to infuse more soul into his writing. With Herbie's assistance, he assembled a crack team of writers and musicians to record his album *Street Talk* at Record One Studios in Los Angeles, including Craig Krampf from his old band Alien Project, longtime Carpenters lyricist John Bettis, noted country writer Randy Goodrum, and Larrie Londin, one of the late Elvis Presley's favorite session drummers. The album includes ten tracks of vocals-oriented, soulful rock and roll, all written or cowritten by Perry, who also recorded his own backing vocals. "Foolish Heart," with a soaring vocal line, and "She's Mine," by Perry and Randy Goodrum, hit numbers 18 and 21, respectively, on the *Billboard* Hot 100; and "Strung Out," by Billy Steele, Krampf, and Perry, peaked at number 40. (Also noteworthy was "Don't Tell Me Why You're Leaving," by Perry, Krampf, and guitarist Danny Kortchmar. Although it didn't make the *Street Talk* original release, the song, in which Perry sounds like James Brown, appeared on a later reissue.) Released by Columbia on April 6, 1984, *Street Talk* sold very well, peaking at number 12 on the *Billboard* 200 on June 9 and rocketing to platinum certification a month later. It also earned Perry another Bammie for Outstanding Male Vocalist.

The centerpiece of *Street Talk* is "Oh Sherrie," by Perry, Krampf, Goodrum, and Bill Cuomo, who had played synthesizer on Kim Carnes's number-one 1981 hit "Bette Davis Eyes." Modeled on the Four Tops' 1967 Motown hit "Bernadette," the lyrics were addressed to Perry's girlfriend Sherrie Swafford, who had been present at the start of the all-night writing session and featured in the resulting video. (The title may have been partially inspired by a dish at Galatoire's, a "jacket required" restaurant in the New Orleans French Quarter where Perry surely dined while Journey was shooting the videos for *Frontiers*. One item on their menu is "Turtle Soup *au Sherry*." Cuomo denies this, telling me he only added "oh" for timing.)

Perry had originally intended to include a saxophone solo, but guitarist Waddy Wachtel, a veteran session player who had worked with Ringo Starr, Jackson Browne, Bob Seger, and others, insisted on the guitar solo that brings the song together. It peaked at number 13 on the *Billboard* Hot 100, behind "Let's Hear It for the Boy" by Deniece Williams (number 2) and Cyndi Lauper's "Time after Time" (number 1).

True to his feelings after the silly videos recorded for the *Frontiers* album, Perry refused to do stylized videos for *Street Talk*. Instead, in a move that would have made Marshall McLuhan proud, he used the medium to attack the style. The opening notes from "Oh Sherrie" play at the start of what appears to be a medieval wedding in full costume, Perry dressed as a prince replete with bejeweled gold crown. But just before the lyrics, he stops the action, protesting that the whole thing is "ridiculous," and takes off the crown, gown, and necklace to reveal modern street clothes. Confronted by an apoplectic director, he apologizes to the hair-and-makeup team and excuses himself politely when asked to chat with a journalist. Leaving the stage, he sits at the foot of a stairwell in what is revealed to be a modern building, and starts singing, as on the album, without accompaniment: "You should have been gone/Knowing how I made you feel." When the real Sherrie Swafford enters through art deco brass-and-glass front doors, finally getting the stardom she was denied in New Orleans, he sings to her, first from a balcony, then descending the stairs, ultimately leaving the building with his arm around her shoulders to the frustrated exclamations of the video director.

Perry had long opposed members of Journey engaging in solo projects. "I used to think solo albums would defuse the nucleus of the band," he told Dennis Hunt of the *Los Angeles Times*. "I thought they would make the group seem scattered and not together. I was a real gung-ho Journey person. I wanted us all to stay together and I was against anything that might pull us apart." But when Schon and Smith did solo projects and still returned to make another blockbuster Journey album in 1983, he was less reticent. "I waited a long time but I finally figured I might as well do one too. If they [didn't worry] about it, why should I?"

Recording a solo album provided Perry the chance to get back to his musical roots. "The main difference between *Street Talk* and a Journey album is that my songs are more romantic and personal," he told Craig Moderno of *Rock* magazine. "They have more of the emotionalism that you associate with early Motown songs." The lyrics were "more honest, more American," he told Rich Sutton of *Song Hits*, noting that "America is . . . a melting pot of music." Jeff Tilton, writing in the *Oakdale Leader*, found "the influence of Smokey Robinson and the Miracles in 'I Believe,'" calling "'Captured by the Moment' the most gratifying song on the album," dedicated to "Martin Luther King, the Beatles, Otis Redding, Janis Joplin, Jim Morrison, Jimi Hendrix and others." In "You Should Be Happy," on the other hand, Tilton saw Perry as inspired by Journey's *Dream, After Dream*, another favorite of the singer's.

For once, the critics' response matched that of the fans. Indeed, the worst Pete Bishop of the *Pittsburgh Press* could manage was to call it "pretty much standard fare with little substance, 'corporate rock' to you cynics. So is Journey. But, like Journey's albums, it's well-done standard fare." Even rock and roll legend Chubby Checker, known for "The Twist," got in on the plaudits, calling Perry "a tremendous lead singer" after hearing the album.

In January 1985 the tremendous lead singer joined three dozen other superstars to record an album to benefit Ethiopian famine relief. After several prominent British pop and rock stars formed "Band Aid" to record the smash hit "Do They Know It's Christmas?" that December, pop star Lionel Richie (formerly of the Commodores) and superstar producer Quincy Jones (whose credits included Michael Jackson's smash hit album *Thriller*) organized American artists into USA for Africa to record "We Are the World." Told to "leave your egos at the door," Steve Perry joined Tina Turner, Bruce Springsteen, Michael Jackson, Cyndi Lauper, Ray Charles, Kenny Loggins,

Kenny Rogers, and more, and was among the artists selected by Richie for a solo line in the song and the even smaller group invited to record a song for the resultant album ("If Only for the Moment, Girl," cowritten with his *Street Talk* colleague Randy Goodrum). "We Are the World" flew up the charts, reaching number one on the *Billboard* Hot 100 on April 13, 1985, pushing the album to the same spot on the *Billboard* 200 two weeks later. During the taping, Perry demonstrated a knack for leadership and an ear for the studio, honed after years of practice; he actively helped Richie correct issues with Huey Lewis's tonality and direct Cyndi Lauper for her own noteworthy vocal solo.

Perry's success as a solo artist raised concerns among fans and the press alike that he might leave Journey permanently. "It will be interesting to see if he gets back together with Journey," said Kathy Lee Gifford after interviewing the singer on *Good Morning America*. "Rumors are abounding." Indeed, Perry himself seemed to be pining for retirement altogether: "I'm thinking of moving to Portugal, permanently," he told journalist Phil Harvey. Ross Valory, hearing this, kidded that Perry should go there and "open a cork factory" (about half of the world's cork is produced in Portugal).

It did not help that Perry stoked the fire even when trying to put it out. Describing his work on *Street Talk* as "freedom," he told Dennis Hunt that he'd be back in "bondage" come fall to record a new Journey album—not a happy insinuation. On the one hand, he was planning to "go back and record with those guys as planned," but on the other, "I like calling the shots in terms of writing and producing and what the band plays. It may be hard working with a band again . . . where everybody has a say in what happens." To make matters worse, Perry had learned that one member of Journey had privately panned *Street Talk*. Perry would not reveal who it was, intimating only that "it's not drummer Steve Smith." Seeking to quell rumors of a breakup, the members of Journey filmed a scene together for the Christmas season as an alternate ending to the video for Perry's "Foolish Heart." After Perry sings the song alone on a stage—all accompaniment invisible in perhaps the least stylized music video ever made—he walks into the wings to find the rest of Journey awaiting him with champagne. They congratulate him, and together send a "Happy Holidays" toast to the audience, after which Perry says "Let's go cut a track. Italian food!" As they walk offstage, Schon tousles Smith's thinning hair, aiming to project band camaraderie.

Steve Perry had yet another opportunity to demonstrate his willingness to continue with the band that had given him his fame, fortune, and professional satisfaction when the Journey Force fan club received a unique letter. A young fan named Kenny Sykaluk was dying of leukemia in a Cleveland children's hospital, and his one desire was to meet the members of the band whose music he so adored. The nonprofit Make-A-Wish Foundation reached out, and the band immediately agreed to visit the boy. Perry, Schon, Cain, and Valory flew to Cleveland and brought with them a singular present. Handing him a Sony Walkman and slipping the headphones over his ears, they watched as Sykaluk's eyes lit up as he became the first person outside the Journey organization to hear an outtake from the *Frontiers* sessions. The song was "Only the Young," an up-tempo by Perry, Schon, and Cain, and the theme speaks to the boy's plight: "Only the young can say/They're free to fly away." The band "played it for him, and, it was rough," recalled Perry. "It was really rough, because, you know, he was in heaven. He really was in heaven." As for Schon, "It changed my outlook on life. It makes you realize that the things you were making a big deal out of maybe were not so big." Kenny Sykaluk died in that bed the next day, the headphones still on his ears, the cassette still in the Walkman.

This was a very emotional episode for Cain. "Here was this little kid just struggling for every breath he could, and we were doing everything we could not to break down and bawl in front of him," he said. The writer of "Open Arms" and "Faithfully" naturally kept his emotions close to the surface, ready to be tapped for their creative potential. But this experience was something different. "Still to this day I can always see his face . . . and I can see his pleasure of hearing that song. I mean he just melted into his bed. And that song will always be his song," Cain said, breaking down in tears. "That's the worst thing I've ever seen. It's just not fair, you know, for kids to live with that kind of pain, it's just not fair." Clearly, the Sykaluk episode tapped into Cain's memories of the fire at Our Lady of the Angels. His emotions for this little boy—until that moment a stranger to the sensitive pianist—were standing in for the feelings of guilt and trauma he had long struggled with over the victims of the school fire.

Like so many of the band's biggest hits, the lyric to "Only the Young" speaks directly to the workaday experiences of the audience: "Another night in any town . . . /Sharing the same desire, burning like wildfire." And like

"Don't Stop Believin'" in particular, it played to the audience's very specific white American nostalgia, continuing the same Reaganesque "Morning in America" theme: "In the shadows of a golden age/A generation waits for dawn." After its private premiere at Sykaluk's bedside, the song was released on the soundtrack to the movie *Vision Quest*, where it is the opening theme and a good fit, despite the film's overall failure at the box office (it earned just under $13 million). The song plays to scenes of the protagonist—a white teenage boy—running through the streets of a typical American town (in this case Spokane, Washington) as he trains for a wrestling meet, in an echo of Sylvester Stallone as Rocky Balboa running through the streets of Philadelphia, training for his next fight. And like the theme—and music—of the *Rocky* series, *Vision Quest* fits with the general mode of popular culture of the time: the idealization of a segregated suburban lifestyle found in numerous "Brat Pack" films like *Sixteen Candles*, *The Breakfast Club*, and *Pretty in Pink*, replete with stereotypical depictions of token nonwhites. "Only the Young" quickly ascended the charts, peaking at number nine on the *Billboard* Hot 100 on March 23, 1985.

*   *   *

"Steve Perry: He's Loyal to Journey," blared the headline in the *York Dispatch* on November 20, 1984. And indeed, Journey—or at least four members of the band—were in Sausalito's Plant Studio that month. The studio's general manager, Jim Gaines, who had recently produced Huey Lewis and the News' multiplatinum album *Sports*, was serving as coproducer—with Perry—on a new Journey album.

Perry had in fact been reticent to return. Working on his solo album had given him a taste of control over the entire creative process, and its success had verified his abilities there. He wanted to both maintain that control over his own work—even if that work involved Journey—as well as continue to explore the R&B- and Motown-influenced sound he enjoyed singing. And while Journey had certainly changed since he joined the band, and even more once Jonathan Cain started writing, it was still very much a rock band. Plus, Journey already had someone in control: Herbie Herbert.

When Perry started writing music again with Cain and Schon, it became clear that they were willing to change the sound to keep Perry in the band, but the leadership and control issue remained a major stumbling block—not so much for them but for Herbie. Ultimately Perry presented the manager with an ultimatum: become an employee of the band rather than its boss, or the popular singer would walk.

To ensure that Perry would return to Journey and keep the cash flowing, Herbie agreed. Recall that Journey had been incorporated in the State of California as "Nightmare Productions" almost as long as it had been in existence. In 1985, the five current members of the band, plus Herbie, each had equal votes. Any changes to what constituted "Journey" would require the agreement of four of these six. Because of the ultimatum, and knowing full well that Journey could not continue in 1984 without Perry, Herbie joined Schon, Cain, and the singer in providing the crucial fourth vote for Perry's terms.

Smith and Valory, the other two shareholders, capitulated. "None of us felt strong enough to carry on without him," said Smith. "Basically we gave him all the power. Financially, we needed a hit record. We didn't want to start all over again. We all had house payments." Valory had been in Journey before Perry and "felt it was possible to go on without him" but saw that having Perry back was the simplest route to continued success.

And so, on January 15, 1985, Nightmare approved an agreement with the newly formed "Elmo Partners," consisting of Perry, Schon, and Cain. Named for the robot/alien character depicted on the cover of *Frontiers*, Elmo Partners was granted the exclusive right to perform and record as Journey for an undisclosed sum "until the date upon which none of Stephen Ray Perry, Neal Joseph Schon, or Jonathan Cain is actively engaged in a professional musical career utilizing the name 'JOURNEY.'" In effect, Herbie, Smith, and Valory agreed that Perry, Schon, and Cain could call themselves Journey, exclusively or with others. Journey—meaning Elmo—booked Plant Studio in Sausalito and served notice to their longtime coproducer, Kevin Elson, that his services were no longer necessary. (Elson remained close to Herbie and later produced recordings for Eric Martin's group, Mr. Big.)

Although he continued to officially serve as Journey's manager, Herbie was no longer "in the driver's seat," as Steve Perry was making the important decisions now. To protect what was left of his still large fiefdom, he gave up the lavish Nightmare headquarters and his office with the view of the Golden Gate Bridge. He formed Herbie Herbert Management, a corporation separate from Nightmare, from which he could manage such artists as Europe,

Roxette, Eric Martin, and Gregg Rolie (who was working on a second solo album and considering a return to Santana) without worrying that Perry (or any other members of the band) might move to take further control over Nightmare.

His protective instincts were spot on. The band soon decided to sell Nocturne, the affiliated company now providing lighting displays for major acts like the Grateful Dead. Herbie and Schon agreed to buy them out, incorporating as Schon & Herbert, Inc.

With Elmo—meaning Perry—now having the power to hire and fire members of Journey, Valory became the first casualty. "We're thinking of firing Ross Valory," Perry told "Oh Sherrie" cowriter Bill Cuomo when the keyboardist came to the studio for a visit. As it happened, Valory chose to bow out on his own after learning that the music would more closely resemble Perry's solo work than much of what he felt had made Journey *Journey*. He left after the first week of recording, although he held out the prospect of rejoining the band after the release of the album, expecting that any tour would include many of the hits that he still enjoyed playing. Even though he would still be making money as a Nightmare shareholder—and thus, unlike Aynsley Dunbar, had no grounds to sue—he knew he could make a larger share by touring with the group rather than simply sitting home collecting royalties. Perry replaced him first with session player Bob Glaub and then with Randy Jackson, a local African American bass player who had sat in for one song on *Frontiers*. Once the album was completed, however, Perry refused to consider a reunion with Valory, and the founding bassist was not invited to join the band on tour after all.

Steve Smith was the next to go, and his separation was more painful. He appeared at the studio, ready to work, only to find that Perry, Schon, and Cain had already written most of the songs, his professional input was not wanted, and in some cases, the Three had already recorded demos at Cain's home studio with a click track or a synthesized drum, and Smith was asked to simply mimic what they had already put down. "I felt a lot less involved, and there was much less leeway in what I could contribute," he said. "They felt that the drum machine itself was part of the compositions. I started feeling that it wasn't a band, and it certainly didn't have the same band approach as when we wrote collectively." Smith reported that after two months in the studio, "it was decided that they would bring in another drummer to re-do four of the songs" to get a sound closer to the one they had originally done on the demos. "But they had no intention of just doing four songs. When they got Larrie [Londin], they wanted him to play everything again," he told Robyn Flans of *Modern Drummer*. "Nobody called me to talk about what was going on. It became very impersonal . . . my attorney was informed that they wanted me to retire from the band," adding that Perry "really hurt me . . . because he insulted me personally."

Perry's side of this story should not be discounted. Of all the members of the band, by the end of the *Frontiers* tour, he was facing the most pressure as a public figure. He had also suffered tremendous loss in the years since. By the time the band convened in the studio in November 1984, Perry's mother was dying of cancer. It didn't help that the sight of the singer in a cancer ward sparked rumors that he was suffering from throat cancer himself (his idol, Sam Cooke, had dealt with a similar canard in 1962). At a time when he needed his privacy most, it was the one thing least available to him. What's more, his longtime girlfriend Sherrie Swafford—the muse for his hit "Oh Sherrie" and star of its video—had left him. Although he was not the only one in the band to have suffered loss—three of his fellow musicians had been through divorces, Cain's particularly painful after learning that Tané, the subject of a song about staying true, had in fact been unfaithful, and Herbie lost both of his parents in those years—he ultimately felt he had to make his own tough choices. "I produced the album, took the heat and lost a good friend," he told Joel Selvin. "Steve Smith doesn't want to be my friend."

From Perry's perspective, he was the most popular member of the band, he was the moneymaker, and if Journey wanted to continue, they would have to do so according to his rules. He had "secretly left the band" after *Frontiers*; all the press hype that he wasn't coming back to Journey at that time was actually true. As for letting go of Valory and Smith, once he was writing tunes again with Cain and Schon, he said, "We were ready to roll. But they weren't, so we decided to continue without them," adding, "We have nothing to say to each other." Unlike Schon and Cain, Valory and Smith were unwilling to accept the musical changes that Perry insisted were necessary for Journey to remain at the pinnacle of stardom.

And what were those necessary musical changes? Perry's vision for the music was based on *Escape*, *Frontiers*, and *Street Talk* but also the impact of Michael Jackson's *Thriller*, Prince's *Purple Rain*, and USA for Africa's *We Are the World.* These three albums alone made it seem like African American pop and soul artists were on the verge of integrating popular music again.

Purple Rain was a phenomenon. Prince released the album in June 1984, and it rocketed to the top spot on the *Billboard* 200, blocking albums like Perry's *Street Talk.* A month later, Warner Brothers released the film *Purple Rain*—in which Prince played the lead role. It was a box office smash, raking in more than $70 million and cementing the soul artist's status as a superstar. With his coiffed perm and oversized motorcycle, Prince combined the sensitivity and ambiguous sexuality of Steve Perry with a masculine rock guitar proficiency that rivaled Neal Schon's. But unlike Perry and Schon, Prince was African American, the legitimate heir to Chuck Berry and Jimi Hendrix. To match that raw power, Perry resolved to make Journey a soul-rock band, playing a louder, harder version of the music from *Street Talk.*

Once in the studio with the personnel issues sorted out to Perry's satisfaction, however, the band still had difficulty getting the sound right. Part of this was because Perry kept interrupting production to hop on his own motorcycle to be with his dying mother, an understandable response to her illness that nevertheless left the other members of the band feeling as much in limbo as they had during the long hiatus. And it wasn't just his personal affairs that were impeding progress; it was also his dual focus as the record's producer. "He's on the phone trying to coordinate stuff when he's supposed to be writing lyrics," lamented Cain. "And it started to bug me after a while. I had to say, '[Stephen], can we get back here?'"

Perry also butted heads with Schon, after which "the guitarist absented himself from much of the creative give and take, content to whip out his customary guitaristics in the studio and leave it at that," according to Selvin. "I hated Perry so much that I was going on binges," the guitarist reported. "I'd come to the studio after having stayed up all night, and he'd look at me and say, 'I can see you're not going to be good for anything.' Then I'd cut my solo on the first take. He has no respect for anyone he works with."

To make matters worse, Plant Studio—the storied location where Fleetwood Mac once recorded *Rumours*—was shut down by federal marshals when its owner, Stanley Forbes Jacox, was discovered to have been using it to traffic in quaaludes and methamphetamine. Herbie arranged for "a representative of the group" to get in and remove the existing Journey tapes—following an extensive strip search. Although "[f]ederal officials said the musicians and technical workers at Plant were in no way involved in Jacox's alleged drug activities," it took some time before recording could resume elsewhere. "We got to the studio one day and the Feds were there," said Cain. "It was scary. We were shut down for nearly a month." Meanwhile, according to Selvin, "the budget went through the ceiling."

When finally released in April 1986 after nearly eighteen months of work, the end product was impressive. *Raised on Radio* contains eleven songs written by Perry and Cain, including three also cowritten by Schon. In addition to Randy Jackson on bass, Larrie Londin, a Country Music Association Award–winning drummer who had been a session player for the likes of Elvis Presley and many others, provides an uninspired drum line on eight of the songs, with Steve Smith appearing on the remaining three. Ironically, the Tubes drummer Prairie Prince, who had sat in for several gigs back in 1973 before Aynsley Dunbar joined the band, provided the artwork for an album cover depicting the Hanford, California, radio station that, also ironically, played little of the music that inspired its hometown hero (it was largely a Portuguese station).

"Girl Can't Help It" is an up-tempo, easy listening song with Larrie Londin on drums that rose to number 17 on the *Billboard* Hot 100. Penned by Perry and Cain, this is *not* a cover of Little Richard's song "The Girl Can't Help It," which appeared on the soundtrack to the 1956 Jayne Mansfield movie of the same name, but is inspired by its themes. "Positive Touch," a jazzy up-tempo by Perry, Cain, and Schon, with Smith on drums and Glaub on bass, includes Dan Hull on saxophone.

"Suzanne," a mid-tempo by Perry and Cain, would have fit on *Street Talk* if not for the guitar solo. The single rose to number 17 on the *Billboard* Hot 100. Next up is "Be Good to Yourself," an up-tempo, radio-friendly rocker by Perry, Cain, and Schon, featuring Randy Jackson on bass and Larrie Londin on drums. Cain's synthesizer sounds like a harpsichord during the bridge, and the guitar solo serves as a fade-out. With its self-affirmation lyrics ("Be good to yourself/When nobody else will"), the song rose to number 9, making it the album's only top-10 hit.

"Once You Love Somebody," a mid-tempo by Perry, Cain, and Schon, has a funky bass line by Jackson and includes Londin on drums, while "Happy to Give," a ballad by Perry and Cain, is another soulful one that would have been fine on *Street Talk*, with a confessional lyric, operatic vocals, a simple synthesizer line, minimal bass and drums from Jackson and Londin, and a brief, synthesized horn solo instead of a guitar solo.

Side 2 begins with "Raised on Radio," a rocker by Perry, Cain, and Schon that includes the first harmonica part since Gregg Rolie left the band, and lyrics comprised of titles from 1950s and 1960s rock and roll and Motown hits. Dan Hull provides saxophone and harp, and Jackson and Londin cover bass and drums. Ironically, Londin's former boss, Elvis Presley, had recorded a song with a similar theme in 1973—the year Journey was founded.

"I'll Be Alright without You," a bluesy mid-tempo by Perry, Schon, and Cain, has Jackson and Londin on bass and drums, with Cain adding some vocals. The song did well, rising to number 14. It is followed by "It Could Have Been You," another soulful number in the mold of *Street Talk* by Perry, Schon, and Cain, with a funky guitar and synthesized harpsichord, and Jackson and Londin on bass and drums. "The Eyes of a Woman," a haunting ballad by Perry, Schon, and Cain, is synthesizer- and vocals-driven, with Bob Glaub and Steve Smith on bass and drums. The album ends with "Why Can't This Night Go On Forever?," a piano- and vocals-driven ballad by Perry and Cain, with Bob Glaub and Steve Smith on bass and drums, and a haunting guitar line and operatic vocals. It too received some airplay, rising to number 60.

The album did very well overall, peaking at number four on the *Billboard* 200 on May 31, 1986, down slightly from *Frontiers* (number two) and *Escape* (number one), but still better than any of the band's previous offerings. Hungry Journey fans gobbled it up as soon as it hit the shelves, and the stream of hits earning airplay did not hurt sales. It was certified gold and platinum by RIAA on June 23, 1986.

Unlike in the past, the band did not immediately go out on tour in support of the album, and given the immediate sales, they did not have to. But there was clearly a desire to tour among the remaining members. Conscious of the cultural appropriation, Perry was determined that this new "soul-rock Journey" be interracial, so he asked Randy Jackson to stay on for the tour. The bassist eagerly agreed (although, unlike Ross Valory, he was never offered any shares in Nightmare—or Perry's Elmo Partners, for that matter). Finding a drummer was a bit harder, as session player Larry Londin was unavailable. They tried out Omar Hakim, a local African American drummer, but Perry found him "inadequate," according to Schon. For a time they settled on

Barbadian drummer Atma Anur, but he, too, failed to make the cut. "Journey's a special band," said Perry, and "we need a special drummer."

Finally, in midsummer, they hired noted session drummer Mike Baird, and Herbie booked the band for a national tour extending into winter 1987. They kicked off in August at the Calaveras County Fair, filming a minidocumentary where Perry talked about winning the Battle of the Bands there with his high school band, the Sullies. From there they went to Portland and Seattle and then across the country, including what had been an annual winter jaunt to Hawaii. In Pittsburgh, demand for Journey tickets was so high that not only was a second date added at the last minute but a local radio station set up porta-potties for folks camping out for tickets, and a Roy Rogers restaurant volunteered to "provide coffee and doughnuts for the weary waiters."

The setlists were eclectic for a Journey show, including not only the band's catalog of hits and a smattering of songs from the new album but also some rock and roll and Motown classics like Elvis Presley's "Jailhouse Rock" and the Four Tops' "Reach Out I'll Be There." As when they performed a song from Schon's work with Jan Hammer during the *Frontiers* tour, now they performed Perry's "Oh Sherrie," "Strung Out," and occasionally "Foolish Heart" to appreciative crowds. The de rigueur drum solo was replaced by a full rhythm section showcase to assuage skeptical fans concerned over the loss of founding member Valory and the legendary Smith. "Fabulously funky bassist [Randy] Jackson . . . put tremendous life into the performance," Joel Selvin reported, before engaging in a bit of wishful thinking: "His ebullient spirit was clearly one of the major sources of Journey's new life."

To what extent was Steve Perry's musical style a cultural appropriation of Black musical traditions—in other words, could his performances be described as a sort of modern minstrelsy? Historian Michael Bertrand defines four characteristics of white artists engaged in cultural appropriation: (1) a lack of "popularity with African-American audiences and record buyers"; (2) lack of interest "in black culture before endeavoring to become a professional performer"; (3) the failure to exercise "power, right, or motivation to question music business practices or those who devised them" in the interest of making the industry more racially equitable; and (4) limited musical taste, focused exclusively on the African American styles. Unlike Elvis, for whom none of these characteristics proved true on analysis, Steve Perry met three of the four.

First, although his talent was respected by Black musical powerhouses like Quincy Jones and Lionel Richie, as evidenced by their decision not only to include him in USA for Africa but to invite him to submit an original song for inclusion on the *We Are the World* album, Perry had little purchase in the African American listening community, either as a member of Journey or as a solo artist. Second, Perry never publicly demonstrated any interest in Black culture outside of his admiration of Black performers like Sam Cooke and Jackie Wilson. Third, almost as soon as he had achieved a modicum of power in the industry, he began questioning and challenging "business practices [and] those who devised them." He engineered the firing of producer Roy Thomas Baker, steered Journey toward a more soulful sound, and then became a producer himself on *Raised on Radio*. But the closest he came to using this power to help African American professionals achieve parity in the industry was his token hiring of Randy Jackson to play bass on the album and ensuing tour. Even then, however, Jackson was not offered any of the lucrative benefits of full membership in the band. Only the fourth category fails to match, as Perry's musical tastes were eclectic and not limited to the Motown and soul he so often favored. In sum, while it might be unfair to label it as virtual blackface, Perry's work clearly fell within the realm of cultural appropriation.

As always, the band had its detractors. Scott Mervis of the *Pittsburgh Post-Gazette* wrote that "Perry has one of those voices that makes dogs wince," but "Neal Schon, formerly the second-string guitarist in Santana," impressed the fans "by quoting 'Dazed and Confused' as a lead into 'Raised on Radio,'" adding that "Journey, in its 13th year, is credited with 're-defining the Bay Area sound,' which included Jefferson Airplane, Santana and the Grateful Dead. Two out of three ended up sounding like Journey," but "[w]ho ever said it needed re-defining anyway?"

Negative reports had never phased the band before, as they hardly affected the bottom line; they didn't seem to faze Perry, Schon, or Cain this time either. At the Bammies, Journey took the awards for Outstanding Group, Outstanding Male Vocalist, Outstanding Guitarist, and Outstanding Keyboardist. Even Randy Jackson was nominated for Outstanding Bassist (but lost out to Jack Casady of Jefferson Airplane and Hot Tuna). "For Journeymen Perry and

Cain, this is a fourth Bammy—they will now join Grace Slick in the BAM Hall of Fame, ineligible for future awards." Journey did not perform at the ceremony, as they had in years past; instead Schon, Cain, and Jackson played with drummer Narada Michael Walden and singer Michael Bolton. At his acceptance speech, "Perry fought back tears while he read the names of all the current and most of the former members of the supergroup, as though he were reading a list of dead soldiers."

But the accolades were bittersweet, as it was clear by winter that Perry was exhausted again and ready to stop. "I'm done," he told Herbie. He met with Schon and Cain at the marina in San Rafael, telling them, "I can't do this anymore. I gotta get out for a while." When queried by Cain, he added, "I need my life back . . . I'm just toast." And now that he was in charge, he had the clout and the power to unilaterally end the tour. So he did.

In a rare moment of reflection, the normally comedic Ross Valory provided his own take on what happened with Steve Perry:

> The "American dream" rock and roll quest to be rich and famous, a lot of people think they're immune to what happens when you get that much money. You burn yourself out getting there. Or they find themselves famous and don't wanna be famous. You know, they don't wanna sign autographs, and hey, ya know, you signed up for this and ya gotta pay for it. 'Cause a lot of people don't know what the price is when they step up to the plate. The wear and tear is not physical . . . the wear and tear is a mental, emotional thing. You really just let go of a lot of relationships that require presence and constant nurturing. You say goodbye to people. People get sick and die when you're gone. And just a lot of things go by the wayside. And then there's all the strife of power and money and control.

Steve Perry had so desperately wanted to be a rock star, but when it finally happened, he burned himself out and lost the daily connections to his loved ones. After his mother died, he knew that this was not the life he wanted. And he may have been wise to get out when he did: "Touring professionals," including musicians and roadies, have been "found to be at high risk for mental health issues . . . and their associated risk factors," according to a recent study in the *Journal of Psychiatric Research*, which noted "a much higher risk of suicide than the general non-touring community."

He had taken control of the band that had welcomed him as its savior. Step by step, like Shakespeare's Macbeth, he had forced out or otherwise neutered anyone with rival claims to the throne, including the all-powerful manager and founding members alike. But the task, once accomplished, left him friendless in his castle.

Steve Perry walked off a Journey stage for the last time in Anchorage, Alaska, on February 1, 1987, not quite ten years after his audition with the band at Long Beach Arena. Jonathan Cain made a beeline for the hotel lobby to sign autographs, where he stayed until 2:30 in the morning, when his hand went numb. "It was a sad, sad night," he told Selvin. And just like that, with nary a bang nor a whimper, and without any official announcement, the Journey was over.

For now, at least.

Second Set

"Running Alone," 1987–1994

A 45-year-old rock 'n' roller, who the hell wants to see that?

—*Gregg Rolie*

How does one keep busy after being in Journey? For Jonathan Cain, it was a return to his roots as a songwriter. Unfortunately, many artists in the late 1980s were leery of too close an association with the "Journey sound," but he managed to keep the paychecks coming in. He penned a hit for the Australian rock star Jimmy Barnes, for whom he had already produced two hits on the singer's 1985 album *For the Working Class Man*, "American Heartbeat" and the title track, helping make the album a number-one hit on the Australian charts. Barnes liked what Cain offered and asked the keyboardist to cowrite seven of the ten songs and play keys on his follow-up, 1987's *Freight Train Heart*, which also made number one in Australia—and was a bit of a reunion that included Neal Schon on guitar, Randy Jackson on bass, and the Babys' Tony Brock on drums. Next, Cain was asked by NBC to rewrite "American Heartbeat" as a theme for a new TV show, *Glory Days*, because Bruce Springsteen wouldn't release the rights to his song of the same name (the show did not survive the 1987–1988 season). Then Cain flew to Los Angeles for an uncredited turn at the keyboard for the Whitesnake single "Give Me All Your Love," later lamenting that he was in and out of the studio so quickly that he never even met the band (which then included former Journey drummer Aynsley Dunbar).

He had more longevity with Michael Bolton, cowriting and performing on the singer's hit album *The Hunger*—along with, again, Schon and Jackson, as well as Mike Baird, drummer for Journey's truncated *Raised on Radio* tour. *The Hunger* proved a breakthrough album for Bolton; his cover of Otis Redding's "(Sittin' on) the Dock of the Bay," which includes Schon, Cain, Jackson, and Baird (arguably "Journey with Michael Bolton"), is a masterpiece; the brave decision to allow an electric guitar solo, when the original had contained none, earned an accolade from Redding's widow, who said it "brought tears to my eyes. It reminded me so much of my husband," who had died in 1968, "that I know if he heard it, he would feel the same." Schon, Cain, and Jackson also feature prominently in the song's video, where Schon plays one of his own brand of guitars.

Personally, as with any life, Cain's had its ups and downs during this time: he lost his father and steadfast cheerleader, Leonard Friga, to cancer, but he fell in love again, this time with Elizabeth Fullerton, who would make him a father three times over after they married in 1989. And there were other activities: he recorded a public service announcement for a canned food drive organized by Safeway Supermarkets and the Rainbow Records chain, appeared in full medieval costume at a Renaissance fair in Marin County, and was caught playing golf at an invitational tournament with none other than Gregg Rolie, his predecessor in Journey.

Cain also found Schon willing to keep up their longtime collaboration. The two were regular performers at Four Star, a "hot new dance club at Embarcadero Center" in San Francisco, and they joined Herbie Herbert and Eric Martin at a softball game to benefit the Los Gatos Vanished Children's Alliance and the Oakland Missing Children's Project. When local rock photographer Randy Bachman died after being struck by a drunk driver, the two "Journeymen" played a show in his honor.

Schon, of course, was always busy with one project or another but found time to join Carlos Santana, Rolie, Eric Martin, and members of the band Night Ranger to play a benefit for former Journey production manager Jim McCandless, felled by a heart attack at age thirty-five, who had left behind a penniless wife and two kids. The benefit took place at the Omni the night after Steve Smith played there with his jazz band, Vital Information.

Schon had some professional setbacks. He auditioned both for Mick Jagger's new band and to rejoin Santana, failing to land either gig. But he found success in his personal life, remarrying and having a son, Miles. And he put some time into his signature guitar brand, heading off to Los Angeles to meet up with George Harrison and Eric Clapton to demonstrate Schon Guitars. Then he went into the studio to record his first solo album, *Late Nite*.

The supergroup Bad English started when Cain had a chance meeting with John Waite in New York in the summer of 1988, backstage at an appearance of the band Heart. After the disintegration of the Babys, Waite had been nearly as successful as Journey, recording four solo albums, including the 1984 smash *No Brakes*, which featured the number-one *Billboard* hit "Missing You." The chance meeting proved fruitful; by August they had recruited former Babys bass player Ricky Phillips and started rehearsing new material with guitarist Steve Farris and drummer Pat Mastelotto (formerly with Mr. Mister, famous for their 1985 hits "Broken Wings" and "Kyrie"). But Cain really wanted Schon in the band. After being asked several times, the Journey guitarist finally acquiesced, bringing along his "protégé" Deen Castronovo, drummer for a Portland, Oregon, speed metal (sometimes called *shred* metal) band called Wild Dogs that he "discovered in a little rehearsal space in San Rafael." By the end of 1988, still without a name, the band had a contract with Epic Records, a Columbia subsidiary. According to an "insider," "We don't know whether this is Journey with John Waite or the Babys with Neal Schon."

The name originated while the bandmates were playing pool one night. According to Cain, who had played many a pool hall in his early years in Chicago, "I was trying to show Neal how to put English on a cue ball—how to give it sidespin—yet every time he hit the ball, it went in the opposite direction. 'That's bad English,' I said, and then commented how that sounded like the name of a rock group." By February they were in the studio.

The album *Bad English* begins with a hard rocker, "Best of What I Got," by Waite, Cain, and Schon. It has a strong beat and a catchy tune. Like most of the tracks on the album, it is a love song with a lyric full of double entendres that leave little to the imagination ("Put my key inside your door/Feels so good."). "Heaven Is a 4 Letter Word," a rocker by Schon, Cain, Waite, and Los Angeles–based songwriter Mark Spiro, has a playful lyric that focuses on, literally, four-letter words: "It's *like love* and *kiss*/And it *feels like this*/Baby *don't wait* too *long*." "Possession," a love ballad by Waite, Cain, and Phillips featuring a soft acoustic guitar, has a lyric that would seem like stalking ("I've got to be with you . . . /You're my obsession/I want possession of you") if not for its underlying sensitivity: "It's my soul that you own." "Forget Me Not," a hard rocker by Waite, Cain, and Spiro, continues the theme of yearning bordering on obsession: "You can feel me there and you know I'm waiting . . . /Our eyes connect and we both know what this is." But "When I See You Smile," by Diane Warren, is a straightforward love ballad with no trace of the awkward. "Sometimes I want to give up, I want to give in, I want to quit the fight/And then I see you baby and everything's alright." Side 1 concludes with "Tough Times Don't Last," by Cain, David Roberts, and Waite, another hard rocker, this time with an insistent synthesizer line.

"Ghost in Your Heart," by Waite, Cain, and English songwriter Martin Page, starts side 2 with a haunting rocker pining for a love lost, followed by "Price of Love," an earnest ballad by Waite and Cain. Then come four serious rockers: "Ready When You Are," by Cain, Waite, Schon, and Nashville-based songwriter Todd Cerney; "Lay Down," by Waite, Schon, and Cain; "The Restless Ones," by Waite, Cain, and Phillips (with more haunting lyrics); and "Rockin' Horse," by Schon, Waite, and Cain. The album concludes with "Don't Walk Away," a jazzy number by British composer Andy Hill and poet Peter Sinfield.

Critics had little positive to say about Bad English. Calling them "a band of jaded jet-setting rock stars going through the motions" and "a Pyrrhic victory of technique over melodicism," John Evosevic of the *Pittsburgh Press* mused that "'Heaven Is a Four Letter Word' refers to 'the almighty B-U-C-K.'" And even steadfast fan Joel Selvin had had enough after Schon sent in a taped greeting for the 1990 Bammies, which "turned into a giggling plug for an upcoming concert appearance."

But "When I See You Smile" lived up to its potential and then some, hitting number one on the *Billboard* Hot 100 on November 11, 1989, and bringing Waite, Cain, and Schon another taste of superstardom. Indeed, for Schon and Cain, it was their first number-one hit; Journey had never scored one. (The timing was auspicious: in taking the top spot, they knocked out the Herbie Herbert–managed Roxette's "Listen To Your Heart" —which was Herbie's first number-one hit.) Ironically, Cain had been reluctant to record it. "It was sappy and sweet and didn't fit where we were going with the group," he said. "We were hard rock and wild and dangerous and sexy and nobody could mess with us"—except for this one ballad. But John Waite was adamant: "I gotta sing this," he said. "It's a hit." And it was, but Cain was right about the reaction: "People came to our concerts and sang all the words to 'When I See You Smile' while looking at us the rest of the set with an expression that said, *I didn't realize you were a rock band!*" Although Cain later complained that "[o]ne song can put you in a box you'll never get out of again," in fact Bad English was no different in that regard from Journey—nor, indeed, from the aspect of Journey's success that Cain had best contributed to: the prom hits and wedding ballads that brought in tens of thousands of fans (and millions of dollars) but often overshadowed the band's edgier tracks. And after all, Bad English had rock songs in the *Billboard* Hot 100, too, just none that reached number one like "When I See You Smile."

Cain's reticence to record "When I See You Smile" was, probably without his realizing it, of a piece with a prevalent attitude among rock critics and so-called authentic rockers. In rock music, performers could sing the occasional cover song, but their authenticity rested with their ability to write their own music, from the Beatles to Bruce Springsteen to Nirvana (as opposed to pop and country, where singers often performed work written by others). Cain, who prided himself on his compositions, chafed at the thought that his new band's biggest hit was written by someone else. There was also no small amount of misogyny at play—again, likely unconscious, but nevertheless real. Rock stars' performed sexuality was explicitly male and hetero. "When I See You Smile" can also be seen as "wild and dangerous and sexy"—to quote Cain—but because it was a ballad written by a woman, at some level Cain likely found it threatening to his masculinity. The song, to him, bespoke a feminine sexuality that he surely found titillating in a sexual partner—his first wife, Tané, was certainly "wild and dangerous and sexy"—but not when performed by five macho rock stars.

To accompany the brief tour, the band released five videos: "Best of What I Got," "When I See You Smile," "Heaven Is a 4 Letter Word," "Price of Love," and "Forget Me Not." These were semistylized: not as bad as Journey's *Frontiers* videos earlier in the decade but not simple "on the road" or "in the studio" videos either. They all feature the same female model, for whom all of the musicians apparently pine, but especially Waite, the lead singer standing in the sunroof of a limo driving through what appears to be Greater Los Angeles; and lots of water making the model—and Schon's obviously phallic guitar—very wet.

By the time the band went into the studio to record a second album, problems began to plague them, and fissures appeared. According to Cain, John Waite did not like the group's first album and was disappointed in Cain's performance in particular. A truck full of their equipment was stolen from a parking space right in front of bassist Ricky Phillips's house. Their new producer, Ron Nevison, quarreled with Waite until the singer walked out of the studio; then he started correcting the legendary Schon on his guitar playing. "[N]obody tells Neal Schon how to play the guitar."

Released in 1991, *Backlash* provided more of the same muscular hard rock as the band's first album. The name unknowingly invoked the reality that hard rock had become "backlash music"—the music of the white backlash against the civil rights era. But the band knew nothing of that; they just wanted to rock. "So This Is Eden," by Waite, Cain, and English songwriter Russ Ballard, includes the lyric "As we made love on the balcony/With a drink in my hand, like they said it would be"—piano and hard rock guitar. "Straight to Your Heart," by Waite, Schon, Cain, and Mark Spiro—who also provides backing vocals—is a revisiting of the stalking theme. "I watch you move, I watch you dance, I watch you drift away/And I'd give anything for you, and you know that's bad when it gets that way." The video features an ecstatic Cain; he preferred these rockers. Waite plays the brooding, melodramatic protagonist, but at the end, with the object of his affection standing on a darkened Hollywood street corner, neck exposed, looking like prey, he seems a vampire preparing to strike. "Time Stood Still," by Waite, Phillips, and session keyboardist Jesse Harms, on the other hand, uses a Moorish acoustic guitar to invoke a Mexican beach romance. "We found a little seaside bar high above the rocks/You were drinking white wine, and I was doing shots."

"The Time Alone with You," by Waite, Cain, and Diane Warren, is a ballad intended to recapture the magic of their number-one hit "When I See You Smile." The song features prominent piano, a standard rock guitar solo, and an urgent lyric: "Your kiss can captivate me and your touch can set me free/I count the hours, baby, 'til you are next to me." Then follow six hard rockers: "Dancing Off the Edge of the World," by Waite, Cain, and Schon; "Rebel Say a Prayer," by Waite, Cain, and Ballard; the bluesy "Savage Blue," by Waite, Cain, and Schon; "Pray for Rain," by Waite, Cain, and Spiro; "Make Love Last," by Waite and Cain; and "Life at the Top," by Waite,

Cain, Spiro, and Tim Pierce. Chuck Eddy's review in *Entertainment Weekly* captured the album best. "At its most intense, John Waite's world-worn, white-bread croon captures suburban heartache as profoundly as soul music ever captured the heartache of Georgia's back roads or Chicago's ghettos. . . . Taken together, the album—with its unceasing references to rain and rivers—inevitably bogs down," he added, "but heard one at a time over the FM in the Ford, even its platitudes, given Waite's delivery, add up to a hack-rock miracle or two."

Because of the band's continuing fissures, John Waite left Bad English even before *Backlash* was released, dashing any hopes for a second tour. He was particularly incensed with Cain. "He was always leaving early and coming late," the singer recalled. "He was a very difficult person to get on with. And in the end, I just said, 'Fuck it,'" but "I walked away from a very successful thing. I took it all very personally, and I was very angry at the situation." In retrospect, Waite felt the project was doomed from the start. "[W]e could never agree on anything. We never shared the vision of where we were going or why." He later claimed he was just looking for a two-month break, after which he would have been willing to do a brief tour, but even if that were the case, Neal Schon, at least, had learned enough from his recent experience with Steve Perry to not wait around while a singer took a "break."

Cain took the opportunity to restart his solo career, recording an album in his own Wild Horse Studio, *Back to the Innocence*, which includes a rendition of his Journey hit "Faithfully" and a heartfelt tribute to his late father, "My Old Man." He put together a band and appeared at Slim's and the Great American Music Hall in San Francisco, ultimately releasing the album with Intersound Records in 1995. He then joined drummer/producer Narada Michael Walden to play a cancer benefit at New George's, and cowrote a song for Peter Frampton, "Can't Take That Away."

As for Schon, he and Deen Castronovo teamed up with Johnny and Joey Gioeli—two brothers the guitarist had "discovered" while on tour in Pennsylvania, whose sister he would soon make his third wife—and bass player Todd Jensen, a friend of Castronovo's who had played with David Lee Roth. They called the band Hardline, and as the name suggested, they played unapologetic hard rock. *Double Eclipse*, produced by Schon, is one rocker after another, with a few power ballads (emphasis on *power*) thrown in for good measure. Most of the original material—nine of the twelve tracks—was written by Schon and the Gioeli brothers, with Cain contributing on two and fading rock superstar Eddie Money on one. The exceptions are "Dr. Love," a guitar-heavy mid-tempo by Mark Baker, Brian Connors, and Mike Slamer, and "Hot Cherie," a cover of a song originally performed by the Canadian rock band Streetheart. Hardline's version, an ode to a potential liaison with the sexy titular "Cherie"—pronounced "Sherry"—may have seemed to Schon a necessary rebuke to Steve Perry's sappier hit—and a bit of needling directed at his former bandmate, almost as if to say *I'm out working here, why don't you join me?* It rose to number 25 on the *Billboard* Hot 100. The lyrics, like the Bad English tune "Best of What I Got," leave little to the imagination. "You're gettin' me hot, Cherie . . . /I'm ready to rock you long and rough." The only other track to chart was "Takin' Me Down," an allusion to cunnilingus by Schon and the Gioeli brothers, which made it to number 37. One respite from the overtly sexual is "31-91," an acoustic guitar instrumental written by Schon in honor of music impresario and unofficial Santana manager Bill Graham, who had been born in 1931 and died in 1991 in a helicopter crash. A Japanese edition of *Double Eclipse* also includes the bonus track "Love Leads the Way," by Schon and the Gioeli brothers.

For Schon, *Double Eclipse* was a one-album project, and the Gioeli brothers continued on as Hardline without him. He had other fish to fry. First up was joining a "band of dinosaurs" called the "Paul Rodgers Rock and Blues Revue," featuring the former lead vocalist for Bad Company. The group played the Metropole in Pittsburgh and the Great American Music Hall and Shoreline Amphitheatre in San Francisco, where they jammed with Steve Miller, and then joined Santana at the Woodstock '94 festival in Saugerties, New York. Back in the Bay Area, Schon reconnected with several old friends at a benefit for the ailing former manager of Big Brother and the Holding Company, Chet Helms, in a band called "Squid Vicious," defined as "Neal Schon and Ross Valory of Journey, Bobby Scott of Santana and Greg Errico of Sly & the Family Stone."

*   *   *

Working with Columbia Records, Herbie Herbert arranged for the release of another compilation album. *Journey's Greatest Hits* includes only tracks from the Steve Perry era, most of which were originally recorded after Jonathan Cain joined the band. The album includes three songs from *Escape*, three from *Frontiers*, three from *Raised on Radio*, and four from *Infinity*, *Evolution*, and *Departure* combined. The album also includes two hits that had not previously been on a Journey album: "Only the Young," the theme from the film *Vision Quest* which the band had played for the dying Kenny Sykaluk, and "Ask the Lonely," from the film *Two of a Kind*.

Journey's Greatest Hits peaked at number 10 on the *Billboard* album chart on February 11, 1989, placing it squarely among the band's best-selling albums. It was simultaneously certified gold and platinum on January 23 and was already multiplatinum by June 13. It became a mainstay in the CD jukeboxes ubiquitous in the 1990s and resulted in continued financial success for Journey by increasing sales of the previous albums. As Herbie later put it, "What I was able to do for them in death was more fantastic than in life."

Continuing the trend, the label released another compilation, *The Ballade*, in Japan. Consisting of ballads, as its title implies, the album includes fifteen tracks from the six Journey albums recorded with Steve Perry in the United States: three each from *Infinity*, *Escape*, *Frontiers*, and *Raised on Radio*, two from *Departure*, and one from *Evolution*.

In 1992, Columbia released *Time*^{3} (pronounced "time, cubed"), a three-disc boxed set that compiled hits and other pivotal songs from across the band's history. As with *Journey's Greatest Hits*, the Perry era is given prominence, with only six of its fifty-six total tracks heralding from the band's early years. The collection includes four tracks from *Journey*, *Look into the Future*, and *Next*, all of which had previously appeared on the *In the Beginning* compilation; five from *Infinity*; five from *Evolution*; and eight from *Departure*, five of which are live versions from *Captured*; both original songs from *Captured*; one from *Dream, After Dream*; seven from *Escape*; four from *Frontiers*; seven from *Raised on Radio*, including previously unreleased live versions of "Girl Can't Help It" and "I'll Be Alright without You"; and both original songs from *Journey's Greatest Hits*.

The collection also includes eleven songs previously unreleased on Journey albums. "Cookie Duster," by Valory, is a fast-paced, creative jazz instrumental that showcases all four instruments—guitar, organ, bass, and drums. "For You," by Schon, Rolie, and Robert Fleischman, originally intended for the

Infinity album, showcases Fleischman's singing talents—a first for Journey fans accustomed to Steve Perry's lead and the occasional Rolie or Schon backup. "Velvet Curtain" from the same era, by Perry, Rolie, and Aynsley Dunbar, is an alternate version of "Feeling That Way," a short track with vocals by Rolie and harmonies by Perry, Schon, Valory, and Dunbar. It has the same beginning as "Feeling That Way," except with a twangy acoustic guitar accompanying the opening piano melody, and after the first verse, it moves into a brief chorus: "Please let me stay/Just another day." The first disc also includes Journey's version of Sam Cooke's "Good Times," originally performed on the *King Biscuit Flower Hour* radio show. Disc 2 includes "Natural Thing," a soulful ballad by Perry and Valory that features Rolie on keyboards. Originally recorded for *Departure*, the song was the B side of the single "Don't Stop Believin'," from *Escape*.

Disc 3 includes "La Raza del Sol," an up-tempo by Perry and Cain, which was the B side of the single "Still They Ride," from *Escape*, and consists of English lyrics with the exception of the repeated song title, roughly translated as "sun people." "Only Solutions," an up-tempo by Perry, Schon, and Cain, was from the soundtrack to the 1982 film *Tron*. (Neither was a hit, either on the radio or at the box office.) The disc also includes "Liberty," an acoustic, patriotic ballad by Perry, Schon, and Cain, and "All that Really Matters," a funky electric up-tempo rocker by Schon and Cain, with Cain on lead vocals; both were originally recorded for *Frontiers*. There are also two instrumentals by Perry, Schon, and Cain: the jazzy "With a Tear" and the synthesizer-heavy rocker "Into Your Arms." Both were recorded during the long months in the studio for *Raised on Radio*, with Randy Jackson on bass, but left unfinished until Schon and Cain completed them as instrumentals in 1992. Not nearly as successful as their 1989 compilation, *Time*[3] peaked at a modest number 90 on the *Billboard* 200 on January 9, 1993, and was certified gold on February 10.

*   *   *

After leaving Journey, Ross Valory "started a family . . . and for nearly two years didn't pick up his bass except when musician friends dropped by," because Journey left a "bad taste." In 1987 he "took a touring job with Michael Bolton" in support of the album to which Jonathan Cain and Neal Schon had lent their talents—"and played on Todd Rundgren's '2nd Wind' show and album." After that, he teamed up with Prairie Prince, the drummer for the Tubes who had briefly played in Journey in 1973 and more recently designed the cover for their album *Raised on Radio*. They recruited Kevin Chalfant, a Streator, Illinois, native with a voice eerily reminiscent of Steve Perry's. Chalfant had moved to San Francisco in 1981 to pursue a career as a rock singer and had achieved limited success fronting a band called 707. The new band, the VU, also included pianist Tim Gorman, who had performed with the Who on their 1982 album *It's Hard*; on guitar was Stef Burns, an alumnus of Sheila E.'s band, and Chicago native Josh Ramos, borrowed from a band called Le Mans. Their name VU was taken for the abbreviation of "volume unit," a measurement on a music producer's soundboard; it is unlikely, given the sonic dissimilarity, that it was a callout to the early punk rock act Velvet Underground. The VU cut an album, *Phoenix Rising*, that remained unreleased for nearly twenty years. Of its combination of guitar- and bass-heavy rockers, plaintive piano-driven ballads, and Chalfant's insistent vocals soaring over it all, one reviewer found it "a faithful continuation of Journey's 'Frontiers' album." Another compared their sound to that of Heart or Starship, and indeed none other than Cher recorded a version of its first song, "Who You Gonna Believe," for her 1991 album *Love Hurts*.

But the failure of the VU to gain any traction was a tough financial blow to Valory who, thanks to poor investments, unpaid taxes, an overly aggressive (and probably incompetent) accountant, and continuing alimony payments, lost his "ancestral home"—the house he had grown up in that had hosted practice sessions for Frumious Bandersnatch and Steve Miller. He had bought it from his parents during his flush years with Journey, but he filed for bankruptcy soon after. If he had been able to hold on just a bit longer, the massive sales of *Journey's Greatest Hits* might have remedied the situation.

Gregg Rolie, who had left Journey a few years earlier, had remained close to his old friends, keeping Herbie Herbert as manager for his solo career and working as a producer for Eric Martin's band under the auspices of Nightmare Productions. He married girlfriend Lori, became a father, and briefly returned to Santana in 1982 for the album *Shangó*. In 1985 he finally released his debut solo album, *Gregg Rolie*, on which Carlos Santana and Neal Schon appear as guest artists. But because he was still uninterested in touring, the record sold poorly—despite some moderate airplay of one track. Rolie was in a professional quandary because he did not want to be tied too closely to the sounds of the bands he had helped make successful. The album resembles neither Santana nor Journey, as he is clearly trying to declare his independence (without returning to his William Penn roots either, ahem). Music writer Ross Muir called it "the mirror of Tané Cain's debut . . . incredibly similar in . . . 80s production sound . . . and, I hate to say it, pretty disposable." But Rolie stayed active in the music scene and was often reported sitting in when Neal Schon or Eric Martin performed locally, for instance, at the McCandless benefit or at Bammie Award ceremonies (where his work continued to earn the occasional nomination). Rolie released a second poorly promoted (and largely unsold) solo album, *Gringo* (again featuring Santana and Schon, this time on the same song), which Muir acknowledged was "a better offering than the debut . . . a mix of melodic soul-rock and Prince."

Rolie returned to Santana again in 1987 for *Freedom* (which ironically took the name Herbie had intended for Journey's *Raised on Radio*). Credited as merely an "additional musician," this time he joined all the members of the original band (except Michael Carabello and David Brown) on the subsequent tour.

That tour caused bad blood with Carlos over a promised "bonus" that turned out to be nothing more than a satin tour jacket. "Fielding a question about how competitive egos often break up rock bands and how they planned to avoid that, [drummer Michael] Shrieve got serious. 'Often creativity comes out of that exact tension,'" he told Joel Selvin. "'There's a way to bring that all together and create a new sound.' 'Yeah,' echoed Rolie, the dry comic of the group. 'fistfights.'" Still, this iteration of Santana performed well together. *Freedom* sold enough to chart at number 95 on the *Billboard* 200 and earned the group three 1989 Bammie nominations, including Outstanding Group and, for Rolie, Outstanding Keyboardist. But when he failed to get any nibbles shopping around a demo for a third solo album in 1990, it was clear he needed to try something different.

That's when Herbie introduced him to Chalfant, the singer for Ross Valory's band, the VU. An ardent 49ers fan, Herbie brought Rolie and Chalfant together at his box on the fifty-yard line at Candlestick Park for a 1990 home game. Rolie had been tooling around on a song that Chalfant now helped him finish, "Show Me the Way," and they were looking to sell it for songwriter credit. Herbie and Jimmy Iovine, who had recently founded

Interscope Records with Ted Field and David Geffen, "suggested Rolie and Chalfant record it themselves." They recruited Ross Valory and Josh Ramos from the VU, and reached out to another old friend from Journey, Steve Smith, to provide the drum line. Quickly signed to Interscope, the Storm went into the studio in January 1991 and released their eponymous first album that September.

The Storm, following the same "suburban heartache" vein as Bad English, imagined how Journey might have sounded if Rolie had remained in the band (and if Journey had remained together). Although lacking the arrangements that Schon and Cain gave their project with Waite, the group produced a somewhat wider variety of styles. The album begins and ends with a nice touch: the sound of rain falling on concrete. Vocal harmonies bring in the first song, "You Keep Me Waiting," by Rolie, Chalfant, and Bob Marlette (who had written songs on Schon's solo album *Late Nite*). On most tracks, Rolie delivers the opening vocals and stretches his upper register more than he did on his three albums singing with Perry, raising the point of transition to the even higher notes of Kevin Chalfant. "I've Got a Lot to Learn about Love," a radio-friendly hit also by Marlette, Rolie, and Chalfant, rose to number 28 on the *Billboard* Hot 100. This one is much closer to the low-high vocal give-and-take of "Feeling That Way" or "Just the Same Way," albeit with a bit more Rolie. "In the Raw," by Marlette, Rolie, and Chalfant, is a playful take on sexual desire, the object being a woman "wearing nothing but some cowboy boots/Maybe a smile and that's all . . . /That's my baby—in the raw." The bridge takes the form of a news report: *The arresting young lady was apprehended by police officers, who said she did not resist.* "You're Gonna Miss Me," by Rolie, Chalfant, and Ramos, is an up-tempo rocker designed to showcase Chalfant's voice, while "Call Me," by Rolie and Andre Pessis, is a ballad with Rolie on lead vocal for the entirety. Pessis had worked with the keyboardist on his first solo album and continued to write for Eric Martin and Mr. Big. Then for "Show Me the Way," the ballad Rolie had written with Chalfant that earned them the contract, he hands those duties over to Chalfant. The rocker "I Want You Back," by Marlette, Rolie, and Chalfant, is more of a vocal partnership, with frequent handoffs and a high tenor chorus. "Still Loving You," another soft ballad by Pessis and Rolie, has a rousing chorus and full vocal duties by Rolie. "Touch and Go" is a hard rocker by Marlette, Rolie, Ramos, Chalfant, Valory, and

Smith that utilizes the harmonies of the band members as much as their songwriting, while giving Chalfant full duties as lead vocalist. "Gimme Love," by Marlette and Rolie, is a rocker that again gives full lead to Rolie, although Chalfant sings backup throughout the track. "Take Me Away" provides a mid-tempo by Daniel Ticotin, Premananda Johannes, and Marlette, and the album concludes with "Can't Live without Love," a ballad by Rolie and Chalfant with shared lead vocals.

Valory was happy that the Storm so quickly achieved success but harbored some bitterness that the VU—a group with a similar sound and similar talent—had languished. "It's all so much luck and politics," he told Ward Triplett of the *Kansas City Star*. "Talent has nothing to do with getting signed, getting on the air or selling records."

Once the album was cut, Steve Smith departed the band, owing to pressures on his time from the jazz ensemble Steps Ahead and his own band, Vital Information. (He did give guitarist Josh Ramos a token of his appreciation: four bottles of wine dedicated to Journey in 1981 by Bill Graham.) Fortunately, there was an experienced drummer ready to replace him: Ron Wikso, who, like Smith, had studied at Berklee School of Music in Boston and who had recently played for superstar singer Cher. Wikso came recommended not only by Smith himself but also by Bad English and Hardline drummer Deen Castronovo; Mr. Big's drummer Pat Torpey put Herbie in touch with him. New drummer onboard, the Storm recorded a video for "Show Me the Way" and went on tour in 1992 opening for Bryan Adams.

The Storm's second album, *Eye of the Storm*, saw Bob Marlette continue to assist with the writing, and the songs have fewer lead vocals by Rolie. "Don't Give Up" is an insistent anthem with a rousing chorus by Marlette, Rolie, and Chalfant; "Waiting for the World to Change," by Rolie, Chalfant, and Wikso, is a wistful ballad; "I Want to Be the One," a mid-tempo by Marlette, Rolie, and Chalfant, has the familiar vocal give-and-take. "To Have and to Hold," a wedding-ready ballad by Rolie and Chalfant, features a yearning vocal by Chalfant, followed by three rockers by Marlette, Rolie, and Chalfant, all with shared lead vocals: "Livin' It Up," which notes that President Bill Clinton plays saxophone but has marital troubles ("We've got a rocker in the White House/But it could be the doghouse"); "Love Isn't Easy"; and the formulaic sports anthem "Fight for the Right." Then comes a ballad with shared vocals, "Give Me Tonight" by Rolie and Chalfant, followed by the mid-tempo rocker

"Soul of a Man," by Rolie, Chalfant, and Wikso, with shared lead vocals and somewhat clichéd lyrics ("Pick yourself up and get back in it/Why would you quit when you know you can win it"). "What Ya Doing Tonight" is a heartfelt ballad by Marlette, Rolie, and Chalfant, while "Come In Out of the Rain" is a rousing up-tempo by Rolie and Chalfant with shared vocal duties and a lyric that speaks to the band's name and theme. The album concludes with "Long Time Coming," a satisfying mid-tempo by Marlette, Rolie, Ramos, and Chalfant with an R&B sensibility. "It's been a long time coming/Sure feels good to be home."

But Interscope was moving toward Gangsta Rap and refused to release the album. The band eventually got it out, through the British label Music for Nations, in 1995, by which point the musicians had all gone on to other projects.

Ultimately the Storm, while rewarding for the longtime Journey fans who enjoyed their music and notwithstanding their one hit song, came together two years too late to enjoy the success Rolie, Valory, and Smith had previously achieved with Journey. The seventeen-year-olds of 1981 were now consumed with mortgages and professional careers, while the seventeen-year-olds of 1991—at least a large proportion of the white ones, the intended "suburban" audience—were taken more with the grunge rock coming out of Seattle and perhaps the heavy hair rock of Bad English. The band also, frankly, did not have star power; Rolie was well known in industry circles, but he was no John Waite. "There was a stigma attached to the band because people said 'these are members of Journey, but it's not Journey,'" said Valory. "We didn't gain the recognition we deserved. Record executives would say that although it was good music, it wasn't really what they were selling at the time."

*   *   *

With the clarity of hindsight, Neal Schon must have looked back at this period and wondered what would have happened if, rather than joining the Gioeli brothers in Hardline, he had instead joined Rolie, Valory, Smith, and Chalfant from the Storm. The group might even have been able to call itself *Journey*—if Jonathan Cain had come on board, too, perhaps as rhythm guitarist. Schon and Cain constituted a majority of the three-shareholder Elmo Partners, and Schon, Cain, Valory, and Smith were a majority of the six-shareholder Nightmare (Herbie, increasingly frustrated with the absent Steve Perry, would have surely voted his shares with them too).

Something close to this lineup did occur for one night in October 1993 at Bimbo's 365 Club in San Francisco, when "a reunited Journey" featuring Schon, Rolie, Cain, Valory, and Smith, with Chalfant "[s]ubstituting for recalcitrant vocalist Steve Perry," performed at a "roast" of Herbie Herbert. Even Aynsley Dunbar sat in for a few numbers. Joel Selvin called their performance "brief but sensational"; Jancee Dunn of *Rolling Stone* reported that "clone Kevin Chalfont [*sic*] stepped in, and few noticed the difference."

But something even bigger was brewing when Schon—with Herbie as manager—brought together Rolie, Michael Carabello, Michael Shrieve, and Chepito Areas in a band that might have been called "Santana without Santana." Hoping to capitalize on *Santana's Greatest Hits*, the 1974 compilation that was, alongside *Journey's Greatest Hits*, enjoying a resurgence in CD jukeboxes, they named the group "Abraxas" after the second Santana album and topped the bill at the reopening of the Fillmore Auditorium in 1994, Herbie introducing them by noting that "[t]he last band to headline a concert at the Fillmore before releasing an album was the original Santana."

Abraxas caused quite a stir in San Francisco's musical scene. Rolie was nursing a grudge after his most recent experience with Carlos in 1988, noting that a promised album never materialized. So his songs, intended for that Santana album, would now be recorded by Abraxas. And he also nursed a grudge about credit for the original success of Santana, arguing that Carlos had "been trying to rewrite history forever, that he did all this by himself." Carabello agreed, seeing the reunion as an opportunity to set the record straight. "This band wasn't created around Carlos Santana. . . . It was about the music and the people." Columnist Joel Selvin thought Abraxas would force a critical reconsideration of Carlos's career, which he felt had been lackluster since the breakup of the original band.

Tensions soon came to a head between Carlos and his former bandmates. After Carabello, in an obvious snub, called Schon "the most talented" guitarist he had ever played with, Carlos pointedly replied, "We have nothing in common . . . except the music we played together back then," adding that "it's like trying to dance with a cadaver. . . . I wish them well, but this is not who I want to hang around with anymore." When the majority of the original group, who (much like the shareholders of Journey's Nightmare Productions) remained equal partners in the company that controlled the songs, "voted to accept the offer" to sell music for a beer commercial, the spiritually minded Carlos "wrote a letter to the sponsor on his own, threatening to go public with his objections to the use of music to sell alcohol." The brewer withdrew the offer, and his former bandmates took Carlos to court. Michael Shrieve, who had remained with Carlos the longest after 1972's *Caravanserai*, tried to play peacemaker, noting that "there is a strong possibility that Gregg and I will be doing something with Carlos later this year," But Rolie had less patience. "He was asked to sit in on a couple of tracks," Rolie said of Carlos. "He declined."

Heading into Gush Studios in Oakland, Abraxas laid down tracks that heralded a solid return to the musical style of the original Santana, updated with a 1990s rock sensibility. Schon, Shrieve, and Rolie, at least, remained knee-deep in the currents of hard rock; Carabello, Areas, and Johnson had that same Afro-Cuban rhythm of years past. The music is as eclectic as ever, with every member of the band participating in the songwriting except Johnson; Chepito's son Adrian also cowrote a track. There is a guitar-and-drums instrumental tribute to Gabor Szabo, titled for the Hungarian guitarist's last name; and a remake of the Santana classic "Jingo," the conga-heavy song that Carlos first heard when listening to Carabello playing with the *congueros* in Golden Gate Park. AllMusic.com reviewer Gregg Juke called the album "well-crafted, produced, and performed" with "much of the fire that made Carlos Santana's original entrée into the musical nexus of Latin, jazz, and rock so exciting in the first place," opining that "[w]hile Neal Schon more than adequately handles the Santana role on guitar, this recording really highlights the singing, playing, and writing talents of keyboardist/vocalist Gregg Rolie."

Ultimately the band had to change its name to "Abraxas Pool"—to avoid being sued by Santana cover bands! "There were several bands in Europe that were called 'Abraxas,'" explained Rolie. "We wanted to avoid legal problems." The album languished for nearly three years before finally being released in 1997 with a cover featuring Egyptian hieroglyphs designed by Jim Welch, who knew a thing or two about Egyptian imagery, having helped produce all the Journey album covers since *Infinity*. But by the time it came out, Schon and Shrieve had moved on, and Abraxas Pool ceased to exist. The real Santana reunion would have to wait.

Meanwhile, that critical reconsideration of Carlos Santana's career, which Joel Selvin had predicted, never came. In 1999, at the behest of Clive Davis,

Carlos recorded an album of duets with several popular music stars like Dave Matthews, Lauryn Hill, Eagle-Eye Cherry, and Eric Clapton. His duet with Rob Thomas, "Smooth," spent twelve weeks on the *Billboard* Hot 100, while the album enjoyed the same run on the *Billboard* 200. Carlos was launched back into stardom, where he has remained ever since.

"One More," 1994–1997

Those songs are gonna be embedded in everybody's heads and hearts forever.

—*Neal Schon*

And just what had happened to "recalcitrant vocalist Steve Perry," as Joel Selvin called him? It would seem "reclusive" was a better descriptor. After the truncated *Raised on Radio* tour, the singer attended to his family and personal life, both of which he kept very private. He actually considered going to medical school at Stanford—ironically following one of Journey's original guitarists, George Tickner—but "[w]hen it came to cadaver studies, though, I just couldn't do it." Aside from fleeting appearances on albums by Sheena Easton, Crosby, Stills, Nash & Young, and the Irish folk/New Age rock group Clannad, he avoided professional appearances, becoming the subject of repeated "Where Are They Now?" columns in syndicated newspapers. "Where Steve Perry is, and what he is doing is unknown," wrote Joe Limongelli. "I surmise he is relaxing in the California Hills some where [sic], collecting royalties from the great records he made." Bruce Britt called him "conspicuously absent" and "missing in action," listing him among his favorite "Missing Minstrels of Music." Former bandmate Jonathan Cain requested understanding, opining that "Steve was . . . pretty tired of the responsibility of being the sheriff of Journeytown," but Herbie

Herbert considered Perry's absence irresponsible, calling it his "civic duty" to return to Journey.

Perry did check in occasionally by granting an annual interview to the *Journey Force Newsletter*, the house organ of the band's official fan club, formerly run out of the Nightmare office and now maintained by steadfast Journey fan Lora Beard. He reported on his many trips around the San Joaquin Valley on a motorcycle with his father (although he was unclear whether this was his musician birth father or the farmer stepfather who largely raised him); that he enjoyed flying helicopters; how he had successfully buried the hatchet with a former bandmate, visiting Steve Smith's house and speaking approvingly of the drummer's home studio; and that his regular visits to an ailing grandfather in Southern California were slowing progress on his second solo album, which always seemed just around the corner. He also found time to visit his ancestral homeland. "I've driven up the north coast of Portugal," he said, adding "Portugal is nice." But he didn't stay, as he had earlier threatened, nor did he invest in a cork factory, as Ross Valory had suggested.

And then there were the "sightings." When Bon Jovi performed at the Shoreline in Mountain View, California, Perry came onstage for the encore; they sang "Sam Cooke's 'Bring It on Home to Me' and the Four Tops' 'Reach Out, I'll Be There.'" And the maître d' of Masa's, an exclusive restaurant in the city, found Perry a table when he showed up in a limousine.

Rumors circulated that he had lost his voice or his creative spirit. Herbie attributed the singer's longtime absence to "creative debility," saying "I think the long and the short of it is that Steve Perry decided his creative well was dry. . . . It's a bitter pill." A sympathetic Cain told Bruce Britt that "being a singer is very demanding, and Steve wasn't like [the Rolling Stones'] Mick Jagger, just prancing around. He'd bleed a little every time he sang."

Perry was, in fact, recording music. By 1989 he had cut enough tracks for a new solo album, but conflicts with the record label prevented their release for well over a decade. What would have been the album *Against the Wall* yielded seven songs on his eventual greatest hits album, "When You're in Love (for the First Time)," "Against the Wall," "Forever Right or Wrong (Love's Like a River)," "Summer of Luv," "Melody," "Once in a Lifetime, Girl," and "What Was," and three songs eventually attached to a rerelease of a later album, "Can't Stop," "Friends of Mine," and "If You Need Me, Call Me," a rerecording of the Alien Project demo that had gotten Herbie's attention back in

1977. All save the Alien Project demo were written with Randy Goodrum, with whom he had collaborated for 1984's *Street Talk*. Additional cowriters included legendary guitarist-producer Michael Landau; "Oh Sherrie" cowriter Bill Cuomo; Randy Jackson and Larrie Londin, who had worked with Perry on Journey's *Raised on Radio*; Rick Nowels, a veteran songwriter and producer who had worked with Stevie Nicks and Belinda Carlisle; Nashville-based country songwriter Josh Leo; and Alien Project drummer Craig Krampf. The music, taken together, demonstrates a developing maturity for Perry's solo material. It is both a product of its time and also groundbreaking, with full, soaring vocals and complex instrumentation.

When sixty-year-old San Francisco musical mainstay and legendary rock impresario Bill Graham died in a helicopter accident in 1991, prompting Neal Schon to dedicate a Hardline song to his memory, Steve Perry briefly came out of retirement to take the stage with Schon and Cain to perform "Faithfully" and "Lights" at the tribute concert in Golden Gate Park. The crowd was subdued during the performance, which was understandable because not all were Journey fans and it was an outdoor, daytime show. Perry twice held out the microphone, expecting the audience to sing the chorus of "Faithfully," but the response was tepid and frankly embarrassing; it did not help matters that the singer had forgotten some of the words to the song's second verse. A few in the crowd—about one in ten—waved their arms to the music. During "Lights," Perry almost begged the audience to join him for the refrain; it was about their hometown, after all. "Just one time, please sing it," he implored, to no avail. Schon delivered a forlorn solo, and some observers seemed as sorry for the diminished Journey as they were for the loss of Bill Graham. Maybe if they had bass and drums and better amplification or they appeared later in the evening, with lasers, strobe, and their trademark giant screens, the audience might have responded. Maybe it was the musical key: Cain and Schon detuned both songs below their original versions to accommodate Perry's maturing voice. Perry ended the second song saying "God bless you, Bill, we love you," and Cain and Schon something similar; Cain put his arm around the shoulders of a clearly demoralized Perry as they walked offstage past Herbie and former Journey tour manager Pat Morrow.

Steve Perry needed a comeback as much for his own self-esteem as to meet the demands of his adoring fans. In 1993 he returned to the studio to record what actually became his second solo album. Released on July 19, 1994, *For the Love of Strange Medicine* shows a Perry with a raspier and slightly lower voice than the one he had displayed on *Raised on Radio* but still clear, formidable, and in the tenor range. Like *Street Talk*, the album is an exploration of Perry's musical interests, but now they are significantly broader, emphasizing blues, Motown, and even some jazz, as in the intro to "Somewhere There's Hope." But the album begins with a strong rocker, "You Better Wait," about the dangers of Hollywood for the young, starry-eyed teenagers who flock there seeking fame and fortune. The song peaked at number 6 on the *Billboard* rock chart on July 16 (and number 10 on the pop chart a week later). "Missing You," a ballad with long, well-crafted vocals cowritten by vocalist Tim Miner, hit number 24. The album peaked at number 15 on the *Billboard* 200 on August 6 and was certified gold on September 20. The tour included Hardline's Todd Jensen on bass, twenty-three-year-old Lincoln Brewster on guitar, Moyes Lucas on drums, and Paul Taylor on keys.

Reviewers were not impressed. Tracy Collins of the *Pittsburgh Post-Gazette* complained that "[t]he disc is filled with overwrought ballads that begin to grate quickly, especially when you want to hear the screaming guitar of Neal Schon, who served as the perfect balance for Perry's voice so long ago." Sympathetic Selvin lamented that the album "disappeared virtually without a trace, almost on release." The brief tour—truncated when the singer developed bronchitis—was a treat for his most die-hard fans but few else. With a setlist that included eleven Journey hits, six songs from his solo repertoire, Sam Cooke's "Cupid," the Everly Brothers' "Let It Be Me," and Marvin Gaye and Tammy Terrell's "Ain't Nothing Like the Real Thing," Perry showed he could still do the job but was less energetic than during his Journey tours, mostly keeping to center stage and nervously clutching the microphone wire in his alternate hand. The high notes also weren't as high; the band played the Journey hits a half step below the recordings.

And the show was campy, which drew the ire of rock critics, especially when he asked the audience to sing, "I miss you Stevie," joking with the jealous men in attendance that "[i]f you were up here you'd do it too." Sporting a horse-tail of hair with neatly shaved sides, just before his Journey set he performed a playful act with a topcoat and tails that descended from curtain rigging: in a reverse striptease, he sexily put it on, removed his scrunchie and handed it to a devoted female fan in the front row—from which he collected lots of flowers at the end. Reviewer Ed Masley called him a "master of lame" (earning the ire of his readership); Selvin, perhaps unfairly, went after the band, calling Lincoln Brewster "some hapless youth, old enough to have learned guitar to Journey records," and Moyes Lucas "a merely adequate drummer [who] attempted to recreate the fluid grace of sturdy Steve Smith," finally declaring the show, in a kiss of death, "unintentionally hilarious."

But for the women who came to the show with flowers for their idol, it was anything but. Whether or not they had seats close enough to the stage to give them to him at his curtain call, these fans knew, at some level, that their relationship with the man on stage was one-sided. The reason they brought the flowers was the same reason little girls go to the ballet dressed in tutus: it builds anticipation, helps them feel connected to the performers during the show, and leaves them with a warm feeling afterward. Bringing flowers for Steve Perry helped these women recapture the feelings they had when they first saw him with Journey, whether that was on an actual stage back in the '80s, on a lipstick-covered poster from *Tiger Beat* in a junior high locker, or in one of Journey's atrocious music videos.

*   *   *

Steve Perry's latest solo album may have met with little success in comparison with his comeback tour, but then, neither did Jonathan Cain or Neal Schon meet with much success in their own solo efforts. The eleven instrumental tracks on Schon's 1995 album *Beyond the Thunder*, released by Higher Octave Music, explored the guitarist's blues roots, this time with more of a jazzy feel. Absent was much of the hard rock he had been doing with Bad English and Hardline. Schon and Cain coproduced the album at Cain's Wild Horse Studio in Novato, California, and cowrote all eleven songs, except for two which Schon wrote on his own. Cain provided keyboards, Steve Smith provided drums on five of the tracks, and old friends Chepito Areas and Michael Carabello sat in on a couple of the tunes. Ross Muir called it "a beautiful 'world music' instrumental work that showcases Schon at his most melodically expressive and, at times, delicate; set within interesting ambient, soul-pop, Latin and jazz rhythms and lighter arrangements that let the 'Schon sound' truly shine."

The former members of Journey seemed to be communicating with one another through their music. The final track of Perry's *For the Love of Strange Medicine*, "Anyway," contained a lyric that seemed almost an entreaty to Perry's fellow Journeymen: "I'd like to say I'm sorry/I'd like to make amends." And in the liner notes to *Beyond the Thunder*, Schon wrote, "I think Steve Perry is going to like this record." Such communication was necessary because there was precious little of the traditional kind. Indeed, Cain was actually denied a backstage pass to see Perry when the singer played the Warfield in San Francisco on his *Strange Medicine* tour.

When they weren't communicating through lyrics, liner notes, or denials of credentials, they were communicating through lawyers and official documents. In early 1994, acting as president of Nightmare Productions, Herbie wrote the Elmo Partners—Perry, Schon, and Cain—to officially terminate their license to perform and record as Journey, noting that none of them had "actively engaged in a professional musical career utilizing the name 'Journey'" since 1987. His date was wrong; in fact, the three had performed as Journey at the Bill Graham Tribute in 1991. But his sentiment was correct, and there were ample grounds to terminate the contract. In serving notice, Herbie singled out "Mr. Perry," who "has consistently frustrated all attempts of the group known as 'Journey' to perform, thus preventing successful exploitation of the rights licensed to you by Nightmare, Inc." With that, Journey was again controlled by Nightmare Productions—consisting of Herbie, Perry, Schon, Cain, Smith, and Valory as equal shareholders.

With a Journey reunion in mind—using Kevin Chalfant as lead vocalist if necessary—Herbie convened a shareholder meeting. He and the company's lawyer were physically present, Schon and Valory were present "by proxy" (which meant they authorized Herbie to vote on their behalf), Perry was notified but did not attend, and Cain and Smith sent letters agreeing to a shareholder resolution to accept the termination of the Elmo contract and "re-form Journey." Herbie then proceeded to vote all shares (except Perry's) in favor of the resolution "that this corporation re-form 'Journey' as a performing and recording group."

Despite his lack of involvement in the machinations at Nightmare, Perry had in fact been seriously considering working with Journey again. During his *Strange Medicine* tour he "was missing more and more being the singer in Journey than I ever thought I would." And he was certainly aware of what Herbie was doing. "They're putting together, I think, the band, they're working on securing the name," he told the Canadian television show *Much*

Music. "They have a singer who is very similar in style to mine, I think in their minds."

In early 1995 Cain received an unexpected phone call. "Hey, Jon, it's Steve," said the voice at the other end that Cain knew so well. "I've been thinking that maybe we should talk about getting back together." Perry remembers it differently, saying that Cain was away at a golf tournament when he called; wife Liz answered and passed on the message. After meeting over coffee, the two reached out to John Kalodner, Sony* Music's head of A&R (artists & repertoire), who had first achieved success with Geffen Records in the 1980s, when he helped Aerosmith return to superstardom. Kalodner talked Perry into agreeing to reunite with the entire classic band—all the musician shareholders of Nightmare—rather than trying to reinstate the Elmo Partners contract. Perry later called Kalodner "the Henry Kissinger of rock," invoking the Nixon administration's national security advisor and secretary of state who had negotiated between Egypt, Saudi Arabia, and Israel during the Yom Kippur War, implying that convincing Perry to work with Schon, Cain, Valory, and Smith again may have been as difficult to achieve as peace in the Middle East. Even Gregg Rolie was invited to participate, "but friction with Perry ended his involvement," according to Joel Selvin. "'Some people get along better with others,' said Schon."

Perry had only one condition this time, and it didn't involve being in total control, as had been the case a decade earlier when they recorded *Raised on Radio.* As far as the singer was concerned, Herbie had to go. The manager's attitude toward the singer, expressed in press interviews and most recently in his letter to the Elmo Partners, was too much for Perry to abide working with him again. But that was just fine for Herbie, who was more than happy to retire as Journey's full-time manager while continuing to serve as president of Nightmare. The group hired Irving Azoff, the longtime manager of the Eagles who had recently engineered the *Hell Freezes Over* reunion of that multiplatinum band.

Before long, five members of Journey were meeting "under wraps in the Novato home studio of Jonathan Cain," with Schon telling Joel Selvin, "We're getting along great." The summer of 1995 found them at Ocean Way Recorders in Los Angeles. "We were supposed to play on a particular day in September, though we were going to get into town the night before and set up

---

* The Japanese conglomerate had purchased Columbia Records in 1988 and thus owned the contract with Journey.

the instruments on the rehearsal stage," reported Steve Smith. "But you can't get people to just set up their stuff and not start playing, so it ended up that the four of us set up and started jamming right away . . . and then Steve Perry called to find out what was going on, and we said, 'Come on over.' So it actually started a day early," he said. "[I]t felt really good . . . the chemistry was instantaneous." Perry admitted that "we have our conflicts [but] we got together anyway and were able to move out of it and move forward with it." The group found themselves working full time again, "11:00 to 5:00, five days a week," according to Smith, who found that the rhythm section was again respected as part of the songwriting process. Although Perry, Schon, and Cain—the "core of writers"—often still wrote the music as a trio in Cain's studio, they left out the drum and bass parts so Valory and Smith could add their own creativity. Smith, now a more confident, seasoned drummer, even insisted they use a click track, avoiding what had been a major bone of contention a decade earlier during the *Raised on Radio* sessions. And their producer, Kevin Shirley, made them rehearse the completed songs together as a band before recording them. "[T]here was a lot of grumbling, but we did it," Smith said.

Sony Music released Journey's *Trial by Fire* on October 22, 1996, to multiple "launch parties" at Hard Rock Café locations around the country, followed quickly by the usual critical panning. Despite "Schon's sometimes-meandering solos and Perry's often weak, overwrought lyrics," Tracy Collins of the *Pittsburgh Post-Gazette* found "enough exceptions here to make you really want to like the disc." Jeremy Helligar of *People* magazine heard "nothing revolutionary or unpredictable" in the album, admitting that "had these fortysomethings embraced grunge, trip hop or some other newfangled sound, it would have been as unbecoming as trying to squeeze into their old skin-tight hip-huggers." But Perry had a ready-made reply. "We're going to sink or swim being what we are," he told Melinda Newman, "and not by trying to reinvent ourselves and not by trying to be the flavor of the month."

The album begins with "Message of Love," an up-tempo rocker cowritten by lyricist and Carpenters alumnus John Bettis, starting with a screeching guitar lick followed by a haunting vocal chorus, and a nod to "Separate Ways (Worlds Apart)." The song made it to number 18 on the *Billboard* mainstream rock chart. It is followed by "One More," a heavier rocker with a harsh biblical lyric ("Wicked prophets kill . . . /Holy vengeance is the justice of hell").

"When You Love a Woman," a piano-driven ballad with violin accompaniment, became the album's bona fide hit when it peaked at number 12 on the *Billboard* Hot 100—and number 1 on its Adult Contemporary chart—on December 13, 1996. With a lyric and sound not unlike the classics "Open Arms" and "Faithfully," the song received copious airplay and proclaimed the band's return; David Browne of *Entertainment Weekly* said it would "make a perfect wedding song for old fans preparing to march down the aisle" (he was right; I was among such "old fans"). And despite coming out in the era of the hip "Macarena" dance and the screechingly insistent tunes of Alanis Morissette, it earned the band their very first Grammy nomination in the "Best Pop Performance by a Group or Duo with Vocal" category (they lost to another "reunion," the Beatles' "Free as a Bird" from their *Anthology 1*).

"If He Should Break Your Heart," a bluesy mid-tempo, also made the Adult Contemporary chart, rising to number 21 on April 18, 1997. Then follows "Forever in Blue," a rocker with some bluesy overtones and interesting vocal rhythms; "Castles Burning," a rocker about a failing marriage, something four members of Journey were now intimately familiar with, and which includes an urgent Perry voiceover (*You know I love you, you know you're my girl, I'd never hurt you*); "Don't Be Down on Me Baby," a ballad with extended vocal notes; and "Still She Cries," an easy-listening ballad with acoustic guitar and piano. Next up is "Colors of the Spirit," a mid-tempo attempt at communion with Native American spiritualism by Perry, Cain, Schon, and Bettis; "When I Think of You," a piano-and-vocal ballad by Perry and Cain that Perry later said was a tribute to his late mother; and "Easy to Fall," a ballad with string accompaniment recorded at Skywalker Sound in Marin County with a vocal similarity to "Don't Be Down on Me Baby." Then comes the rocker "Can't Tame the Lion," featuring an ironically tame Schon on electric guitar, which made it to number 33 on the *Billboard* Mainstream Rock chart on February 22, 1997; and "It's Just the Rain," a ballad by Perry and Cain with rainfall sound effects.

Finally, the title track, an easygoing ballad with acoustic guitar and a haunting lyric inspired by the New Testament ("Let the light shine out of darkness/Fallen down but not destroyed") sums up the writers' feelings about the reunion. The song also contains the somewhat ambiguous line "Hello, Mr. Moon ... /I've come back to talk to you." Unconfirmed rumors had it that Perry had entered Alcoholics Anonymous at some point in the late

1980s, partly explaining the difficulties the singer had had finishing his second solo album; "Mr. Moon" may refer to a famous former astronaut he met
in a celebrity-sensitive AA meeting, possibly his sponsor.

The Jim Welch–designed album cover includes multiple themes, much
like Santana's *Abraxas*: a baby in a beached boat by a lagoon with palm
tree, playing with a string held by a cat-headed, bird-feathered woman; two
shirtless "natives" (perhaps representing the song "Colors of the Spirit")
standing atop a cloud and pouring something ("Just the Rain"?) from urns;
an Earthlike planet on the horizon; and in the foreground, tipped over and
slightly buried on the beach, a jar of clay with the Journey scarab affixed to
the side.

Listeners who did not quickly remove the compact disc from their players
were treated to a common practice of the era: after thirty seconds of silence
there is a "hidden" track: "Baby I'm a Leavin' You," a reggae by Perry, Schon,
and Cain that bears no resemblance to either Journey's "I'm Gonna Leave
You" from *Look into the Future* or "Babe I'm Gonna Leave You," the Led
Zeppelin/Joan Baez tune. And those who bought the album in Japan (or had
the "Japanese version" shipped in) found a "bonus" track, also by "the Three,"
the fast-paced grunge rocker "I Can See It in Your Eyes." This one was later
covered by garage punk rock band Guff on their 2007 album *Symphony of
Voices*, featuring none other than Steve Perry on backing vocals.

The album debuted in third place on the *Billboard* 200 chart on November
9, 1996, behind Westside Connection's *Bow Down* in second and *The Best
of Van Halen Volume 1* in first. This was Journey's highest debut, but it was
also the album's peak. It fell steadily over the next twenty-seven weeks, finally
leaving the chart the following May—but not without first being certified gold
and platinum on December 12, 1996, marking a successful reunion for a band
that so many critics and fans had long thought finished.

*   *   *

When a reunion album is released, can a reunion tour be far behind? The
members of the band said they were game, and they certainly seemed to
be getting on well enough. Manager Irving Azoff's other major rock group,
the Eagles, had resumed a full-time touring schedule after their reunion
album, so all signs pointed toward an opportunity for longtime fans to see

their favorite band in person again and for a new generation to witness the Journey magic live. Perry told Melinda Newman that the group would tour in 1997 because "[t]his time feels so much better." Schon predicted an arena-and-stadium tour, Cain adding that "we sound big in a coliseum and our music sounds glorious there and that's where we belong." But prospects for a reunion tour were dashed when they learned that Steve Perry, who had been injured while hiking in Hawaii prior to recording the album, needed to undergo hip replacement surgery. "Steve Perry isn't physically up to touring," reported syndicated columnist Brad Schmitt. "He apparently injured his hip a year or so ago, and it's still bugging him."

But Perry refused to schedule the surgery. The singer might have been leery of general anesthesia; a small percentage of all surgery patients die "on the table" due to medical accident, malpractice, or just bad luck, and even wealthy celebrities, with top-flight care, were not impervious to such mishaps—and certainly not impervious to such fears. He had kept the pain at bay with physical therapy during the *Trial by Fire* sessions, but the prospect of jumping around onstage night after night in one town after another was a different matter entirely.

Cain, for his part, was not short of ideas. Remembering the band's experience with Kenny Sykaluk, the boy with leukemia for whom they had premiered "Only the Young," he suggested Perry go public about his condition and come onstage at an award show or other venue to raise money for a charity, perhaps one that would benefit children with disabilities. And if he didn't want to tour, would he at least be willing to record another album? But these ideas mostly fell on deaf ears. Perry did join the band on a soundstage to film a video for "When You Love a Woman," but he had to retreat to a private room between takes to have his hip packed in ice.

Perry felt that his medical decisions were not the band's business, which was technically true; his bandmates could not force him to undergo surgery. But the singer also kept them in the dark during this critical time while their new music was on the airwaves, not telling them or their new manager what he was thinking. Again the other members of the band were left waiting for a lead singer who perhaps, they now started to wonder, had never really intended to tour with them at all. "We had our high-octane engine running, but the driver wasn't even near the vehicle," Cain said. "Soon the gas tank was empty, and the car shut down."

Even so, Perry was working—just not with Journey. He was happy to go into the studio to record a song with David Foster for the film *Quest for Camelot*. Ironically, the song was titled "I Stand Alone," which Ross Muir called "a sweeping, fully orchestrated ballad featuring a striking and . . . defiant vocal." Still, manager Azoff told Australian journalist Andrew McNeice in November 1997 that the singer was "on medical leave" from Journey. "[C]ontrary to rumors, the band has not broken up."

There is some evidence that Steve Perry never intended to go out on tour with Journey but merely wanted to record the album and move on—and that was certainly Herbie's opinion. Perry had long maintained that the grueling life on the road is what caused him to leave Journey, first in 1983, after the *Frontiers* tour, and then in 1987, when he had prematurely ended the *Raised on Radio* tour. An album alone would be timely and lucrative, and *Trial by Fire* was certainly both of those things. Perry had probably been willing to engage in promotional activities from the get-go but truly was sidelined by the injury; after that, he may have used the injury as an excuse to avoid touring. Indeed, even after eventually getting the surgery, he did not go out on tour or make any attempt to rejoin his bandmates.

Perry was hardly the first rock star to prefer recording to touring. After British multi-instrumentalist Mike Oldfield released *Tubular Bells* in 1973 on then fledgling Virgin Records, he simply returned to his parents' home. He refused to tour or do any publicity events despite having a top record, with one song, featured in the hit film *The Exorcist*, becoming a top-10 hit in the United States. But Oldfield just wanted to sit in the country and build a duck pond. More famously, in 1966 the Beatles left the road for good, and their subsequent albums sold well anyway.

Finally, in early 1998, Schon, Cain, and Valory, with the support of Azoff and the implicit approval of Nightmare coshareholders Herbie and Smith, decided they needed to move on—as Journey without Steve Perry. Cain was tasked with making the phone call. And thus, the reunion that had begun when Perry called Cain now ended when Cain called Perry. "We're not going to go behind your back," he said. "So if you hear we're auditioning for new singers, it's true." The band did not have the right to force the singer to undergo surgery, but by the same token, Perry did not have the right to prevent them from moving on without him. "Do what you have to do," Perry told Cain, after pleading his case to no avail. "Just lose my phone number."

As with the start of the reunion, Perry remembered it differently. While admitting that he was "in denial about" the seriousness of his hip injury, he spent much of that period going from doctor to doctor, hoping for a better prognosis that would allow him to avoid major surgery. "And then finally, months went by, and the band got impatient. I got a phone call from Jon, and I could tell Neal was on the phone . . . I could hear him breathing, I think. And Jon was telling me, 'We want to know what you wanna do. We've tried out a few singers.'"

The timing of when they started auditioning singers mattered. If Cain called Perry to let him know that they were *about to* audition singers, then that was honorable, and Perry was being petulant. But if Cain called to tell Perry they had *already started* auditioning singers, as an attempt at some sort of leverage, then Perry's request that Cain "lose my number" was an understandable reaction. Of course, Perry remembered that differently too. "Don't call it Journey. Because if you do, you will fracture the stone. And I don't think I'll be able to come back to it if you break it," he said. "If you crack it—it's got so much integrity. We've worked so hard." For Perry, Journey was Neal Schon, Jonathan Cain, and himself. Others were expendable, as he had shown—but not any of "the Three." So if they moved on with another singer, as far as he was concerned, that would "fracture the stone"—it wouldn't be Journey.

Getting the votes at Nightmare to reform Journey without Steve Perry was not a problem, and the singer knew it. But he still had considerable leverage in the fine print of the Elmo Partners contract. Although that partnership—Perry, Schon, and Cain—no longer had a license to record and perform as Journey, their legal commitments to one another were still binding. Perry might have prevented Schon and Cain from moving on as members of Journey—or at least bogged them down in drawn-out legal proceedings.

And so, the Elmo Partners made an agreement among themselves to satisfy Perry and allow the guitarist and keyboardist to continue as the "New Journey." Schon and Cain would be required to give Perry fully half their earnings from the band's first two albums and tours; the former lead singer would then get 25 percent for the third album and tour, and 12.5 percent for every album and tour thereafter. Schon and Cain also agreed that Perry would be able to edit (and potentially veto) any Journey press release related to a new lead singer for one year.

To ensure that Schon and Cain didn't pay Perry from the band's collective revenues—still controlled by Nightmare, which Perry co-owned—they were required to form a new, separate company together. As a dig at Perry, they called it Nomota LLC, the acronym standing for "No More Tails," referring to Perry's trademark retro stage outfit.

But clearly Perry was having the last laugh. Herbie, astonished at the sheer moxie of what he saw as a cash grab, compared Schon and Cain to prostitutes and Perry their pimp. As always, he was colorful and bombastic. "They're working the street for him," he said.

Drum Solo
Steve Smith

I've been fired from a lot of gigs. And I learned a lot from those situations.

—*Steve Smith*

"One of the reasons that one plays music," said Steve Smith, is to "get beyond the everyday experience of life and you just go to this, like, spiritual zone where the musicians are meeting in some other place and then the music is happening and you're just watching, in a way."

Whitman, Massachusetts, is about as far away from California as one can get without crossing the ocean. But this leafy suburb of Boston is similar to Lafayette, Palo Alto, and Hanford in other ways. Although it lacks Northern California's ubiquitous mountains and Spanish mission heritage, during the 1950s and 1960s it was a suburb not unlike many other suburbs around the country, with heritage aplenty—including the origin of the Toll House chocolate chip cookie.

Stephen Bruce Smith, born in 1954, was raised on Whitman's Harvard Street, which ran two miles from downtown Whitman's tony, upper-middle-class colonial houses all the way to rural East Bridgewater, with its streams and fields and barns. Smith might have spent an idyllic childhood playing ball with Harvard Street's many other children of the postwar baby boom, but instead he took up the drums. Inspired while still in the fourth grade at an assembly at his elementary school, he started lessons with local drum teacher Billy Flanigan, at a drum shop around the corner from his dad's job at the *Brockton Enterprise*. Flanigan was a jazz drummer, so Steve identified early on as a jazz drummer—until he heard Ginger Baker and Ringo Starr and Charlie Watts, who gave him an appreciation for rock drumming. He got his first drum set in the sixth grade, and joined his first band in eighth grade, a group of kids called the Road Runners. In high school, still taking lessons, he played with the Bridgewater State College Band just down the road and earned extra cash playing drums for a circus. After graduation, dad Bruce and mom Lorraine convinced him to apply for admission to Boston's prestigious Berklee School of Music, about an hour away on the city's commuter rail line, known to locals as the "T." He got in, which gave him the opportunity to study with noted jazz drummer Alan Dawson, among others. "The best thing about Berklee was that there were so many musicians," Smith told *Modern Drummer*'s Robyn Flans. "Every night I could find people to play with . . . whether it was a gig or just a jam session." Already good, his time at Berklee gave Smith the polish and experience to land his first paying gigs, including two years in a big band led by Lin Biviano, a trumpeter who had played for Buddy Rich and Maynard Ferguson. "We toured the East Coast and the Midwest." When a full scholarship beckoned at the University of Tulsa, he tried it out but quickly returned to Boston, forfeiting the money.

Smith's professional career took off quickly after Berklee. In 1976, thanks to a friend's recommendation, he snagged an audition in New York City with jazz violinist (and Frank Zappa alumnus) Jean-Luc Ponty, winning a spot with the accomplished star. "I was able to get the gig with Ponty because I read well. He put a lot of charts in front of me, I mean, odd [time signatures] and some very difficult music, and I could read everything." Smith moved out to the West Coast to record Ponty's album *Enigmatic Ocean*, joined by noted guitarists Allan Holdsworth and Daryl Stuermer (also recommended by Zappa) and Australian pianist Allan Zavod (who had been a professor at Berklee prior to Smith's time there). "It was a great experience," Smith recalled. "I had to be real consistent and I was learning a lot." But he found Ponty's authoritarian style grating: "one thing I learned that I didn't want, was to work for somebody who was always telling me what to do and telling everyone what to play." After Smith joined fellow bandmates in complaints, Ponty fired the lot of them.

Smith moved on to serve as sideman for the Dutch progressive rock band Focus—one of the many bands that had once sought Aynsley Dunbar—when they recorded their album *Focus con Proby* with singer-songwriter P. J. Proby. He then found himself in an enviable position: his talents were sought by Grammy-winning jazz trumpeter Freddie Hubbard as well as guitarist Ronnie Montrose, an alumnus of Van Morrison's and Edgar Winter's bands whom rock promoter Bill Graham had pushed to go solo. "I really wanted to play with Freddie, because he's a great trumpet player. But . . . I didn't want to be just a sideman. Ronnie approached things like a band." He took the plunge and went with Montrose. "Ronnie's band was more group oriented and he would let me have a lot to say and let me play more." The choice also took Smith deeper into rock drumming, for which he had developed a taste after working with Focus. "I would've loved to have played with Freddie Hubbard, but I had to make a choice and I just somehow had the feeling that I could always do that or something like that," he recalled. "So for me, playing with Ronnie Montrose was a more unique opportunity."

In the winter of 1978, Smith went out on tour with Montrose, opening for the Greg Kihn Band. Montrose had just recorded an all-instrumental, jazz-rock fusion album, *Open Fire*, so despite his being very much a rock guitarist, Smith's jazz and swing background was a natural fit for his 1978 tour. Pianist Jim Alcivar and bassist Brad Stephenson rounded out the group, which sold out a February 23 appearance at the County Fairgrounds in Reno. "The rhythm section consisting of Steve Smith on drums and Brad Stephenson on bass was dynamic," gushed local reporter Gary Iratcabal in the *Reno Gazette-Journal*. "The final encore would have been a fairly normal closing except that 'Rocky Road' contains a drum solo performed by Smith that was the best solo this reviewer has heard yet . . . making maximum use of the drum kit which included a double bass."

That writer also unwittingly included in his review a promising note for Steve Smith's future. "On March 1, Montrose will join Journey and Van Halen for a 10-week tour of the eastern states." Join them they did, and the praise continued. "All three bands had excellent drummers and all three performed excellent solos," wrote Jeff Barcus about Journey's Dunbar, Alex Van Halen, and Smith in the *South Bend Tribune* after the March 19 show at Morris Civic Auditorium, down the street from Notre Dame. And in Murray, Kentucky, Montrose "stole the show" with his "fine back-up band," according to Steve

Wingfield of the *Paducah Sun*. These were important notices, considering how Journey was coming to dominate the reporting as their *Infinity* tour progressed.

Smith's future arrived that fall when Joel Selvin reported in the *San Francisco Chronicle* that the Montrose drummer would be replacing Dunbar. After recording the unaired episode of the *King Biscuit Flower Hour* radio show with Journey, he joined the band as their permanent drummer when they started their next tour in Reno, sans Montrose and Van Halen.

There was no doubt that Smith could adequately fill Dunbar's seat. His background as a jazz drummer, now tempered with his rock experience with Focus and Montrose, made him even more attractive to a hard rock band still spending much of their stage time playing the progressive rock and jazz fusion numbers that had filled their first three albums. As Steve Perry said, "Smith was a fusion drummer who was with Montrose . . . that's where we saw him play every night and I turned to Neal and said 'this is the guy we should have in our band. This is what we need.'"

But the choice undermined the band's arguments for Dunbar's incompatibility. If Dunbar was wrong for Journey because he was too progressive, too jazz oriented, why replace him with another progressive, jazz-oriented drummer?

Because he was raised in America. According to Smith, "I had a natural ability to play the feels of US music simply because I was brought up in the United States. It's . . . my culture and my times, and so I was able to play with an R&B-ish feel, if that was necessary. And I think that was the issue. Aynsley's feel wasn't really what Steve Perry liked. He wanted more of a rhythm and blues kind of feel." Dunbar may have had origins in the British blues, but Smith had origins in American *everything*.

Smith's desire for a freedom in his playing, the individualism in his technique which drove his resentment of Jean Luc-Ponty's authoritarianism and pushed him to choose the more democratic Ronnie Montrose over Freddie Hubbard, would seem a poor fit for a band that ostensibly jettisoned Dunbar for too much independence in his solos. Still, the decision was made, and Smith handled his Journey duties with aplomb, continuing his studies of the accomplished rock drummers of the era. "I was listening to everyone from Charlie Watts to investigating how Nigel Olsen played ballads with Elton John." The results can be heard on every drum line from *Evolution* to *Frontiers* and earned him the nicknames "machine gun" and "Animal" (after the drummer from the Muppet Show band).

*   *   *

Steve Smith's solo forays began while still quite busy with Journey. He joined longtime Santana member Tom Coster—who had replaced Gregg Rolie in Santana back in 1972—on the keyboardist's solo albums *T.C.* in 1981 and *Ivory Expeditions* in 1983. (Few at the time seemed to notice the irony of pairing Rolie's replacement with Dunbar's; they certainly did not ask for the comparison by titling either of the albums, or any subsequent collaboration, *Replacements*.) Then Smith returned to his first musical love, heading back east to reunite with bassist Tim Landers and saxophonist David Wilczewski, friends from the Berklee School, to form a jazz band called Vital Information, with guitarists Dean Brown and Mike Stern. Granted a contract with Columbia Records, they recorded their eponymous first album in September 1982, immediately following Journey's *Escape* tour, and released it in January 1983. When Journey finally took a real break later that year, Smith brought Vital Information together again, replacing Stern with Dutch guitarist Eef Elbers, and went out for a few dates. When they headed back to the studio in Rhode Island, Journey's Kevin Elson helped with the mixing, and Jim Welch—responsible for so many Journey album covers—provided the art. *Orion*, their second effort, was released in September 1984, following another Vital Information national tour. With all of this, Smith still made himself available to friends in the business. When his Marin County neighbor Barry Jekowsky formed a classical ensemble called Primary Percussion, of course Smith agreed to sit in. (Jekowsky went on to found the California Symphony in 1986.) And when fusion bassist Jeff Berlin needed a drummer for his first solo album, *Champion*, produced by Smith's old bandleader Ronnie Montrose in 1985, of course he agreed to do that one too. And he brought an accomplished guitarist in tow: Neal Schon, who sat in on the song "Subway Music."

Smith did not miss a step after being fired from Journey in 1985. In addition to his continued work with Vital Information, he joined Steps Ahead, a jazz combo where he was just one of several talented musicians and could develop in relative anonymity without the Journey audience that often attended Vital Information shows, hoping for the occasional rendition of Journey drum showcases like "Line of Fire" or "Dead or Alive." He kept busy with lucrative session work, playing with artists as varied as Shaw/Blades, Y&T (managed by former Journey comanager Lou Bramy), Zucchero,

Mariah Carey, Stanley Clarke, Allan Holdsworth, and Randy Brecker, as well as benefit shows for causes like the McCandless family, a teen crisis hotline in Palo Alto, and the Hamilton Family Shelter in San Francisco's Haight neighborhood. His continuing friendships with Ross Valory and Gregg Rolie led to his involvement in the Storm, and he remained close with Schon and Jonathan Cain, regularly sitting in on their projects as well, including the Herbie Herbert roast in 1993—a fact that no doubt helped when he rejoined Journey in 1995 for the reunion.

When Journey moved on without Steve Perry, Smith decided to leave Journey too (although, as in 1985, he kept his shares in the company). This was not out of some sense of loyalty to the singer nor because he felt that the band could not move on without Perry but simply because without Perry in Journey, he was more interested in continuing his career as a jazz drummer. He saw, perhaps better than his bandmates, that *Trial by Fire* was a temporary reunion. He was willing to be in Journey with Steve Perry but didn't see the point of it without him. Even during the recording sessions, despite feeling like a respected, equal partner, he had approached the work more as a session drummer, with detachment, and to avoid the emotional issues given the musicians' long history together.

After leaving Journey for the second time, Smith continued to be active and prolific. When he wasn't recording and touring with Vital Information, he was working with a new band of his own creation, Buddy's Buddies, a tribute to the music of the legendary drummer Buddy Rich. He toured abroad—including such destinations as China, Russia, and Britain—and offered drum clinics around the United States, where he became known in performance for a bit he called "Mr. High Hat"—a drum solo demonstrating the "countless sounds that can be achieved solely with a high hat," as one reviewer put it, "juggling the sticks while playing, using props, and even using his foot!" Otherwise, he could often be found in San Francisco at Yoshi's Jazz Club on Jack London Square or at Jazz at Pearl's, sitting in with the likes of the Michael Zilber Quartet or George Brooks's Summit. He filmed a DVD, *Steve Smith's Drumset Technique/History of the U.S. Beat*, and he joined a group called Yo Miles!, in tribute to the music of Miles Davis, formed by guitarist Henry Kaiser and trumpeter Wadada Leo Smith. His personal life was also a success in these years. Although his first marriage to Susan Gurnack had ended in divorce, he was remarried, to Diane Kiernan.

"Signs of Life," 1998–2003

It's music they grew up to. Fell in love with. Had sex with. Got married to. Graduated from high school or college with. It's a moment frozen in time, and when they remember those moments, they remember those songs.

—*Jonathan Cain*

The years following the decision to move on without Steve Perry were characterized by one failed attempt after another to restore the band to superstardom. While popular culture fetishized the hits sung by their former lead singer, the "new" Journey did the yeoman's work of touring, year after year, literally touring their new singer's voice away. Without planning to or desiring it, Journey—like most rock music—had entered a period in their history where they were best described as a "nostalgia act." Their core fan base was in or near middle age and mostly set in their tastes. As teenagers, their identities still in development, these fans had greeted new albums with a sense of excitement, tearing off the plastic and opening the cardboard slit to savor the smell of new vinyl before enjoying that tactile moment of lifting the disc out of the sleeve to place it carefully on the turntable, all the while anticipating the first sounds. Now in their thirties, forties, and fifties, their musical tastes represented a bygone era that defined their generation. It was still a part of their identities, but it represented their youth. They wanted to hear this music on the radio (usually on "oldies" or "classic rock" stations) and were willing

to revisit that feeling by seeing the band in concert. But by and large, they had
no interest in the band's new output.

There are basically three categories of nostalgia acts. The first category, that
of either the "one-hit wonder" or the band with only a couple of very recognizable hits, defines musical acts past their prime that are relegated to appear
as opening acts for the bigger concert draws, eating proverbial crumbs from
the master's table. An anecdote from the popular animated television program
The Simpsons demonstrates this phenomenon. The character Homer Simpson
goes to see the Canadian band Bachman-Turner Overdrive at a fairground,
and once the show starts, demands that they play their hit "Taking Care
of Business"—and then, during the song, that they skip the verses and just
play the chorus. Later, after the band has played their other major hit, "You
Ain't Seen Nothin' Yet," Homer demands they play the same song—again.
(Bachman-Turner Overdrive actually had six *Billboard* Top 40 hits, but only
these two remained in regular rotation on classic rock radio stations.)

The second category of nostalgia act is that of continued success with new
music. Usually it is singer-songwriters, or solo acts that have separated from
their bands, that constitute this category, but sometimes whole bands fit the
bill. The best example of these is Aerosmith, who followed their "superstar"
years (and 1980s "superstar comeback") with occasional tours and albums
that continued to sell well and influence current musical tastes. Journey might
have fit this category if Steve Perry had stayed with the band—or if they had
agreed to do a reunion album together every five years or so.

Instead, by touring and recording without Steve Perry, Journey fell into a
third category. They had so many hits from their early years to play live—the
band called them "the dirty dozen"—that they could perform a full set, night
after night, and draw enough of a crowd to be headliners, even without their
longtime lead singer. But they wouldn't see significant album sales without
him and could not influence the popular zeitgeist as they once did. "There
was just one thing the 7,141 people who turned out Tuesday night at the Blue
Cross Arena at the Community War Memorial didn't want to hear," opined
journalist Jeff Spevak after a Journey, Styx, and REO Speedwagon concert
in 2003. "One of the guys in these bands saying, 'And now here's something
from our new album.' No, when you're 45 years old and paying $56.50 for a
ticket, time stopped in 1979, when Styx's 'Babe' was at the top of the charts."
Or in 1981, when it was "Open Arms."

There was an upside. Thanks to nostalgia, the tours finally became lucrative. In the 1970s Journey lost money on the road, using their concerts to promote their albums, to build up a following that would go to the record store the morning after the show. They cut corners by sleeping on buses and underwrote costs with sponsorships by companies like Budweiser beer. In the 1980s, when the albums were largely selling themselves thanks to radio airplay, the tours broke even, making their profit on merchandise sales, which Herbie Herbert carefully controlled. By the 2000s, with the advent of the World Wide Web, even the merch was selling itself: longtime fans (and millennials trying to be "cool") could buy T-shirts, mugs, and mouse pads directly from the band's website. Now the purpose of the tours was to make money, and ticket prices reflected that.

The generation of fans who supported these nostalgia acts was hardly the first to do so. Fans of doo-wop groups and other 1950s-style acts like the Platters and the Four Tops consistently turned out to hear their music in middle age while Journey was still appealing to teenagers (and these fans, now mostly in their seventies and eighties, still do—even while some of the "official" acts contain not a single original member, they all having long since passed away).

*   *   *

"Journey confirms new lead singer," proclaimed *MTV News* on April 24, 1998, reporting that one "Steve Augeri, previously with the band Tall Stories," had taken over vocal duties. Replacing Steve Smith on drums was none other than Deen Castronovo, who had played with Neal Schon and Jonathan Cain in Bad English and with Schon in Hardline; most recently, the drummer had served a stint playing for Ozzy Osbourne (until Ozzy's wife, Sharon, fired him for being "a messed up, arrogant punk"). The new lineup had already recorded a song for the soundtrack to the motion picture *Armageddon*: "Remember Me," a rocker by Schon, Cain, and Night Ranger's Jack Blades. The soaring vocal line gave listeners an ample introduction to the talented replacement and proclaimed the band's intent to resume recording and touring. And Castronovo proved more than capable in the drummer's seat, adding a strong background vocal to the harmonies of Cain, Schon, and Ross Valory. Despite stiff competition from the movie's theme song, "Don't Want to Miss a Thing" by Aerosmith, "Remember Me" peaked at a modestly impressive number

39 on *Billboard*'s Rock chart. "There's a different energy to this band," said
Schon. "We're more daring. We're stretching a bit and we're going to take
the audience on a different journey." Valory, nurturing his reputation as the
band's jokester, concurred. "Like so many San Francisco treasures," he said,
"this band has been retrofitted for earthquake safety."

Steve Augeri, whom Deen Castronovo once called "Steve Perry with a
perm," was born in 1959 in Brooklyn, New York, where an uncle instilled
an early appreciation for music, teaching him the guitar, and "picked us up
by the scruff of the neck one Sunday evening and plopped us in front of the
TV to watch The Beatles on the *Ed Sullivan Show*." Augeri was only six years
old, but the experience clearly left an impression. He spent freshman year
of high school at the prestigious Music & Art, known as "the Castle on the
Hill," in Harlem's Manhattanville section. Initially studying alto saxophone,
his "axe" was promptly stolen, and when the school refused to replace the
valuable instrument, he took up the bassoon—presumably less likely to be
taken. By the late 1970s Augeri was getting session work as a rhythm guitarist at Record Plant Studios in Midtown, down the street from the cavernous
Sam Ashe Music store. "It was an amazing place, the Record Plant. You'd see
anybody and everybody walk through those doors back then," he said. "AC/
DC, Aerosmith, Stevie Nicks, John Lennon," adding in typical Brooklynese,
"Forgetaboutit!" The neighborhood also had a long and storied history in
music recording, having included the original headquarters of both Columbia
Records and RCA Victor. This led to an early opportunity playing rhythm
guitar in a band called Kicks, fronted by singer Marge Raymond. When
Raymond was snapped up by members of Aerosmith to form the spinoff
band Renegade, Augeri stepped into the lead singer role, attracting AC/DC
and Aerosmith managers Steve Leber and David Krebs. Soon after, he put
together a band called Maestro, "which consisted of three wonderful Brazilian
musicians [including] Junior Homrich, who did the music for the [1985] John
[Boorman] film *Emerald Forest*." During the 1980s, Maestro evolved into the
rock band Tall Stories, after Augeri met guitarist Jack Morer while shopping
for a new guitar at Sam Ashe. They released an album with Epic Records in
1991 that yielded one single, "Wild on the Run," that peaked at number 22
on the *Billboard* Mainstream Rock chart (but made no traction on the all-
important Hot 100). And in the same year, they opened for Mr. Big, the Eric
Martin vehicle that Herbie Herbert managed.

There was no question that Journey influenced Steve Augeri's career choices, and that comparisons with Steve Perry ultimately doomed his youthful attempts at rock stardom. Perry had set the standard for rock tenors, forcing them to sing in a very high—and for many singers, damaging—key. Regularly compared to Perry, like his Bay Area contemporary Kevin Chalfant of the VU and the Storm, Augeri was attempting to replicate Perry's success in an era that had no use for soaring, angelic rock vocals.

Tall Stories ultimately met with a similar fate to that of the Storm and the VU, albeit without the famous names attached. Recording power ballads and rockers with vocal harmonies seemed passé to many in the industry during the era of grunge rock and the Seattle sound of Nirvana. When Tall Stories floundered, another band threw Augeri a lifeline. Tyketto, a hair band not unlike Bad English and Hardline, had lost lead singer Danny Vaughan, whose wife had been diagnosed with cancer. With two albums already under their belt with Geffen records, being the vocalist for Tyketto seemed like a real shot for Augeri. "I drove down the Jersey shore . . . and got acquainted with the band," the singer recalled. "Jammed at a few Asbury Park rehearsal studios. Wrote lyrics on the beach." Then it was off to Pachyderm Studios in Minnesota to lay down tracks for what became 1995's *Shine*. But the band, which had once opened for Bon Jovi, sputtered. They released a live album in 1996, *Take Out and Served Up Live*, and disbanded.

At age thirty-seven, having tried for two decades to find success in an unforgiving industry, it seemed a good time to "grow up a bit and move on," he told *New York Times* journalist James Barron. He was married and had a child now. So he returned to Brooklyn and went into his father's line of work, painting houses. Thanks to a well-placed cousin, he got a salaried job at the clothing retail chain the Gap, doing light construction at stores throughout the city.

That's when he got a phone call from an old friend, guitarist Joe Cefalu. Raised in New York, Cefalu now lived and worked in the Bay Area and had become friends with none other than Neal Schon. Cefalu had learned that Journey was seeking a new lead singer but that unlike Van Halen, which had replaced David Lee Roth in 1985 with Sammy Hagar to produce a different sound, Journey was looking for someone who could replicate Steve Perry's contribution. Cefalu shared a Tall Stories tape with Schon, who was quickly convinced he had found his new Steve. Initially Augeri shrugged it off; he was out of the business. Indeed, when he received another phone call from Schon himself, at first he thought it was a prank. But when the next call came—this time from Jonathan Cain—he knew it was for real. He packed his bags to join Journey—the band that he idolized, the band whose distinctive sound had caused his struggles, the band that now offered him a ticket to stardom. After a five-day audition in Marin County, punctuated by a flawless rendition of "Open Arms," he got the gig.

Journey hit the road in 1998 for the first time in eleven years, with a tour they called "Vacation's Over"—sixty-one appearances, including four in Japan. Finances were tight without their storied and celebrated former lead singer. Manager Irving Azoff had initially demanded a $75,000-per-show minimum from the venues, many of which balked at the possibility of making no return. The band had faith that the fans would show, but the venues and promoters did not. Ultimately Cain convinced Azoff to pull back on the demand and called "Vacation's Over" the band's "break even tour." Expenses and per diem were the only guarantees for the musicians. "Not a comeback tour, but more like a rebirth tour," Cain said. "We were rebuilding."

Although clearly trying to make up for lost time, the band encountered some trouble with the arenas they had once filled with ease, at least in their hometown: lagging ticket sales for a planned show at San Francisco's Bill Graham Civic Auditorium forced the band to perform at the Warfield, the more intimate venue that Schon and Valory had often played with the original lineup in the early 1970s. As for the reviews, they were snarky but encouraging. John Young of the *Pittsburgh Post-Gazette* expressed the typical sentiment, writing that Steve Augeri "looked like Kenny G imitating Robert Plant, but sounded remarkably similar to Journey's better-known power crooner," adding that the performance of their song from *Armageddon*, "Remember Me," "sounded like a leaden leftover from 'Raised on Radio.'" A sign of what was to come, he reported that vast numbers of concertgoers took a bathroom break during the "mid-show, two-song instrumental set," concluding that "[i]f Journey truly intends to stick around, here's hoping they'll find a way to add some rough edge to their sound and write some more melodic songs. In the meantime, Journey offers no less than a fine, fun nostalgia trip." With Foreigner opening, the following year's "Under the Stars" tour was more successful: sixty-three dates, all in the United States, from May through November 1999, in somewhat larger venues.

Much had changed in the intervening years that influenced the band's interactions with its fans. The web was no longer a tool for hobbyists but had become a ubiquitous platform for instant global communication. Not only did major corporations (and rock bands) set up websites, but so did the fans, and one popular format was the "forum." Named for the ancient Greco-Roman gathering place where citizens would debate policy and philosophy, forums (users typically eschewed the elitist-sounding Latin plural *fora*, owing to the decidedly nonelite nature of the format) allowed anyone with an internet connection to converse on a given topic—or on any topic. In the past, Journey had controlled—somewhat—the public reaction to personnel changes through the careful cultivation of the press. Now the fans could express themselves to anyone who cared to download a web page through a dial-up modem.

The online fan response to the band's separation from Steve Perry was mixed, to say the least. On the one hand, many fans were grateful that the band was finally touring and recording again. Some had been too young to see Journey live during their heyday, and they jumped at the chance to at least see Schon, Cain, and Valory—no matter which Steve was out front or who was behind the drum set. Some who had admired the band since their earliest albums justified the change by noting that Journey had existed before Perry and it could continue without him.

But by far the most vocal (if not the largest) group of fans who expressed themselves though this new medium (although not on the band's official website, then at journeytheband.com, where dissent was quickly deleted by webmasters), were the so-called Perryheads: those who did not believe any "real" version of Journey could exist without Steve Perry. "I was worried about [Augeri] getting shot," recalled Cain. "We took a lot of flack. We used to get hate mail. Somebody got my number and would call me: 'You son of a bitch!'" These fans were truly fanatic, and supporting the version of Journey with Steve Perry was part of their identities. They saw the replacement of the iconic singer as a personal affront. We challenge identities at our peril.

Aside from the fervent fans who were paying attention, of course, was the much larger group of listeners for whom Journey's music was casual entertainment, and the band coming to town was just an excuse for an evening out of the house, perhaps away from the kids. Yet even these concertgoers expected to see Journey with Steve Perry. And since the ticket price was significant (between $30 and $50, about $56–$94 in 2023 dollars), many felt that without Perry onstage, they weren't getting their money's worth. After some walked out of the show and demanded a refund, and New York "shock jock" Don Imus told his listeners that "this isn't Journey" prior to their two sold-out shows at the city's storied Beacon Theater (where Perry had also sold out during his *Strange Medicine* tour in 1995), the band began including the names of the current musicians in advertisements.

Those who stayed in their seats, however, found they were in for a treat. Steve Augeri was a highly talented, emotive front man who knew how to work a crowd. For the most part, he sang the hits the fans remembered just like Steve Perry had in the past, and in a few instances made minor updates to the lyrics: "When the summer's gone, she'll be there standing by the light" (from "Feeling That Way") became "When the summer's gone, she'll be there, *Journey* by the light"; to the line "All night (all night), every night" (from "Any Way You Want It") he added "that's right!" Not a few casual fans were overheard leaving the shows saying things like "that new Steve, he's not bad." It helped that drummer Deen Castronovo, also a tenor, was a fantastic singer in his own right; he sang unison with Augeri on the highest notes to help re-create the robust vocal sound of Perry in his heyday, while Schon, Cain, and Valory provided the additional harmonies they always had. After a show at the Jones Beach Amphitheater in Wantagh, New York, I wrote that "Steve Augeri is almost a carbon copy of Perry. The sideburns, the hair, the profile, the build, the dance style, the voice. They couldn't have picked a better replacement. I could barely tell the difference."

The band headed to New York City in 2000 to record their first full album since Perry's departure. Columbia Records—owned by Sony but now having reassumed their longtime name—released *Arrival* in Japan in the fall of 2000. Journey now became the victims of a new phenomenon—internet music sharing. The online Napster platform made it possible for listeners to share MP3 versions of their favorite songs throughout the world for free. At a time when internet download speeds were significantly slower than today, with most users relying on dial-up modems rather than dedicated cables, MP3 formatting removed enough digital information to keep the per-song download times acceptable with minimal loss perception to the human ear. Although Napster soon ran afoul of the authorities and was shut down, eventually giving way to more legitimate internet music downloads, by the end of

2000, many fans had already downloaded the entire album. But now Journey became beneficiaries of what might otherwise have been a crisis. Because the fans had the music in advance, and because the fans could use the internet to critique the work, the band learned that the American audience—or at least those fans who had stayed with them after the break with Perry—found the album too soft, with too many ballads. And so they mixed in some harder rock tunes as they prepared for its American release in the spring of 2001.

The album begins with a rocker with strong bass beat called "Higher Place," by Schon and Night Ranger's Blades, who had cowritten their effort for the *Armageddon* soundtrack, "Remember Me." The song starts off the album with a toe-tapping lyric: "I try to reason why/Don't you know I can't go on this way." The next track, "All the Way," a ballad by Schon, Cain, Nashville-based Aerosmith songwriter Taylor Rhodes, and Augeri, gives the singer an opportunity to demonstrate his vocal bona fides, with a soaring tenor refrain in a return to the ballads of the classic Journey era. Next up is a mid-tempo number, "Signs of Life," by Schon, Cain, and Cain's wife Elizabeth—marking the first credited contribution by a Journey spouse since Diane Valory cowrote "Wheel in the Sky." The lyrics, like the title, address the departure of Steve Perry: "It's been forty days since I heard from you/ This waiting game you put me through." However, the message is hidden in a love song: "I'll miss your love/Miss your touch/But this holdin' on it hurts too much." Then comes "All the Things," an up-tempo by Schon, Cain, and Andre Pessis, who had cowritten songs with Gregg Rolie and Kevin Chalfant for the Storm. "Loved by You," a ballad by Cain, Tammy Hyler, and Kim Tribble, is followed by the dirge "Livin' to Do," by Schon, Cain, and Tribble. This one has chord changes reminiscent both of Journey's early years before Steve Perry joined the band and Schon's "Blues for Miles" from his recent solo album *Piranha Blues*, as well as a mournful lyric inspired by the recent death of his father Matthew, who had worked with Journey on *Dream, After Dream*, and was given a cowriter credit. "A church in the rain, a sad congregation, an old friend I knew/When I look at the end, I understand now, I got livin' to do," followed by a Rolie-style organ solo by Cain, leading to a fade-out.

The Japanese and American track lists deviate at this point, with only the US version including "World Gone Wild," another toe-tapping rocker by Blades, Schon, and Cain; both then feature the up-tempo "I Got a Reason" by the same writers. Liz Cain joined Schon and Jonathan writing the wedding ballad "With Your Love," and both versions also include "Lifetime of Dreams," by Schon, Cain, and Tribble, and "Live and Breathe," by Schon, Cain, and Augeri. The American release then includes the rocker "Nothin' Comes Close," also by Schon, Cain, and Augeri, and the up-tempo "To Be Alive Again," by Cain, Augeri, Tribble, and the Hooters vocalist Eric Bazilian (this one also appears as the final track of a later edition of the Japanese version). Both versions include the jazzy "Kiss Me Softly," a ballad by Blades, Schon, and Augeri; the Japanese version includes another ballad, "I'm Not That Way," by Schon, Cain, Augeri, and Tribble; and both conclude with "We Will Meet Again," by Schon, Augeri, and Tribble, providing a fitting statement that Journey is promising to survive their separation from Perry, even if, as with "Signs of Life," the message was otherwise buried in a love song: "Was it the words she said or was it all in the way in which the lady said them?/Her eyes that spoke to me were sending my heart a thought so deep I can't forget them."

Despite its professional composition and excellent sound, and the willing engagement of the band members in all the normal promotional activities (which Perry had refused to do after *Trial by Fire*), *Arrival* was a commercial disappointment, peaking at number 56 on the *Billboard* 200 on April 20, 2001—the poorest showing for a Journey album since 1977's *Next*—the band's last album before they hired Perry. "Higher Place," like "Remember Me" from *Armageddon*, saw some activity on *Billboard*'s Rock chart, peaking there at number 23, and "All the Way" moved up the Adult Contemporary chart, peaking at number 22, but none of the album's songs cracked the *Billboard* Hot 100. *Rolling Stone*, for once, had a positive review, opining that "*Arrival* is dense and smoothly produced with a hint of hard-rock heft and catchy hooks a-plenty." But the reviewer's concerns proved sadly prophetic: "The question is whether there's still an audience for Journey or whether the Sheryl Crows and Dave Matthews of the world have left *Arrival* with no place to go."

There was at least one negative review. *House of Shred* said "All the Way" sounded like the boy band 'N Sync and called "Nothing Comes Close" too much like Robert Palmer's 1986 hit "Addicted to Love." "To top it off, it's a sonic mess. The whole thing sounds muddy and thick." But the fans—at least those who had accepted Journey without Perry—were overwhelmingly positive. I wrote at the time that it was "the perfect showcase for Augeri's talent and hopefully . . . a harbinger of things to come."

The Japanese release of *Arrival* presaged a major international tour. In the fall of 2000 and the winter of 2001, Journey played four dates in Central America; the new year saw them play seven dates in Japan. The subsequent United States tour coincided with the release of the US version of the album, and they played sixty-four dates between May and October (including an appearance in Acapulco, Mexico).

The *Arrival* tour included two opening acts: legendary guitarist Peter Frampton and singer-songwriter John Waite, who had fronted Bad English with Schon, Cain, and Castronovo, and the Babys with Cain. Waite had continued to enjoy a successful solo career but had not seen superstardom since Bad English. Fans looking for "When I See You Smile" or any of the other Bad English tunes during either the John Waite or the Journey set, however, were disappointed; while Schon often came out to play a song or two with Waite, Cain did not join him, and Waite did not appear during the Journey set. Asked if this was due to lingering bad blood over the Bad English breakup a decade before, Cain feigned ignorance, arguing that the two bands were on completely different travel schedules. But if Schon could make the venues in time for Waite's set, surely Cain—who once prided himself on sitting in the audience before the sound check of each show to remind himself of the audience perspective—could have done the same.

Journey joined with kitsch when a couple on an episode of *Blind Date* attended a Journey concert as part of the program. A syndicated television dating show that paired singles and sent them on a series of adventures to determine romantic compatibility—usually without success—series editors would "enhance" the program by adding sex-referent animation and silly thought bubbles in post-production, leading thoughtful viewers (if there were any) to wonder why anyone in their right mind would agree to be on the show. The "contestants" whose date was filmed on August 15, 2001, attended a Journey concert at the Greek Theater in Los Angeles that night, among their other activities; the episode aired on November 14.

In the interim, of course, came the events of September 11, 2001. Several Al Qaeda terrorists, under the leadership of Osama bin Laden, organized the deadliest strike by a foreign actor on American soil since Pearl Harbor, flying hijacked airplanes into the World Trade Center towers in New York City and the Pentagon, headquarters of the Department of Defense; other national targets, including the White House and the US Capitol, were spared, but a plane intended for one of these was retaken by passengers and forced down in central Pennsylvania, with all aboard perishing.

The aftermath of the attacks, traumatic for so many, resulted in a tightening of security by the band's management. Some of this made sense; at the Hartford, Connecticut, show on July 7, opening act Peter Frampton had encouraged the fans to come closer to the stage, asking security guards to abandon the ten-foot perimeter; the fans pushed forward, and one jumped up to stand next to the guitarist, raising two triumphant fists to the sky before being hustled off the stage by embarrassed staff. And after the September 12 show in York, Pennsylvania—a state fair show the day after the attacks, at which Journey performed with a "show must go on" attitude—fans who merely walked around the shed got to mix and mingle with the band, separated by nothing more than a thin line of plastic tape.

The crackdown after September 11, based on fear, was like killing a mosquito with a sledgehammer. Trying to avoid being a soft target, venue security increased, usually with underpaid, undertrained individuals. But Journey concerts hardly resembled the sort of high-profile locations that attracted terrorism. This ultimately proved harmful to the band, as they found there was a fine line between encouraging their fans to be as involved as possible in various marketing activities like the "Street Team"—fans selected through the internet to hold preshow parties (at their own expense) and distribute flyers and various giveaways and given early access to front-row seats—and keeping the musicians safe from that one potentially dangerous fan.

Other reactions made more sense: in memory of the lives lost on what became known simply as "9/11," Schon began playing "Amazing Grace" during the Journey set. And the band joined Styx and other "classic rock" groups that October to play "Volunteers for America," a concert that raised $500,000 to benefit the American Red Cross and the first responders—a new term to enter the American lexicon after 9/11, collectively describing police, fire, and medical professionals. That "Amazing Grace" was based on a poem by a reformed slave ship captain was never mentioned.

Despite all the attempts at promotion and the successful tour, sales of *Arrival* were not enough to stop the executives at the label from making good on a threat their predecessors had made before the band hired Perry: they dropped Journey. Columbia Records would not distribute future Journey albums; the group would need to find another way to get its music to listeners. Schon made the unlikely claim that it was the band that dropped the label, and not the other way around, because of poor promotion of the album and a minuscule offer for the next one; and the band's official stance was that the break was "a mutually agreed upon decision." In other words, "you can't fire me—I quit."

*   *   *

Between 2001 and 2002, the band recorded an extended-play (EP) record, *Red 13*, at Jonathan Cain's Wild Horse Studio. An EP is a short album, considered "extended" because the length originated in the era of the 78 rpm single, before the advent of the long-playing album (LP), when the typical record had only one song on each side. *Red 13*, so titled, according to Schon, because it was Journey's thirteenth album (including *Dream, After Dream* but excluding compilations and live albums), has the feel of assembled outtakes from the *Arrival* sessions, with some of the same guest writers—Andre Pessis and Taylor Rhodes—joining Cain, Schon, and Augeri. The release was billed as a gift to the fans who had stayed loyal despite the loss of Perry and the band's longtime record label. Even the album cover was a tribute to the fans, the result of a contest—and it was largely those fans alone who heard it. "Intro: Red 13," by Cain, is an exciting drum moment that was played over the speakers as the band prepared to take the stage during subsequent concerts; it is followed immediately by the up-tempo "State of Grace," by Schon, Augeri, and an increasingly religious Cain; the song includes the lyric "state of grace" played backward, recalling the original Journey's cover of the Beatles' "It's All Too Much." Then comes "The Time," another rocker by Schon, Cain, Augeri, and Gary Cirimelli, followed by the contemplative ballad "Walkin' Away from the Edge," by Cain, Schon, Pessis, and an uncredited Geoff Tate of Queensryche, with acoustic guitar, and lyrics that speak to recovery from drug abuse; and the up-tempo "I Can Breathe," by Schon, Cain, Augeri, and Rhodes.

The band initially released *Red 13* as a "fan exclusive" starting in August 2002, selling copies at concert merchandise tables and through the band's online store. The initial design for the album cover was a simple red bar and two thin red circles on black background bearing the title "RED 13 JRNY."

When the album was released commercially that December by Frontiers Records, an independent Italian label mostly working with classic rock bands (now increasingly called "melodic rock"), it had a new cover designed by fan and artist Christopher Payne: a winged scarab mostly obscuring a setting sun.

Likely due to lack of promotion by a major North American label, *Red 13* did not attract sufficient attention to merit mainstream reviews. But those it did garner noted its "retro" feel, comparing it positively to the Roy Thomas Baker–produced *Infinity* and *Evolution*. The review at FoundryMusic.com (now defunct) called "the overall vibe of this disc . . . loose, flowing and raw," while RevampScripts.com in 2002 called the album "reminiscent of the Journey of the mid to late 70's." Nevertheless, by the end of 2003, the band was giving away the EP for free.

The 2002 "Under the Radar" tour, with Peter Frampton and Cheap Trick sometimes serving as opening acts, included fifty-six dates between April and November: mostly clubs, casinos, and state fairs, all in the lower forty-eight except for two quick stops in Ontario, Canada, and a three-night trip to Hawaii to play Honolulu's Blaisdell Arena and the Maui Arts & Cultural Center. On some of the dates, Schon, Cain, and Augeri would pull up stools to play an acoustic set, with Cain on rhythm guitar and Valory and Castronovo taking a break; these sets included rarely performed material like the title track from *Trial by Fire* and "Liberty" from the *Time^3* box set.

Concertgoers got a treat at one stop that coincided with a local appearance of the Gregg Rolie Band, which included Michael Carabello and Chepito's son Adrian Areas; not only did Rolie, Carabello, and the younger Areas join Schon and Cain onstage for a "Santana set," including "Black Magic Woman," "Everybody's Everything," and the Journey song "La Raza del Sol," but even Chepito himself came out of retirement to sit in. And when fans who gathered at New York City's Hard Rock Café sent Augeri an invitation to join them, the gracious singer, unable to attend, called the restaurant and bought them champagne.

On August 24, Valory stopped the show to wish Vincent Price a happy birthday. "Vincent was near me and I thought he might need medics after that one," wrote one fan in a subsequent online review, adding "he was totally on cloud nine thanks to that thoughtful acknowledgement by Ross." Considering that Price had actually been dead for nearly nine years and that, in any event, his birthday was in May, the person in the crowd was more likely Vincent

Barrett Price, his son, whose birthday was just a few days later, on August 30—unless, of course, the noted horror actor had somehow returned from the dead for the sole purpose of attending a Journey concert. Given his 1983 participation in Michael Jackson's "Thriller," at least the rock concert part is not farfetched. Chalk it up to Valory's unique sense of humor.

The success of the Under the Radar tour prompted Journey to consider larger venues for 2003. Still lacking a major label, they fell back on one of the techniques they had pioneered in the late 1970s and sought a corporate sponsor. Budweiser had been a poor fit during their early years owing to the age of their fans at the time, but with concertgoers now almost exclusively of legal drinking age, a brewer would have been appropriate. However, Azoff Management decided that an even more appropriate corporate sponsor— especially given that Schon was now a recovering alcoholic—would be the cable TV channel VH1 (short for "Video Hits 1").

The band formed a "package deal" with two other popular nostalgia acts. Styx and REO Speedwagon had already toured together successfully, taking turns as headliners and performing a "big band" encore together, one song from each band's repertoire. Now, "Classic Rock's Main Event" featured Journey as headliners and saw Styx and REO swapping turns as opening and middle acts for a four-and-a-half-hour superconcert for an average ticket price of $48 (about $80 in 2023). As each band now included their own elaborate onstage equipment, the sound booth displayed a large digital timer at each of the fifty-eight shows, ticking down to the end of each performance (and each "scene change") to keep the musicians and crew on time—especially important in venues with strict curfews.

Neal Schon jetted off to New York City to start the tour with a jam with Styx's Tommy Shaw and REO Speedwagon's Kevin Cronin at a club in Greenwich Village, taped by VH1 to help promote the tour. During a layover after a show in Englewood, Colorado, responding to a fan invite, the band showed up at a Denver bar, plugged in, and performed what became a free concert; Schon even served drinks to the astonished patrons. Demonstrating the purchasing power of the mature fans even beyond the hefty ticket price, the tour culminated with all three bands playing—and presumably enjoying—a "weeklong Caribbean cruise" for Carnival.

Reviews were mixed. Julia Ann Weekes of the *New Hampshire Union Leader* filed a positive notice, as did Alexander Choman of the *Wilkes-Barre*

Citizens' Voice, who wrote that the first act—REO Speedwagon—set a standard that Styx and Journey struggled to meet, but felt that Augeri was a fine replacement for Perry. Michael Eck of the *Albany Times Union* wrote that "[w]hen Journey, Styx and REO Speedwagon join forces, they offer hits aplenty with a healthy side dish of nostalgia of the 1970s and 1980s." But Jeff Miers of the *Buffalo News* disliked Journey's performance, accusing Augeri of singing "thinly-veiled karaoke" and adding that "[t]he soul just wasn't there," ironically expecting from Journey an embodiment of African American musical styles that the overwhelmingly white fan base, although loath to admit it, also wanted.

Cain spoke to this point as well. "We are a soul band," he told an interviewer, without mentioning that "soul" in this context meant popular music performed by African American musicians for largely African American audiences. Of course, Schon was a fan of the "Queen of Soul," consciously modeling much of his solo work, and his guitar parts for Journey, after what he considered to be Aretha Franklin's vocal style; and for the musicians, after all, the genre mattered less than the music itself. The "soul band" comment is indicative of an attitude likely shared by Cain and Schon, that they wished the music they played live had more appeal across racial lines. But it also represented an attitude among the fans, that Journey (and "classic" rock music altogether) represented an evolution from integrated rock and roll, an evolution accessible only to white musicians. In an era when minstrelsy was finally being decried by mainstream whites as the racist cultural appropriation it was, enjoying the "soulful" aspects of Journey music allowed the white fans to embody a "safe" amount of Blackness without violating white cultural norms. White artists had long ago laid claim to the evolution of the blues; now, it seemed, they were claiming the evolution of soul as well.

White cultural norms also include a toleration of violence, and Journey fans could occasionally behave like soccer hooligans. Tragedy nearly struck during a Journey concert in Detroit, when several men got into a brawl that left twenty-year-old Joe Rumbley stabbed in the heart and a woman described as "40ish" sliced in the arm. Drunk, angry, and apparently jealous that the young man was ogling his girlfriend, thirty-nine-year-old James Locklear, who had snuck a knife past security, went on a rampage. Rumbley "said he felt a thump on his chest . . . and fell back against his friends, who toppled like dominoes, wrote Jim Schaefer in the *Detroit Free Press*. "I saw all the blood

on the floor and I thought, man, someone got screwed up," recalled the victim. Rushed to a nearby hospital for emergency open-heart surgery, he made
a remarkable full recovery and a year later was back on his college football
team. Locklear, his assailant, "pleaded guilty . . . to stabbing Rumbley and
resisting arrest." Azoff Management said the band members were unaware of
the brawl while it occurred but were quick to send their wishes for a speedy
recovery to all the victims.

Without a label to promote their shows, and with little interest in *Red 13*
beyond the hardcore fans, the band nevertheless proved their continuing
value. They grossed "about $380,000 per show" in 2003, according to *Pollstar*,
for an approximate $22 million for the year. Smith, Herbie, and Perry each
took their cut as co-owners of Nightmare but left enough for a salary for
each of the five performers of about $1 million per year—more than a decent
amount. Perry took a 12.5 percent cut of Schon and Cain's performance salaries thanks to the agreement of the Elmo Partners—a cool quarter million for
not performing himself. Schon and Cain still likely netted more overall than
Augeri, Castronovo, and Valory, however, because of performance royalties
for the songs they had written—royalties prorated for each of the songwriters for the band's hits. At least as early as *Escape*, the group had abandoned
the earlier "Nightmare owns all royalties" model—likely thanks to Aynsley
Dunbar's lawsuit.

*   *   *

On February 18, 2001, the MTV-affiliated cable television channel VH1 aired
the latest episode in their *Behind the Music* series, this one focusing on Journey. The typical format of the program was to tell a version of a band's history, usually building to a crisis involving the abuse of drugs or alcohol by one
or more of the players and culminating in some sort of a resolution in which
the band either successfully reunited with the recalcitrant member or moved
on with no feelings hurt. The problem with the Journey story, for the show's
producers, was that although some of the musicians had alcohol problems
and most used cannabis recreationally, none admitted to letting their drinking significantly interfere with their work or progress into the abuse of more
serious narcotics. Searching for a "hook," the show's producers focused on
the departure of Perry. The result was something of a "hit job" on the singer,

making him out as a diva and control freak (not unlike another contemporary genre of so-called reality television, the "bridezilla"). And while some of that was justified, they crafted the band's history to suit the favored storyline. The episode ended with Perry saying that he "never felt like [he] was part of the band" and then cutting to his former bandmates who reacted with typical shock at what appeared to be a ridiculous statement, despite it having been clearly taken out of context and played for them for their reactions and the resultant shock value. What the interviewer had asked Perry was how he felt about the camaraderie of the *original* Journey he joined in 1977, to which his response—in that limited context—was understandable, despite that fact that he eventually became not only very much a part of the band but also its leader and driving force.

Several of the current and former members of Journey remained busy with other projects. Cain continued his solo career, with albums recorded in his Wild Horse Studio at home in Novato, California. These allowed him to stretch creatively but yielded little pecuniary reward. *For a Lifetime*, his third album with Higher Octave Records, contained mostly instrumental wedding songs, released in 1998, including one, "A Day to Remember," for Schon's marriage to Amber Kozan (his fourth), and "Open Arms"; then came 2001's *Anthology*, a compilation of the solo material he had released since the initial Journey hiatus in 1987, on One Way Records, an independent label based in Albany, New York; and *Namaste*, a collection of New Age songs he released on his own label, Wildhorse, through his website. In 2002, after a decade of watching Disney movies with his children, he recorded *Animated Movie Love Songs*, also on One Way, substituting his piano for the vocal lines. That December he recorded his kids' schoolmates singing for an album, *If Every-day Were Like Christmas*, which he never released commercially but sold to parents to benefit the school. And in 2004, with another independent label, AAO Music, he released the instrumental soul-jazz album *Bare Bones*, which included another Journey song he had cowritten, "Who's Crying Now."

The overwork had a reason: his second marriage, to Liz Fullerton, had become strained. Cain reported that when he would return from his long months on the road, during which his kids would sleep in his bed with Liz, he would have to play the tough dad and force them to sleep in their own rooms. "I was stunned at how little regard there would be for how hard I had worked for the money we were blessed with." A relatively minor complaint, to be sure, and one likely similar to those of married couples of all social circumstances. But Cain's subsequent response was highly ironic. The author of "Faithfully," a song about being true to his wife despite the temptations of the road, and whose first wife had betrayed that trust, now himself was unfaithful. "My initial affair" with an ex-girlfriend, he later wrote, "turned into numerous ones." Before long he was even enlisting his son Weston in keeping his affairs secret. Eventually he came clean in couples therapy, and he and Liz divorced.

Valory also found time for work outside of Journey's tight annual touring schedule. Like Cain, he built a home studio, which he called the Hive, with the help of old friends: George Tickner, cofounder of Journey and Frumious Bandersnatch and now retired from a career as a surgical technician; and onetime Journey relief keyboardist Stevie Roseman, who had recently worked with Schon on *Piranha Blues*. Of course, they started to write and record music together and in 2005 released an album as VTR (Valory, Tickner, Roseman), called *Cinema*. Old friends Prairie Prince and Steve Smith pitched in on drums for nine eclectic, instrumental tracks that combine jazz, New Age, and—of course, given Tickner's proclivities—a touch of psychedelia.

Rolie was also keeping busy—with the band he had formed after the draining of Abraxas Pool, the Gregg Rolie Band. His 2001 album *Roots* was released by 33 Street Records, the in-house label for retailer Tower Records. It was Herbie who made the connection with the short-lived label, through which Tower sought to shore up its leaking business model in the digital era. The band for the album included Santana's Michael Carabello and Chepito's son Adrian, guitarist Dave Amato of REO Speedwagon, Alphonso Johnson on bass, and the Storm's Ron Wikso on drums. Schon contributed guitars for one track.

They took the album out on the road, with a show that included some of the biggest Santana and Journey hits, first in Northern California and then nationwide. Kevin Chalfant, who got the rest of the former members of the Storm to allow him to use that band's name, often served as opening act and came back onstage to sing Steve Perry's lines during the Journey numbers of Rolie's set. Those in attendance loved it, but it failed to garner sufficient press to book the larger arenas that Santana and Journey continued to fill. This left his tour vulnerable to interruptions. In October 2002, for instance, when the "D.C. sniper"—actually two gunmen, John Allen Muhammad and

Lee Boyd Malvo—terrorized Greater Washington, Rolie was forced to cancel a planned swing through the area. He did it "[f]or the safety of my fans, my band—I'm not a target, but we can't put people at risk," he told me after a show in Connecticut the following month, explaining that "when you have a series of dates, and they're all in small places, you only get paid so much. If two of them fall out, then logistically you can't go to the others because . . . it'll break the bank. So—one fell out here, one fell out there—pretty soon, they all fell apart." And when former Santana and Journey roadie Jack Villanueva fell ill, Rolie willingly flew in to join Carlos, Herbie, and Michael Shrieve at a luncheon in Jack's honor at the San Francisco restaurant Fior d'Italia.

But mostly it was about having fun. In a deliberate recollection of one of his reasons for leaving Journey, the keyboardist required that his bandmates follow only one rule: no meetings.

Herbie, meanwhile, singing blues under the alter ego "Sy Klopps," released three albums between 1993 and 2000, then joining Grateful Dead drummer Bill Kreutzmann in a band they called the Trichromes. In 2002 they released *Dice with the Universe*, also with 33 Street Records. The album contained eleven songs cowritten by their guitarist Ralph Woodson and Grateful Dead lyricist Robert Hunter, with several other writers participating, such as Pete Sears of Jefferson Starship, bassist Mike DiPirro, and the ubiquitous Neal Schon. The Trichromes played a reggae-influenced bluesy folk-rock not unlike that of the Dead, with one reviewer calling them a "distinctly Bay Area coagulation"—which is primarily where they performed their original songs as well as the Grateful Dead numbers they covered.

The Napster phenomenon may have simultaneously helped and hurt Journey's first effort following Steve Perry's departure, while provoking the artists' and labels' lawsuits that led to its demise, but it certainly caught Herbie's attention. He saw beyond the copyright infringement to the moneymaking potential of internet music sales. At the same time as his former copartner in Journey management, Lou Bramy, was advising the team that would eventually become the multibillion-dollar music-streaming service Pandora, Herbie launched Muzic.com, which licensed the back catalogue of rock singer Joan Jett and attracted some investment. Partnering with a twenty-four-year-old Brian Villanueva (an unconfirmed but likely relative of former Journey roadies, the brothers John and Jack Villanueva), Herbie acknowledged that he faced an uphill battle against larger players simultaneously hoping to capitalize on the changes to the industry that the internet portended. It was an interesting attempt, but where Herbie failed was in his twentieth-century thinking. Whereas Herbie busied himself signing individual artists, much as Columbia Records and the other major labels had done to achieve their initial success in the 1940s and 1950s, the businesses that succeeded in the internet music game were those that recognized its game-changing potential: Amazon, which applied the internet to the existing retail practices of the big-box store, its music download operation becoming the Tower Records of the internet, replacing the grungy-but-knowledgeable salespeople with the wisdom of fellow buyers; and Pandora, which licensed music for membership, becoming the Netflix of music (or a more comprehensive, online version of the old Columbia House record club, which famously had an introductory offer of twelve albums for a penny, so long as the members agreed to buy a certain amount at full purchase price—and receive a featured album at full price unless they returned a monthly card to opt out).

Onetime Journey lead singer Robert Fleischman also was active in the early 2000s. Having previously fronted the bands Channel and Vinnie Vincent Invasion, he released a solo album in 2002, *World in Your Eyes*, with Frontiers Records, the same independent Italian label that released Journey's *Red 13* EP. The songs included a mix of hard rock and ballads, not too far from the type of music Journey had been putting out since he had been fired from the band in 1978. "I hope a lot of Journey fans gravitate to it," he told me when it was released; when they didn't, he branched into electronic ambient instrumental music in 2004 with *Kinetic Phenomena*, much of which consisted of repetitive sounds that could have been used for a gym workout.

This era also saw the growth in popularity of Journey tribute bands. A number of cover bands, long a staple of the rock scene, coalesced to perform a repertoire consisting entirely (or overwhelmingly) of Journey songs, playing to the same nostalgia as the actual band. A phenomenon not limited to Journey, what made the many Journey tribute bands around the country (and beyond) unique was that they often included lead singers who bore an uncanny resemblance to Steve Perry—from the mullet to the leopard-print shirts to the topcoats and tails. The illusion worked, and it even earned the lead singers the odd record contract. Certainly the best example of this was a singer named simply Hugo, who sang with the Long Island, New York–based tribute band Evolution. Attendees at the small clubs and bars these bands played could squint a little, ignore the occasional instrumental slip, and imagine themselves at a Journey concert in days of yore. And, after all, not even Journey had the *real* Steve Perry anymore; fans at the Journey concerts also had to engage—somewhat at least—in a suspension of disbelief. For his part, Hugo was physically imposing, a good three inches taller than Perry, and several wider at the shoulders, but Danny Gagliano, of the Northern New Jersey–based Worlds Apart, matched Perry's build more closely (and had a white coat with tails to boot). The suburban Chicago-based Infinity kept their wide 1980s repertoire for the second half of their show, but the first half was all Journey, during which they compensated for singer Bob Biagi's poor resemblance to Perry with a professional laser light show. And then there was the Virginia-based Frontiers, with a lead singer—Jeremey Hunsicker—who didn't need any of the accoutrements, because his clean tone and vocal style seemed to clone the sound of Perry in his prime. That band traveled further afield than most: "Our travel limitations are within about five hundred miles," Hunsicker told me, "but with the right planning, anything is possible." Frontiers released a DVD of their show, which they sold at a merchandise table and by mail order, and Hunsicker teamed up with Swedish songwriter Juhani Nahkala to record a CD of their own original music: *Elemental.*

"Don't Stop Believin',"
2003–2007

He always does this "woe is me" bullshit about "Oh, they don't like me." Well, you're invited. I mean, come on.

—*Neal Schon*

Will he show? Excitement slowly built on the morning of April 25, 2003, in front of the Bill Graham Civic Auditorium on Grove Street in San Francisco, where Journey was expected to arrive to commemorate their thirtieth anniversary with the unveiling of a plaque on the Bay Area Music Walk of Fame. Prior inductees included "Bill Graham (1997), Carlos Santana (1997), Jerry Garcia (1997), Janis Joplin (1998), John Lee Hooker (1998), Jefferson Airplane (1999), & Metallica (1999)." But the fans who turned out wanted to see *him.* Steve Perry. Their only question was, *Will he show?*

As the members of Journey arrived one by one, excitement built in the crowd. Aging wunderkind guitarist Neal Schon was there, leering as usual, along with the boyishly good-looking pianist-songwriter Jonathan Cain, with his Prince Valiant haircut, unchanged since 1983, and bass player Ross Valory, the band's craggy-faced comedian. Few paid much attention to the "new guys," Brooklyn-born singer Steve Augeri, as always in a tight button-down shirt, and "bad boy" drummer Deen Castronovo, covered in tattoos.

Jovial Herbie Herbert's rotund figure was instantly recognizable, as was Aynsley Dunbar, still the same rock star, if somewhat older and more road-weary.

No longer trolling for underage groupies, the Liverpudlian drummer who had played with Zappa and Bowie and was twice short-listed for Led Zeppelin had recently lost his four-year-old son to pontine glioma, a rare form of cancer.

The die-hard fans also surely recognized organist-singer Gregg Rolie, still wearing the same mullet that had caught the breeze on that rainy afternoon thirty-four years before at Woodstock—and still sporting the easy smile of a man who knew how fortunate he had been to have started not one but two superstar bands.

But as the minutes ticked by and the ceremony started, one thing was abundantly clear: Steve Perry, the one member of the band that everyone wanted to see, was a no-show. *Again.*

That evening Journey played the Warfield and invited all former members of the band to sit in. Again, rumors persisted. Would Perry come out? Rolie couldn't make it, but Dunbar turned up, and as Castronovo graciously stepped aside for him, it was clear that Schon had apparently—finally—buried the hatchet with the band's original drummer after the lawsuit that had so scarred their friendship. And other old friends came out of the woodwork, including the jumping *conguero* Mike Carabello and VD-prone *timbalero* Chepito Areas of the original Santana Blues Band, as well as Sammy Hagar, now known more for his star turn as the replacement singer in Van Halen and less for the 1984 album he had cut with Schon, Kenny Aaronson, and Mike Shrieve.

As the current and former members of Journey played the band's hits and some of their earlier material, one thing was abundantly clear: Steve Perry, still the one that everyone wanted to see, was a no-show. *Again.*

An arguably bigger honor was in store when on June 19, the Hollywood Chamber of Commerce announced that Journey would join José José, Nancy Sinatra, and Britney Spears as 2004 inductees in the "recording" category of the Hollywood Walk of Fame. Perhaps Perry would show this time?

Getting a star on Hollywood Boulevard, near Grauman's Chinese Theater and the Capitol Records Building and around the corner from the spot where Frumious Bandersnatch got their first big break opening for the Byrds, was actually not so difficult: all it took was $15,000 and a petition. The money covered the cost of planting the brass star in the sidewalk, and security for the unveiling. The petition was no difficult hurdle, given Journey's long-term popularity. By that time, "[a]ccording to the Recording Industry Association of America, the band [had] sold more than 40 million albums in the United States alone, about as many as Jimi Hendrix and the Who combined."

Journey scheduled the unveiling for January 21, 2005. As before, all former members were invited to participate, and this time, while Rolie couldn't make it, cerebral drummer Steve Smith, Aynsley Dunbar, and even vocalist Robert Fleischman and guitarist George Tickner confirmed their attendance in advance. Fleischman even agreed to sing "Wheel in the Sky" with the band that evening at the House of Blues.

This time, the reclusive Perry actually gave a few interviews. Problem was, when asked if he was coming to the unveiling, he refused to answer. Fool me twice, shame on me, so most fans—and certainly the band members themselves—expected another no-show.

In a last-ditch effort to rope him in, Schon went public to goad his former bandmate and writing partner into attendance. "You know, all day on the radio I've been inviting him. He always does this 'woe is me' bullshit about 'Oh, they don't like me. . . .' Well, you're invited. I mean, come on."

Jonathan Cain, always one to show more understanding, had a similar take: "I don't think he comes. . . . He's not good at confronting situations like this, you know? Never was. I mean, it's just part of his personality."

Reporter Dan Reines, who polled the fans in the crowd, found the response unanimous. Would Steve Perry attend? "No way," said one. "Zero percent chance," said another.

As the current and former members of Journey assembled around a podium and a red carpet covering the bass star in the pavement on Hollywood Boulevard near McCadden Place, one thing was abundantly clear: Steve Perry, still the one that everyone wanted to see, was a no-show. *Again.*

But then, at the very last moment, to everyone's surprise—there he was, wading through the crowd with a security officer. The long hair was gone, replaced with a crew cut, and despite crow's feet at the eyes, everyone knew that face. Dressed in a black suit, black shirt, and black necktie, he took the podium to address his fans, clearly aware of his own importance to the event.

"Being in the band [was] the most wonderful thing that ever happened to me, and . . . I really mean this from the bottom of my heart. You can have all the stuff that we knew it took, from management and the crew and the best players, but without you, you don't got shit! This star really belongs to you, and I wanna thank you for making it happen."

The crowd roared, the flashbulbs popped, and then it was over. Perry disappeared back into obscurity and Journey—with its replacement singer—went back out on tour.

But in the months that followed, something strange began to happen. Perry took to hanging out near the star and watching people take pictures with it. Sometimes he even joined in, to the disbelief of everyone around. Aidin Vaziri of the *San Francisco Chronicle* called it "creepy," but for the Journey fans who were lucky enough to experience it, it was an honor. More importantly, what did it bode for Journey's future?

*　　*　　*

And where had Steve Perry been since leaving Journey the second time? Mostly retired, and characteristically reclusive. He had eventually gotten the hip surgery and fully recovered but had made no moves to reunite with the band and indeed was difficult to reach for his former bandmates, even to talk business.

He had released several compilations of his previous work, starting with *Greatest Hits + Five Unreleased*. This collection of his solo material included hits from his blockbuster 1984 album *Street Talk*, including "Oh Sherrie" and "Foolish Heart;" most of the material from the unreleased album *Against the Wall*; some songs from his 1994 album *For the Love of Strange Medicine*; the soaring "I Stand Alone," from the soundtrack to the movie *Quest for Camelot*; a demo cowritten with the Babys' Tony Brock, "It Won't Be You," previously released as a B side to a single; and "If You Need Me, Call Me," the Alien Project demo that got him that fateful Journey audition back in 1977.

Then came *The Essential Journey*, a two-disc expansion of *Journey's Greatest Hits* with the addition of material from the *Trial by Fire* reunion and the *Captured* live album—but without any of the songs from before Perry joined the band. Coming as it did mere months after the release of *Arrival*, it was clear to fans that Columbia Records, which released the collection, did not view any of the post-Perry material as "essential"—in essence saying that Perry was essential to the success of Journey. Not an unreasonable sentiment, and one shared by a good many of the band's fans.

In 2002, Perry worked with former Ambrosia singer-guitarist David Pack on his album *The Secret of Movin' On*, eventually released in 2005, supplying backing vocals on the song "A Brand New Start." One reviewer wrote that the song "needs less Pack and a lot more Steve Perry, who only provides glimpses and traces of vocal contributions in the background"—a fair assessment. Mostly Perry harmonizes in the chorus. For a few moments in the second half, he seems ready to break out into one of his trademark solos, but he holds back.

In 2003, hanging out in the studio with guitarist Jeff Golub, who was working on the bluesy "Can't Let You Go"—initially intended as an instrumental for his album *Soul Sessions*—Perry suddenly said, "Man, I could really hear this vocal line going along with your guitar." The engineers quickly brought in a microphone and recorded him, justifying a statement that summer by John Kalodner (the A&R guru who had brought Journey together for the *Trial by Fire* reunion): "If Steve Perry wanted to sing, or wants to sing at ANY TIME, any manager, promoter or agent would be ecstatic" (emphasis in the original).

Perry did work with Kalodner again that year to develop and release the DVD *Greatest Hits 1978–1997*, a collection of Journey's music videos, including the stylized ones from *Frontiers* that he hated (including the atrocious "Separate Ways" video with the "air instruments" and the oblivious model walking in and out of frame). There were also the studio videos from the Gregg Rolie era, like "Feeling that Way," "Wheel in the Sky," and "Lights," and the concert videos from the *Raised on Radio* tour. Then he produced *Live in Houston 1981: The Escape Tour*, from a concert originally televised by MTV.

The work proved emotionally draining for the singer, as it forced him to recall aspects of his past he thought were long behind him. "It dragged me through a plethora of emotions that I didn't expect," he said. "When I heard 'Open Arms' I got choked up." But not enough to pursue another reunion with his former bandmates.

Despite these signs of life in his professional pursuits, Perry's personal life remained a mystery to the outside world—just the way he liked it. In 2007, he threw the crowd off the scent when he pretended to let it slip that he was married. Recounting how he kept secret a planned media use of a Journey song, he told the *Pittsburgh Post-Gazette* that "I didn't want to blow it. Even my wife didn't know. She looked at me and said, 'You knew that and you didn't tell me?'" But in later interviews he claimed (more truthfully) never to have been married. He had been deposed too often in legal proceedings around his former bandmates' many divorces to have any desire for the institution.

The reference to "my wife" was clearly designed, like his references to pizza and beer during interviews he gave in the early 1980s, to appeal to the sensibilities of his fans, an attempt to make himself an everyman. In 1982 he saw his fans as people who ate pizza and drank beer rather than the hot tea with honey he preferred for his throat. Now, in the 2000s, he knew his reputation still mattered for sales of prior albums as well as his stake in revenues from the band's current performances, so he made himself into a family man with a wife at home. He let fans imagine, perhaps, a mature version of ex-girlfriend Sherrie Swafford. He was certainly experienced at presenting a false identity; Jonathan Cain called it "the persona that Steve Perry had built as a singer [as] the boy next door with a broken heart who never got the girl."

Did Perry create the fiction of a wife and an active sex life because he was in the closet? If he were anything other than straight, he would have most likely wanted to keep that secret during his many years as a struggling singer and the superstardom that followed, worried that it would be unacceptable to his fans. And during the 2000s, when his cut of Journey's tour revenue came as often as not from their performances at county fairs in "red states"—areas of the country that did not accept "alternative" lifestyles—he may have feared that coming out would hurt ticket sales.

He needn't have worried. Given the continued popularity of Elton John, David Bowie, and the late Freddy Mercury, the bulk of Perry's female fans would likely have stuck with him. Those who saw him as a sex object—and many did—understood at least on some level that their attraction would never actually be reciprocated, regardless of whether he was straight or gay. Other than the tiny percentage who become groupies and the even smaller number who actually become girlfriends or wives, the women attracted to rock stars typically channel their desires toward their own boyfriends or husbands. Sexually satisfied at home after the show, they still buy the next album or splurge on the next ticket.

Aside from feminine traits like the conditioned, shoulder-length hair and the unbuttoned, knotted shirts that gave the appearance of a plunging neckline of an evening gown over a hairless chest, Perry gave several hints that he was at least bisexual.

A case in point is Perry's role in the film *Monster*, which includes a sympathetic take on lesbianism. Perry consented to the two specific uses of "Don't Stop Believin'" in the film. First, a portion is heard starting as background music in a roller rink and then at full volume as the main characters move outside to share their first kiss, under a streetlight, ogled by homophobic teenagers. Then it is played in its entirety during the closing credits. The decision to play Tommy James and the Shondells' "Crimson and Clover"—a title often erroneously thought to be a euphemism for a vagina—during the movie's only lovemaking scene (a lesbian sex scene) may have been at Perry's suggestion, as he was also credited as the film's music consultant. (The film's depictions of hetero sex consisted of rape and prostitution—not lovemaking.)

It is possible—but unlikely, given the film's overall context—that he enjoyed watching the kissing and lovemaking; many straight men are aroused by lesbian sex. But Perry also referred to his new short hairstyle as "butch"—a slang term often used in the gay community to designate the more masculine member of a lesbian couple.

This evidence may amount to nothing more than alliance; Perry may be "straight but not narrow." He fathered a child in the 1970s (unbeknownst to the media for four decades), but sexuality is a spectrum, not a binary. In the end, where he falls on that spectrum is his own business and that of his lovers. And Sherrie Swafford still isn't talking.

Just like during the 1987–1995 hiatus, there were also the Steve Perry "sightings." In December 2000 he had a cameo on the WB Network television show *Roswell*. While two of the main characters are Christmas shopping in a hardware store, Perry walks into the background to pay for an item at the cash register, turns slightly toward the camera, and then walks offscreen. Two years later, a sharp-eyed fan saw him at a San Francisco Giants game, and the following March he joined fans during the seventh-inning stretch of a spring training game in Scottsdale, Arizona, to sing "Take Me Out to the Ball Game."

Then, in 2005, when the Chicago White Sox adopted "Don't Stop Believin'" as an unofficial anthem for their improbable bid for the pennant, in something of a betrayal of his San Francisco fans, Perry showed up in Houston at the World Series to sing the song with the team. "They've always believed," he told a reporter, before going across the street to drive a few nails at a Habitat for Humanity worksite. Another contrived moment to nurture his reputation

among fans and the press? Perhaps. But the house got built and someone got
to move in, so did his motives really matter?

But there was something about that song. "Don't Stop Believin'" suddenly
seemed to be gaining a whole new popularity more than two decades after its
initial release. It certainly gave a renewed celebrity to its singer.

Its resurgence began when it was used to poke fun at 1980s music in the
Adam Sandler film *The Wedding Singer*. When it appeared on NBC's TV
show *Scrubs* in 2003, Nielsen reported that "retail sales of Journey's 'Greatest
Hits' increased 51 percent in the first full week after the show aired." And
there was its use in *Monster*. Charlize Theron took home a Golden Globe for
her work on the film and thanked Perry in her acceptance speech; Perry was
the surprise guest when director Patty Jenkins held a Q&A for film students
at the University of Kansas.

The following year, 2005, proved "a busy summer for the song," according to the *New York Times*. In MTV's "reality" show *Laguna Beach: The Real
Orange County*, one of the stars listened to it on camera; it made *Family Guy*
as karaoke and was included in "the soundtrack to 'Star Wars: A Musical
Tribute' . . . and as the hook for Capone & Noreaga's 'City Boys' on the Heatmakerz' 'Crack Mixtape Vol. 1.'" Perry also fielded a request for the song to
appear on the Fox television drama *The O.C.*

Each use of the song, or reference to it, in popular media boosted the
number of its iTunes downloads, a new *Billboard* category. It went as high as
number 13 on August 26. But the song's biggest moment of the decade—perhaps its biggest moment since its initial release in 1981—was still to come.

*   *   *

In 2005, Journey released another full-length album, *Generations*. Neal
Schon said the title symbolized how the band, now more than thirty years
old, had attracted multiple generations of fans and benefited from the talents of generations of musicians. Continuing the group's slide without Steve
Perry, however, none of the songs received any radio airplay. Although
replacement singer Steve Augeri did participate in writing five of the album's
thirteen tracks—including one, "Butterfly (She Flies Alone)," which he wrote
solo—and Kim Tribble and Night Ranger's Jack Blades cowrote one, Schon
and Jonathan Cain now emerged fully as Journey's main songwriting duo.

What makes the album interesting is that, despite Augeri's songwriting involvement, each of the other members of the band sings lead vocals on at least one track (although Augeri sings lead on each of the tracks he wrote or cowrote). Recorded at the Record Plant in Sausalito, where they had recorded *Raised on Radio* until the drug bust, the album also saw the return of Kevin Elson to the booth. Elson had been the band's live sound engineer for the *Infinity* and *Evolution* tours and producer of *Departure*, *Escape*, and *Frontiers*.

The album begins with two up-tempo rockers sung by Augeri: "Faith in the Heartland," by Schon, Cain, and Augeri, and "The Place in Your Heart," by Schon and Cain. There follow two mid-tempos by Schon and Cain: "A Better Life," sung by drummer Deen Castronovo, and "Every Generation," sung by Cain, with lyrics that are an attempt to recapture the magic of "Don't Stop Believin'": "Kids hanging out on a Saturday night/Cruisin' 'round town, just feels right." Next is "Butterfly (She Flies Alone)," Augeri's light ballad; "Believe," by Augeri and Tommy De Rossi, which speaks to the bonds of friendship ("I believe in you/Believe in me"); and "Knowing That You Love Me," a ballad with long, soaring vocal lines, written by Cain and sung by Augeri. "Butterfly" and "Believe" have the distinction of being the first songs without a Jonathan Cain writing credit since the keyboardist joined the band in 1980—a change that would not last.

"Out of Harm's Way," a rocker by Schon and Cain sung by Augeri, is another attempt to recapture the fans of "Don't Stop Believin'"—this time by writing about the experience of Iraq War vets. Following the attacks of September 11, 2001, the United States invaded Afghanistan, where the Taliban government had allowed Al Qaeda terrorists to set up their base camp. But US president George W. Bush and his advisors then made a false case for Saddam Hussein's possession of weapons of mass destruction to justify a war in Iraq, which had nothing to do with 9/11.

And so there was a danger that the band would appear to be taking sides in a political dispute. Much like in the 1960s with Vietnam, the nation was divided between citizens who opposed the war and those who supported it. In an era when the Dixie Chicks famously lost airplay and album sales for what some of their fans deemed an unpatriotic onstage statement, Journey's "Out of Harm's Way" carefully treads the middle ground, speaking only of veterans' sense of duty, but the idea inherent in the title is straight out of a

Bush "talking point" about the war. The president told the American Legion that our soldiers would "fight them over there so we do not have to face them in the United States of America." The lyrics include that theme: "So he signs up to fight . . . a desert war with another land . . . /Keepin' them all out of harm's way."

But other lyrics focus on the deindustrialization around the country that forced too many of our young men and women into the military in the first place: "The plant in town closed ten years ago . . . /For the last nine months he's tried to find a job." The song concludes by focusing on the difficulties of reentry: "Certain scents and smells trigger flashback spells/That rewind the tragedy."

Despite the danger of partisanship, the song is a remarkably empathetic piece tapping into the same postindustrial angst that had made Journey so successful in the 1970s and 1980s. But because it was sung by Steve Augeri and not "the other Steve," it never received the airplay that would have brought it to the ears of those for whom it was written.

The rocker "In Self-Defense" was, like the two "new" tracks released with the $Time^3$ box set in 1992, cowritten by Perry back in the '80s. In this case it was actually released at the time as part of Schon's second album with keyboardist Jan Hammer. Cain and Schon pulled it from the archives and recorded it with Journey, with Schon handling lead vocals. Next up is "Better Together," a mid-tempo by Schon, Cain, and Augeri, sung by Augeri. Then comes "Gone Crazy," a frenetic rocker by Schon, Cain, Tribble, and Schon's wife Amber, and sung—surprisingly—by Ross Valory. Schon and Augeri wrote "Beyond the Clouds," a ballad with soaring tenor vocals.

The album concludes with "Never Too Late," a rocker written by Schon, Cain, and Blades with a sound reminiscent of Survivor's 1980 hit "Rebel Girl" and sung by Castronovo, who proves to have quite the set of tenor pipes himself. The Japanese release of the album also includes a fourteenth track, "Pride of the Family," a ballad written and sung by Cain with singular acoustic and electric guitar lines provided by Schon.

As with 2002's *Red 13*, Journey initially released *Generations* at its concerts—this time as part of the ticket price: fans were handed the CD in a sleeve when they entered the venues where Journey was performing with Def Leppard that summer. Management hoped this would count as album sales and move the release into the *Billboard* album chart. The gambit largely failed; the album spent all of one week on the chart, at number 170, a far cry even from the lackluster performance of *Arrival* in 2001.

With the end of the 2005 tour—another fifty-eight appearances interrupted only by an emergency appendectomy for Cain—Journey released the album to retail through another independent label. But the separation from Columbia Records was clearly having adverse repercussions on the group's ability to promote new music.

In addition to the lack of a record label, the album lacked the admixture that had made their previous work so successful: that element of the Motown tradition that Steve Perry had brought, and the blues that inflected the original Journey. With *Arrival*, Schon and Cain had somehow managed to find that musical chemistry that their fans loved, but with *Generations*, they seemed to have lost it.

Journey had other problems. Fans who wondered why the band shared lead vocal duties on *Generations* were soon given their answer. Steve Augeri's lip-synching was spotted by astute fans as early as the 2003 "Friends and Family" show at the Warfield the night the band received a plaque on the Bay Area Walk of Fame. Wrote one reviewer at the time, "Many of us who stood so close to the stage noticed that Steve's voice sometimes did not match the movement of his mouth." When Augeri started hiding behind a larger-headed microphone, this change also did not go unnoticed. The singer had previously been using both arms to emphasize the emotive power of the lyrics, but now he displayed a much more careful posture, lest his lips be seen clearly.

Dean Ohlrich, a California-based Journey fan, broke the story on the web forum MelodicRock.com after comparing previous recordings with those from a recent performance in Manchester, England, during the band's first visit to the United Kingdom since the *Frontiers* tour in 1993. The response from other fans was heated, and eventually, after the conversation moved over to another website, MelodicRock.com's publisher, Andrew McNeice, no casual fan of the new Journey, urged the band to address the allegations.

At first they explained it as the stress of trans-Atlantic travel on Augeri's voice, but when other observers compared previous shows with earlier performances and found them note-for-note identical, it was clear that Augeri had been lip-synching for several years. And since "the odds against producing precisely the same vocal delivery would be astronomical," wrote Scottish music writer Ross Muir, "[i]f it's not a synchronised line, we're dealing with an extraordinary talent who can deliver exactly the same pitch perfect vocal including nuances and inflections night after night. If that was the case I'm guessing Steve Augeri's job before getting the Journey gig wouldn't have been Maintenance Manager for the Gap."

The band's official statements claimed that it was "industry standard" to supplement the live performance with backup recordings. After the Warfield show in 2003, "Rocko, a JRNY stage employee . . . confirmed that Steve [Augeri] was involved in a digital stage process . . . to enhance the singer's voice to make it sound as close to the original version of the song as possible."

Journey bassist Valory, for his part, blamed the messenger. "It turns out the person who stirred up the tape issue is not a journalist and didn't have the correct information," he told an interviewer, ironically *not* from a main-stream publication. "It appears to me some people have too much time on their hands, sometimes fans can be over-obsessed with the band of their dreams and they can get to be too imaginative or creative in order to provoke a response. It's like they're clutching at straws, and even inventing those straws!" Lest he be misunderstood, Valory added, "I don't, of course, wish to disparage the bulk of our fans." The fans were fine with him, as long as they paid for tickets and albums and didn't look too closely at what went on behind the curtain (or the microphone).

Lip-synching had long been a part of life in a successful band. In the MTV era, of course, artists were expected to lip-synch their own music during film-ing, and the director of Journey's stylized "Separate Ways (Worlds Apart)" video had expressed surprise when Perry actually sang during filming so that he would not appear to be lip-synching.

But a series of episodes in which artists were exposed lip-synching live—or substituting others' vocals for their own—did not go over well. The duo Milli Vanilli were caught in 1990 lip-synching to vocal lines recorded by others; they were forced to return their Grammy for Best New Artist, and three state legislatures considered bills making the practice illegal unless the artist clearly stated an intent to lip-synch.

Two years later, when opera tenor Luciano Pavarotti was caught lip-synching to his own recordings at a concert in Italy, it prompted a thought-ful piece in the *New York Times* comparing live musical performance with spectator sports. "[W]hen Mr. Pavarotti opens his mouth, we insist on not knowing what will come out. Public performance is more of a sporting event than we like to admit. We talk about beauty, but we all keep score."

In 2004, after Britney Spears's manager admitted that her act included both live and prerecorded vocals, éminence gris Elton John accused Madonna of the same, opining that "Anyone who lip-synchs in public on stage, when you pay £75 [about $60] to see them, should be shot," in keeping with the notion that a live rock act should be as true to the recorded version as possible—without actually *being* the recorded version. After Ashlee Simpson lip-synched during a performance on *Saturday Night Live*, her manager father claimed she had a sore throat but had refused to cancel the performance. So while Journey was right that performing live to a prerecorded track had become common enough to at least arguably be considered an industry standard, the practice was hardly uncontroversial.

Steve Perry called it for what it was: fake. "There's a lot of careers built on artists that . . . would run tapes, a lot of them were fake and would have mouth and ear pieces with little microphones in front of their faces and dance around." Robert Fleischman, too, decried the practice, the coauthor of "Wheel in the Sky" telling me, "It would be nice to usher in another era of bands that actually write good songs rather than just looking good and lip syncing most of the time."

Why this happened was no mystery: Steve Augeri had blown out his voice, singing Journey songs in their original key on a grueling tour schedule, year after year. Recorded when Perry was in his twenties and thirties, the songs were exceedingly difficult for a singer in his forties, and Augeri developed vocal nodules. These "hard, rough, noncancerous growths" on the vocal cords entered American popular culture with Mario Puzo's book *The Godfather*, where the character Johnny Fontane, a singer and nephew of the progenitor Vito Corleone, cannot get through more than a song or two without developing a severe sore throat. But the Journey money machine—the live act—had to keep rolling; as Schon said, "This is how I make my living, you know, and I need to pay the bills." Now approaching his fourth divorce, those bills were significant indeed.

Finally forced to admit that something was wrong, the band declared Augeri to be suffering from a "throat infection" and sidelined him shortly after their return to the states for the start of their 2006 tour. "We were hoping he'd be in well condition to handle the rigors of the road but unfortunately it appears to be a chronic condition requiring total voice rest," read the press statement. At his last show with the band, the jig was up, and there was no lip synching; his voice cracked and strained. Deen Castronovo sang the lead vocal along behind him, and when the pain in his throat was too intense for the high notes, he pointed to the drummer to take over.

Journey named Talisman singer Jeff Scott Soto as temporary replacement "while Steve Augeri recovers," the *Decatur Herald and Review* reported. Although he underwent surgery to remove the nodules, it quickly became apparent that the band had no intention of bringing Augeri back. "We did well with Steve Augeri while he was up and running, but when the voice goes there's no more songs. Our songs are all built around vocals, and so we had to fix it. It was a really ballsy move," Schon said, with no shortage of self-congratulation, "but I think it was the right one." Time would tell. Meanwhile they covered their bases and had Augeri sign an agreement to never reveal that he had been lip-synching.

*   *   *

Jeff Scott Soto, like Steve Augeri, was born in Brooklyn, New York, and was also deeply influenced by Steve Perry. Like Augeri and Kevin Chalfant and, indeed, any number of rock tenors of the era, he found that the resemblance to Perry's clean crooning sound got in the way of superstardom; unlike them, however, he switched his style, becoming more of a screamer. His first big break came in 1984, at age nineteen, when he was tapped by Swedish guitarist Yngwie Malmsteen for a collaboration that resulted in two albums, *Rising Force* and *Marching Out*. In 1988 he cofounded the Swedish hard rock band Talisman, which enjoyed immense popularity in Europe and released seven studio albums, two with Polydor Records and the rest with independent labels (including two with Frontiers, the Italian label that released Journey's 2003 EP *Red 13*). In 2001 he sang vocals for the fictional band in the Mark Wahlberg film *Rock Star*. He did a stint with Neal Schon's Soul SirkUS as a temporary break from Talisman, which he considered his permanent gig, until Schon tapped him for Journey. Talisman cut its 2006 tour short but promised to play their remaining dates when Soto returned (after Steve Augeri recovered from his supposed throat infection).

Jeff Scott Soto had something else in common with Steve Augeri and, for that matter, Steve Perry: he was not quite white, at least not in the Nordic sense. Perry was the child of Portuguese immigrants and Augeri's forebears hailed from southern Italy. Soto was Latino, which in the Americas usually indicates mestizo, or mixed European and Native American ancestry. Like Perry and Augeri—and, for that matter, like the Grateful Dead's Jerry Garcia—he identified as white, but his dark hair and eyes bespoke a Mediterranean swarthiness that brought a sense of the exotic to the Rust Belt crowds that Journey attracted—mainly the descendants of northern and eastern Europeans. Without realizing it, white fans found this attractive yet safe. As when the band had welcomed African American blues legends Albert King, Luther Allison, and Pinetop Perkins to the stage in Chicago in 1978 and then just as quickly hustled them off so they could get back to their "progressive" white rock, the audience found the introduction of race thrilling but harmless, minor when it came to Soto and Augeri and Perry, temporary when it came to the Chicago bluesmen. Like a ride at an amusement park. Or a horror movie. Or, more bluntly, a minstrel show.

But Soto had a job to do, and he knew how to do it. He hit the ground running. "They flew me in and two days later with no rehearsal and only a run through minutes before we went out on stage in front of 22,000 people, and I played my first Journey show."

Soto already worked well with fellow Soul SirkUS veterans Neal Schon and Deen Castronovo but quickly won over Jonathan Cain as well. "He just responded like Rocky Balboa [the fictional boxer played by Sylvester Stallone in the *Rocky* film franchise] and started swinging and worked his way through it. He really brought it together and I think every show he does gets a little better and it's impressive." As if to prove the point, when the singer slipped on the stage at a rainy show at the Hollywood Bowl, he popped right back up, shucked his shoes, and finished the set barefoot. The heroics were not lost on Castronovo, who said that if not for Soto, "I'd be sittin' at home fighting with my wife." Maybe, maybe not: as he had with Augeri, Castronovo shared lead vocals duties with Soto, singing "Faithfully" from behind the drum set, this time with the camera and spotlight on him; arguably he could have done so—and the rest of the repertoire—from the front of the stage if necessary. (In any event, his reference to domestic discord was an unfortunate choice of words, given his later arrests for intimate partner abuse.)

The new combination worked so well that by the end of the tour, the band dropped the pretense that Augeri would be returning. On December 19, 2006, they issued a press release announcing that Soto was now Journey's "official lead singer." After a career of too many comparisons to Steve Perry, like Augeri before him, Soto was ecstatic to finally be able to use the resemblance to its best effect. "I'm extremely excited about what I'm gonna be able to bring to this band," he told Andrew McNeice. And indeed, he and Schon and Cain had already started writing the next Journey album. His future with Journey seemed bright.

Not that there weren't naysayers. At the news that Soto had replaced Augeri, *Boston Globe* writer Geoff Edgers snarkily wrote that "this might be filed under the category of 'who cares?,'" explaining that "[w]hat Journey needs is to lure back Steve Perry. He can still sing. Honest. I got him to croon a few lines back in 2005. But Jeff Scott Soto? Is it ever a good sign when the 'rave reviews' the press agent cites are from the Grand Rapids Press?" Frankly, most fans could see his point.

Fans and reviewers alike could be forgiven a sense of whiplash when, not six months after the announcement, Journey fired Soto. He sang his last show for the band on May 12, 2007. Schon and Cain claimed the split was amicable. "He did a tremendous job for us and we wish him the best," Schon said. "We've just decided to go our separate ways, no pun intended. We're plotting our next move now." Cain added that "Jeff was always the consummate professional and we hope that he remains a friend of the band in the future. We just felt it was time to go in a different direction." Likely having signed a nondisclosure agreement, Soto did not contradict them, allowing only that the decision took him by surprise. Years later the singer admitted he still didn't know why he had been fired.

Soto's mixed loyalties may have played a role in the decision. When he stepped in to relieve Augeri in July 2006, Talisman was forced to postpone a series of dates in Europe; knowing that Journey would be touring Europe again in April 2007, Soto agreed to sing for Talisman there in May to make up those dates. And although he was clear that this would be a farewell tour for Talisman, no previous member of Journey had joined the band without making a clean break from whatever he had done before—and survived long. Prairie Prince briefly tried to have it both ways in Journey's first months but ultimately had to choose one or the other, and he rejoined the Tubes; Steve

Smith left Montrose and Jonathan Cain left the Babys when Journey came calling. Robert Fleischman, who attempted to maintain separate management, was out in mere weeks.

Side projects were allowed, but for "employee" band members like Augeri, Castronovo, and now apparently Soto, such side projects were best if they involved one of the principals. Castronovo was safe when he did side projects with Schon, and had Soto survived, he would have surely been allowed to join a Soul SirkUS reunion with the drummer and guitarist. But leading another band with its own fans? That was too much for Neal Schon to tolerate. And if anyone needed to be kept happy at this point, it was Schon.

One of Soto's comments during his Journey stint may be more illuminating as to why he was let go so quickly. "What I'll be able to contribute into hopefully, not necessarily reinventing Journey, but kind of reopening what once was. . . . I'm hoping to help turn it around the same way Sammy Hagar turned Van Halen around," the singer said, later adding, "When we did the European tour, it was our own set and we all agreed to vary it up and do some things that wouldn't normally be heard at a Journey show, and I was really happy about that."

Soto had unknowingly stumbled into the very dynamic that Schon was trying to avoid after the break with Perry. Back in 1971, Schon had watched as the relationship between Carlos Santana and Michael Carabello threatened the cohesiveness of his first major band. Then, when Perry walked away from Journey in 1987, Schon had watched helplessly as the band he cofounded was put on indefinite hiatus waiting for Perry to return. After *Trial by Fire*, the guitarist had learned his lesson: no more waiting. If Perry would not tour, the band would go on without him—but it would not replace him with another strong personality. From now on, the lead singer would be an employee—a million-dollar employee but an employee nevertheless—whose ego would not get in the way of Journey's continued success.

In 1998, when the band announced the hiring of Steve Augeri, many Journey fans wondered why they had not selected Kevin Chalfant. Not only had Chalfant already been in the Storm with Ross Valory, Gregg Rolie, and Steve Smith but he had also performed with Schon and Cain at the roast honoring Herbie Herbert in 1993. And Chalfant had proven he could handle Perry's high notes on "the dirty dozen." But his was an independent spirit and he would have modeled his stint as Journey frontman on Sammy Hagar's experience when he replaced David Lee Roth in Van Halen, playing the hits in concert, yes, but taking the band in new directions, owning and inhabiting the role in his own way.

That's not what Schon wanted. Schon wanted a Perry clone, and he got it in Augeri. When Soto started comparing himself with Sammy Hagar, his days with Journey were numbered. If anyone was going to "turn it around," it would be Neal Schon, not Jeff Scott Soto.

*   *   *

On June 10, 2007, less than a month after Jeff Scott Soto's last performance with Journey, HBO aired the final episode of the popular Mafia TV show *The Sopranos*, one of the most celebrated, and debated, endings in television history. Set in northern New Jersey, the series follows a modern-day "godfather," Tony Soprano, in his travails as the leader of a secondary Italian crime family in decline. While not a comedy per se, much of the plot was comedic, starting with the premise that the lead character would be in treatment with a classic Freudian psychoanalyst (not unlike a contemporary Mafia comedy film, *Analyze This*, starring Robert De Niro and Billy Crystal). Over six seasons, the protagonist gets deeper into his own angst even as the world of the American Mafia is fading.

In the final scene, Tony, actively hunted by rival gangs, the Federal Bureau of Investigation, and possibly even members of his own "crew," sits in a diner in Bloomfield, New Jersey. Joined first by his wife, then by his son, while his daughter struggles with parallel parking outside, various people whose presence seem ominous enter the diner; one of them, in a long-outdated Members Only jacket, heads to the men's room, in a nod to a murder scene from *The Godfather*.

Through it all, Tony's jukebox selection plays. Thumbing through the options, which include Sawyer Brown's version of the Oak Ridge Boys' "Somewhere in the Night," Heart's "Who Will You Run To" (written by Diane Warren of Bad English's "When I See You Smile"), and Tony Bennett's version of "I've Gotta Be Me," he settles on Journey's "Don't Stop Believin'." The scene concludes to the sound of Steve Perry singing his eighth or ninth "Don't stop," and the screen goes black, leaving the viewer to wonder what—if anything—happens next.

The choice of "Don't Stop Believin'" spoke volumes. *The Sopranos* existed in a postindustrial suburban world. The song had been written for fans like the fictional Tony, the teenagers of the late 1970s and early 1980s, not necessarily future mafiosi but youngsters similarly trying to find their place in a world where the opportunities that had propelled their parents into middle-class jobs seemed to be vanishing. Tony Soprano represented those fans who saw Journey at the Capitol Theater in Passaic, New Jersey, in 1978, rhythmically slapping the stage to demand another encore. Now in middle age, they faced new crises, having abandoned cities like Passaic (or Newark, in Tony's case) for the suburbs and finding them culturally wanting. The song, like the band that performed it live, appealed to a nostalgia for a mythical time before the concerns and challenges of either adolescence or middle age.

Watching at home in San Diego, Steve Perry knew what was coming. While the episode was in the final stages of editing, producer David Chase approached him for permission to use the song. Initially the singer refused, "concerned that this could be a finale bloodbath or a [St.] Valentine's [Day] massacre." He demanded to be told how the scene would play out, but Chase did not want to let the secret slip; the actors and crew were contractually kept from "spilling the beans," but Perry was not. Ultimately Perry convinced Chase that he would keep quiet, and the producer relented. Cowriters Neal Schon and Jonathan Cain had already given their permission for the song to be used, and Perry's permission came on Thursday, June 7, only three days before airtime. Once Perry learned of the ending, he agreed that it was "just perfect" and stayed true to his promise.

The series finale of *The Sopranos* brought Journey once again into the cultural zeitgeist, even as it confirmed their status as a "nostalgia act." The day before the show aired, "Don't Stop Believin'" was downloaded on iTunes 1,000 times; the day after, 6,531 times, rising to number 17 for the week. *Journey's Greatest Hits* "also cracked the Top 20." And according to Nielsen, radio airplay of the song "increased 192 percent Monday through Thursday over the first four days of the previous week." Before long "Don't Stop Believin'" had become "the bestselling digital track from the 20th century," as one reporter put it, and remains so as of this writing. "Not Michael [Jackson]. Not Bruce [Springsteen]. Not Whitney [Houston]. But the rock band that still has us holding on to that feelin'."

Schon had taken a big risk firing Jeff Scott Soto, the sort of move he liked to call "ballsy." But it was his move to make. Herbie and Perry had destroyed each other fighting over the band's leadership. Herbie's replacement, Irving Azoff, ran a multiclient organization that provided support for the band's operations but little guidance or direction.

For better or worse, it was Schon's band now. And with "Don't Stop Believin'" featured on the *Sopranos* finale, Journey was more popular than ever.

But without a lead singer, they were dead in the water.

Guitar Solo
Neal Schon

He really wasn't going to high school. He was there, but he wasn't going to high school.

—*Gregg Rolie*

Carlos Santana wrote, "I could not be another Lightnin' Hopkins or Gábor Szabó or Michael Bloomfield . . . [t]hey had their own sounds and integrity. I needed to get mine together. I would have to be Carlos Santana and do it so well that no one would mistake me for anyone else." And he did. So what of Neal Schon, the Santana "second lead guitarist" who found his greatest success playing popular rock hits with Journey? At some level, Schon has never been truly original. His sound is too much like Eric Clapton, whose licks he learned note for note in his formative years. On the other hand, for the purpose of producing fantastically popular rock songs, it has served.

Much of the founding myth of Journey is predicated on Schon's claim— repeated many, many times over the years—that as a teenager he found himself in the enviable position of being sought by both his idol Eric Clapton and by Carlos Santana. Born on an Oklahoma Air Force base to a music teacher and jazz clarinet player, Neal Schon played oboe as a child before turning to rock music, finding that he "wanted to be Jimi Hendrix." This kept him from his studies. "The only classes that I ever went to . . . were Art and Music. So, I'd spend half the day down in the music room cutting my other classes . . .

and my teachers used to cover for me!" After the family moved to San Mateo, California, in 1961, Schon found himself "constantly on the streets of San Francisco with my guitar, trying to get into the clubs that you're not allowed into until you're 21," the prodigy said. "But I would eventually make friends with all the club owners so they'd let me in and I'd play with anybody who would let me." Before long he was sitting in with Elvin Bishop and B. B. King. That's how he met Gregg Rolie and Michael Shrieve, who introduced him to Carlos Santana, who started inviting him to jam with his group during gigs.

According to Schon, the teen was hanging around with the band in the Wally Heider Studios in Berkeley one day when Bill Graham brought in Eric Clapton to meet them, and he started jamming with his idol. The next day Schon wandered back into the studio and was told Clapton was looking for him, wanted him to come to a performance at the Berkeley Community Theater that night. Clapton called Schon on stage and the teen proceeded to play all the Brit's solos, note for note. That evening, Schon claims, Clapton asked the youth to join his band Derek and the Dominos, in a slot originally filled in the studio by Duane Allman. That's when Carlos Santana realized "that if we wanted to keep Neal with us we only had one choice," which left Schon in perhaps the most enviable position of any teenage guitarist in rock history—not unlike where drummer Steve Smith found himself in 1977—courted by two established musical acts. "I wanted to play with Clapton more than Santana but I could tell Clapton was going through some problems," Schon said. "I'm pretty good at scoping out a situation and feeling whether it's happening or not. I felt that it wasn't happening with Clapton and it was with Santana because I knew him." Age and location were also, seemingly, a factor: "If I had gone with Eric I would have had to move to England and I was only 15 and I don't think I was ready to do that," he said (misremembering his age in 1970, which was actually 16).

But Derek and the Dominos keyboardist and singer Bobby Whitlock tells a very different version of the story. "His daddy brought him to one of our shows and we were on . . . our American tour, and tried his best to talk Eric into letting him play with our band. . . . But he sat in with us, and it was just—it didn't fit . . . his playing was entirely wrong for us." Asked if Clapton ever offered Schon the gig, Whitlock was certain he did not. He never saw such an offer, and Clapton was never alone with either of the Schons. "If Neal Schon was anywhere [with Clapton] he was backstage and I saw him and stuff. We always kept tight—Eric didn't have a dressing room and so on, and—it wasn't like that. We carried our own suitcases and we only brought two guitars."

Getting nowhere with Clapton, in all likelihood Schon's father used the claim of a gig with the British star as leverage for another job for his son. Of course, what happened next is without doubt: Neal Schon joined Santana as second lead guitarist and was never without work thereafter. Santana led to Azteca and plenty of session work and then to Journey.

*   *   *

At the height of Journey's popularity, the guitarist proved the most prolific of the band's members at the solo game. In 1981, Schon teamed up with keyboardist Jan Hammer of the Mahavishnu Orchestra and British session bassist Colin Hodgkinson to record a side project as Schon & Hammer. With Schon covering vocals and Hammer doubling as drummer, the three went into the studio during one of the short breaks from the *Escape* tour to record *Untold Passion*, released by Columbia Records that November. The nine songs are guitar- and synthesizer-driven hard rock, with some creativity and copious talent. The ever-effusive Herbie Herbert called it "the Police meet Cream and Jimi Hendrix." Schon used the opportunity to explore the guitar synthesizer, a new instrument that allowed guitarists to generate sounds similar to those of which keyboardists had long been capable. All three musicians took writing credits on the record, which includes four instrumentals among the nine total tracks, and won the 1982 Bammie for Best Debut Album.

The following year, after Journey's second *Escape* tour, they got together for one more album. Released in December 1982, *Here to Stay* includes more radio-friendly songs like "No More Lies," which Journey performed during the 1983 *Frontiers* tour. At one performance of the song, captured in the *Frontiers and Beyond* documentary, Schon plays through the pain and flowing blood of a head wound from a glass bottle thrown from the audience. Schon's Journey bandmates also participated in the album, Steve Perry cowriting two tracks. "Self Defense," cowritten by Perry and Jonathan Cain, could be considered a Journey song, as it also includes Perry on backing vocals, Smith on drums, and Ross Valory on bass. It was coproduced by Journey soundman Kevin Elson and missed out on inclusion in Journey's *Frontiers*—but is a good fit on *Here to Stay* (and also eventually landed on

Generations). The album cover plays on the similarity of the group's name to the baking soda Arm & Hammer, featuring a tattooed muscular arm holding a sledgehammer. The tattoo is the band's logo from *Untold Passion*—a heart punctured by lightning bolts.

Reviews were generally positive. Pete Bishop of the *Pittsburgh Press* called *Untold Passion* "extremely rewarding" and found *Here to Stay* "a solid album, several steps above workmanlike." But as with Journey's early work, critically acclaimed albums scored poorly with the general public. *Untold Passion* made it to number 115 on November 28, 1981, while *Here to Stay* made it only as high as number 164 (number 30 on the *Billboard* rock albums chart).

As Hammer went on to score the soundtrack for the hit television series *Miami Vice*, which aired on NBC from 1984 to 1990, Schon next teamed up with singer/guitarist Sammy Hagar, bass player Kenny Aaronson, and drummer Denny Carmassi. He had previously collaborated with Hagar on one track on the singer's 1980 solo album *Danger Zone* (and Hagar had previously employed both Aynsley Dunbar and Cain). Hagar and Carmassi had been in the original, pre–Steve Smith iteration of Montrose and then had collaborated on two of Hagar's solo albums. But by the time Schon came off Journey's *Frontiers* tour, Carmassi had joined Nancy Wilson and Ann Wilson full-time in the band Heart. Schon asked original Santana drummer Michael Shrieve to join up instead, and they formed the supergroup Hagar Schon Aaronson Shrieve—their four last names without punctuation, but often simply abbreviated as "HSAS." Hagar and Schon both being "type A" personalities and successful rock guitarists, they agreed that Hagar would provide all the lead vocals and Schon all the guitars. These two principals both took coproducer credits for the album *Through the Fire* and wrote eight of its nine tracks (the ninth being a cover of Procol Harum's "Whiter Shade of Pale"). Schon later posited that he alone actually produced the record and that Hagar was never in the studio. "He just wanted his name there, that's—Sammy's crazy, he's like, you know, egomaniac," said the pot of the kettle. "Yeah, he loves himself." They recorded the album live in November 1983 at clubs in San Francisco, San Jose, and San Rafael—with proceeds donated to local arts and sports programs. They mastered it at Fantasy Studios, stripped the tracks of the audience sounds, and secured its release through Geffen Records, where Hagar had a contract as a solo artist. Like Schon & Hammer, this is hard rock, but unlike that prior collaboration, there are no keyboards. *Through the Fire* unsurprisingly sounds like a combination of Van Halen and the hard rock numbers on *Escape* and *Frontiers*. And indeed, Hagar went on to replace David Lee Roth as longtime Van Halen lead singer—but not before recording a concert with HSAS for MTV.

Reviews were mixed. One, noting that HSAS was managed by Herbie's Nightmare Productions, called it "the biggest bonafide supergroup to come together since Asia and, perhaps, the most pre-packaged band since the Monkees." The *Chronicle*'s Joel Selvin called the band "less than the sum of its parts, to put it kindly." But Pete Bishop liked the group and its sound, except for a few of the instrumental tracks, and the album garnered Schon yet another Bammie for Outstanding Guitarist.

*   *   *

Late Nite, Schon's 1989 solo album, is bluesy, jazzy, and of course guitar-heavy, with some experimentation. All of its eleven tracks were written by Schon and Bob Marlette, with Gregg Rolie and Glen Burtnik joining for "Softly," a ballad with some airplay potential; Rolie for "I'll Be Waiting"; Burtnik for "I'll Cover You"; and Jonathan Cain for "Rain's Comin' Down" and "Smoke of the Revolution," on which Cain's keys accompany background vocals by an up-and-comer named Sheryl Crow. Six of the tracks are instrumental, some with only background vocals, including the ten-minute "The Theme," which recalls some of Schon's guitar explorations during the Journey years prior to Perry's arrival; an updated, synthesizer-heavy version, "Inner Circles," comes later on the album. Randy Jackson plays bass, and Marlette plays keyboards on all tracks except "Smoke of the Revolution," which also introduces Deen Castronovo. Otherwise, Steve Smith and Omar Hakim—another local drummer who had been rejected by Perry for Journey's *Raised on Radio*—sit in on sticks and skins.

In 1999 Schon released another solo album, *Piranha Blues*, with twelve songs cowritten by Schon and Richard Martin-Ross of the short-lived LA band Skatt Brothers (which had included Craig Krampf of Steve Perry's previous band Alien Project). Martin-Ross supplies a rough rock vocal over the otherwise bluesy hard rock on the album. Prairie Prince provides drums, Ross Valory bass, and Stevie "Keys" Roseman, who had worked with Journey on

"The Party's Over (Hopelessly in Love)," the lone studio track on *Captured*, sits in on the Hammond B3 organ.

Shortly after completing work on Journey's *Arrival*, Schon released a rather unique solo album, *Voice*. It consists of ten instrumentals, each a popular standard or recent hit, from Lucia Dalla's "Caruso" to Roberta Flack's "Killing Me Softly" to Bryan Adams's "(Everything I Do) I Do It for You," with Schon replacing each vocal line with his guitar. Ostensibly he recorded the album to honor the singers he had worked with over the years, but in light of the recent separation of his band from its most famous singer, fans could not help but wonder if he was making another statement entirely—that his guitar is voice enough. Regardless of intent, the album was a tour de force, peaking at number 15 on *Billboard*'s New Age chart on August 24, 2001, and earning a Grammy nomination in the Best Pop Instrumental Album category, Schon's first as a solo artist. "Perhaps the most important thing this album demonstrates about Neal Schon is his very human complexity," I wrote at the time, adding that "[w]hat Voice shows us is . . . how versatile a musician he is." The Grammy ultimately went to guitarists Larry Carlton and Steve Lukather for *No Substitutions—Live in Osaka*, but Schon, a good sport and longtime friend of the winners, said, "It was an honor for me just to be nominated," adding, in an unfortunate if apt choice of words, "I did leave with a trophy . . . my wife," the model Amber Kozan, then pregnant with the couple's first child.

Always looking for more to do, and now looking for an income stream unencumbered by his deal with Steve Perry, in 2002 Schon reconnected with Sammy Hagar. Hagar had enjoyed a successful run in Van Halen in the intervening years; now they teamed up with Van Halen bass player Michael Anthony and Journey's Deen Castronovo—always willing to follow Schon into any venture. Calling themselves Planet US, they initially enlisted famed Guns N' Roses alumnus Slash as a second lead guitarist, but when he proved unavailable, they took in Joe Satriani. The group quickly wrote and recorded two songs, one of which seemed like a good fit for the soundtrack to the movie *Spider-Man* but was ultimately rejected, according to Schon, for being too "heavy." After a few performances, including the California Music Awards (formerly the Bammies) and as an opening act for Hagar's solo act, the group tried to find more time together in the studio—but they failed, what with Journey's tour schedule that summer. Schon kept writing heavy rock for them, but Hagar's return to Van Halen in early 2003 (he called it "the Van Hagar reunion") doomed the venture.

Schon reworked some of the songs for the next Journey album, *Generations*; one he released as part of yet another side venture with Castronovo: Soul SirkUS, which came together in 2004 with Jeff Scott Soto and bass player Marco Mendoza, who had played with Ted Nugent and Whitesnake. Soul SirkUS released a single album, *World Play*, initially through a band website and then in 2005 with Frontiers Records, before breaking up for Castronovo and Schon to return to their main gig. That same year, Schon released yet another solo album, *I on U*, this time with Favored Nations Records, the imprint of guitarist Steve Vai. The album includes twelve instrumental tracks ranging from jazz to fusion to techno, nine of which were cowritten by Schon and Igor Len and three by Schon on his own. Schon plays guitar, bass, and synthesizer; old friend Omar Hakim handles drums.

*   *   *

One of the downsides of becoming a successful teenage rock god may be stunted emotional growth, and unlike mere mortals, Schon could always move on from violated friendships and unhappy marriages—he just had to keep paying alimony and child support. He claimed in 2008 that he had amassed a large enough fortune to retire, thanks largely to the continuing income from the stage lighting company Nocturne, which he still owned with Herbie Herbert; when they sold it in 2011, it had become "the world's premiere concert touring video service company," listing among its clients such major acts as "Paul McCartney, Lady Gaga, Bon Jovi, Madonna, Eagles, Van Halen, Metallica, KISS, Britney Spears, Bruno Mars, Ricky Martin, Janet Jackson, Elton John, Tim McGraw, Radiohead, Red Hot Chili Peppers, Nickelback, Kid Rock, NKOTBSB, James Taylor, Sting, Nine Inch Nails, Carrie Underwood, Def Leppard, Linkin Park, Alice in Chains . . . and many others." But he kept adding ex-wives whose maintenance he could not out-race, even with the fastest sports car in his garage. The millions he earned on the road and from royalty payments never seemed to be enough; while he claimed to be a workaholic because he had so many musical ideas, in fact he bolstered his income from each of his several solo albums during this period (at least from the hardcore Journey fans and industry professionals who bought them; none enjoyed sales comparable to his Journey records from the band's heyday).

Schon had two children with Amber Kozan, the model who had become his fourth wife in 1998. After their 2008 divorce, she managed to finish a bachelor's degree in history from Augsburg College and started work on a teaching certificate but was suspended for failure to make her tuition payments. When she asked the guitarist for more money in 2013, Schon took her to court, saying he had already paid her "more than $1.3 million over the past five years." A judge supported the guitarist, noting that Amber's annual expense report claimed such frivolities as "$9,600 for eyeglasses, $9,600 for birthday parties, $7,200 for clothing." When the *London Daily Mail* reprinted a blog post by Amber's mother, Judy Kozan, the former mayor of Waseca, Minnesota, in which she hinted that Schon was a "deadbeat dad," Schon sued for libel, arguing that she had been going after him online "for years." They settled out of court for an undisclosed sum.

Next up was *Playboy* centerfold Ava Fabian. This fifth "marriage" was less complicated, as the couple only had a "humanistic union" of dubious legal validity in Paris in 2011 which produced no children and lasted all of two months. If he was keeping count, he might have decided to ignore this one for its brevity and questionable legality. But the marriage mattered to Fabian—a friend of Amber's—who was devastated by her mate's next escapade.

On November 24, 2009, President Barack Obama welcomed Indian prime minister Manmohan Singh to the White House for an official state visit. Among the millions of Americans *not* invited to the state dinner that evening were Virginia vintner and sometime Middle East peace advocate Tareq Salahi and his wife, Michaele, who was being filmed as a participant in the television show *Real Housewives of D.C.* They showed up anyway—and got in, shaking hands with Singh and Obama. Apparently one guard waved them through despite their not being on the invitation list, because there was a light drizzle and pressure to move the increasingly moist VIP line; they passed the second checkpoint seemingly because they were well dressed and looked like they belonged there. They went through a metal detector and were cleared. The press called it what it was: a failure of the Secret Service.

Two years later, the publicity-hungry couple were back in the news. In September 2011, Tareq Salahi went to the police and declared Michaele missing. As it turned out, she was not missing at all. She had run off to join Neal Schon on tour. Apparently the two had dated in the 1990s, and he now told the press that he had always been in love with her—despite intervening marriages for each of them. Before long, Schon was describing Michaele as his fiancée, and Journey management was requiring journalists to sign a waiver promising not to photograph the audience—lest they catch a shot of her. The jilted Tareq, for his part, told the press that he was protected by a prenuptial agreement before veering toward the absurd when he claimed that the family *dog* had died of a heart attack over Michaele's betrayal.

The affection between Schon and Michaele Salahi certainly appeared genuine. At an interview in which the guitarist was speaking about his early years with Santana, a member of the audience started a question with "When you were young, and you were fifteen—" at which point Schon jokingly cut him off, asking, "What do you mean, when I was young?" The host intervened. "Let's ask his fiancée. Is he still young?" to which the blushing Michaele, standing in the wings, gushed, "Very."

They married in December 2013, at the Palace of Fine Arts in San Francisco. The 365 guests included the current members of Journey, Sammy Hagar, Bob Weir of the Grateful Dead, *The Apprentice* contestant (and future Trump advisor) Omarosa Manigault, and Brian McKnight. Steve Perry was not present but was probably invited, given Schon's continuing public statements about his desire to mend fences with his former partner. The Tower of Power performed, as did Journey, and Schon himself played a solo. The entire event was broadcast on pay-per-view because money mattered to Schon—and why not? Afterward the couple incorporated as N & M Productions and showed City Hall just how much money mattered. They sued San Francisco, claiming they had been overcharged for the wedding, which their lawyer actually called a civil rights violation. Just as Journey was a corporation as much as a band, Neal and Michaele Schon were now a corporation as much as a marriage. The city settled, returning $290,000. The White House gate-crasher surely felt she had made a sound investment, despite Schon's prior failed marriages. And he seemed to have finally met his mate. But as with Journey's lead singers, time would tell if the sixth would be the charm. She took to following her husband on tour as the band's unofficial photographer, the better to keep his eye from roving too far.

*   *   *

Neal Schon never let more than a year or two pass without releasing a solo album completely different from the last, with collaborators continually drawn from his deep well of Bay Area friends. He also kept trying to build a reunion of any sort. Back in the 1990s, he had masterminded the "Santana without Carlos" reunion called Abraxas; in 2014, he finally convinced Carlos to reunite with much of that original band. Carlos, Gregg Rolie, Michael Shrieve, Michael Carabello, and Schon joined current Santana bassist Benny Rietveld and *timbalero* Karl Perazzo to release the album *Santana IV* in the spring of 2016, consciously giving it a title that evoked the band's first three albums before the breakup. The album's highlights include a cameo by singer Ronald Isley for two tracks and no shortage of the exciting Latin and Afro-Cuban rock that this combination of musicians had made famous nearly fifty years before. Rolie's "hey baby . . . sit on my lap" lyrics seem somewhat creepy now that the organist was approaching seventy, but the album gar-nered positive reviews in the *New York Times, Rolling Stone,* and the *San Francisco Chronicle,* and peaked at number five on the *Billboard* 200. The group appeared live at the Las Vegas House of Blues to promote the album and opened for Journey three times, but after that the reunion fizzled; Rolie toured as part of Ringo Starr's All-Starr Band that summer, Schon returned to Journey, and Carlos moved on, as he always did, with a rotating group of musicians.

After Journey's 2017 induction into the Rock and Roll Hall of Fame, Schon tried another reunion, this time with a unique combination of former mem-bers of Journey. On February 9, 2018, he and Gregg Rolie teamed up with bass player Marco Mendoza, with whom Schon had previously worked in Soul SirkUS; a keyboardist named John Varn; and Deen Castronovo on drums and lead vocals to play a benefit for North Bay Fire and Rescue and the victims of recent wildfires, at the Independent in San Francisco. John Waite was an expected "special guest," but he bowed out at the last minute for another gig. Calling the grouping "Journey through Time," they performed a few Journey hits but mostly "deep cuts" like "Lady Luck," "Daydream," and "Still They Ride," even finding time for two Dunbar-Rolie compositions from the pre-Perry era: "Hustler" and "People."

What Schon really wanted was another reunion with Steve Perry. "I do hope that him and I can work together in the future on something different, even if it's only a song for a movie or whatever."

Indeed, a central tension after Perry left Journey the second time was between Schon's virtual ownership of the band, on the one hand, and its popular association with Perry, on the other. Even though the current Journey includes both its original guitar genius—Schon—and classic songwriting wizard—Jonathan Cain—it is the voice of Steve Perry on the radio, Pandora, and Spotify, and on CD and MP3 players worldwide. So despite Schon's desire to "own" Journey, he knows that for most fans, Perry continues to be synonymous with the band Schon helped found. Having shown so much early promise as a child prodigy thrust into superstardom with Santana, Schon remains frustrated by Perry's continued association with the band in the minds of the fans, even decades after the singer left Journey for good.

"After All These Years," 2007–2017

I'm just here to celebrate the legacy of Journey.

—*Arnel Pineda*

If California's Central Valley produces almonds and rock singers, the Philippines produces street kids—and rock singers. Arnel Pineda was born in Manila to a downwardly mobile family. The oldest of three boys, his parents scraped out a living as tailors, but when his mother died and his father sold everything in a failed attempt to pay the rent and feed the children, the thirteen-year-old was thrust out onto the dirty streets. "He collected scrap metal, bottles, and old newspapers, usually bringing home the equivalent of thirty cents a day," according to a *GQ* magazine profile. His road to solvency was paved by his tenor singing voice and an uncanny ability to mimic the styles of many a famous singer. Before long the diminutive Pineda was fronting a teen cover band attired in pastel-colored knockoff Members Only jackets. It was a living, and it kept his younger brothers fed, clothed, and housed, so they could avoid the worst of Arnel's year sleeping with other homeless kids in Manila's Luneta Park, where he had used the fountain to drink and bathe.

The Philippines was something of a mecca for cover bands and karaoke, beginning in the 1960s when the islands catered to American servicemen on leave from fighting in Vietnam—a tradition that continued well into Pineda's lifetime. "They want to hear you singing other bands' songs that made it to number one. Like Beatles, Led Zeppelin, Journey," he said.

Pineda gained some local fame with a cover band that relocated to Hong Kong in search of the limelight. In 1999 he impressed the executives at Warners enough to release an album, *Arnel Pineda*, which garnered some local airplay. Failed relationships, minor stardom, and custody battles over two sons born in the early 1990s drove him to alcohol and drugs, and by the early 2000s he had nearly done permanent damage to his vocal cords; a doctor told him he was finished as a singer. But he recovered, with a devotion to clean living, and nursed his voice back to full strength. By 2007 he was back in the Philippines with a new band, the Zoo, which performed covers of what was now considered classic rock and released an original album in 2007 that barely made it to the States. Devoted fan Noel Gomez recorded their performances and posted them on YouTube. Now pushing forty, Pineda settled down and married his supportive girlfriend, Cherry. With a baby on the way, he started writing heartfelt original tunes. But the owners of the bars and clubs where the band played, as well as their rowdy customers, had no interest in Pineda's music. "If you only play original songs, [audiences in the Philippines] will not appreciate you 100 percent," he said. The prospect of a record contract was never even a consideration. Dejected, Pineda considered giving up his dreams and leaving music for good.

Jeremey Hunsicker, on the other hand, was hardly raised on the streets of Manila or any other city in a developing country. The product of a middle-class background, Hunsicker made a decent living as a mild-mannered sales representative by day while indulging his rock star fantasy by night. He fronted the Journey cover band Frontiers, which traveled as far as five hundred miles from their home base in Roanoke, Virginia—and which attracted attention. Jonathan Cain's daughter Madison, now living in Nashville, had seen him perform on YouTube and went to a Frontiers show to check him out. Impressed, she told her father about Hunsicker's near-perfect vocal resemblance to Steve Perry, and in May 2007 Cain and Neal Schon flew to Charlotte, North Carolina, to see the band, awkwardly trying to stay inconspicuous. They approached him afterward and congratulated him on the show, exchanging phone numbers. Weeks later, when the finale of *The Sopranos* aired, Hunsicker called Schon to congratulate *him*. "And he got on the phone and said, nonchalantly, 'Yeah, we just let Jeff Scott Soto go,' and I was floored," reported the singer. Before long, the band had invited Hunsicker to San Francisco to audition for Journey. Soto, already a friend for several years, told him, "I hope they treat you better than me." Robert Fleischman might have given the same warning.

The audition lasted a week, during which Hunsicker and his pregnant wife were given tours of downtown San Francisco and Marin County, and he cowrote the rocker "Never Walk Away" with Schon and Cain. Then he joined the band at Cain's Wild Horse Studio to record the song's demo.

It was an exciting week, and Hunsicker allowed himself to believe the job was his. Just like in the film *Rock Star*, where a tribute singer gets hired to join the main act, his oldest dream seemed on the verge of coming true. The band assured him they weren't auditioning anyone else. Schon said it was "a bit scary because he was almost too much like Perry. He was almost like a duplicate, probably the closest of anyone out there. And what was kind of strange was he also looked like him a bit." All the other tribute singers had already been considered and rejected, and there would be no open auditions. Nor was the band soliciting demo tapes; unlike in the past, the advent of ProTools—basically the Adobe Photoshop of recorded music—allowed demo tapes to be easily altered to make a singer pitch-perfect. (Indeed, Journey had some experience in that department, the discovery of which ended Steve Augeri's tenure with the band.) Instead, Schon trolled YouTube, calculating that raw footage was less likely to be doctored.

One other option—barring another reunion with Perry—was never considered: Kevin Chalfant, the former lead singer of the Storm and the VU, who had sat in for Perry when Journey played the Herbie Herbert roast in 1993. Chalfant was at that very moment recording an album of Journey covers, demonstrating that he still had the vocal range for the material.

Upon his return home, Hunsicker received a phone call from Cain. He was to come back to San Francisco in two weeks to finish writing and recording Journey's next album. He would receive a six-figure retainer in anticipation of joining the band on tour in the spring of 2008; in the meantime, he would need to wrap up his affairs in Virginia. The next call was from manager Irving Azoff: "Welcome to Journey." Reflecting on the audition in San Francisco, Hunsicker said, "I had dined with rock and roll royalty, men who had the power to change lives with a single phone call, and with no more thought than it took to order Chinese carry out."

Three hours later his dream became a nightmare—to coin a phrase—when he got a call from John Baruck, the Azoff executive who directly managed Journey. "Schon had decided things were moving too fast" and the band would need "to take a breather." Hunsicker called Schon and said he didn't want to be "jerked around." With a baby on the way, he needed to know where he stood and could not afford to give up his day job if the Journey gig did not pan out. He called Cain, complaining that "you made me jump through every hoop and I passed every test with flying colors, and then you pull this shit," only to discover that "nobody in the band knew that Neal had done this." Cain encouraged Hunsicker to stay available, and they kept talking through the summer of 2007. But then the calls stopped. And then came another press release.

What had caused Schon to have cold feet about Jeremey Hunsicker? Initially, the singer thought Schon was worried that his wife would interfere with the band's ability to function as a team. "Neal was really bothered by my wife and her pregnancy." He "had this paranoia about me having to bring my wife on tour or something, or her having to approve my stage clothes." The couple was affectionate during the audition week, and she may have come off as somewhat clingy. But Hunsicker was clear, when asked, that his wife's concerns were not anything to worry about; she was no Yoko Ono (or, for that matter, Sherrie Swafford). "[H]ey, she's seven months pregnant and she just found out five weeks ago that her sales rep husband may leave to tour the world for the next four or five years," Hunsicker said.

Later, another possibility emerged. "Come to find out . . . it was pretty much Neal's girlfriend the whole time . . . . She didn't like how my wife and I got along . . . I found out that yeah, this girl of Neal's at the time pretty much was getting him all worked up about things, and she was actually kind of proud of her role in the whole situation."

The situation was surely also a nail-biter for Jonathan Cain, who now found himself in the opposite position from when he auditioned for the Babys back in December 1979. That band had cut its third album without a regular keyboardist and saw two hits with radio airplay but no way to go on tour. Now that *The Sopranos* finale had aired, Journey had a golden opportunity to exploit the renewed success of "Don't Stop Believin'"—but no one to sing it.

But Schon had good reason to keep the band on the edge. Ultimately his decision was swayed neither by his concerns about Hunsicker's wife nor his own girlfriend's jealousy. Just like in 1977, when Herbie first heard that Steve Perry demo tape, Schon had found another singer. He had continued scouring the internet for footage of various tribute and cover band singers and came across one who intrigued him even more than Hunsicker: Arnel Pineda.

"I went on YouTube for a couple of days and just sat on it for hours," said the guitarist. "I was starting to think I was never going to find anybody." Whether he already had it in mind, or it simply happened in the eleventh hour, he came across the grainy videos of Pineda singing "Faithfully" and "Don't Stop Believin'" at the Hard Rock Café in Manila. What struck him was that not only did Pineda sound just like Steve Perry but he also had, thanks to the tough competition for cover bands in the Philippines, the emotive qualities that had been so important to Perry's act: the heartbreak of "Faithfully," the joy of "Open Arms," the desperation of "Separate Ways (Worlds Apart)." Not to mention the engagement with the audience. Seeing Pineda's other cover work—the Zoo was not a Journey tribute band but a classic rock cover band—one could see how he inhabited so many of the characters familiar to late baby boom and Generation X rock fans: Van Halen's David Lee Roth, U2's Bono, Chicago's Peter Cetera, the Doors' Jim Morrison. These were qualities that Hunsicker, for all his resemblance to Perry, lacked; the Virginian delivered all the notes but did so with his own personality, rather than imitating Perry's. And these were the qualities Schon had been seeking in a replacement: not someone who might do for Journey what Sammy Hagar did for Van Halen or Phil Collins did for Genesis—in other words, not Jeff Scott Soto—but someone who could make the fans comfortable despite Perry's continued absence.

On June 28, 2007, Schon wrote an email to Noel Gomez, the Zoo fan who had posted the YouTube videos of Pineda. "I am the guitarist Neal Schon from Journey," he wrote. "Don't know if your [sic] aware or not but Journey has been very active.... This is not a joke. We would love to get Arnel to come out in the near future to audition for the singer position in our band that is now available."

When Pineda saw Schon's email, he didn't believe it was really him. At first, like Augeri in 1998, he thought it was a prank. But Schon had included his private phone number, and Gomez convinced Pineda to make the call. "What if it really was Neal and he wanted to offer you the chance of a lifetime?" After several clarifying questions, the singer agreed to try out. Schon got the band's management and lawyers involved and they arranged a travel visa. When a Filipino customs agent asked him why he was heading to the United States, Pineda replied that he was going to audition for Journey. The agent asked him to sing some of their tunes.

*   *   *

On the first day of Pineda's audition, Cain was skeptical. "I think the biggest concern of mine," he said, "was how do you take somebody from a third-world country and throw him into this circus? It's a big circus, you know." His fears were especially pronounced after Pineda failed to demonstrate his promised dynamism in the studio. "He seemed out of it, and his voice wasn't there. So far, it's not clicking for me, I wasn't hearing it, you know." But Schon felt the singer was simply exhausted from the trans-Pacific flight. On the second day he was better, and on the third, he had won over the keyboard-ist. Just to be sure, Cain sent Pineda to Los Angeles for a session with his vocal coach, Joel Ewing. "If you're looking for the voice of Journey, you've found it," was the unhesitant professional evaluation. "He's your man." On December 5, 2007, Journey announced that Arnel Pineda was the new lead singer of Journey. Within weeks they were in Plant Studios recording the next album.

Revelation begins with the explosive and catchy "Never Walk Away," by Schon, Cain, and Jeremey Hunsicker, which places Neal's solo in the beginning—the opposite of the band's megahit "Who's Crying Now." Cain and Schon clearly wanted the album—and Pineda's impact—to begin with a bang. The lyrics speak to Cain's deteriorating marriage to Liz. "Will she go or will she stay?/Fool herself for one more day . . . /Don't give up, never walk away." Notably, it features the same chord progression as "Be Good to Yourself," from *Raised on Radio*. Cain's marriage might have been floundering, but Journey was back!

Next, as had become usual for Journey albums, is a ballad by Cain and Schon, "Like a Sunshower," with a soft vocal by Pineda accompanied by Cain's insistent piano. What is clear from the lyrics was that as much as their earlier music had appealed to teenagers, Cain understood that their next breakthrough—if they were lucky enough to get it—would need to demonstrate more maturity and appeal not only to the aging Journey fans willing to keep shelling out for the new music but also to those who were looking for some new professional output from these talented musicians. "I know you care, 'cause you stand your ground/When we talked enough, I wanna make up."

"Like a Sunshower" is followed by "Change for the Better," a hard-driving rocker by Schon and Cain, continuing their role as songwriting duo; indeed, of the ten tracks original to the release, they wrote eight together (including one with Hunsicker and one with Pineda). "Change for the Better," with its uplifting self-actualizing lyric, is followed by another rocker by Schon and Cain, "Wildest Dream," a song reminiscent of "World Gone Wild" from *Arrival*. This one has an angry sound (replete with Jerry Lee Lewis–style rockabilly piano) but a vulnerable lyric that could either be an entreaty to a lost lover or another "na na na na na" to Steve Perry. "We had our time to shine before we started fading/Could not see eye to eye, pretending nothing's wrong."

This is followed by Pineda's take on "Faith in the Heartland," the rocker from *Generations* by Schon, Cain, and Steve Augeri. Schon and Cain clearly felt that the song had potential that had not been realized in its previous itera-tion; now with Pineda at the microphone, it helps make *Revelation* fantastic. The song demonstrates Pineda's emotional range. Its lyrics speak to what it is to be American, what it is about America's heartland—whether that be the heartland of a "small town girl" or "city boy," to cite "Don't Stop Believin'." Pineda's version includes a fadeout celebrating "Their faith, their dreams, believe/They're keeping their faith alive." Yes, it's red meat for red state fans. But it is also about a kid from the backstreets of Manila and what it really means to be an American—to be a striver, to come from somewhere else to add your distinctive originality. And that's exactly what Pineda brings to his version of the song.

The album's "Open Arms"—its adult contemporary hit along the lines of *Trial by Fire*'s "When You Love a Woman" and *Arrival*'s "All the Way"—is "After All These Years," Cain's solo composition. It is a wedding song but a specific kind of wedding song. It's a "renewal of vows" song. It is a prayer for his wife Liz to stay with him. "A faded wedding photograph, you and me in our first dance . . . /We've learned to take the laughter with the tears." Of course, the lyric "Make a living up and down the gypsy high-ways/Somehow in my heart I always keep you near" is a sentiment straight out of "Faithfully," Cain's first solo composition for Journey. And one which ironically bit him in the backside, as his fidelity to first wife Tané McClure went unrequited; this time around, he's celebrating the trust of second wife Liz, which he has violated. The song got some airplay, hitting number 9 on the *Billboard* United States adult contemporary chart, and number 34 in Canada.

Next follows a rocker by Schon and Cain, "Where Did I Lose Your Love," with a lyric that is either a pining for lost love—or yet another dig at the missing Steve Perry. "Love forgives but never forgets . . . /I still regret the night you walked away." It hit number 19 on the adult contemporary chart. Then comes the haunting "What I Needed," by Schon, Cain, and Pineda, with a tone reminiscent of *Arrival*'s "Livin' to Do," and a lyric that continues the overall theme of the album, Cain's deteriorating marriage, sung in an almost churchlike choral style: "You lifted my spirit up/Brought out the best in me," concluding with the refrain "Your love was what I needed/Hear me calling."

Perhaps the only loser on the album is "What It Takes to Win," a paean to hard knocks training for game day by Schon and Cain that sounds like it was written for a television commercial for a workout program—or a Chevy pickup. "When you want to prove you're the best that's ever been/'Cause you know what it takes to win."

Pineda's vocal role on the album concludes with the penultimate song, an inspirational ballad by Schon and Cain, "Turn Down the World Tonight." The final song, "The Journey (Revelation)," written by Schon, is an instrumental exploration, and mostly (if unsurprisingly) a guitar showcase.

Beyond the original numbers, *Revelation* served an important purpose, notably in its second disc. On this one, the current lineup—Pineda, Schon, Cain, Ross Valory, and Deen Castronovo—rerecorded eleven of the band's greatest hits, most of the "dirty dozen" that they played night after night to cheering crowds. Having sung these songs for many years, Pineda was more than up to the task. In rerecording these hits, Schon and Cain were finally able to cut into what Herbie Herbert considered Perry's "pimp" profits. Although Perry would always get a cut of the composition royalties when they performed the songs he had written or cowritten, and would continue to get 12.5 percent of Schon and Cain's performance and recording income because of the Elmo Partners Agreement of 1998, he would no longer receive performance royalties when they played the songs he had originally recorded, because now, they could legally argue, they were playing the songs they had rerecorded without him—on disc 2 of *Revelation*. These included two from *Infinity*, one from *Departure*, four from *Escape*, two from *Frontiers*, one from *Raised on Radio*, and "Only the Young" from *Journey's Greatest Hits*. The time was ripe, and Pineda's pipes were fresh. As Herbie often said, "You gotta make hay when the sun shines." And indeed, the sun was shining once again in Journey-town.

Following a well-timed appearance on the CBS *Sunday Morning News* (which featured Pineda's real tears as he recounted the story of his late mother inspiring him to sing), the band released *Revelation* to retail in the United States exclusively at Walmart stores. The album quickly resurrected Journey on the *Billboard* 200, peaking at number five on June 20, 2008—the same date the magazine ranked it the number-one independent album. It also made *Billboard*'s Top Rock Albums chart, peaking at number two a week later. And it was simultaneously certified gold and platinum on December 18, 2008. As a double album, each sale counted as two units, but it was nevertheless impressive; the band had not received any RIAA certification since their 1996 release *Trial by Fire*—their last with Steve Perry. As a bonus, the package included yet a third disc: a DVD recording of the band's current lineup performing on March 8, 2008, at Planet Hollywood in Las Vegas. In Europe, the album was released by Frontiers without the DVD; it nevertheless did well on the charts there.

Notwithstanding the album's success, reviews were mixed. Ben Ratliff of the *New York Times* allowed that "though the album doesn't transcend [its] purpose" to promote an upcoming tour, "it is, actually, good," adding that "Mr. Pineda, who sings hard and with the appropriate vulnerability, gives it some distinction. Beyond that, the band seems to have taken rock vitamins: it feels alive." Jody Rosen at *Rolling Stone* found space for a backhanded compliment, saying the record was "pure schlock, but the craftsmanship is formidable." As for the rock music websites that had arisen to challenge the mainstream press on the subject, Rob Rockitt of HardRockHideout.com improbably claimed the album "rivals those of their hit making years with Steve Perry," ultimately pronouncing it "one of the best Melodic Rock discs so far this year."

Pineda soon proved as revitalizing for the band's live act as he was in the studio. Exploding onto the stage at their opening night in Viña del Mar, Chile, the singer's frenetic traversing made Schon, Cain—and especially

Valory—seem like statues in comparison. "He was just racing around this large, circular ramp," said Valory. He ran across its breadth unencumbered by microphone cords and unafraid of tripping over those of his bandmates, all of whom were now, like Pineda, playing wireless. The mic stand was a mere prop to be waved like a trophy or, like Aerosmith's Steven Tyler or the late Freddie Mercury, held upside down (albeit without any handkerchiefs attached). Pausing only to shake hands with the fans in the front row, Pineda must have made the sound technicians cringe, so often did he flip his microphone in the air as if it were a drumstick, only to catch it effortlessly. Cain worried that the new singer would all-too-quickly run out of breath, but, remarkably, he didn't. "I never thought in a zillion years that this guy would be able to sing our material and find air to be able to roam like that," said Schon.

"I was grinning from ear to ear," said Castronovo, who knew firsthand the difficulty of Journey vocals. "[H]e was like choom-choom-choom! Jumping off the riser . . . it's like David Lee Roth and Bruce Lee put together!"

"Adrenaline," explained Pineda, nonchalantly.

When Schon played his solos, Pineda was there too—and not to upstage the gum-chewing former prodigy but to appreciate him, alternately pointing at the guitarist, kneeling behind him, or playing a bit of air guitar beside him, and always—always—with an incredible expression of joy, constantly looking at the crowd as if to say, *Can you believe we're here listening to the legendary Neal Schon play guitar?*

That connection he made with the audience was genuine, and they felt it. He was first and foremost a Journey fan, just like them. The attitude also served to underline his very public gratitude for being there and awareness that he was not the original singer of these hits. He not only won the fans over but became their connection to the band, channeling them as much as he did the Absent One. "Anytime Steve Perry wants to walk in, I would be glad to step out," he told Paul Liberatore of the *Marin Independent Journal*. "It's his band. I'm just here to celebrate the legacy of Journey."

It was not lost on the press that Pineda was the first man of color to serve as the band's lead vocalist—and one of very, very few nonwhite rock stars (Jeff Scott Soto, like Jerry Garcia before him—although proud of his Latino heritage—was treated by the press as white). This was, after all, the year that Barack Obama successfully ran for president, becoming the first man of color to hold that office. "In a clicky, viral, cell-phone-delivered media moment where even the twice-weekly cult-of-the-amateur hour that is American Idol seems like a rusty piece of star-making machinery . . . Journey—Journey!—seem like innovators, in touch with the forces shaping the culture," wrote Alex Pappademas of *Gentleman's Quarterly*. "For a band prominently featured in people's memories of the Carter administration, this is pretty impressive," adding "this latest frontman hire still seems like the first smart move Journey have made in years." But still, the writer added a note of warning: "[H]owever comfortable Pineda's been made to feel during the past few months, he must know on some level that Steve Augeri and Jeff Soto once felt comfortable, too."

The *Revelation* tour included a whopping sixty-seven dates in 2008 and seventy-one dates in 2009. They spent June 2008 in Europe, visiting Spain, Germany, the Netherlands, England, Scotland, and Ireland, immediately returning to the states for a summertime tour with Heart and Cheap Trick. They started 2009 in Asia, with three dates in Japan in March. Then after a three-day break, during which Pineda returned home and got to meet the president of the Philippines, the band joined him to play their first-ever gig in that country, at the Mall of Asia Field in Manila—where they recorded another DVD. After a show in Macao, the band played five nights in Hawaii, then a quick stop in California before departing for Europe again to play Sweden, Norway, Ireland, England, France, the Netherlands, Spain, Switzerland, Germany, and Belgium. Then it was back to the states for another summer tour and no real break until October. None other than Oprah Winfrey had them on her storied talk show, where they repeated the tale of how Schon found Pineda on YouTube, and performed—of course—"Don't Stop Believin'."

The *GQ* article featured a picture of Pineda sprawled on a chair in a dressing room, dueling humidifiers spraying over him. Already forty when the band hired him, he was no spring chicken. Offstage, conscious that he was singing notes night after night that Perry had recorded in his twenties and thirties, Pineda behaved like Pavarotti, taking care of his "moneymaker." He avoided excessive talking, stayed away from alcohol, wore a scarf to keep his throat warm, swallowed raw honey by the spoonful, and choked down a variety of vitamins. The same masseuse who accompanied the million-dollar band to rub Valory's forearm before shows also massaged Pineda's neck to keep it warm.

Cain took the new singer under his wing, running Pineda through a series of vocal exercises before each show with a small keyboard backstage, and treated him like the hot commodity he was, keeping him away from the temptations of the road (perhaps also still smarting from his own failure to avoid them). Cain made sure that the staff put the lyrics for each song on the stage teleprompter in case Pineda ever stumbled with the second-string hits with which he had less experience, and the two rehearsed one new song each day. Castronovo, who had filled in on a few numbers during Jeff Scott Soto's brief tenure, continued to sing favorites like "Mother, Father" from behind the drum set, allowing Pineda time for costume changes.

The 2008 tour brought in more than $50 million, an average of $746,837 per show—with tickets averaging $49.99—making Journey the eighth-highest-grossing tour of the year. Notably, the better-grossing acts charged more per ticket; Journey appealed to folks who could scant afford to pay $90 to see Janet Jackson, let alone $173 to see Madonna, especially during a Great Recession caused by a home loan crisis; but now they had expanded their audience beyond the red state county fair crowd to include Filipino Americans and other recent immigrants.

Pineda's presence in Journey—and the increase in immigrants and other people of color in attendance—did not go unnoticed by those county fair folks and the other predominantly white fans. "I think he should be from here," said one, drinking beer with her friends before a show. Asked if she thought that was a racist sentiment, she defensively replied, "Not at all, but it would just be better if he was." Online, the animus was more open. "Only Pilipinos will support tis crappy singer [sic]," wrote "ayimloveayu" in all caps, followed by nine exclamation marks, and the epithet "Pinoy monkeys!" "Fruggerugger" wrote, "No one gives a rats ass about a copycat voice! [sic]," adding, also in all caps, "Sucks bif=g time, ukkk." Pineda's wife, Cherry, "was so freaked out with all these racist comments that she told [him] to bring a bulletproof vest." Paul Liberatore called it "an undercurrent of racism."

This reaction is unsurprising given how rock music had for so long been perceived by its largely white audiences. Certainly, the choice of the new frontman went over better in Viña del Mar and Honolulu—not to mention Manila—than it did in Raleigh and Indianapolis.

In the end, with the album selling platinum and the tours pulling in more than ever before, whatever racism the band faced paled in comparison to their renewed success. For the first time since Steve Perry's departure, Journey had recaptured the popular zeitgeist. The question now was what they would do with it.

* * *

After two intense years on the road promoting *Revelation*, in October 2009 the band went on an extended break, reconvening in 2010 to produce a new album. Recorded in Berkeley's Fantasy Studios (where the band had cut *Escape* and *Frontiers*) and in Nashville, where the Cain family had relocated, *Eclipse*, like its predecessor *Revelation*, comes out of the gate strong with a catchy rocker. "City of Hope," like all but three of the album's eleven tracks, was written by Neal Schon and Jonathan Cain. The inspirational lyrics include the now obligatory throwback to an old hit of continuing importance to the band: "Never stop believin' change will come/There's a city of hope beyond our fears." What follows is the guitar-driven "Edge of the Moment," reminiscent of the band's darker, deeper sound on *Frontiers*, and "Chain of Love," a rocker with a soft vocals-and-piano introduction.

The classical-infused ballad "Tantra" speaks to Cain's deepening religiosity, a song that comes about as close to Christian rock as the rest of the band would allow. "Across the universe, the same force that moves the earth . . . / Look for some kind of sign from the heavens above." The mid-tempo, catchy, and uplifting "Anything Is Possible" got some airplay, peaking at number 21 on the Adult Contemporary chart on September 30, 2011. "Resonate," a rocker, returns to the theme of "Faithfully" ("Even though we're miles apart/I reach for you and there you are"), but with a harder edge. "She's a Mystery," a ballad with an acoustic guitar and a hard rock bridge by Schon, Cain, and Pineda, allows the singer to explore his upper register, while the up-tempo "Human Feel" serves as a cri de coeur for the age of the smartphone: "I'm needing more than the virtual world I'm seeing/Could someone just let me talk to a live human being?"

Next up is "Ritual," a rocker that combines a love song with the continuing religious theme ("We've got something sacred/You've become a ritual"), followed by "To Whom It May Concern," also classical-inspired, and also religious: "Our fathers have embraced the messiah and made the peace with Allah/They even sought to be like Buddha to follow the old ways of Krishna."

The song, written by Schon, Cain, Pineda, and another songwriter named Pineda (alternately credited as Erik, Allan, or Eduardo, of no apparent relation to the singer), also contains a soaring chorus: "To whom it may concern, I'm sending out a prayer/The world finds peace in my lifetime." The album's vocal songs conclude with "Someone," another catchy up-tempo of a piece with Journey's "trademark" rock-pop sound, and an even catchier "hook" chorus: "Once you let someone love you, you'll find an open door/A place in your heart you've never been before." The final track is, like its counterpart on *Revelation*, an instrumental written by Schon: "Venus." With no resemblance to the 1969 Shocking Blue hit of the same name, the song replays the guitar theme from "To Whom It May Concern" and the piano theme from "Believe," from *Generations*.

Overall, Cain called *Eclipse* "a concept record with some spiritual themes to it. Pretty tough, hard-hitting stuff. This is Journey with big combat boots on. And helmet and a rifle." Riffing on one of his favorite numbers, "Tantra," he added that the album speaks to "the belief that life is kind of a weave, a circle of energy, a life force that's woven with the universe in all of us. We dove deep into it."

As with *Revelation*, reviews were mixed. In *Rolling Stone*, Caryn Ganz called the album "bloated," while *Parade* magazine said it was pretty much what the band was known for, "vintage arena rock"—whatever that is. Online, reviewers were more kind, with Phil Ashcroft on the British fansite Rocktopia comparing its darkness favorably with that of *Frontiers*, seeing a pattern from the *Escape-Frontiers* sequence repeating in *Revelation-Eclipse* nearly three decades later. Also on that side of the pond, Scottish reviewer Ross Muir, one of the writers who had broken the lip-synching story in 2006, astutely noted that "the voice of Journey . . . on Eclipse isn't Arnel Pineda. It's Neal Schon."

Initially released, like its predecessor, as a "Walmart exclusive," the album did almost as well on the charts as *Revelation*, peaking at number 13 on the *Billboard* 200 on June 10, 2011—and at number 4 on *Billboard*'s Top Rock Albums chart and number 4 on its Independent Albums chart the same week. However, it was on the charts only briefly; sales were lackluster. The Walmart stunt did not work this time, and the album did not muster even a gold certification—five hundred thousand units—from RIAA. Whatever chemistry it was that had launched these vintage rockers back into the popular conversation in 2008 clearly failed to do so this time around.

No worries: the live act continued to rake in tens of millions of dollars. In 2011 they broke another band record, making eighty-six appearances for their "most successful year in terms of gross ticket sales," according to reporter Mike Devlin. Reflecting their increasing international focus, the tour began with ten dates in South and Central America and the Caribbean in March and April. Joined by Foreigner and Styx—who stayed with them through the summer—they then performed twenty-two shows in Europe, hitting every Western European country except Spain and Austria. The highlights included an appearance on NBC's *Today* before screaming fans in New York City's Rockefeller Plaza. The band performed "Don't Stop Believin'," a truncated "City of Hope," and "Faithfully," and finally showed the limits of Pineda's prowess: however talented he was, he should not have been performing live, outdoors, in the morning—or at least not the high notes at the end of "Faithfully." To be fair, however, he pulled it off better than Steve Augeri had on a similar outdoor stage for a morning talk show ten years before.

The shorter 2012 tour with Pat Benatar and Loverboy, by contrast, included only forty-eight appearances, all stateside. Then it was a fifty-date Europe-North America-Pacific tour in 2013, including their first-ever appearances in New Zealand, Australia, and Singapore. Then fifty-one dates in 2014 with Steve Miller, who now got to open for his former bandmate, Ross Valory. At the Theodore Roosevelt Hotel in New York City, the band received a "Legend of Live" award from *Billboard* magazine for their touring prowess. Appealing to their red-state fan base, they also played an event at the 2012 Republican National Convention in Tampa, which nominated Mitt Romney for president. Management issued a careful statement that tried to have it both ways. "It's not an endorsement of any candidate and/or party—it's just another private show." And at a very steep price: "A package of six tickets to both shows (Journey and B-52's) starts at a minimum of $45,000."

Ever conscious that his newfound fame and fortune might come to an end sooner rather than later, Arnel Pineda hedged his bets. The lessons of Steve Augeri and Jeff Scott Soto were not lost on him. He recorded an EP of Christmas songs and a full solo album, *AP*, both released on indie label Imagen Records.

He also remained humble. He started a foundation to help struggling kids back home across the Pacific. "I've seen enough pain and, you know, poverty in the Philippines that . . . I never dreamed that big," he told Oprah Winfrey. "All I wanted . . . was to get out of it and to live decently every day." It's easy to be cynical about jaded rock stars like Neal Schon and argue that the entire "rags to riches," "plucked from YouTube" story was contrived by the management team of a corporate rock megalith as a marketing ploy to bring the band back to the pinnacle of success—especially given how they treated Jeremey Hunsicker and Soto. And that certainly may have been part of the calculus. But for Pineda, the poverty was real, and the success was sudden. He did indeed go—like Steve Perry before him—from rags to riches. And, like Jonathan Cain, he never stopped believin'.

*   *   *

In 2012, high on painkillers following back surgery, Journey drummer Deen Castronovo got into an altercation with his girlfriend. "[H]e was charged with reckless endangerment, interfering with making a police report, second-degree criminal mischief and harassment" and sentenced to community service. Unlike Neal Schon, who had given up drugs and alcohol in 2007, Castronovo descended deeper into the morass of addiction, trying in vain to fill an emptiness with "alcohol, cocaine, pain medication and meth." When his doctors cut off his prescriptions, he turned to the black market for more painkillers.

Castronovo's difficulties were a long time coming. "I have never liked who I am [so] I immersed myself so much in being a drummer and singer," which, because of Journey's merciless tour schedule, never allowed him the time to seek regular treatment; he had been "on and off the wagon for 22 years." This came to a head when, on June 14, 2015, he assaulted his fiancée. According to the Marion County, Oregon, district attorney, he "threw the victim into a wall 14 times, pulled her hair, sexually assaulted her and forced her to have sex with him," and was "high on meth when he was arrested." Released the next day on $20,000 bail, he immediately violated the judge's restraining order when he "texted the woman 122 times and called her 35 times." This time he spent two weeks in jail before being released on July 10 on a much more substantial bail of $200,000; he was fitted with an ankle bracelet and required to go directly to rehab at the Hazelden Betty Ford Springbrook facility in Newburg, Oregon. In October, he pleaded guilty to domestic abuse and was given four years' probation on the condition that he continue to stay away from his former fiancée and "undergo domestic violence and drug counseling."

By that point, of course, Journey had been forced to move on; a rock band cannot tour without a drummer, and Castronovo's behavior had the potential for the opposite effect on the band's reputation as Neal Schon's recent wedding, let alone Arnel Pineda's rags-to-riches story. They hired Omar Hakim, one of the drummers Steve Perry had rejected for the *Raised on Radio* tour in 1986. Hakim had built a solid reputation since then, having worked with such bands as Dire Straits; recently he had handled percussion duties on Schon's 2015 solo album *Vortex*. Schon called the New Yorker a "hidden gem." He took over in June shortly after Castronovo's second arrest, playing with Journey at a June 20 show at the Hollywood Bowl, and continued with the band through the summer tour—twenty-one dates through August 3, mostly in Canada, followed by an October 22 show at the Warfield in San Francisco. Hakim and Schon did double duty on that tour, with Schon's band from his solo album serving as Journey's opening act.

And what of Journey's classic-era drummer, Steve Smith? Now bicoastal, living part-time in New York City, Smith continued to tour with his jazz band Vital Information, even at one point forming East Coast and West Coast versions. This sometimes resulted in confusion: in 2012, the *New York Times* listed Vital Information as appearing on June 5 at that city's Iridium Lounge, while an advertisement for Smith's longstanding hangout in San Francisco, Yoshi's, listed them as appearing there on the same day. Remarkable as he was, it is doubtful he took advantage of the three-hour time difference to hop a plane immediately after the New York set. And responsible as he was, it is doubtful he would have allowed himself to be booked that way, even if he intended to make that flight.

Smith also continued to use the financial comfort from his years in Journey to engage in artistic, but not particularly lucrative, musical pursuits. He released a DVD, *Standing on the Shoulders of Giants*, as an attempt to explain what modern drummers owed to their jazz forebears. In keeping with his calling to pass on his wisdom, he joined the board of the Collective, a rhythm school in New York City's Greenwich Village, and teamed up with noted Indian tabla player Zakir Hussain for a percussion showcase at the new San Francisco Jazz Center and a drum camp in upstate New York near Woodstock.

But he always found time for friends. In addition to appearances with guitarist Mike Stern and saxophonist Bill Evans, Smith appeared on two of Neal Schon's solo albums—2012's *The Calling* and 2015's *Vortex*. In 2012, with Schon and former Babys and Bad English bassist Ricky Phillips, he played at the memorial service for his old boss, guitarist Ronnie Montrose. And then he teamed up with guitarist Vinnie Valentino and organist Tony Monaco to record the 2015 album *Groove: Blue*.

Smith was Schon's first choice to replace Deen Castronovo. When the embattled batterer was first arrested, however, Smith was on tour with Vital Information, with immediate plans to tour Europe with the Buddy Rich Alumni Big Band, followed by more New York appearances, including one with a group called Coltrane Revisited. He begged off for the summer but did not accept any more bookings. In November 2015, calling Omar Hakim a "temporary fill-in," Journey announced the return of Steve Smith as the band's official drummer, with a planned tour in 2016 supported by the Doobie Brothers.

Before Castronovo's troubles, Schon had not been actively looking to replace any band members, but the drummer's arrest and subsequent jailing provided an opportunity that he simply could not pass up. With Steve Smith back, the band now included four of the five members of the classic Journey lineup—the version of the band that had recorded *Escape*, *Frontiers*, and *Trial by Fire*. Not only would this help quell some of the lingering doubts of the fans, but if it put some additional pressure on Steve Perry to do another reunion album—or even just a handful of appearances with the group—so much the better.

Schon also had an ulterior motive to bringing Smith back: band politics. After years of infidelity on the road and the added stress of a son struggling with addiction, Jonathan Cain divorced his second wife, Elizabeth, in 2014; the following spring he married Pastor Paula White, a televangelist and Donald Trump confidante. That June—the same month as Castronovo's arrest—Trump famously descended the escalator in his New York tower to declare his candidacy for the Republican presidential nomination. Shortly thereafter, Trump named Paula White Cain to his Evangelical Advisory Board.

Schon had long maintained that Journey's music was not political. Although the band appealed to "red state" fans and working-class white ethnics increasingly inclined to vote Republican, maintaining an apolitical official posture allowed the band to appeal to the immigrant community through Arnel Pineda as well. Their appearance at the 2012 Republican National Convention had been carefully positioned as just another private event. But now his bandmate Jonathan Cain had become connected to the most disruptive and polarizing figure in modern American politics.

Although all six co-owners of Nightmare theoretically had a say in the activities of the current band, in practice, band decisions were made by the five current musicians with manager Irving Azoff and his designee for Journey, John Baruck. But because Pineda, Castronovo, Hakim, Azoff, and Baruck were employees—if extremely well-paid employees—the real decision-makers were the current members who were also co-owners of Nightmare: Ross Valory, Jonathan Cain, and Neal Schon. If push came to shove, could Schon depend on Valory—also ostensibly apolitical, but with family ties to the California Republican Party—to help him keep the band out of the increasingly polarized American political struggle?

The return of Steve Smith changed that calculus. Like Valory, Smith was officially apolitical—his life was devoted to his music. But unlike Valory, Smith held very clear progressive values, evident in his devotion to the African American origins of jazz and his appreciation for international music. Put another way, while Cain had moved to Nashville and then central Florida—red and redder—Smith split his time between New York City and San Francisco, two of America's great liberal bastions. So in the event that Cain might attempt to push the band toward the unthinkable—the endorsement of a presidential candidate—Schon could depend on Smith to help keep them neutral and officially out of politics.

Indeed, this calculus bore fruit within months of Smith's return, when the band turned down an invitation to play the 2016 Republican National Convention in Cleveland. Asked why, Schon was explicit: "I'm not into taking any one side in politics, and having politics get in involved [sic] with music," adding that "Steve Smith and Arnel . . . were with me, too, and . . . Irving Azoff agreed with the three of us," implying that Cain and Valory were willing to play a concert at the convention where Trump received the nomination for the presidency. Schon also, in the same interview, took another swipe at Cain: "I feel that way about . . . religion, too. We can't be tied to any one religious group," he said. "Music is my savior, and it's everybody's savior."

*   *   *

In 2016, in a surprise upset, Republican Donald J. Trump won the presidency of the United States, defeating Democrat Hillary Rodham Clinton in the electoral college, although Mrs. Clinton handily won the popular vote. As a shocked Trump took the stage at a ballroom in New York City's Trump Tower to announce Clinton's concession, rock listeners were being given the opportunity, for only the fifth time, to cast ballots for the 2017 class of the Rock and Roll Hall of Fame—ballots that would be combined in a weighted algorithm with those of the Hall's regular voting members, mostly industry insiders and the critics who for years had panned Journey as sellouts to "corporate rock."

But times had changed. The second life of "Don't Stop Believin'" and the band's international appeal thanks to Arnel Pineda had made critics far more receptive and appreciative of Journey's role in rock history. With the aid of their fans, Journey won a place in the Hall that winter. As Steve Smith put it—subtly telegraphing the cosmopolitan drummer's political leanings—"We won the popular vote."

The Hall, which reserves the right to name individual members of the bands it inducts, announced that their definition of "Journey" included the musicians who had recorded the band's first five albums with Steve Perry: Jonathan Cain, Aynsley Dunbar, Neal Schon, Steve Smith, Ross Valory, Gregg Rolie—who had already been inducted in 1998 with Santana—and of course Perry himself. The exclusion of George Tickner of the original Journey, and Steve Augeri, Deen Castronovo, and Arnel Pineda of the reformed nostalgia act, indicated the Hall's opinion that Journey's major contributions to rock history had all occurred with Perry in the band. Schon told reporter Ed Masley that he argued about this with representatives of the Hall, pushing for the inclusion of every band member who had appeared on a Journey record, and that the Hall, which had initially planned on admitting only the five who had recorded *Escape*, *Frontiers*, and *Trial by Fire*, had compromised by including Rolie and Dunbar.

The exclusion of Herbie Herbert was not a snub of the founding manager. When nonmusicians are inducted into the Hall, it is for lifetime achievement under the banner of the Ahmet Ertegun Award, named for a cofounder of Atlantic Records (and of the Hall itself). The late Bill Graham, that impresario of the San Francisco sound who nurtured the careers of such acts as Jefferson Airplane, the Grateful Dead, Santana, and Journey, was given the award posthumously by John Fogerty and Carlos Santana in 1992; Clive Davis, the president of Columbia Records who refocused the label at a pivotal turning point in rock history, was given it by Patti Smith in 2000.

As the April 7 date for the induction approached, however, the press—and presumably the fans—were not concerned with debating which members of Journey got snubbed by the Hall; rather, the discussion swirled around Steve Perry. Would he show up? Would he perform with the band? The singer had not seen his former bandmates since the 2005 unveiling of their star on the Hollywood Walk of Fame; he had not performed live with them since the Bill Graham tribute at Golden Gate Park in 1991.

He had not performed live with Journey, but he had performed live. On May 25, 2014, Perry surprised fans of the rock band the Eels when he walked onstage during their encore at the Fitzgerald Theater in St. Paul, Minnesota, to sing their "2000 cult hit 'It's a Motherfucker'," and Journey's "Open Arms" and "Lovin', Touchin', Squeezin'." The following week in Washington, DC, when he repeated the surprise, this time adding Sam Cooke's "Only Sixteen" to his set, Eels' lead singer Mark Oliver Everett jokingly introduced him by saying, "Live, for the first time in *six days*, Steve Perry."

The critics welcomed his return to the stage. "While Perry's vocals have grown gruffer and scratchier with age," reported Jon Blistein of *Rolling Stone*, "his pipes still packed the same potent, pained arena-ready punch." When the Eels appeared in Los Angeles on June 11, fans of Steve Perry and Journey bought tickets in eager anticipation, hoping that the "surprise guest" would make yet another appearance, this time in his home state. They were not disappointed. Now Everett introduced him "for the first time in eleven days and the first time in Los Angeles in twenty years." This set swapped "Lights" for "Open Arms," with Perry noting that he had written the original version of "Lights" for LA, later changing it to "city by the bay" when he joined Journey.

Everett, who went by the stage name "E," had been reticent to allow Perry to perform with the band. "[W]hen I was younger, one thing I never really appreciated was Journey," he said. "And I felt like I didn't know what to say to him . . . so I just avoided it for years." Introduced by Patty Jenkins, Perry's friend who had directed the film *Monster*, he agreed to let Perry attend rehearsals, and they struck up a friendship. Eventually, through conversation and his own listening, E came to appreciate the music of Journey. Before long he made it clear that Perry was welcome to sing with the band any time he wanted, but it was years before Perry would take E up on the offer. After "Eels guitarist Jeff Lyster managed to bait Mr. Perry into singing Journey's 'Lights' at one of these rehearsals," the stage was set, according to *New York Times* reporter Alex Pappademas. It was "this great moment—a guy who's become like [ultra-rich recluse aviator] Howard Hughes, and just walked away from it all 25 years ago, and he's finally doing it again."

But these were rare appearances, more akin to the Steve Perry "sightings" reported in the press from time to time than any sort of permanent return to the spotlight; as with his impromptu appearance with Bon Jovi in 1989, they did not presage any "comeback" tour. Where Perry spent most of his professional time in these years was pretty much where he had spent the previous decade: working with Sony Music to repackage his old material, writing new material, and recording some (but not releasing it). The difference was that he was becoming more comfortable talking about it publicly. He gave multiple interviews around the release of Journey's *Greatest Hits 2* in 2011, going over the process for choosing the seventeen songs in collaboration with Schon and Cain—through their representatives—and even taking a few of the harder questions, such as those related to his long-ago relationship with Sherrie Swafford and the reasons for the band's breakup in 1998. But he stuck to his story and revealed little new.

What he wasn't saying, however, was that he was going through a particularly traumatic time. Through the good graces of Patty Jenkins, Perry had fallen in love again—this time with Kellie Nash, a psychologist suffering from advanced-stage breast cancer. The romance was fast and intense, but it was doomed by her medical condition. Although she had previously been in remission, the cancer had returned with the same fiery intensity as her love affair with Steve Perry, and was in her bone marrow. She died in December 2012 but not before extracting a promise from her devoted lover: that he would return to music. The promise led to his decision to appear onstage with the Eels. And it was in that context, when the news broke that Journey would be inducted into the Rock and Roll Hall of Fame, that rumors started to swirl around the possibility of him performing with the band. Now that Steve Smith was back, the band was only missing one of its classic members; what better opportunity than his induction into the Hall of Fame, where even Gregg Rolie and Aynsley Dunbar were expected to sit in for a number or two?

*   *   *

Eight current and former members of Journey, along with seven wives, Herbie and Jeanne Herbert, and Irving Azoff and John Baruck and their "plus ones," gathered at the Barclays Center in Brooklyn, New York, home of the Nets basketball team, on the evening of April 7, 2017. The basketball court was covered with round tables, like at a wedding reception, with a stage and proscenium arch at one end; the artists and guests sat at the tables and the ticketed fans filled the stands. The locker rooms were converted into dressing rooms. For most of the performers, who had long played arenas and stadiums, this setup was nothing new; this was certainly the case with Journey, Pearl Jam, and Yes, if perhaps less so for fellow inductees Joan Baez, Electric Light Orchestra, and Nile Rodgers, who was given an award for musical excellence despite the Hall's rejection of his band, Chic.

In the hours before the induction, the bands rehearsed their planned numbers. Journey rehearsed "Separate Ways (Worlds Apart)," "Lights" with Gregg Rolie and Aynsley Dunbar, and, of course, "Don't Stop Believin'." Steve Perry did not rehearse, but he was there, with his own dressing room. The band was ready at any point to swap him in for Arnel Pineda—onstage at the Barclays Center or for the permanent touring job, if he wanted it. At one point, Neal Schon disappeared into Perry's dressing room; he emerged after about ten minutes, uncharacteristically tight-lipped. Then Perry himself emerged; he had been told that Pineda was looking for him. The Voice and the Replacement met—for the first and only time—in a hallway backstage. They embraced, Perry later saying that Pineda greeted him "like a grandfather" (although their age difference was fewer than twenty years). Then the band took their seats on the basketball court while Perry inexplicably stayed hidden backstage.

First came a tribute to Chuck Berry, who had died two weeks before; then ELO performed before being inducted by Dhani Harrison, son of Beatle George. Next Jackson Browne took the stage to introduce and induct Joan Baez, who sang a version of "Swing Low, Sweet Chariot," altering the lyrics to state that "even Donald Trump can be saved." She played two more songs,

joined by Mary Chapin Carpenter and the Indigo Girls. Then Geddy Lee and
Alex Lifeson of the Canadian band Rush appeared onstage to induct British
progressive luminaries Yes. Like Journey, Yes had seen many musicians come
and go, but unlike Journey, two groups had recently been touring with the
same name, as competitors. After that, Snoop Dogg inducted Tupac Shakur
posthumously, and Alicia Keys played a medley of the late rapper's songs.

The big moment had arrived. Although the Barclays Center was filled by
more fans of Pearl Jam than of Journey, a hush descended over the crowd as
Pat Monahan of the San Francisco band Train took the stage. "Tonight," he
said, "I'm here to live out a lifelong dream of mine to induct the heart of San
Francisco music into the Rock and Roll Hall of Fame." What followed was
a touching five-minute tribute to the band and its history, in which Monahan even sang parts of "Faithfully" and "Lovin', Touchin', Squeezin'" to the
delight of the crowd; Schon and wife Michaele in particular thought he had
quite the voice for Journey tunes. "I'm just a kid from western Pennsylvania,"
Monahan continued. "I moved to San Francisco because the song 'Lights'
made me think that maybe I could fit in there and be someone." Referring to
the "na na na na na" of "Lovin'," he said, "They didn't even need lyrics, that's
how badass this band is!" Monahan concluded, passionately, "It isn't just my
honor to induct these gentlemen tonight. It is my appointed duty to induct
the heart of San Francisco music into the Rock and Roll Hall of Fame. And
it's about damn time! Ladies and gentlemen, Journey."

One by one, six current and former members of the band walked past a
beaming Herbie Herbert to join Monahan on stage—but Steve Perry came out
of the wings, arriving there first. Schon embraced Perry at the microphone to
an adoring, standing ovation. Then Perry ducked behind Schon and Cain to
shake hands with Rolie and hug Steve Smith while Cain put his arm around
Ross Valory's shoulder. Taking the microphone, Schon was overcome with
emotion. Fighting back tears, he lost track of the words on the teleprompter
and decided to wing it, thanking Steve Perry, Gregg Rolie, Herbie Herbert,
Michaele, his kids, the Hall, Irving Azoff, John Baruck, and Journey's longtime producer Kevin Elson. Aynsley Dunbar thanked "my family, my friends,
my managers, my ex-wives, Zildjian cymbals and drums." Rolie thanked
Herbie Herbert and Neal Schon for "saving me from the restaurant business."
Steve Smith gave the most cerebral of the acceptance speeches, discussing
the diversity of the 2017 class, along with a brief history of rock and roll. He

thanked "talent scout Neal Schon" for "noticing what I was bringing to rock and roll" when he was opening for Journey as part of Montrose. He thanked Jonathan Cain, and when he thanked "Arnel Pineda for keeping the legacy sound of Journey alive and moving forward," Perry was first to applaud. Valory's speech was a bit awkward, with some odd jokes, but he thanked his parents "who shared music with us . . . from Miles Davis to Mozart," and he added that Herbie Herbert also deserved the award, thanking him for putting his "blood, sweat, and tears" into Journey. Jonathan Cain thanked "the Cubs for winning the World Series so we could get in the Hall of Fame," comparing the band to Chicago's longtime baseball underdogs. He mentioned the fire at his childhood school Our Lady of the Angels, and thanked his late father, his brothers, his children, Paula White Cain, the Babys, Journey, and the many professionals who had helped him along the way. He also thanked Steve Augeri and Deen Castronovo—and God.

Finally it was Steve Perry's turn at the microphone. After he expertly milked the long ovation, he began with "Hello, Rock and Roll Hall of Fame! You sure look good to me tonight." He spoke of how moved he had been when he first heard Schon play. He thanked Herbie Herbert: "He did not have to call me; he gets tapes all the time. . . . Now, Aynsley Dunbar, Gregg Rolie, Steve Smith, Neal Schon, Jonathan Cain, Ross Valory—are you fuckin' shittin' me? Any singer would give his ass for that shit! I mean they play so well, so I wanna thank them for all the music we've written." Then, "I must give a complete shout out to someone who sings his heart out every night, and that's Arnel Pineda." He thanked his "longtime attorney Lee Philips"; the Sullies, his old high school band; the "original Journey road crew;" and he expressed "condolences to the families of . . . Jim McCandless, Jackie Villanueva, and recently the great Bennie Collins." He thanked Fan Asylum, the Journey fan club that had grown to support fans of other acts. And he thanked the fans: "You're the ones who put us here. . . . I've been gone a long time . . . but I want you to know you've never not been in my heart."

As Andy Greene of *Rolling Stone* reported, "What followed can only be described as unbearable tension. The band disappeared backstage and didn't emerge for a couple of long minutes. . . . The tension grew greater when they finally came out and kicked into a long intro to 'Separate Ways' without any vocalist onstage." Another minute ticked by, as Schon and Smith passed solos back and forth, guitar to drums and back again. Would Steve Perry perform?

Finally, when Jonathan Cain began those unforgettable synthesizer notes, out he ran, in a pink business suit, the longtime lead singer of Journey, none other than . . . Arnel Pineda. They finished the song, Schon played a solo riff, and then he introduced Rolie and Dunbar, dedicating "Lights" to Steve Perry. Rolie played like he was still in the band, but Dunbar played with a certain tension that he had not had in the early years with Journey, certainly in contrast to Smith's smooth jazz style. But Dunbar still showed the raw power that had made him such a formidable drummer for David Bowie and Frank Zappa. Then Cain started playing the opening piano notes to that ubiquitous "Don't Stop Believin'" as Smith returned to the drum set for their final number. Later in the evening, Schon and Cain joined Pearl Jam, Lifeson and Lee of Rush, Trevor Rabin of Yes, and Dhani Harrison to perform a rather cacophonous version of Neil Young's "Rockin' in the Free World."

The induction of Journey into the Rock and Roll Hall of Fame may not have been the reunion that the fans—or Neal Schon—had wanted, but for those who were still "believin'" in the eventual return of Steve Perry to the fold, it was a step in the right direction. With Steve Smith back in the band, four of the five musicians of Journey's classic period were touring and performing as Journey. And the affection that Perry and Schon still had for one another was evident on the stage that night.

Or so it seemed.

Encore

"Castles Burning," 2018–2023

The way things went down was really not that kosher.

—*Neal Schon*

After the election of Donald Trump, Jonathan Cain's wife, Pastor Paula White, gave the invocation at Trump's presidential inauguration. When the inevitable invitation to visit the White House arrived that summer, Cain specifically did not ask Neal Schon or Steve Smith to join him; instead, he only asked Ross Valory and Arnel Pineda to attend. For Valory, who did not publicly comment on his political values, accepting the invitation was in keeping with his longstanding family connections to the California Republican Party; his mother had been a fundraiser for Ronald Reagan's gubernatorial runs. Pineda's acceptance was somewhat more surprising, given the president's attitude toward immigrants from places like the Philippines (Trump famously referred to them as "shithole countries"). But for a kid from the backstreets of Manila to get a chance to visit the White House, it was an incredible honor—regardless of its current occupant. The singer later noted that he was interested in meeting a Filipino member of the White House kitchen staff and spent his time in the Oval Office admiring the desk and the other furniture rather than interacting directly with the president.

If Cain handled the situation poorly by not inviting Schon and Smith—or at least informing them beforehand and making it clear that the visit was not "Journey" but rather three musicians and their families—Schon handled the news far worse. He took to Instagram and Twitter and denounced his bandmate for getting Journey involved in politics. Noting that the band had regularly refused invitations to visit the White House during the Obama administration, he decried the pianist and blamed Cain's increasing evangelism for a growing rift in the band. But they continued to tour together, with Schon and Cain finding their live act far too lucrative to let a public Twitter fight spoil it. One reporter, trying to dig up dirt, observed that the two remained on opposite sides of the stage at performances—failing to note that Cain's piano had been on stage right for decades, and Schon's pedals and other hardware on stage left. They still played together in the center when Cain picked up the rhythm guitar for the rockers.

Cain compared the incident to a marital squabble. "It's kind of like if you have a fight with your wife. . . . You have to weather it and overcome it," he said, momentarily forgetting his two divorces. But he noted that the musicians lived separate lives offstage. "I have a life with Paula in Florida. He's got a life with Michaele in San Rafael," he told *Rolling Stone*—a geographical statement which doubled as a political statement, given the different partisan leanings of the California Bay Area and suburban Orlando, where the Cains lived. To his credit, Cain avoided public outbursts of the type Schon was unleashing. Founding manager Herbie Herbert, no fan of Trump's, weighed in from his comfortable retirement, lamenting that the band had returned to a familiar state of dysfunction, only this time it wasn't caused by Steve Perry but by Neal Schon.

Schon's public tantrums continued in 2018. When Aretha Franklin died on August 16, the guitarist arranged for a pictorial tribute on the big screens during his solos at two Journey shows. Favorable press stated that during these tributes, *Journey* displayed the slideshow of the Queen of Soul. Schon, at first through a publicist and then on his own, berated journalists who dared suggest that the tribute was anything other than his, Neal Schon's, own decision and action—and ordered them to issue corrections. "It seemed odd that Schon would go out of his way to make sure readers knew his bandmates had nothing to do with it," reported Jay Cridlin of the *Tampa Bay Times*. Schon claimed that each member of the band who got solos was allowed to use the time according to his own wishes, as if it was not a band called Journey but rather a bunch of separate musicians with completely disparate interests. So he turned a positive media story about how he had honored Aretha's memory into a negative one about a petulant former child star having a midlife crisis.

The story made the pages of *Variety* and *Spin*, and *New York Times* columnist Frank Bruni made it the centerpiece of his article on celebrity misbehavior, "Death in the Age of Narcissism." Andy Cush at *Spin* compared Schon's demand to something that "might as well have come from Kim Jong-Il's publicity shop," referring to the reputation-conscious North Korean dictator. After some digging, Cush found several similar "corrections" in recent years. Schon seemed to particularly bristle at the suggestion that either his current bandmate Valory, or even his legendary former colleague Gregg Rolie, were cofounders of the band, telling journalists that they should instead refer to Valory and Rolie as Journey's "original" bass player and keyboard player: "I myself started the band with ex-manager Herbie Herbert," he claimed, disingenuously. This was nothing new: in 1997 he had told writer Willie G. Mosely a similar version of Journey's founding, even going so far as to claim that it was he, and not Herbie, who had asked Cain to join the band in 1980 when Rolie announced his retirement (Cain, for his part, recalled that it was road manager Pat Morrow).

Online responses called Schon a "douche" and a "diva." That second insult, so frequently leveled at his former bandmate Steve Perry, with its obvious feminine overtones, must have particularly stung the macho guitarist who performed his sexuality through serial marriage.

*　　*　　*

The following year, Steve Perry proved that he still had music in him when he announced the release of his first solo album in twenty-four years and embarked on an interview blitz across the United States and United Kingdom. The album had taken five years of work—punctuated with an extended break in the middle so the singer could get a second hip replacement—and all the musicians and other technicians who worked on it had signed nondisclosure agreements to keep the project quiet. But it was worth the wait.

Traces begins with "No Erasin'," a catchy up-tempo with nostalgic lyrics cowritten by David Spreng that give ample evidence that Perry could still sing, and sing well, if somewhat raspier than in his youth. Guitarist Thom Flowers, who played on several tracks and coproduced the album, said Perry's singing "reminded me of watching a thoroughbred horse work." Perry could also still write rock tunes, but alas, as with his previous solo effort, something was missing—and it was far too easy to argue that that "something" was the contribution of former bandmates Neal Schon and Jonathan Cain. Still, the hype surrounding the album and the sheer thirst of Perry's fans for more material pushed the song to number 18 on the *Billboard* Hot 100 on November 2, 2018—a stronger showing than Journey's first bona fide hit, "Lovin', Touchin', Squeezin'."

"We're Still Here," a mid-tempo cowritten by Brian West, grows on the listener and has a steady beat and a soulful, gospel sensibility apparent in the backing vocals "Brother to brother/Sister to sister"—plus a Schon-like, albeit too brief, guitar solo. It did even better than "No Erasin'," going to number 14 on April 26, 2019, a higher showing than anything Perry had released as a solo artist since "Foolish Heart" (number 2 on February 8, 1985). Next up is the contemplative "Most of All," cowritten by Perry's longtime writing companion Randy Goodrum, with a nod to Barbra Streisand's "The Way We Were," ample Perryesque overenunciation of diphthongs (he pronounces "Many years won't heal with tears" as "Many yee-ahs won't hee-al with tee-ahs"), and a mild, funky rhythm guitar. Then comes "No More Cryin'," cowritten by Grammy nominee Dan Wilson, with a funky beat and upbeat guitar solo, again all-too-brief, belying the fairly depressing lyrics ("No more cryin'/'Cause I won't love again"). This one includes parts performed by something called "The Steve Perry Philharmonic Orchestra." What would be side 1 on an LP concludes with the mournful "In the Rain." This one contains some of Perry's trademark soaring vocals, the ultimate tribute to his departed lover: "Didn't know you were crying/Tell me why we're standing again in the rain."

The album continues with "Sun Shines Gray," a toe-tapping rocker of a love song cowritten with metal guitarist John 5, who also—in an unlikely pairing with Steve Perry—provides his signature guitar sound honed with David Lee Roth and Marilyn Manson. "You Belong to Me" is next, a plaintive, appealing ballad that begins with a simple vocal and piano and is quickly joined by violins, drums, and, later, a subtle, groovy guitar. The chorus is punctuated by a harmonic vocal bridge. "Easy to Love" provides a soaring vocal chorus over a groovy jazz rhythm. Then comes a Beatles cover, George Harrison's "I Need You." *Traces* concludes with "We Fly," a sad, mournful, nearly a cappella tribute to his late girlfriend, with muted guitar notes: "With you I had it all . . . /You were the reason, love was our season."

The version sold in Target stores in the United States includes five bonus tracks, all but one written by Perry alone. "October in New York," cowritten with Patrick Williams, evinces a midcentury Broadway sensibility with a relaxed vocal, violins, and soft piano, developing into an urbane jazz tune seemingly designed to evoke two people walking hand in hand through New York's Central Park, perhaps watching the skaters at Wollman Rink. Perry later confirmed that it was about his final weeks with girlfriend Kellie Nash, when they had moved to the city to be close to the hospital where she was seeking treatment. "Angel Eyes," by contrast, is an up-tempo, Motown-inspired tune, with a staccato vocal: "After you left, you made her cry . . . /It won't be long, she'll be mine." "Call on Me" is an endearing reggae, despite Perry's unfortunate use of pidgin: "Stay, you no lonely/Pick up de phone." Then comes the gospel-inflected, funky up-tempo "Could We Be Somethin' Again," which, although ostensibly a love song, can be interpreted much as his "Anyway" was in 1994: an appeal to reunite with Schon and Cain. "Could we be somethin' again?/All you gotta do is call" (except that, as Neal Schon claimed, Perry did not share his number with them). Finally, there is "Blue Jays Fly," a mournful lullaby in which Perry again laments the loss of his girlfriend to cancer—written from the perspective of a dream he had before she died. "Wishing you were still here/Just a boy in the dark, in the yard by the tree."

With *Traces*, Perry had brought the Journey story full circle in no fewer than three ways. First, "No More Cryin'" featured Booker T. Jones on the Hammond organ—the same Booker T., known most famously as the leader of Booker T. and the M.G.s, who had opened for Santana in 1971 as half of "Booker T. and Priscilla"—with Schon playing guitar for both acts. Second, with his cover of George Harrison's "I Need You"—for which he received the approval of Harrison's widow Olivia—it was not lost on fans that Journey's 1976 Beatles cover, "It's All Too Much" from *Yellow Submarine*, was also by Harrison. Whereas the original Journey foursome took Harrison's composition and sped it up to make it a true rocker, here Perry reimagines "I Need You" at a sultry, contemplative pace. Finally, the cover art, designed by Jeff Wack in close collaboration with Perry, is evocative of the singer's history in music, including images of a theater in which his father had performed; his high school in Lemoore, California; San Francisco's Golden Gate Bridge; the legendary topcoat with tails; and a stadium lit for a rock show, among others. A rattlesnake coils around a wine bottle, symbolizing a battle with substance abuse never publicly disclosed. An antique radio microphone is on fire, symbolizing a love-hate relationship with the talent that served him so well but apparently caused so much of his pain.

The album did very well on the *Billboard* 200 chart. Released on October 5, 2018, it peaked at number 6 on October 19—better than his previous effort, *For the Love of Strange Medicine* (number 15), and even better than his 1984 debut *Street Talk* (number 12). It was not certified gold, because RIAA only does certifications at the request of the record label, and Perry no longer had a contract with any record label; *Traces* was distributed by Berkeley's independent Fantasy Records. Reviews were generally positive but focused on Perry's dramatic return more than on the album itself; when the critics actually did address the music, Kory Grow's *Rolling Stone* review was typical: "full of dramatic schmaltz, nostalgia and the occasional rocker . . . but in a weird way that's what you want from Steve Perry—you want to feel and remember." Still, Perry had clearly found a winning formula: no need to tour, just do interviews with as many major news outlets and radio stations as possible. When he followed up *Traces* with *The Season*, his 2021 collection of Christmas songs, and additional work with Dolly Parton and the Irish band the High Kings, the pattern was set; his fans knew what to expect. Of course, it helped that Journey was still touring, performing his music and keeping alive the inevitable rumors of a possible reunion.

On that subject, the singer continued to confound. On the one hand, he could get combative. "Please listen to me," he told Andy Greene of *Rolling Stone*. "I left the band 31 fucking years ago, my friend," referring to his 1987 decision to walk away and ignoring the *Trial by Fire* reunion. About Schon, he said, "You can still love someone, but not want to work with them. And if they only love you because they want to work with you, that doesn't feel good to me." As for Cain, "I don't really care to read Jonathan's book," he said, referring to the pianist/songwriter's 2018 memoir, adding, "I'd appreciate if you didn't tell me about it. I don't need to know. It's none of my business."

But he refused to rule out a return to Journey. "The only thing I'm willing to be definitive about is that at this age I am right now [sixty-nine years], I have to do things that I feel really great about, that feel life-sustaining and give me passion."

*   *   *

Any excitement about the potential for another Journey reunion was quickly tempered by other events that threatened to split apart what was left of the band. Frustrated with lackluster sales of his solo albums, his continuing 12.5 percent rent payments to Steve Perry, and alimony for multiple ex-wives, Neal Schon decided to commercialize his group Journey through Time—the group featuring Gregg Rolie, Deen Castronovo, and Marco Mendoza that had performed Journey deep cuts at a 2018 benefit for the Marin County Fire Department. On January 5, 2019, he filed a trademark application for the band name "Neal Schon's Journey through Time," to be owned by Schon Productions, Inc. The company would provide "pre-recorded CDs, pre-recorded DVDs, and downloadable audio and video recordings" under the mark, as well as "Necklaces; Bracelets; Rings; Key chains . . . T-Shirts; Long-sleeved shirts; Tank tops; Sweaters; Jackets; Hooded sweatshirts; Hats; Headwear, namely, caps; Beanies," and "[e]ntertainment services in the nature of live musical performances." He then announced a tour with the group, starting on February 22 in Jackson, California. In doing all this without permission from Nightmare Productions, Journey's parent company, he violated the Journey trademark. Daniel Schacht, of Nightmare's law firm Donohue Fitzgerald, filed an official "Notice of Opposition" with the US Patent and Trademark Office.

Of course, as a founding and continuing member of Journey and Nightmare, Schon had a claim to the Journey name few of his current or former bandmates could match. Indeed, had he formally sought permission from Nightmare to use the name in this way, it would likely have been granted in exchange for a customary percentage of revenues. Even after Schacht sent the Notice of Opposition, Schon could probably still have smoothed everything over had he simply discussed the matter with the other shareholders—or at least enough of them to get a majority to support a fair deal. He was on tour throughout 2018 and 2019 with Jonathan Cain, Steve Smith, and Ross Valory, and continued to enjoy a good relationship with Herbie. Schon was currently serving as secretary of the Nightmare board of directors; he could have worked out the details with his three bandmates and Herbie, contacted Steve Perry's lawyer for additional negotiation, and convened a shareholders' meeting to approve the final deal.

Instead, in a move almost guaranteed to raise objections from his bandmates, Schon attempted to use his authority as an officer of Nightmare to pressure the lawyers to back off their opposition, threatening to fire them. Of course, his post on the board of directors was mostly honorary, without any daily responsibilities or actual authority; Schon could not act without a majority of the board behind him. The number of directors had fluctuated over the years among the six shareholders; the directors tended to be two or three of them plus an accountant who served as Nightmare's treasurer, and sometimes one of their lawyers. In 2019, the board of directors consisted of Cain, Schon, and Valory.

And so, to ensure a favorable vote by the board, Schon buried the hatchet with Jonathan Cain. Put another way, Schon convinced Cain to collude with him to get Nightmare to allow him to register the trademark for Journey through Time, even if that meant firing lawyer Schacht. Any monetary incentives he may have used to appease Cain have not been made public. But Cain knew that if he were to split with Schon, it would have meant the end of Journey—or at least his own membership in it. And his earnings from the Journey tours, even with the continuing payoff to Perry, were in the millions. As long as he could play and sing, he wanted to be up on that stage, earning. But if Schon wanted him out, he would either be out, or the band would end.

When they learned that Schon was using his position on the board of directors to pressure Schacht to drop Nightmare's opposition to the trademark violation, the response from the other shareholders was swift. No matter his importance to the history of the band or its current iteration, Schon could not unilaterally create a new band to profit from the Journey name. A benefit concert was one thing, but this was another matter entirely. And so Herbie, Smith, and Valory, with Perry's consent, requested that Cain call a shareholders' meeting to elect a new board of directors—which would include all six of the shareholders—and thereby ensure that the board would neither allow the Journey through Time trademark nor fire the lawyers who had properly represented Nightmare in the matter.

There was some dispute as to whether Jonathan Cain actually signed the notice to call the shareholders meeting. Lawyers representing Schon and Cain argued that his electronic signature had been added to a document without his consent by an employee at Nightmare's law firm. But that's a technicality; as president of the board of directors of Nightmare, he was bound by fiduciary duty to the corporation to call a shareholders meeting on the request of a majority of shareholders, and Herbie, Perry, Smith, and Valory—a majority—were requesting such a meeting. Had he refused to do so, the four could have called the meeting on their own, so long as they provided adequate notice to all shareholders. The lawyers provided adequate notice, both by "snail mail"—that is, the US Post Office—and by email.

On February 3, 2020, Nightmare lawyer Daniel Schacht convened the shareholders meeting. Valory, Herbie, and Nightmare accountant Timothy Jorstad were present in person; Cain, Perry, and Smith were present by phone. Smith and Perry had given their written proxies to Jorstad, which shareholders are legally allowed to do. Neal Schon was absent, although he was represented—also by phone—by his lawyer, Mark Barondess. (Schon later claimed he was listening in by phone as well, but the official record does not reflect that.) Schacht declared a quorum (a majority of the shareholders) present, so they were empowered to conduct business. By a vote of 4–0, with Cain abstaining, the shareholders then voted all six onto the board of directors: Cain, Herbert, Perry, Schon, Smith, and Valory. The new board, by the same vote totals, then proceeded to elect Smith as president and Valory as secretary and to retain both the accounting firm and the law firm that represented the company.

This was no corporate coup d'état, as was later alleged by Schon and Cain. In fact, under the circumstances, this was a perfectly legal and prudent act. It also demonstrated good faith. Although the purpose was to prevent Schon from using his authority with Nightmare *against* Nightmare, they nevertheless reelected Schon to the board. His opinion—as always—would matter, and his vote—as always—would count.

Another argument that Schon would later make—that Smith and Valory were trying to take over the band—was also misleading. Smith agreed to be president and Valory secretary because they were the only two shareholders currently in the band who were voting with the majority. Valory had actually been secretary before, so he knew the job (minimal though it was). Herbie was retired, and Perry had no desire to engage in a volunteer job connected to Journey, even if largely ceremonial. He was more than happy to give his proxy to Jorstad whenever there were board or shareholders' meetings, but otherwise, so long as the checks kept coming, he no longer had any interest in the management of Journey.

If Schon's actions so far were shocking, what happened next was even more so. He concocted a story that Smith and Valory were looking to retire with payouts similar to what he and Cain had been paying Perry. To engage in this nefarious scheme, Schon claimed, the two had duped Herbie and Perry into engaging in a corporate coup to take over Journey. He then outlandishly claimed that it was not Nightmare Productions that controlled the Journey trademark but actually . . . *Elmo Partners.*

Elmo Partners? Elmo was the group that Perry, Schon, and Cain created in 1985 when Herbie was trying to convince Steve Perry to record another Journey album and was willing to hand over control of the band to do so. And indeed, Elmo Partners *had* controlled the Journey name and trademark—from 1985 to 1994. The contract between Nightmare and Elmo explicitly gave Elmo control "until such time as none of Perry, Schon, or Cain are actively performing or recording as Journey." Except that within two years of signing that contract, none of the Three was performing or recording as Journey, actively or otherwise. Steve Perry left the band, despite repeated entreaties from the fans, his former bandmates, Herbie, and even Columbia Records; Schon and Cain recorded with Michael Bolton—not as Journey but on a Bolton solo album—and then with John Waite—again, not as Journey, but as Bad English. Save their appearance at the 1991 Bill Graham tribute in Golden Gate Park, none of them performed or recorded *as Journey* for nearly a decade—thereby voiding their control of the band. In 1994, acting as president of Nightmare, Herbie terminated the agreement with Elmo Partners, and the six shareholders, eager to proceed with the *Trial by Fire* reunion, *unanimously* agreed with that action. Schon himself acknowledged the reality in a 1997 interview, noting that "we stopped playing together and stopped making records," even as "there was never anything official about the band breaking up." Of course, none of this was included in Schon's legal filing.

Schon worked hard to make sure his gambit worked. He resolved to fire Smith and Valory from Journey, and when Azoff Management refused to do it—a reasonable decision since he actually had no legal right to fire Smith and

Valory—*he fired Azoff Management.* Then he had his law firm—also with no legal right to do so—terminate his bandmates. "Effective immediately, you are no longer members of the band Journey and cannot perform under the name Journey," wrote Louis Miller, one of Schon's lawyers. As founding member George Tickner once put it, "That was the nature of it—they fucked each other over."

Schon then told the press that he and Jonathan Cain were Journey's remaining "principal members." The guitarist had not been able to establish that he was the band's only "founding member," so now he claimed that his input—with Cain and Steve Perry—had been solely responsible for the group's success, adding insult to injury by alleging that "[n]either Smith nor Valory have ever made significant creative contributions to Journey."

In musical parlance, the term "principal" refers to a lead at a particular instrument in an orchestra—principal violin, for instance. But in rock music, there is no hard and fast rule privileging any particular instrument. Some lead vocalists are bandleaders; some are not. Some lead guitarists are bandleaders; some are not. To say that Ross Valory and Steve Smith were unimportant to the success of Journey simply because of the instruments they played is belied by the experience of other bands. The Police, for example, were led by their bassist, Sting; the Eagles were led by their drummer, Don Henley, and rhythm guitarist, Glenn Frey.

Of course, it is undeniable that Valory and Smith did not get songwriting credits on any of the band's hits, all of which (except "Wheel in the Sky") were written by some combination of Perry, Cain, and Schon. But their songwriting impact was not negligible. Valory wrote or cowrote a total of fifteen Journey songs, most of which *after* Steve Perry was hired; Smith cowrote two of the songs on *Frontiers*. Even so, songwriting credits are not the only way to measure contribution. Valory and Smith added arrangements in the studio, and to a lesser extent on the road, that shaped listeners' enjoyment of the music, from the prominent bass line in "Don't Stop Believin'" to the drum fills in "Lovin', Touchin', Squeezin'." Valory sang lead on one song on *Generations* and had a reputation among fans and bandmates alike as the band's jokester, hamming it up onstage whenever he saw a little red light appear on one of the roving cameras.

This is not to say that they weren't replaceable. Both had already been replaced before—Steve Smith twice! And to be sure, Valory and Smith were

less integral to the band than were Cain and Schon. "Journey featuring founding guitarist Neal Schon" could surely sell more tickets than "Journey featuring founding bassist Ross Valory."

Having successfully positioned himself and Cain in the press as Journey's "principal" members, however, Schon quickly hired replacements.
Randy Jackson was a former member of the band (albeit without stock in
Nightmare), having provided bass for one track on *Frontiers* in 1983 and
the entirety of the 1986 *Raised on Radio* album, and having been in the
band during the truncated *Raised on Radio* tour. Three decades later, after
a successful career as the head of A&R for rhythm & blues at Columbia, he
was a nationally recognized celebrity in his own right as a longtime judge
on the hit Fox TV show *American Idol*. Narada Michael Walden, who
received his first name (like Devadip Carlos Santana) from the Indian guru
Sri Chinmoy, had built a successful career as a Bay Area drummer starting in the late 1970s. He went on to become a seasoned producer for the
likes of Aretha Franklin, Whitney Houston, Mariah Carey, Starship, Diana
Ross, and Steve Winwood. By 2020 he was a longtime collaborator with
Neal Schon, having written much of the material on the guitarist's recent
solo album *Vortex*.

Frankly, the choice of Jackson and Walden was inspired. In the era of Black
Lives Matter, a heritage rock band that had once been in danger of becoming a "red state" band had hired two Black musicians. With Arnel Pineda, a
majority of Journey now consisted of people of color. Furthermore, given the
band's tensions over the visit to the Trump White House, the move solidified
Schon's control over the band. Despite his protestations that his music was
not political, Schon had successfully steered his band back to its multicultural
San Francisco roots—if not its musical origins.

Inspired though the choice was, it was uncertain whether it would allow
Schon to keep control of the band. In an echo of what happened with Aynsley
Dunbar forty years earlier, Valory countersued, arguing that only Nightmare
could fire a bandmember and that Elmo Partners no longer controlled the
band. Given Schon's statement in his legal filing that he would never work
with Valory and Smith again, the question of who controlled Journey now
rested with the courts. But less than a month later, the courts shut down—
thanks to the COVID-19 pandemic.

*   *   *

Back in 1985, when Journey had continued on as a threesome with a hired rhythm session, Ross Valory and Steve Smith—unlike George Tickner, Aynsley Dunbar, and Gregg Rolie before them—still retained their shares in Nightmare. So how does one define "membership" in Journey? When Dunbar was fired from the band and defrauded of his shares, he sued; the band—or Herbie—or Nightmare—and their lawyers agreed that the former drummer had a strong enough case to merit a settlement and avoid a jury trial. In 1985, when Steve Perry fired Smith and Valory, neither was removed from Nightmare, nor did either contest the legality of the contract with Elmo Partners that allowed Perry, Neal Schon, and Jonathan Cain to go on as Journey without them. But if Nightmare was Journey, and Journey was Nightmare, were they ever actually out of the band? And what about Herbie Herbert? The manager never played a note on an album or a stage, but he was the single most influential person on the history of the band. Was he a "member" because he was an equal partner in, and often president of, Nightmare?

For that matter, can a musical act be a corporation? Can a corporation be a musical act? During the *Escape-Frontiers* heyday, some critics labeled Journey "corporate rock" because they seemed to craft their sound to the tastes of the audience and were willing to market merchandise and make sponsorship deals with corporations like Budweiser and Atari. Such critics had little idea that the band was, even then, literally a corporation. From a legal standpoint, it no longer mattered who actually recorded the music or who actually performed onstage.

In seeking artistic control, Perry had wrested corporate control from Herbie. But the underlying fact remained that if the band could fire one of its six equal shareholders, it could fire any of them. And in 1998, when Journey went on without Steve Perry, it did.

In 2020, from a legal perspective, Valory and Smith were right, and Schon and Cain were wrong. The Elmo Partners no longer controlled the Journey name, as their contract had been voided in 1987 when all three shareholders had ceased to record or perform as Journey, and that voiding was certified with Herbie's December 1994 letter on behalf of Nightmare. Therefore, Schon had no right to fire Valory and Smith, as he and Cain did not constitute a majority of Nightmare, which owned Journey; the other four partners

(Valory, Smith, Perry, and Herbert) did not agree to the firing. (He also had no right to fire Azoff Management, but Irving Azoff didn't sue, so the point became moot.)

Where Valory's countersuit faltered was not in the law but in popular perception and in the realities of the business. Journey was taking in approximately $30 million per year in touring and merchandise revenue. It would have been very unlikely to do so without Schon; Valory and Smith were more expendable. The only scenario in which the two might have continued without Schon would have involved Perry returning to the band; Dennis Hunt once called Perry "the only indispensable member." But such a reunion remained a pipe dream.

Valory and Smith surely knew that their income as Nightmare shareholders would be in jeopardy if the company fired Schon instead of them. Once Schon's lawyer informed them that Schon would never work with them again, the die was cast. They were out. The lawsuit was merely a legal game of chicken: how close would they get to a jury trial before agreeing to a settlement, and how much would Schon have to pay to get them to back down?

Schon surely knew he could not win on the legal merits. But Valory and Smith also surely knew that if the case actually made it to court, the band would be finished; the two on their own could not successfully go on as Journey. When YouTube commentator David Spuria opined that "if you don't have Neal Schon, you don't have Journey," he was incorrect; if you can have Journey without Steve Perry, you can certainly have it without Neal Schon. But the larger sentiment was true: without Perry, only Schon could stake a reasonable popular claim to the band. A settlement was inevitable, and the pandemic gave the parties time to work one out. In early 2021, they went their separate ways for an undisclosed amount. Valory and Smith are likely making less than Perry but still considerable amounts. And Valory is likely making slightly more than Smith because he participated in the rerecording of the catalog hits with Pineda on *Revelation* in 2008. But as members of Nightmare, Jonathan Cain, Steve Perry, Neal Schon, Steve Smith, Ross Valory, and the estate of Herbie Herbert—who died in October 2021—are equal partners. As of their most recent corporate filing at this writing, Smith continued to serve as the corporation's president and Valory its secretary.

*   *   *

The story of Journey is a story about a band that capitalized on the racial backlash of the '70s by producing music rooted in soul and rhythm & blues for a largely white, working-class audience—an audience that didn't want to listen to Motown because it was "too Black" but was perfectly happy listening to five white dudes play music positively dripping with hot Motown wax.

At the same time, the story of Journey is also a story about the incredible loss of purpose that was part of early rock ideals, what some considered the "spirit of Woodstock." While few thoughtful observers expected rock musicians to work for free, the story of Journey—the shedding of progressive roots and its Woodstock rock star and the evolution of its hippie manager into a tough industry mogul—demonstrates how rock and roll's egalitarian future was fully and thoroughly co-opted by commercial interests. Rather than continuing as a cog in the machine, Steve Perry took the wisest course, getting out before the business consumed him. And unlike Neal Schon, he never had to pay any alimony that would force him back out on the road.

*   *   *

As the song says, "it goes on and on and on and on." During the COVID pandemic, the band recorded a new album, its first in a decade. Named for Herbie Herbert's planned title for the band's 1986 album, *Freedom* was very much Neal Schon's baby, the guitarist cowriting all but one of its sixteen tracks. Recording was difficult, as the band members were quarantining in different cities. "During the pandemic, there wasn't much to do," according to Schon. As a result, engineer Jim Reitzel, who had worked with Narada Michael Walden and Randy Jackson and whose credits included the Santana reunion album, is given significant billing in the liner notes. Six tracks feature Jason Derlatka on backing vocals; he had been assisting with keyboards on tour for several years. The album cover features a reenvisioned Journey scarab with orange, red, and green feathers clutching a pearl and a gem on a royal blue background, with the stylized words "Journey" and "Freedom" in all caps.

The album begins with "Together We Run," by Narada Michael Walden, Randy Jackson, Jonathan Cain, Schon, and Berklee-trained singer-songwriter Rachel Efron. A contemplative piano is joined by Arnel Pineda's insistent vocals, which have improved since *Eclipse*. The theme is catchy, with a rhythmic, almost staccato backing vocal. "Don't Give Up on Us," by Schon, Cain, and Walden, begins with a synthesizer intro similar to "Separate Ways (Worlds Apart)," and lyrics reminiscent of a classic Cain theme: "Two dreamers fierce in love/Now We're Miles Apart." Jackson sat out the ballad "Still Believe in Love," by Schon, Cain, and Walden, with Cain playing synth bass—a first for Journey. "You Got the Best of Me," by Schon, Cain, and Walden, begins with an electronic riff and a strong guitar line. Quick verse lyrics lead to a catchy chorus, and the end includes a neat coda. "Live to Love Again" is a ballad by Cain in the vein of "Open Arms" and "Faithfully."

"The Way We Used to Be," a rocker by Schon and Cain, was released with an animated video a full year before the album. The band members are depicted (significantly younger, as is possible with animation) on their way to—what else—a Journey concert, attended by the video's protagonists who are living the theme of the song: the desire of so many to return to a normal life after the pandemic. The song and video were released in July 2021, as vaccines were just beginning to move through the population.

"Come Away with Me," by Schon, Cain, and Walden, is a hard rocker with a repetitive blues guitar riff and lyrics that speak to a desire for a vacation. Pineda sat out "After Glow," by Schon, Cain, and Walden, with none other than Deen Castronovo handling lead vocal duties. The song is, like "Mother, Father" (which Castronovo had covered for years on the road), a ballad with thoughtful, personal lyrics. Then comes "Let it Rain," by Schon, Cain, and Walden, a plodding, almost mournful rocker about bad news, the pandemic Journey's downbeat answer to Bobby McFerrin's "Don't Worry Be Happy." Still, it's got the feel of a rather undeveloped idea.

"Holdin' On," by Schon, Cain, Jackson, and Walden, has a strong blues guitar riff reminiscent more of Schon's solo work—especially on his *Piranha Blues* album—and good harmonies that speak to heyday Journey. Cain sat out the rocker "All Day and All Night," which he had cowritten with Schon and Walden; the drummer covered the keys. The song has a deliberate R&B beat and an insistent vocal. Then it's "Don't Go," by Pineda, Schon, Walden, and Cain, a rocker with a steady beat, a catchy tune, lyrics of entreaty, and a touch of guitar-and-vocal interplay during the second verse.

"United We Stand," by Schon, Cain, Walden, and Jackson, is an uptempo love song with Cain's distinctive mark, and not a patriotic anthem as the title might otherwise suggest. "Life Rolls On," by Schon and Walden, is something of a minimalist sketch, without anything resembling a soaring melody, complex harmony, or fancy fretwork, while "Beautiful as You Are," a seven-minute suite by Schon, Cain, and Walden, is an excellent way to close the album, starting with a soft balled for two plaintive verses, bursting into a guitar-driven, harmonized, catchy up-tempo before eventually resolving in a tender acoustic guitar finale. The Japanese release also included a bonus track by Cain, "Hard to Let It Go," a piano-focused ballad with a strong backing guitar line and a hauntingly beautiful solo.

All told, much of *Freedom* sounds like one of the recent Neal Schon solo albums coproduced by Walden. The result is a good album with lots of catchy tunes but little that significantly furthers the Journey legacy. Schon forgot the lesson of the 1970s, that instrumentalist indulgence in Journey music might make him feel good, but doesn't have mass appeal.

*   *   *

In August 2021, with vaccines reopening venues around the country, Journey headlined the Lollapalooza Festival in Chicago. Randy Jackson, sidelined for back surgery, was replaced with Marco Mendoza—Neal Schon's bassist from Soul SirkUS (and, more recently, Journey through Time—the cause of the 2020 troubles). But by the time they played *Dick Clark's New Year's Rockin' Eve* in New York City's Times Square that December, Mendoza had been sidelined for Todd Jensen, the bassist who had played with Schon in Hardline and with Steve Perry on *For the Love of Strange Medicine*. Jensen is white. And prizing friendship over felonies, Schon brought back Deen Castronovo—ostensibly not to replace Narada Michael Walden but to augment him. When they appeared at Lollapalooza, the stage literally had two drum sets. Castronovo had been in recovery, and Schon—himself a recovering alcoholic—respected that effort. But that September, Castronovo announced that he had been back on opiates for several months. When he contracted COVID-19 and was replaced by his roadie for the New Year's show, Walden was nowhere to be found, sidelined by a heart condition. Journey was again four-fifths white (actually five-sixths, counting Jason Derlatka). The Jackson-Walden moment became just another exception that proved the rule, as when Journey welcomed several Black blues legends to a Chicago stage in 1978.

And they were still suing each other. In September 2022, Steve Perry filed an action against Neal Schon and Jonathan Cain with the US Patent and Trademark Office, claiming that Schon and Cain had fraudulently trademarked the titles of the hits they had cowritten with him. (He withdrew the claim in January 2023, possibly for an undisclosed settlement.) The next month Schon sued *Cain*, claiming that the keyboardist had abused a band credit card. Cain countersued, arguing that it was Schon who was the profligate spender—likely closer to the truth, given the guitarist's unending expenses. Schon even attempted to get Gregg Rolie back in the band on a regular basis as leverage to remove Cain (the organist did appear at a Journey concert near his home in Austin, Texas, but wisely demurred as to the permanent gig). And when Schon actually went ahead with the release of a recording of the 2018 Journey through Time concert with Frontiers Records and booked a show under that band's name, Rolie—who continued to own his own publishing—sent a cease-and-desist letter arguing that he had never signed off on such a release and would sue if necessary. The concert was canceled.

Meanwhile, Schon descended deeper into paranoia, accusing everyone in sight (including me) of working for former Journey manager Irving Azoff in some nefarious scheme to undermine the former guitar prodigy. As with conspiracy theories involving the Kennedy assassination and the moon landing, there's no point arguing with him. Fortunately, Azoff and I have Schon's houses, cars, and even rock venues fully bugged so we can keep good track of his innermost thoughts.*

Apparently unable to find a bandmate with whom he could remain friendly, when *Billboard* published a long-form article blaming the band's problems on Schon, the guitarist vented his frustrations at . . . *Pineda*.

But the money remained far too good to turn and walk away. Their fiftieth year saw Journey on a national tour with Toto. Schon, Cain, Pineda (despite increasing vocal problems), Jensen, Castronovo, and Derlatka were out there performing and sharing their profits with Perry, Smith, Valory, and the estate of Herbie Herbert.

And someday, thanks to modern technology, when Schon and Cain can no longer perform, surely their digital avatars will go out on tour with five or

---

* To be clear, that was a joke. I have no connection to Azoff management and am not engaged in any espionage activities against Neal Schon; nor can I find any evidence that Azoff is listening in on Schon.

six or twelve or twenty talented musicians who can play the music inspired by Motown and soul, influenced by the Afro-Latin rhythms of Santana, the psychedelic surf of Gregg Rolie, and the British blues of Aynsley Dunbar. Perhaps the show will include a giant-sized Steve Perry avatar, lip-synching to his own original vocal tracks. The fans will demand it—the fans who are still, more desperately than ever, "livin' just to find emotion."

Backstage
Acknowledgments

My ability to tell this story is thanks to so many people, all of whom helped improve it, none of whom are responsible for my copious mistakes.

My first acknowledgment must go to my fellow Journey fans, without whom the band would not have been successful. Some of these have worked on The Journey Zone and have continued to contribute time and energy to this project: Cynthia Lee, Ross Muir, and Jan Weir. Other fans I met on Twitter read and commented on portions, making the book better: José Javier Alvarez, Amanda Burk, Jeremy Green, Ruby Heath, and María Cristina Herrera. Thanks also to Mark Ricche for the full critical readthrough and the four-part interview about the book and the writing process, now on YouTube (https:// youtube.com/playlist?list=PLVPiM8p7tsRKmJO_DRK6GGYIVqfT_mjzT).

At the Rock and Roll Hall of Fame Archives, I was privileged to have the assistance of archivists Laura Maidens, Crystal Matjasic, Justin Seidler, and Jennie Thomas, and I am grateful for the conversation with journalist and fellow researcher Peter Ames Carlin.

Most of this book was drafted while at Governors State University, and I would like to thank my colleagues there for their support, in particular Kieran Aarons, Ben Almassi, Reynolds Andujar, Novia Pagone, Jelena Radovic-Fanta, Jarrod Shanahan, Rebecca Siefert, Bradley Smith, and Christopher White, all of whom read and critiqued an early chapter; supportive friends Alice Keane, Bill "Professor Fraud" Kresse (as ever), Andrae Marak (now at

Roosevelt), and Ellie Walsh; and library colleagues Joshua Sopiarz and Cynthia Romanowski (now at SWAN).

Of course, my move to Monmouth University to serve as dean of the Wayne D. McMurray School of Humanities and Social Sciences has brought new friends who have been helpful and supportive. These include Kristin Bluemel, Ken Campbell, Christopher DeRosa, Geoff Fouad (now at Hunter College), Jon Landau, Rockin' Joe Rapolla, Bob Santelli, Bill Schreiber, Hettie Williams, and most especially my decanal colleague Richard Veit—a rare gentleman who made my transition the easiest possible—Ken Womack, the "Lighthouse of Beatles Studies," and Melissa Ziobro.

Speaking of Beatles Studies, I must give a shout-out to my friends from the 2023 Popular Culture Conference: Allison Bumsted, Kent Drummond (University of Wyoming), Stephanie Hernandez (University of Liverpool), Richard Mills (St. Mary's, Twickenham), and most importantly Katie Kapurch (Texas State), whose groundbreaking work connecting Disney to the Fab Four opened my eyes to the role of gender in rock fandom (and who gave Ken his nickname).

Portions of this book previously appeared in an article published in *Rock Music Studies* in October 2023, copyright Taylor & Francis, available online, http://www.tandfonline.com/10.1080/19401159.2023.2252992. Thanks to journal editor Gary Burns of Northern Illinois University.

As always, members of my grad school herd—sadly thinner with the passage of time—each contributed in ways large and small. In particular, thanks to David Aliano (College of Mount Saint Vincent), Kristopher Burrell (Hostos Community College), Carla DuBose (Westchester Community College), Jacob Kramer (Borough of Manhattan Community College), Alejandro Quintana (St. John's), and Alex Stavropoulos. Thanks also to Scott Matthews (Florida State), who, though never a Journey fan, appreciated the musicality of their album *Next*; and to Edward L. Ayers (University of Richmond), who, on learning of my appreciation of the band, asked why Gregg Rolie left not one but *two* successful bands in his career. I hope this answers the question.

I have continued to benefit from the insights of the reading group at the Mount Sinai Division of Psychotherapy, especially Phil Luloff and, until his death in 2023, Hillel Swiller.

This was originally conceived as a trade book, and I'd like to thank David Congdon (University Press of Kansas) and Carol Sklenicka for the advice that helped me land an agent. Honorable mention goes to that agent, Stacey Glick (Dystel, Goderich, and Bourret) who took a risk even though it didn't pan out, and to Peter Mickulas (Rutgers), Ken Womack (again), and Judith Lakamper (Lexington), who helped me find the book its best home here at Rowman & Littlefield. On that note, thanks to Michael Tan and Ashleigh Cooke of R&L and the two anonymous reviewers. It was a major accomplishment to win the enthusiastic support of infamous Reviewer Number Two. Thanks also to George Witte of St. Martin's Press and Tanya Farrell of Wunderkind PR.

Thanks as always to my dad Jeffrey Golland (Mount Sinai Medical Center) and my wife Lana Rogachevskaya, who each offered critical comments early in the process; my children, to whom this is dedicated; and every member of my family who has supported me at any and every stage of my life and career.

Of course, I must thank the former members of Journey and associated acts who have graciously shared their reflections with me over the years. These are Mike Carabello, Kevin Chalfant, Bill Cuomo, Robert Fleischman, Kurt Griffey, Jeremey Hunsicker, Alphonso Johnson, Josh Ramos, Gregg Rolie, Steve Smith, the late George Tickner, and Ron Wikso. And thank you to everyone who has ever performed with Journey, written for Journey, or worked for Journey. *Still They Ride.*

Band Members, by Album

Album	Lead Vocals	Guitars	Keyboards	Bass	Drums
Journey (1975)	Gregg Rolie	N. Schon/G. Tickner	Gregg Rolie	Ross Valory	Aynsley Dunbar
Look into the Future (1976)	Gregg Rolie	Neal Schon	Gregg Rolie	Ross Valory	Aynsley Dunbar
Next (1977)	Gregg Rolie	Neal Schon	Gregg Rolie	Ross Valory	Aynsley Dunbar
Infinity (1978)	Steve Perry/Gregg Rolie	Neal Schon	Gregg Rolie	Ross Valory	Aynsley Dunbar
Evolution (1979)	Steve Perry/Gregg Rolie	Neal Schon	Gregg Rolie	Ross Valory	Steve Smith
Departure (1980)	Steve Perry/Gregg Rolie	Neal Schon	Gregg Rolie	Ross Valory	Steve Smith
Dream, After Dream (1980)	Steve Perry/Gregg Rolie	Neal Schon	Gregg Rolie	Ross Valory	Steve Smith
Captured (1981)	Steve Perry/Gregg Rolie	Neal Schon	Gregg Rolie/S. Roseman	Ross Valory	Steve Smith
Escape (1981)	Steve Perry	Neal Schon	Jonathan Cain	Ross Valory	Steve Smith
Frontiers (1983)	Steve Perry	Neal Schon	Jonathan Cain	Ross Valory	Steve Smith
Raised on Radio (1986)	Steve Perry	Neal Schon	Jonathan Cain	R. Jackson/Bob Glaub	Steve Smith/Larrie Londin
Trial by Fire (1996)	Steve Perry	Neal Schon	Jonathan Cain	Ross Valory	Steve Smith
Arrival (2001)	Steve Augeri	Neal Schon	Jonathan Cain	Ross Valory	Deen Castronovo
Red 13 (2003)	Steve Augeri	Neal Schon	Jonathan Cain	Ross Valory	Deen Castronovo
Generations (2005)	Steve Augeri	Neal Schon	Jonathan Cain	Ross Valory	Deen Castronovo
Revelation (2008)	Arnel Pineda	Neal Schon	Jonathan Cain	Ross Valory	Deen Castronovo
Eclipse (2011)	Arnel Pineda	Neal Schon	Jonathan Cain	Ross Valory	Deen Castronovo
Freedom (2022)	Arnel Pineda	Neal Schon	Jonathan Cain	Randy Jackson	Narada M. Walden

Index

Brubeck, Dave, 24

Bruce, Jack, 84

Bruni, Frank, 291

Buddy Rich Alumni Big Band, 278

Buddy's Buddies (band), 206

Budokan Hall, 147

Budweiser beer, 6, 111, 129, 149, 209, 221, 301

Buffalo News, 222

Buffalo Springfield (band), 19

Bugatti, Dominic, 140

Built for Speed (Stray Cats album), 148

Bumsted, Allison, 310

Burbank, Calif., 76

Burdon, Eric, 96

Burk, Amanda, 309

Burns, Gary, 310

Burns, Stef, 179

Burrell, Kristopher, 310

Burt Sugarman's Midnight Special, 76, 104, 139

Burtnik, Glen, 253

Bush, George W., 237-238

Butterfield Blues Band, 25, 26

Butterfield, Paul, 25

"Butterfly (She Flies Alone)" (Journey song), 236, 237

"Byrd freaks," 19, 23, 24, 71, 230

Byrds (band), 17, 18–19

C

Caen, Herb, 21

Caesar, Julius, 146

Caiaphas (biblical), 86

Caillat, Ken, 106

Cain, Elizabeth "Liz" (wife of JC), 170, 193, 215, 216, 224, 225, 226, 266, 267, 268, 278

Cain, Jonathan (JC), xii, 2, 5, 9–11, 121, 123, 125, 127, 130, 132–133, 135, 137–138, 140–141, 145, 149–151, 155, 157–161, 164–166, 169–170, 175–178, 183–184, 187–189, 191–194, 197–200, 206, 207, 209, 212–214, 217, 219–220, 222–225, 229, 231, 234, 238, 239, 243–244, 245, 247, 252, 253, 259, 262–264, 264, 266–270, 272, 273–274, 276, 278–279, 280, 282, 284–286, 289–291, 292, 293, 294, 304, 306, 313. See also Jonathan Cain Band

Cain, Madison (daughter of JC), 262

Cain, Paula White (wife of JC), 278, 285, 289, 290

Cain, Scott, 75

Cain, Tané McClure (wife of JC), 121, 125, 144-145, 150, 151, 159, 173, 180, 268

Cain, Tommy (brother of JC), 136–137

Cain, Weston (son of JC), 225, 278

Cal Poly State. See California Polytechnic State University

Cal Stereo, 138

Calaveras County (Calif.), 16, 163

Calgary Herald, 103

California Music Awards. See BAMMIES

California Polytechnic State University, 45

California Secretary of State, 10

California State University, 21

California Symphony, 205

California World Music Festival, 104

California, x, 10, 13, 19, 54, 103, 124, 128, 130, 133, 137, 157, 187, 188, 201, 225, 239, 261, 271, 279, 289, 290

Grossman, Albert, 137–138
Grove Street, San Francisco, Calif., 229
Grow, Kory, 294
grunge (music), 35, 131, 183, 194,
    196, 211
Guff (band), 196
Guns 'n' Roses (band), 254
Guralnick, Peter, 68
Gurnack, Susan. See Susan Smith
Gush Studios, 185
Guy, Buddy, 23

H
Habitat for Humanity, 235
Hackensack Record, 72
Haddad, Richard Michaels, 18
Hagar Schon Aaronson Shrieve. See
    HSAS
Hagar, Sammy, 92, 150, 151, 211, 230,
    245–246, 252–253, 254–255, 257, 265
Haight–Ashbury (San Francisco, Calif.),
    23, 206
Hakim, Omar, 162, 253, 255, 277–279
Halee, Roy, x, xi, 46, 48
Hamilton Family Shelter, 206
Hammer, Jan, 11, 129, 147, 151, 163,
    238, 251–252
Hammond B3 organ, 24, 64, 113, 117,
    254, 293
Hancock, Herbie, 43
Handy, John, 151
Hanford Sentinel, 16, 73
Hanford, Calif., 13–14, 161, 201
Happy Days (television), 78
"Happy to Give" (Journey song),
    161–162
"Happy Together" (Turtles song), 87, 88
Harburg, E.Y., 130, 131

A Hard Road (John Mayall album), 84
Hard Rock Café, 194, 220, 265
"Hard to Let it Go" (Journey song), 305
Hardline (band), 11, 175–176, 182, 183,
    189, 190, 191, 209, 211, 305
Harlem (New York, NY
    neighborhood), 210
Harms, Jesse, 174
Harper, Rod, 26
Harrison, Dhani (son of George),
    283, 286
Harrison, George, 52, 171, 292, 293
Harrison, Olivia (wife of George), 293
Hart, Mickey, 24
Hartford, Conn., 218
Harvard Street (Whitman, Mass.), 201
Havens, Richie, 28
Hawaii, 40–41, 43, 124, 127, 128, 147,
    163, 197, 220, 271
Hazelden Betty Ford Springbrook
    facility, 276
Head First (the Babys album), 139
Healey, Jim, 102
Heart (band), 171, 179, 246, 252, 271
"Hearts to Cry" (Frumious
    Bandersnatch song), 23
Heath, Ruby, 309
Heatmakerz (band), 236
"Heaven is a 4 Letter Word" (Bad
    English song), 171, 172, 173
Heavy Jelly (band), 86
Heavy Metal (film), 121, 130
heavy metal (rock genre), 8, 54, 64, 73,
    74, 87, 129–130, 147
"heavy space," 1, 5, 51, 62
Hegedus, Eric, 103
Heineken beer, 111
Hell Freezes Over (Eagles album), 193

About the Author

David Hamilton Golland is dean of the Wayne D. McMurray School of Humanities and Social Sciences and professor of history at Monmouth University. His prior books are *Constructing Affirmative Action: The Struggle for Equal Employment Opportunity* (University Press of Kentucky, 2011) and *A Terrible Thing to Waste: Arthur Fletcher and the Conundrum of the Black Republican* (University Press of Kansas, 2019). Golland has also published articles in *California History, Critical Issues in Justice and Politics, The Claremont Journal of Religion*, and the American Historical Association's newsmagazine *Perspectives on History*. He makes more than a dozen public appearances each year, ranging from plenary talks to panel papers; has been an invited guest on talk radio; and has appeared on C-SPAN's *American History TV*.

He is founder of *The Journey Zone* (journey-zone.com), the leading source for all things Journey over two decades.